EMPLOYEE RECRUITMENT, SELECTION, AND ASSESSMENT

Personnel selection is changing. Whilst traditional face-to-face interviews are still common, the range of assessment processes that inform the selection of candidates is increasingly diverse, taking advantage not only of new technologies but also new methods and strategies, such as assessment centres and personality testing. This new collection looks at the most important contemporary issues in recruitment, selection, and assessment today, highlighting the latest research from the perspective of both recruiter and applicant.

The book is written by an international range of prominent scholars in this area, and provides up-to-date analysis of key topic areas, including:

- How measurements of intelligence can impact on recruitment policies
- The use and value of personality tests
- An analysis of social interaction in the interview process
- The value and impact of video resumes in recruitment
- How social networks affect how applicants are perceived
- Job analysis and competencies modelling

Part of the *Current Issues in Work and Organizational Psychology* series, this is an important book that shines a light on the latest theory and practice in employee recruitment. It will interest not only students and researchers of Organizational Psychology, HRM, and Business and Management, but will also engage professionals in the field.

Ioannis Nikolaou is an Associate Professor in Organisational Behaviour at Athens University of Economics and Business, Athens, Greece.

Janneke K. Oostrom is an Assistant Professor in Social and Organizational Psychology at the VU University of Amsterdam, the Netherlands.

Current Issues in Work and Organizational Psychology
Series Editor: Arnold B. Bakker

Current Issues in Work and Organizational Psychology is a series of edited books that reflect the state-of-the-art areas of current and emerging interest in the psychological study of employees, workplaces and organizations.

Each volume is tightly focused on a particular topic and consists of seven to ten chapters contributed by international experts. The editors of individual volumes are leading figures in their areas and provide an introductory overview.

Example topics include digital media at work, work and the family, workaholism, modern job design, positive occupational health, and individualised deals.

A Day in the Life of a Happy Worker
Edited by Arnold B. Bakker and Kevin Daniels

The Psychology of Digital Media at Work
Edited by Daantje Derks and Arnold B. Bakker

New Frontiers in Work and Family Research
Edited by Joseph G. Grzywacz and Evangelia Demerouti

Time and Work, Volume 1: How time impacts individuals
Edited by Abbie J. Shipp and Yitzhak Fried

Time and Work, Volume 2: How time impacts groups, organizations and methodological choices
Edited by Abbie J. Shipp and Yitzhak Fried

Burnout at Work: A psychological perspective
Edited by Michael P. Leiter, Arnold B. Bakker, and Christina Maslach

Towards Inclusive Organizations: Determinants of successful diversity management at work
Edited by Sabine Otten, Karen van der Zee, and Marilynn Brewer

Well-being and Performance at Work: The role of context
Edited by Marc van Veldhoven and Riccardo Peccei

Employee Recruitment, Selection, and Assessment: Contemporary issues for theory and practice
Edited by Ioannis Nikolaou and Janneke K. Oostrom

EMPLOYEE RECRUITMENT, SELECTION, AND ASSESSMENT

Contemporary issues for theory and practice

Edited by
Ioannis Nikolaou
and Janneke K. Oostrom

LONDON AND NEW YORK

First published 2015
by Psychology Press
27 Church Road, Hove, East Sussex BN3 2FA

and by Psychology Press
711 Third Avenue, New York, NY 10017

Psychology Press is an imprint of the Taylor & Francis Group, an informa business

© 2015 Ioannis Nikolaou and Janneke K. Oostrom

The right of Ioannis Nikolaou and Janneke K. Oostrom to be identified as author of this part of the Work has been asserted by him/her in accordance with sections 77 and 78 of the Copyright, Designs and Patents Act 1988.

All rights reserved. No part of this book may be reprinted or reproduced or utilised in any form or by any electronic, mechanical, or other means, now known or hereafter invented, including photocopying and recording, or in any information storage or retrieval system, without permission in writing from the publishers.

Trademark notice: Product or corporate names may be trademarks or registered trademarks, and are used only for identification and explanation without intent to infringe.

British Library Cataloguing in Publication Data
A catalogue record for this book is available from the British Library

Library of Congress Cataloging-in-Publication Data
Employee recruitment, selection, and assessment : contemporary issues for theory and practice / edited by Ioannis Nikolaou and Janneke K. Oostrom.
  pages cm
Includes bibliographical references.
1. Employee selection. 2. Employee retention. 3. Personnel management.
I. Nikolaou, Ioannis. II. Oostrom, Janneke K.
  HF5549.5.S38E47 2015
  658.3'11—dc23
  2014046731

ISBN: 978-1-138-82325-9 (hbk)
ISBN: 978-1-138-82326-6 (pbk)
ISBN: 978-1-315-74217-5 (ebk)

Typeset in Bembo
by Apex CoVantage, LLC

Printed and bound in Great Britain by
TJ International Ltd, Padstow, Cornwall

CONTENTS

List of contributors ix

Introduction 1
Ioannis Nikolaou and Janneke K. Oostrom

PART A
Job analysis and recruitment 7

1 Work analysis for personnel selection 9
   *Antonio León García-Izquierdo, Luis Díaz Vilela,
   and Silvia Moscoso*

2 Recruitment processes and organizational attraction 27
   Derek S. Chapman and David Mayers

PART B
The applicants' perspective 43

3 Video résumés portrayed: findings and challenges 45
   Annemarie M.F. Hiemstra and Eva Derous

4 Social networking websites and personnel selection:
   a call for academic research 61
   *Donald H. Kluemper, H. Kristl Davison,
   Xiaoyun Cao, and Bingqing Wu*

5 Applicant reactions to selection methods: an overview of recent research and suggestions for the future   80
   Ioannis Nikolaou, Talya N. Bauer, and Donald M. Truxillo

PART C
Advances in predictors' research   97

6 New developments in intelligence theory and assessment: implications for personnel selection   99
   Charles Scherbaum, Harold Goldstein, Rachel Ryan, Paul Agnello, Ken Yusko, and Paul Hanges

7 Personality testing in personnel selection: Love it? Leave it? Understand it!   117
   Janina Diekmann and Cornelius J. König

8 Trends in testing: highlights of a global survey   136
   Ann Marie Ryan, Ilke Inceoglu, Dave Bartram, Juliya Golubovich, James Grand, Matthew Reeder, Eva Derous, Ioannis Nikolaou, and Xiang Yao

9 Beyond validity: shedding light on the social situation in employment interviews   154
   Klaus G. Melchers, Pia V. Ingold, Annika Wilhelmy, and Martin Kleinmann

10 Situational judgment testing: a review and some new developments   172
   Janneke K. Oostrom, Britt De Soete, and Filip Lievens

11 Assessment centres: the latest developments on construct validity   190
   Deon Meiring, Jurgen Becker, Suzanne Gericke, and Nadia Louw

PART D
The criterion domain   207

12 Selecting for innovation: methods of assessment and the criterion problem   209
   Kristina Potočnik, Neil Anderson, and Felisa Latorre

13 Typical and maximum performance   228
   Ute-Christine Klehe, Jessica Grazi, and Tusharika Mukherjee

Index   245

CONTRIBUTORS

Paul Agnello, Baruch College, City University of New York, USA

Neil Anderson, Brunel University, London, UK

Dave Bartram, CEB's SHL Talent Measurement Solutions, and University of Pretoria, South Africa

Talya N. Bauer, Portland State University, USA

Jurgen Becker, University of Johannesburg, South Africa

Xiaoyun Cao, University of Illinois at Chicago, USA

Derek S. Chapman, University of Calgary, Canada

H. Kristl Davison, University of Mississippi, USA

Eva Derous, Ghent University, Belgium

Britt De Soete, Ghent University, Belgium

Luis Diaz Vilela, Universidad de la Laguna, Spain

Janina Diekmann, Universität des Saarlandes, Germany

Antonio León García-Izquierdo, Universidad de Oviedo, Spain

Suzanne Gericke, University of Pretoria, South Africa, and EOH Human Capital Solutions, Pretoria, South Africa

Harold Goldstein, Baruch College, City University of New York, USA

Juliya Golubovich, Educational Testing Service ETS, USA

James Grand, University of Akron, USA

Jessica Grazi, Justus Liebig Universität Giessen, Germany

Paul Hanges, University of Maryland, USA

Annemarie M. F. Hiemstra, Erasmus University Rotterdam, the Netherlands

Ilke Inceoglu, Surrey Business School, University of Surrey, UK

Pia V. Ingold, Universität Zürich, Switzerland

Ute-Christine Klehe, Justus Liebig Universität Giessen, Germany

Martin Kleinmann, Universität Zürich, Switzerland

Donald H. Kluemper, University of Illinois at Chicago, USA

Cornelius J. König, Universität des Saarlandes, Germany

Felisa Latorre, ITAM, México City, México

Filip Lievens, Ghent University, Belgium

Nadia Louw, Stellenbosch University, South Africa

David Mayers, University of Calgary, Canada

Deon Melring, University of Pretoria, South Africa

Klaus G. Melchers, Universität Ulm, Germany

Silvia Moscoso, Universidad de Santiago de Compostela, Spain

Tusharika Mukherjee, Justus Liebig Universität Giessen, Germany

Ioannis Nikolaou, Athens University of Economics and Business, Greece

Janneke K. Oostrom, VU University Amsterdam, the Netherlands

Kristina Potočnik, University of Edinburgh, Edinburgh, UK

Matthew Reeder, APT Metrics, USA

Ann Marie Ryan, Michigan State University, USA

Rachel Ryan, Baruch College, City University of New York, USA

Charles Scherbaum, Baruch College, City University of New York, USA

Donald M. Truxillo, Portland State University, USA

Annika Wilhelmy, Universität Zürich, Switzerland

Bingqing Wu, University of Illinois at Chicago, USA

Xiang Yao, Peking University, China

Ken Yusko, Marymount University, USA

INTRODUCTION

Ioannis Nikolaou
ATHENS UNIVERSITY OF ECONOMICS AND BUSINESS, GREECE

Janneke K. Oostrom
VU UNIVERSITY AMSTERDAM, THE NETHERLANDS

The field of employee recruitment, selection, and assessment has traditionally been one of the most energetic and active domains of research and practice in the field of Work and Organizational Psychology. Numerous psychology graduates are employed in human resource management (HRM) consultancies, HRM departments, and in specialized work psychology/psychological testing firms, involved in staffing, recruitment, selection, and assessment in countries worldwide. Moreover, it has also been one of the first fields to attract researchers' and practitioners' attention both in Europe and the United States (Salgado, Anderson, & Hülsheger, 2010). Therefore, the *Current Issues in Work and Organizational Psychology* series would not be complete without a book devoted to the field of employee recruitment, selection, and assessment.

In the most recent review of selection research published in the *Annual Review of Psychology*, Ryan and Ployhart (2014) claimed, however, that despite the long-standing employee selection research and practice, the field is still full of controversies, exploring "settled" questions, working on "intractable" challenges, expanding into literatures and organizational levels far removed from those historically investigated, and constantly being pushed by practitioners, who continually are confronting questions to which researchers have not yet produced answers (pp. 694–695). In order to describe the current state of affairs, Ryan and Ployhart (2014) describe selection research as a "highly active senior who has not been slowed down by age" (p. 695).

The development of the field is evident in the increasing number of studies appearing in both mainstream work and organizational psychology journals but also in specialized journals (e.g., *International Journal of Selection and Assessment*). Also, a number of influential handbooks have recently been published both in the United States and Europe. Moreover, the number of conference papers and symposia presented at international conferences, such as the Society for Industrial and Organizational Psychology (SIOP), the European Association of Work and Organizational Psychology (EAWOP), the Academy of Management (AoM) and the International Congress of Applied Psychology (ICAP), dealing with issues related to employee recruitment, selection, and assessment has been steadily increasing during the last few years.

Recent research in employee selection has also shifted its focus from the traditional selection paradigm, that is, the relationship between the predictor and the criterion, towards other important issues. For example, there is increased interest in different selection methods (e.g., situational judgment tests), in the role of technology and the Internet in recruitment and selection (e.g., video resumes and the effect of social networking websites), in the applicants' perspective (e.g., trust, fairness, and applicant reactions research), in the use of new statistical and methodological approaches (e.g., multilevel analysis and diary studies), in ethical issues and adverse impact, in high-stakes selection, and so forth.

Another recent development in the field, with a European focus, has been the creation of the *European Network of Selection Researchers* (ENESER). The ENESER's objective is to advance selection research in Europe, to bring together researchers carrying out applied research in the field of employee recruitment, selection, and assessment, and to act as a network for work and organizational psychologists conducting research in this field. The ENESER has already organized three small-scale conferences (Athens, 2011; Sheffield, 2012; Ghent, 2014) and aims to continue organizing conferences on a biannual basis, along with symposia and practitioner-oriented fora at international conferences (e.g., EAWOP, SIOP, AoM, ICAP). Both the editors and many of the authors of the current volume are members of the ENESER.

Structure of the book

We have structured the content of the current volume into four parts. The first part (Part A) of the book deals with the cornerstone of any personnel selection process, work analysis, along with a chapter on recruitment and organizational attraction. The second part of the book (Part B) deals with the applicants' perspective. Specifically, the three chapters of this part deal with video resumes, with the role of social networking websites, and with applicant reactions to selection methods. The remaining two parts deal with the traditional domains of predictor-criterion research in selection. In the third part (Part C), we explore recent developments regarding predictors, namely intelligence tests, interviews, situational judgment tests, and assessment centers. In the fourth and last part (Part D), our contributors review the literature on criteria, specifically on the role of innovation as a criterion and the typical versus maximum performance issue.

More specifically, García-Izquierdo, Díaz Vilela, and Moscoso, in the first chapter of our book, discuss the important role of work analysis in personnel selection. They initially describe the two main types of work analysis, namely task-oriented and worker-oriented analysis. Within the concept of worker-oriented analysis they elaborate on the concept of competency modeling, a widely used methodology within the HRM field. Subsequently, the authors discuss the sources we can use in order to elicit work analysis information and the various methods we could employ during this process. They distinguish between qualitative (i.e., observations and interviews) and quantitative methods (i.e., job-task inventories, Fleishman's Job Analysis Survey, personality-based methods, and the widely used Position Analysis Questionnaire). However, the most comprehensive source of job-related information is the Occupational Information Network (O*NET) and García-Izquierdo, Díaz Vilela, and Moscoso present it in detail. The remaining sections discuss issues related to reliability-validity and work analysis, and how job analysis can facilitate both the recruitment and the assessment of employee fit in the selection process.

Chapter 2 of our book discusses the important role of recruitment in the selection process. Written by Chapman and Mayers, it focuses especially on applicant attraction but also on the series of systems – specifically, systems, processes, and strategies – that are designed to maximize the size and the quality of the applicant pool. Chapman and Mayers initially discuss the important role of designing jobs with recruitment in mind, that is, designing jobs in such a way that they are going to attract large numbers of qualified applicants. The authors emphasize the important role of pay in the attraction of candidates. Subsequently, Chapman and Mayers summarize the organizational characteristics that seem to have an impact on organizational attraction, such as organizational image, organizational culture, and company location. They also emphasize the important role of the recruiter in the attraction process, such as recruiter friendliness. In the final sections of their chapter, the authors discuss the characteristics of an effective recruitment message, a number of issues associated with the recruitment of employed individuals and headhunting, and the impact of new technologies, such as online recruitment, gamification, and social media. They conclude with a number of proposals for future research in the field of recruitment and attraction.

The second part of our book deals with the applicants' perspective. A recent important development in the field of selection research and practice is the use of video resumes. Hiemstra and Derous, in Chapter 3, review the recent research on this topic, which is gradually attracting increased attention. They first introduce the concept of video resumes along five major dimensions: goal-content, format characteristics, standardization, administration, and interactivity. They also contrast video resumes with conventional interviews. Subsequently, Hiemstra and Derous review the relatively limited research in this field and conclude with an agenda for future research on video resumes.

Chapter 4 deals with a "hot" topic in selection research, which is a typical example of how practice drives research in our field. Kluemper, Davison, Cao, and Wu discuss the important impact of social media and social networking websites in employee selection. Social networking websites, such as LinkedIn and Facebook, are being used extensively for screening and recruitment purposes. The chapter explores a range of issues related to social network screening, such as reliability, validity, generalizability, utility, socially desirable self-presentation, and applicant reactions. It also reviews the emerging literature in these areas in an effort to inform academics and practitioners while providing fruitful avenues for future research.

The third and final chapter of this section (Chapter 5), written by Nikolaou, Bauer, and Truxillo, explores the topic of applicant reactions. The authors review the current literature and research on applicant reactions in relation to the major theoretical approaches in this area. They also present the main predictors and outcomes explored in relation to applicant reactions. They include a section on future research on this topic; specifically, they emphasize the role of the Internet and social networking websites, methodological issues, and the impact of applicant reactions from a practitioner's perspective.

Part C of the book deals with the most well-researched area in selection research: a number of different predictors that are frequently being used in selection procedures. Our aim is to focus on the most important predictors in personnel selection research. Scherbaum and his colleagues, in Chapter 6, review recent research in intelligence theory and assessment. They review some of the innovations and developments in the conceptualization and measurement of intelligence that have the potential to impact employee selection. Moreover, they explore recent conceptualizations of psychometric approaches to intelligence, the developments in neuropsychological and cognitive approaches, and modern intelligence test design principles as well as the implications of these developments for personnel selection.

Another often-used predictor in selection practice is personality testing. This is a well-studied topic in employee selection research as well, and Diekmann and König, in Chapter 7, discuss the controversies often associated with the use of personality testing in employee selection. They review the main arguments for and against the use of personality assessment in research and practice and present the findings of their own research on the usage of personality testing in Germany. They describe and discuss several important characteristics of personality tests, beyond standard criteria such as reliability and validity, which might influence the allure of often-used personality tests for practitioners, including the presentation of results, aspects of application, and the process of finding a personality test. They encourage researchers and practitioners to better understand the concept of personality in organizational settings and conclude with suggestions for future research on this topic.

Along the lines of the previous two chapters, in Chapter 8, Ryan and her colleagues present the results of a global survey conducted among HR professionals in more than 25 countries. This is a major update of a previous study conducted by Ryan, McFarland, Baron, and Page (1999). In their chapter, Ryan and her colleagues explore the decision-making behind testing, how tests are used in selection, the role of technology, and common test policies and practices. The chapter concludes with a set of recommendations for research and practice.

The most important predictor in selection research is definitely the employment interview. Chapter 9, by Melchers, Ingold, Wilhelmy, and Kleinmann, explores the social situation involved in employment interviews. Following the literature review on this topic, they explore the two perspectives (i.e., interviewer and interviewee),

Employee Recruitment, Selection, and Assessment: Contemporary Issues for Theory and Practice (Current Issues

focusing especially on the self-presentational behaviors being used. They also explore how technology-enabled interviewing might influence the social interaction during the employment interview.

Apart from testing and the employment interview, a new selection method has recently attracted increased interest from both researchers and practitioners. In Chapter 10, Oostrom, De Soete, and Lievens review evidence concerning reliability, construct-related validity, criterion-related validity, subgroup differences, fakability, and acceptability by situational judgment test takers. They focus on several promising new developments regarding the way situational judgment tests are designed and scored. The chapter concludes with a list of areas that need to be addressed in future research.

The last chapter of Part C (Chapter 11) discusses the widely used method of assessment centers. Meiring, Becker, Gericke, and Louw present assessment centers as a selection method and subsequently focus on recent research on their construct validity. They claim that the debate on the construct validity of assessment centers is probably overrated. They argue that recent theoretical and methodological advances in the assessment center literature suggest that previous approaches used to assess the internal structure of assessment centers may be inappropriate, have limited value, and probably fail to recognize the multidimensional nature of assessment centers.

The fourth and last section of the book (Part D) includes two chapters that deal with the important role of the criterion in employee selection research and practice. Most of the previous research on this topic has focused on predicting job performance. However, more recently researchers and practitioners are also interested in additional criteria, such as extra-role performance and citizenship behaviors. In Chapter 12, Potočnik, Anderson, and Latorre discuss the role of innovation as a significant criterion in selection. They first review the assessment of innovative performance and individual-level innovation literature. Subsequently, they discuss how innovation potential can be assessed through different selection methods. Finally, they conclude with a number of suggestions for future research in this field along with practical implications of this topic.

Finally, in Chapter 13, Klehe, Grazi, and Mukherjee discuss the typical versus maximum performance issue in employee selection research and practice. What employees *can* do as opposed to what they *will* do is a major issue both in research and in practice. The authors present empirical findings about the distinction between typical and maximum performance, address frequent issues in the empirical study of typical versus maximum performance, and link this literature to fundamental theories of motivation in order to develop directions for future research.

Summarizing the evidence presented across these chapters, we can safely claim that employee recruitment, selection, and assessment is a well-developed and thriving area in work and organizational psychology. The contributors of this book originate from twelve different countries, representing four different continents, a valid indication of a "healthy" development in our field. We hope that the current book on *Employee Recruitment, Selection, and Assessment* of the *Current Issues in Work and Organizational Psychology* series contributes to its further development.

References

Ryan, A.M., McFarland, L., Baron, H., & Page, R. (1999). An international look at selection practices: Nation and culture as explanations for variability in practice. *Personnel Psychology, 52*, 359–391.

Ryan, A.M., & Ployhart, R.E. (2014). A century of selection. *Annual Review of Psychology, 65*, 693–717.

Salgado, J., Anderson, N., & Hülsheger, U. (2010). Employee selection in Europe: Psychotechnics and the forgotten history of modern scientific employee selection. In J.L. Farr & N.T. Tippins (Eds.), *Handbook of personnel selection* (pp. 921–941). New York: Lawrence Erlbaum Associates.

PART A
Job analysis and recruitment

1
WORK ANALYSIS FOR PERSONNEL SELECTION

Antonio León García-Izquierdo
UNIVERSIDAD DE OVIEDO, SPAIN

Luis Díaz Vilela
UNIVERSIDAD DE LA LAGUNA, SPAIN

Silvia Moscoso
UNIVERSIDAD DE SANTIAGO DE COMPOSTELA, SPAIN

Introduction

Work analysis (WA) is by now a classic topic in I/O literature due to its long tradition and implementation in companies all over the world, particularly when dealing with personnel selection, promotion, or training. Consequently, WA could be seen as the cornerstone of human resources management because crucial decisions are based on information extracted from this type of report. However, the changing nature of jobs now means that human resources practitioners need a more active and updated approach to WA. The main reason for those changes is the huge development of information technologies, which constitute the origin of new jobs that are constantly emerging. These jobs are highly cognitively loaded and are appearing in all parts of the globe. At the same time, most traditional jobs have also been affected in some way by information technology, placing customers at the center and increasing the pressure for organizations to be online. In this way, duties and tasks are now more diverse and complex, meaning that WA faces new challenges if it is to maintain its relevance in the human resources arena.

In this chapter we use the concept of WA as proposed by Sánchez and Levine (2001) because it is a general concept that is useful for various purposes. As is commonly known, *job analysis* has been the most widely used term in the scientific literature, but WA can also encompass all the concepts that are concerned with the analysis of what people do at work. This facilitates the inclusion of different aspects of work such as tasks, abilities, and roles, and even the evolving nature of work over time and across organizations (Sánchez & Levine, 2012). The uses of WA are manifold, but our objective in this chapter is to shed some light on the main issues around WA for personnel selection purposes.

Broadly speaking, we can define WA as the systematic process for gathering information about activities (e.g., tasks, duties, and responsibilities) and the personal attributes an employee must have in order to accomplish the objectives the organization has established for a particular job, through a procedure of analysis, synthesis, and inference. This analysis consists of subdividing jobs into more detailed elements to find out specific and important aspects for further applied decision-making purposes. Usually, the output of this analysis is a complete and detailed description of the job (i.e., job description) and the inferred workers' traits required for successful performance (i.e., job specification). Consequently, we can use WA for both criteria and predictor development, and for calculating the degree of alignment between criteria and predictors. Another key and related issue is the question of person-work fit, a topic that we are going to deal with in detail in this chapter.

Originally, WA was focused on a standard protocol, and it can be traced back to the principles of scientific management in the early years of the twentieth century, with the study of times and movements by Taylor, and by Lillian and Frank Gilbreth, who were the pioneers in the analysis of workflow from a rational and empirical point of view. Some of the forefathers of personnel selection from different parts of Europe, such as Lahy (France), Lipmann and Stern (Germany), and Mira (Spain), made relevant contributions to WA as well (Salgado, Anderson, & Hülsheger, 2010).

Work analysis implies some costs in terms of time and money, so the effort made to develop a well-designed WA project depends on the gains expected from this process. In this sense, jobs that require high cognitive demands, those full-time jobs with open-ended contracts that are long-term oriented and frequently in the upper part of the organization, more easily justify a WA process despite being the most difficult to analyse. On the other hand, part-time and temporary jobs, which are usually less cognitively demanding, are less likely to deserve an exhaustive examination. The information derived from WA can be classified into three categories: job identification, job description, and job specification. Job identification includes information about job titles and physical and/or functional location. Job description includes a job summary and the workflow breakdown into duties and tasks performed by the incumbents. Other relevant information such as job conditions, methods, or techniques can also be included in the job description. Job specification refers to job requirements needed to carry out the job's duties and tasks. It may include the knowledge, skills, abilities, and other characteristics (KSAOs) that are used in personnel selection procedures, such as memory or initiative (Brannick, Levine, & Morgeson, 2007). Nonetheless, from both a theoretical and a practical perspective, some authors and practitioners defend different and apparently opposed points of view. In the next section, we are going to deal with the classical dilemma about the orientation of the WA, that is, towards the tasks or towards the workers.

Task-oriented analysis and worker-oriented analysis

Following Gael (1988) and Brannick and Levine (2002), we can distinguish between task-oriented methods and worker-oriented methods of WA.

Task-oriented job analysis

This approach considers duties, functions, and tasks as the basis for studying jobs in the workplace. Consequently, particular employees' attributes are not of interest, as worker characteristics display variability in how they perform those tasks depending on their experience, knowledge, abilities, personality, and other attributes. The task-oriented approach places the emphasis on the structure of the organization, which remains relatively stable. From this perspective, jobs are independent of the people who perform them. The best-known methods are the following: Time and Motions Study, Functional Job Analysis (Fine, 1988), Task Inventory/ Comprehensive Occupational Data Program (TI/CODAP), Work Performance Survey System, and the Critical Incident Technique (Flanagan, 1954). Particularly important is the Functional Job Analysis, which is used in the development of the Occupational Information Network (O*NET) database, known for its well-structured synthesis perspective for most jobs. When dealing with very important decisions in terms of money or consequences for people or resources, the Critical Incident Technique is an appropriate method.

Worker-oriented job analysis

The worker-oriented analysis approach stresses the individual characteristics an employee must have for adequate performance. We can differentiate between two types of these characteristics: traits and competencies. Traits are based on stable characteristics, such as aptitudes and personality. Although the concept of competence is far from being clear, we can see competencies as those trainable core characteristics, in terms of behaviors, that lead employees to success (Boyatzis, 1982; McClelland, 1973). These are mainly KSAOs, such as attitudes and motivation (Campbell, McCloy, Oppler, & Sager, 1993). Due to the existence of a growing consensus around the competency model, research on worker traits has suffered a dramatic reduction. The fast and continual changes occurring in the content of jobs and the consequent instability in terms of tasks are impelling a growing number of modern organizations to start using Competence Modelling (CM) in their human resources practices (Schippmann, 1999). The main characteristic of CM is that it enables the identification of KSAOs that tend to be broad and that are not necessarily linked to specific jobs or tasks (Brannick, Levine, & Morgeson, 2007). Therefore, CM takes into account organizational goals and missions and seeks to develop a set of competencies to be applied across the organization or units within the organization (Lawler, 1994). Regarding this, Goldstein and Ford (2002, p. 272) stated that "... these more global competencies are expected to not only predict behavior across a wide variety of tasks and settings but also provide the organization with a set of core characteristics that distinguish the company from others in terms of how it operates its business and treats its employees." Thus, CM approaches seem to offer the advantage of going beyond the information provided by traditional worker-oriented job analysis, which focuses on the identification of the most relevant KSAOs for the job. One of the main criticisms of CM has to do with the multiple and sometimes contradictory definitions of competence (Alliger et al., 2012; Schippmann et al., 2000; Voskuijl, 2005). Nevertheless, some authors agree on considering the competencies as part of job performance (Bartram, 2005; Lievens et al., 2010). As Sánchez and Levine (2009, p. 61) put it,

> In essence, whereas traditional job analysis focuses on describing and measuring the requirements of work, CM creates a conduit to influence day-to-day employee performance along strategic lines. Having highlighted how we stand to gain from using them together, we hope to stimulate research on the manner in which Task Job Analysis (TJA) and CM may supplement each other in a host of HR applications.

Sources of information

The most commonly used sources of information in the analyses have been job incumbents, although supervisors, peers, and job analysts are also frequently used as information agents. Recent changes in working conditions and arrangements are blurring job boundaries and emphasizing teamwork, making it necessary to broaden the number and type of informants, including internal and external customers, and the number of activities observed (Pearlman & Sánchez, 2010; Voskuijl, 2005). This changing nature of work makes WA even more important now (Guder, 2012) and increases the necessity of performing analyses systematically.

As Guder (2012) points out, the blurring of job boundaries entails an increasing need for coordination of activities between different jobs, that is, a "crossfunctional coordination of activities" (p. 37). This implies the appearance of a new form of cross-supervision, not necessarily hierarchical in nature, as it could also take the form of an internal customer. This is probably not new, but it has been receiving particular attention recently (e.g., Sánchez & Levine, 2012). This approach would make WA even more complex because it would require the participation of incumbents, direct supervisors, and coworkers whose jobs are related to the target job.

One more effective way of putting together all the possible WA data could be through a panel of experts who would catalyse all the work information from the incumbent, the analyst, and any other source. A panel of this type should include experts on WA as a technique and experts on the organization and on the target job under analysis. This panel should have different meetings before and after each step, making decisions about what is valid and what is not. As Wernimont (1988) states, using panels of experts will add reliability to a process currently based around one individual, without underestimating the importance of the participation of analysts too.

Methods for WA

This section is devoted to the methods for gathering information through the WA process. Pearlman and Sánchez (2010) describe four categories of WA applications: predictor development, criterion development, validity evidence development, and validity evidence extension. The first category constitutes the most used application, and its goal is to describe jobs in terms of the KSAOs needed to perform them properly. That is, when WA is used for selection purposes, a job description is not enough, and job specifications are necessary too. These specifications require KSAOs, and they are to be used as job performance predictors. Therefore, they constitute decision-making criteria affecting candidates' lives as well as organizational effectiveness, and they should have adequate levels of reliability, validity, discriminability, and practicality (Ployhart, Schneider, & Schmitt, 2006). These characteristics should be expected not only for the instruments used but also for the entire process of WA and the derivation of KSAO profiles.

WA procedures should be iterative: departing from observation, a description should be generated that, in turn, should be confronted with reality, reformulated when necessary, and confronted again. This procedure could last forever, but the intervention of several agents in different points considerably reduces the number of iterations. Each phase in WA deserves special attention and care. We need to point out that even when our goal is to obtain a job-specific KSAO profile, the preliminary steps of observation and description of work activities and behaviors are both necessary.

There are two classic approaches to classifying the different methods and instruments for WA: the qualitative and the quantitative. The qualitative approach is based on gathering information through techniques such as interviews or focus groups, where job incumbents provide ample narrative information stressing not only the content of the job but the context as well. On the other hand, the quantitative approach is mainly based on structured questionnaires where job incumbents are strictly restricted to limited answering options, or even using the organization's work results records (number of clients, money, production, accidents, etc.).

Qualitative methods

Observation

WA is an observational process. A work analyst resembles an ornithologist trying to describe an eagle's behavioral pattern through the seasons, with the only difference being that incumbents can think and speak. But these characteristics of the observed performer do not free the analyst from the need for thorough observation of the performance, whatever method and instruments are used. In fact, observation is one of these methods and is frequently ignored. Observation has four advantages over other methods (Martinko, 1988): (1) the first-hand nature of the data, as the information is obtained directly, (2) the opportunity to obtain in-depth qualitative information, (3) the improvement of face validity by providing organizational jargon to the analysts and to the WA reports, which also improves confidence, (4) information can be purely descriptive, as well as serving inferential hypothesis testing purposes. At the same time, observation also has some disadvantages, which Martinko (1988) describes as time, cost, extension of reports, coordination requirements, incumbents' reactivity, and difficulty in capturing non-observable behaviors. Despite these shortcomings, observation is advisable in the first stages of WA because it will provide the analyst with helpful knowledge about the job and will give the required information for asking appropriate questions in the subsequent interview (McPhail, Jeanneret, McCormick, & Mecham, 1989). Finally, observation becomes necessary particularly when there is a lack of consensus and the panel of experts cannot reach a solution.

Interview

The interview can be defined as a meeting between two or more people for the purpose of exchanging information about a job or a series of jobs (Gael, 1988). Analysts should be trained interviewers, and interviews should be well planned in order to obtain enough quality information to accomplish WA goals. When planning an interview, Gael (1988) suggests four considerations: setting explicit objectives, identifying the class of interviewees, specifying the degree of structure that the interview will have and the number of interviewees, and preparing the necessary materials and equipment. Interviews can and should be performed in different stages in WA in order to obtain (*initial interview*) and refine (*verification interview*) information about the work performed. There are a number of publications on how to conduct WA interviews, from Gael's (1988) chapter to, for instance, the practical guide to interviews by the U.S. Office of Personnel Management (2008). Besides this, McPhail et al. (1989) also provide some suggestions for improving interview effectiveness, including the selection of location, the preparation and structuring of the interview, and the scheduling arrangement with the interviewee. Although the selection interview should be structured, in the light of previous research (Motowidlo et al., 1992), the initial WA interview should be unstructured because its purpose is to obtain as much work-related information as possible, while verification interviews should be structured and centered on the inconsistencies or discrepancies found.

Quantitative methods

Job-task inventories

Job-task inventories are basically questionnaires composed of a background information section followed by a task inventory section, that is, a list of tasks arranged by general functions or duties (Christal & Weissmuller, 1988). Tasks are components of jobs and can be described as a set of activities oriented to accomplishing a single goal (Gillan, 2012; Voskuijl, 2005). They are formulated using an action verb, an object of the action, and essential modifiers. For example, a clerical task could be

"Prepare documents for verification and signature of the superior". Task lists are generated by incumbents, supervisors, analysts, a Subject Matter Experts (SME) board, or any combination of these. Once the list is complete, a questionnaire is made using tasks as stimuli, and a Likert-type scale with a set of anchorages for importance, frequency, criticality, and/or complexity. In fact, there will be as many task inventories as types of scales used (one for importance of tasks, one for frequency, and so forth). These questionnaires can be administered to incumbents or to anyone closely familiar with the work under analysis. As a result, the analyst will have an image of the work done in the form of a list of tasks with their associated properties (frequency, etc.), so that core tasks in the job can be easily identified. This is a work description technique and is intended as an initial step in the development of work specifications.

Fleishman Job Analysis Survey (F-JAS)

The Fleishman Job Analysis Survey (F-JAS) is a system for analysing the KSAOs needed to perform jobs (Management Research Institute, 2013). The F-JAS is a 73-item questionnaire measuring three domains of required KSAOs: cognitive, psychomotor, and physical. Within the first domain, seven cognitive ability requirements are measured: verbal, idea generation and reasoning, quantitative, memory, perceptual, spatial, and attentiveness abilities. With regard to psychomotor abilities, F-JAS measures fine manipulative, control movement, and reaction time and speed abilities. Finally, requirements of five physical abilities are measured: physical strength, endurance, flexibility, visual, and auditory and speech abilities. Contrary to its apparent simplicity, the F-JAS is not, in fact, particularly straightforward to implement. Caughron, Mumford, and Fleishman (2012) recommend four steps to be followed in its application: (1) reviewing job description materials and the F-JAS Administrator's Guide. When these materials do not exist, observation, interviews, and/or job inventories should be undertaken; (2) creating a panel, with the suggestion of about 20 SMEs to obtain sufficient levels of interrater reliability; (3) having each SME rate jobs using the questionnaire. Raters must decide whether each ability is required, and if so, to what extent the ability is required; (4) determining mean ability scores obtained from the SMEs for each job, requiring consensus meetings when interrater reliabilities are low.

Practitioners should be aware of the subjective nature of F-JAS data and the reliability threats discussed above. In addition, special attention should be paid to the difficulties that applicants in particular have in separating their own abilities and levels from those required to perform their jobs.

Personality-based job analysis

Several authors have developed instruments with the aim of evaluating personality-related job requirements. Hogan and Rybicki (1998) developed the Performance Improvement Characteristics Job Analysis (PIC) for use in selection and

TABLE 1.1 Questionnaire examples of Performance Improvement Characteristics Job Analysis (adapted from Hogan & Rybicki, 1998)

Would job performance improve if the incumbent _____?	
- Is steady under pressure	____
- Is not easily irritated by others	____
- Is competitive	____
- Takes initiative – solves problems on his/her own	____
- Needs variety at work	____
- Is kind and considerate	____
- Supports the organization's values	____
- Is imaginative and open-minded	____
- Remembers details	____

(*Response Options*: 0. Does NOT Improve Performance; 1. Minimally Improves Performance; 2. Moderately Improves Performance; 3. Substantially Improves Performance)

development. The PIC is a structured questionnaire based on the Five-Factor Model (FFM) of personality (Digman, 1990) and, specifically, on the scales of the Hogan Personality Inventory (HPI; Hogan & Hogan, 2007). The PIC consists of 48 items, which are evaluated using four-point scales that compound seven dimensions in which the most important personality characteristics for the evaluated job are included (Adjustment, Ambition, Sociability, Interpersonal Sensitivity, Prudence, Inquisitive, and Learning Approach). The PIC shows acceptable psychometric properties (Hogan & Rybicki, 1998). In Table 1.1 some of the PIC items are shown.

Another personality-oriented WA instrument is the Personality-Related Position Requirements Form (PPRF; Raymark, Schmit, & Guion, 1997). This form includes 107 items and evaluates 12 personality dimensions, which are based on the FFM: (1) General Leadership, (2) Interest in Negotiation, (3) Ambition (these three dimensions are included within the Extraversion Factor of the FFM), (4) Friendly Disposition, (5) Sensitivity to Interest of Others, (6) Cooperative or Collaborative Work Tendency (these two dimensions are included within the Agreeableness Factor), (7) General Trustworthiness, (8) Adherence to a Work Ethic, (9) Thoroughness and Attentiveness to Details (Conscientiousness Factor), (10) Emotional Stability, (11) Desire to Generate Ideas, and (12) Tendency to Think Things Through (Intellect Factor).

Raymark et al. (1997), using descriptions of 260 different jobs and 12 occupational categories, found evidence that the PPRF reliably differentiates between jobs. They found interrater coefficients ranging from .66 to .92 for the different occupational categories. Their results also showed acceptable reliability for most dimensions. The alpha coefficients ranged from .72 to .92. Table 1.2 includes some items of the PPRF.

TABLE 1.2 Examples of items on the Personality-Related Position Requirements Form (adapted from Raymark et al., 1997)

Effective performance in this position requires the person to:

- Take control in group situations
- Mediate conflict situations without taking sides
- Seek challenging tasks
- Start conversations with strangers easily
- Give constructive criticisms tactfully
- Work as part of an interacting work group
- Have access to confidential information
- Meet specified deadlines
- Keep cool when confronted with conflicts
- Find new ways to improve the way work is done
- Identify and evaluate options before taking action

(*Response Options*: Not Required; Helpful; Essential)

Position Analysis Questionnaire (PAQ)

This instrument can be defined as "a structured job analysis questionnaire which provides for a quantified analysis of individual jobs in terms of a number of 'job elements', often referred to as 'items'" (McPhail et al., 1989, p. 1). The PAQ consists of 195 items. Of these, 187 relate to job activities or to the work environment; the remaining eight items are used to report the type of compensation (PAQ Services, 2013). It is a worker-oriented questionnaire that is intended to describe jobs based on six domains: information sources, mental processes, responses or actions involved in jobs, interpersonal activities in work, work situation and context, and other miscellaneous aspects of work (McCormick, Mecham, & Jeanneret, 1977). Job elements are arranged within these six divisions. Each division contains several factors. These authors described the process of factor analysis that gave 32 division dimensions and 13 overall dimensions. In short, the first 32 dimensions resulted from six division-specific factor analyses, while the 13 overall dimensions are the result of a factor analysis on all the items together. Following PAQ Services (2013), job component validity analyses with the General Aptitude Test Battery (GATB) makes the PAQ useful in identifying appropriate selection tests and cut-off scores, and providing job component validity evidence for ability tests.

Although the Position Analysis Questionnaire has received attention in almost every work/job analysis handbook, little has been said about its application procedure. Following Mecham, McCormick, and Jeanneret (1977), the use of the *Job Analysis Manual* is strongly recommended when completing the questionnaire. As an example, in an unpublished part of a study, data from two experienced analysts showed that using (or not using) the manual caused clear differences in results (Díaz Vilela et al., 2008). These differences were eliminated when both analysts used the manual to answer the questionnaire.

WA databases

Currently, since the Dictionary of Occupational Titles (DOT) has become outdated, the most comprehensive database of this type is the O★NET (Peterson et al., 1999). It is a dynamic system of information, services, tools, and applications for more than 800 occupations that are updated regularly. The system provides occupational profiles filled with information regarding the required knowledge, skills, abilities, work activities, work styles, work interests, background, education and training requirements, and work context. The O★NET content model is organized on the basis of six sets of descriptors: (1) worker characteristics, (2) worker requirements, (3) experience requirements, (4) occupational requirements, (5) occupation-specific requirements, and (6) workforce characteristics. The first three sets are worker-oriented, and the last three sets are job-oriented. Brannick, Levine, and Morgeson (2007) made a complete and comprehensive summary of these descriptors and their categories:

1. Worker characteristics are personal attributes needed for successful job performance. They are divided into three categories: (a) abilities (e.g., oral expression, originality, or memorization), (b) occupational interests and values (e.g., achievement, creativity, or moral values), and (c) work styles (e.g., persistence, cooperation, or integrity).
2. Worker requirements are personal attributes that are developed through experience and that are helpful in performing different tasks. They are composed of three categories: (a) basic and cross-functional skills (e.g., mathematics, reading comprehension, or persuasion), (b) knowledge (e.g., psychology, music, or art), and (c) education (e.g., general mental ability or instructional program).
3. Experience requirements include specific vocational training, work experience, and licensing (e.g., subject area education, licenses required, requirement to obtain license, or related work experience).
4. Occupational requirements are referred to as what the worker does. This descriptor is composed of three categories: (a) generalized work activities (e.g., getting information needed to do the job, making decisions and solving problems, or documenting and recording information), (b) work context (social interaction, radiation exposure, or level of automation), and (c) organizational context (e.g., empowerment, task identity, or skill variety).
5. Occupation-specific requirements refer to some elements that apply to a single occupation or a narrow job family. It includes specific tasks, tools, and technology.
6. Workforce characteristics are not incorporated directly into O★NET. This category is designed to link to other databases with relevant information. This descriptor includes labor market information, occupational outlook, and wages.

Besides offering a conceptual model, O★NET also provides other useful tools and resources, such as O★NET OnLine and O★NET Questionnaires. O★NET OnLine is a web-based application that allows users to search and access occupational data. O★NET Questionnaires are specific occupational analysis instruments which refer to knowledge, skills, abilities, work activities, work context, background, education and training, and work styles.

Another classification is the ISCO-08 (International Standard Classification of Occupations), which replaced the ISCO-88 and was endorsed by the Governing Body of the International Labour Organization (ILO) in March 2008. This is a tool for organizing jobs into a clearly defined set of groups according to the tasks involved in each job. The occupational classification system includes major, sub-major, minor, and unit groups of the different occupations and the descriptions of each one.

Reliability and validity in WA

Reliability and validity are complex domains that depend on a number of factors. At the very least, raters' own KSAOs (Morgeson & Campion, 1997; Sánchez & Levine, 1994), relative position of the informant/information complexity (Dierdorff & Wilson, 2003; Sánchez, Zamora, & Viswesvaran, 1997), and even demographic background (Arvey, Passino, & Lounsbury, 1977) should be taken into account. These factors affect the quality of the data because they produce informational distortion, which is difficult to reduce. Morgeson and Campion (1997) proposed a list of 16 sources of inaccuracies grouped in two categories, social and cognitive. Social sources are social influence, group polarization, motivation loss, impression management, social desirability, and demand effects. Cognitive sources are information overload, heuristics, categorization, carelessness, extraneous information, inadequate information, order and contrast effects, halo, leniency and severity, and method effects (Morgeson & Campion, 1997).

The conceptualization of validity and, particularly, reliability, is an important topic that should be stressed at this point. Reliability refers to the consistency between raters or within raters (Sánchez & Levine, 2012). Such a clear, simple definition conceals a quite complex concept and certain methodological problems. First, consistency between raters has been represented through intraclass correlations, assuming that high correlations between raters' scores indicate agreement. On the other hand, high correlations between test and retest application to the same rater is assumed to show stability in this rater's observations (Dierdorff & Wilson, 2003; Viswesvaran, Ones, & Schmidt, 1996). Yet neither of these assumptions is rigorously true. Starting with the latter, stability within a rater's scores in a test-retest situation may be due to individual biases when a job has changed in nature: different observed reality – same informed scores. In other cases, observed instability can be a raw reflection of reality and therefore have high reliability. In these cases, stability or consistency is not a reliability indicator.

With respect to interrater consistency, correlations are good indicators of the existence of a relationship and of its strength, but only that. Consistency is not agreement (Ployhart, Schneider, & Schmitt, 2006). Interrater correlations with values around $r_{xy} = .90$ may come from appraisers whose means are quite different. When a practitioner trusts interrater stability, as often happens, the assumption is that the mean scores in each criterion should guide the establishment of the cut-off score for selection purposes. Regardless of which analyst is right, it remains clear that the mean represents none of them.

These are real threats to validity and hence to the quality of WA and subsequent criteria development (Harvey, 2012). For this reason, the concept of reliability in WA should be extended to capture not only consistency, but agreement too. This assertion is especially oriented to practitioners in real-life settings, where often the time and economic expense of analysing a statistically adequate number of positions, or the hiring of a number of analysts, is unaffordable. When this can be done, a cluster analysis of variables should result in as many clusters as job facets. A cluster analysis of subjects (analysts) should result in only one cluster when all the analysts agree. In reliability terminology (Revelle, 2013; Revelle & Zinbarg, 2009), the total omega should be high and the hierarchical omega should be low when variables are analysed, indicating the existence of several underlying factors (job facets); but the hierarchical omega should be high and the total omega low when subjects are treated as variables, indicating the existence of a unique underlying component (agreement among analysts). So, what is the solution to this dilemma? Some decades ago, Wernimont (1988) proposed six guarantees of content validity in job analysis oriented to selection procedures: (1) familiarity with the job analysed, which is expected from incumbents and supervisors and should be gained by analysts through observation and/or interpretation of data; (2) the use of a panel of experts instead of a single informant; (3) training observers in behavioral sciences, although this alone is not sufficient; (4) expertise in tests and attribute derivation from WA; (5) knowledge of existing tasks and attribute taxonomies; and (6) after a WA procedure, relationships among tasks and among attributes should show content validity by themselves. Following these guidelines, a WA should start with job familiarization on the analysts' part, and technical familiarization on the experts' part. There is not much literature on how to train experts in the use and interpretation of analysis tools, so training programs should be developed *ad hoc*.

The question of fit

Job fit is a concept that explains whether the intersection between an employee's characteristics and the requirements of a particular job and work environment match or not. The use of concepts like work roles, team-person fit, and person-organization fit (Lievens, Highhouse, & De Corte, 2005) has been suggested as a substitute of the analysis centered on jobs. Anyway, we can distinguish between demands-abilities (competencies) fit and needs/values-supplies fit. When the two interests match, an employee and an organization experience a good job fit. A good job fit coincides with high levels of job and organizational performance and job satisfaction. The classical approach in personnel selection has put the emphasis on matching individuals and jobs (for instance, Lofquist & Dawis, 1969), and even more recently Kristof-Brown, Zimmerman, and Johnson (2005, p. 281) conceptualized fit as "the compatibility between an individual and a work environment that occurs when their characteristics are well matched". However, nowadays the interest has shifted to group and organizational fit. In this sense, it is important to capture some organizational factors within which the work is carried out, such as leadership, strategic planning, focus on customer satisfaction, and emphasis on quality and productivity (Offermann & Gowing, 1993). This could include sharing team or organizational values, expectations, and climate. The organizational level is mainly related to organizational culture, which is made up of internal values, norm beliefs, underlying assumptions, attitudes, and behaviors shared by a group of people. Culture can be observed throughout the behavior that results when a group arrives at a set of – generally unspoken and unwritten – rules for working together. We can see the organizational culture by means of language, symbols, legends, decision making, and work routines. Person-organization fit deals with the compatibility of the individuals and the organization. Muchinsky and Monahan (1987) distinguished between complementary and supplementary fit. Complementary fit occurs when individuals fill a gap in the environment (i.e., the job) or vice versa, whilst supplementary fit is when the individual and the environment are similar. When looking for applicants to match a specific organizational culture, the steps are similar to the process at the individual level. The main difference between the organizational and the individual level is that the former put the emphasis on the lifestyle-world views. Consequently, when analysing candidates to match the organizational culture, the main issues involve personal values, attitudes, and personality.

WA and equal employment opportunities

Finally, we would like to stress the social dimension of fit and WA. When conducting a personnel selection process, it is necessary to take into account the social and legal requirements as well as the individuals and the organizations. This has been brought to the foreground through the concept of Equal Employment Opportunities (EEO). EEO deals with fairness in an increasingly diverse workforce, in terms of demographic issues such as age distribution and the sexual, ethnic, and cultural composition of the workforce. The challenge is about job-relatedness, so organizations must document some linkage between KSAOs and job tasks. However, there must be thoroughness in the coverage of such KSAOs, focusing on the whole person, avoiding invasiveness, and using unbiased instruments.

As Biddle and Kuthy (2012, p. 365) state, a rigorous WA "provides crucial data for ensuring that EEO objectives are being met". This means that if the WA and work specification are inaccurate, some qualified people, sometimes protected groups, may be excluded from succeeding. Consequently, the selection process could be unfair. The European Union (EU) has protected equality in the workplace, developing extensive legislation to prevent discrimination, especially between women and men. This equal-opportunity legislation arose in the seventies with the enactment of some relevant directives such as Council Directive 75/117/EC regarding equal pay and Council Directive 76/207/EEC on equal treatment in employment and vocational training. At the beginning of the present century, there was a renewed attempt to deal with this matter in the shape of Council Directive 2000/78/EC, which established a framework to prevent all types of discrimination. Two years later, Parliament and Council Directive 2002/73/EC amended

Council Directive 76/207/EEC, giving Member States an active role in achieving the objective of equality between men and women when formulating and implementing laws, regulations, administrative provisions, policies, and activities in employment and vocational training.

As stated in EU Directive 2006/54/EC, discrimination can be performed directly, if one person is treated less favorably on grounds of gender, or indirectly, if an apparently neutral provision, criterion, or practice would put persons of one gender at a particular disadvantage compared with those of the opposite gender. Indirect discrimination alone can be acceptable only in the case of the following three assumptions: (1) for professional activities where gender is a factor because of the nature or conditions of the activity to be performed, (2) to protect women, particularly in pregnancy and childbirth, and (3) to promote equal opportunities between men and women (art. 2.6 EU Directive 76/207 on Equal Treatment). Considering all this legislation, we can conclude that decision making in personnel selection should be based on those criteria clearly related with an accurate and thorough WA. That is, the personnel selection decision being made must be based on tools and instruments that present enough evidence of criterion-oriented validity. That means that WA is not only a useful tool in human resource management but is also essential in avoiding discrimination in the workplace.

Recruitment and WA

The inherent relevance of WA, and more specifically of job descriptions, for recruitment purposes demands a specific section in the present chapter. In fact, the job description very often constitutes the basis of the recruitment advertisement and establishes the ways by which the information will appear reflected. As such, it affects the degree of attraction of the recruitment advertisement that is perceived by the potential candidates and, consequently, has important implications for the success of the entire selection process and for the fulfillment of the job vacancy.

Hurtz and Wright (2012) describe how WA can be used to maximize the effectiveness of recruitment, and, therefore, to improve the utility of selection processes, optimizing the percentage of high-quality applicants (highly suitable applicants) that enter the selection process and remain interested in it, and, consequently, stay in the organization. To achieve this goal the authors recommend the use of established taxonomies, because they provide a common and accepted language to describe jobs. On the other hand, the use of informational systems and communication technologies displayed by these taxonomies allows information to be obtained with more substance and fidelity about the job, compared with more traditional methods.

In this sense, Cober et al. (2003) indicate that the organization must focus on the content as well as on the style (e.g., usability, interactivity) of the information used in the recruitment. Hurtz and Wright (2012) provide a framework with four "layers" of work description that can be used as a guide for the use of WA in the recruitment process. The first layer refers to traditional work descriptions and details how the other layers can be built departing from it. The second layer adds an electronic database to the first to organize and disseminate job descriptions, enabling users to download the respective information. The third layer adds color elements, graphics, and interactivity options to the work descriptions (e.g., hyperlinks), which provide additional information on job descriptions. The fourth layer allows the inclusion of multimedia components (e.g., audio, video, and two-way communication technologies such as message boards or online chat tools). Moreover, these authors stress that the use of this framework can make a valuable contribution in the accomplishment of the three main recruitment objectives: (1) attracting appropriate applicants; (2) maintaining their interest in the job offer and in the organization; (3) persuading applicants to accept the job offer. In any case, the basis of this model and of their four layers lies in the information about the job that is provided by the WA.

Conclusions

WA has a long history that has brought researchers and practitioners a handful of well-designed and useful techniques and instruments, which have been adapted to different times and contexts. Consequently, WA has had to cope with different challenges. One of the most important debates is around WA orientation, that is, task-oriented versus worker-oriented WA. From our point of view, both orientations are necessary, and the choice depends on the WA purposes. For instance, when grappling with personnel selection, worker orientation is unavoidable, but many times, they are complementary perspectives.

Simultaneously, models and principles of WA are changing, as everything is changing in the work arena nowadays. Particularly important are the effects of information technologies, as they are placing individuals working worldwide through connectivity. Consequently, jobs, roles, and performance are progressively far from a static place in the organizations and are more related with a dynamic relationship (García-Izquierdo, Ramos-Villagrasa, & Navarro, 2012). Moreover, workers are coping with the necessity of continuous job crafting (Tims, Bakker, & Derks, 2014) to develop their roles and to enhance their performance, in order to maintain their positions in an organization and across organizations eventually. The workforce is making a huge effort of redesigning jobs and professional competencies in a constant pressure to update and respond to organizational and job market demands. This has turned the view from job fit to organizational fit, and in many cases to job market fit, in order to be employable. Organizations are shaping jobs' functions and their structure to the market demands, and simultaneously need to comply with legal restrictions, particularly in the context of diversity and equal employment opportunities. Thus, nowadays WA remains the core of HR policies, and a good (if not necessary) basis for relevant organizational issues. Even more, WA contributes to enhance responsibility assumed by incumbents and to reduce ambiguity when organizing tasks, and it plays an important role in goals achievement indeed.

All in all, the present chapter suggests that WA is necessary for successful recruitment, personnel selection, and promotion processes. WA may also be one of the best means for guaranteeing equality and avoiding discrimination in the workplace.

References

Alliger, G.M., Beard, R., Bennett, W., &, Colegrove, C.M. (2012). Understanding mission essential competencies as a job analysis method. In M.A. Wilson, W. Bennett, S.G. Gibson, & G.M. Alliger (Eds.), *The handbook of work analysis: Methods, systems, applications and science of work measurement in organizations* (pp. 603–624). New York: Routledge.

Arvey, R.D., Passino, E.M., & Lounsbury, J.W. (1977). Job analysis results as influenced by sex of incumbent and sex of analyst. *Journal of Applied Psychology, 62*(4), 411–416.

Bartram, D. (2005). The great eight competencies: A criterion-centric approach to validation. *Journal of Applied Psychology, 90*, 1185–1203.

Biddle, D.A. & Kuthy, J.E. (2012). Using job analysis as the foundation for creating equal employment opportunity in the workplace. In M.A. Wilson, W. Bennett, S.G. Gibson, & G.M. Alliger (Eds.), *The handbook of work analysis: Methods, systems, applications and science of work measurement in organizations* (pp. 365–379). New York: Routledge.

Boyatzis, R.E. (1982). *The competent manager: A model for effective performance.* New York: John Wiley & Sons.

Brannick, M.T., & Levine, E.L. (2002). *Job analysis: Methods, research and applications for human resource management in the new millennium.* Thousand Oaks, CA: Sage Publications.

Brannick, M.T., Levine, E.L., & Morgeson, F.P. (2007). *Job and work analysis: Methods, research and applications for human resource management* (2nd ed.). Thousand Oaks, CA: Sage.

Campbell, J.P., McCloy, R.A., Oppler, S.H., & Sager, C.E. (1993). A theory of performance. In N. Schmitt & W.C. Borman (Eds.), *Personnel selection in organizations* (pp. 35–70). San Francisco: Jossey-Bass.

Caughron, J.J., Mumford, M.D., & Fleishman, E.A. (2012). The Fleishman Job Analysis Survey. Development, validation, and applications. In M.A. Wilson, W. Bennett, S.G. Gibson, & G.M. Alliger (Eds.), *The handbook of work analysis: Methods, systems, applications and science of work measurement in organizations* (pp. 231–246). New York: Routledge.

Christal, R.E., & Weissmuller, J.J. (1988). Job-task inventory analysis. In S. Gael, *The job analysis handbook for business, industry and government* (Vol. 2, pp. 1036–1050). New York: John Wiley & Sons.

Cober, R.T., Brown, D.J., Levy, P.E., Cober, A.B., & Keeping, L.M. (2003). Organizational web sites: Web site content and style as determinants of organizational attraction. *International Journal of Selection and Assessment, 11*, 158–169.

Díaz Vilela, L.F., Calvo-López, B., García-Bello, M.Á., Recuero-Fernández, A., Batista-Orihuela, A., & Gorrín-Hernández, L. (2008). *Intervención psicológica en los recursos humanos de las policías locales de Canarias. (Psychological intervention in human resources of Canary local police).* Santa Cruz de Tenerife: Escuela Canaria de Seguridad.

Dierdorff, E.C., & Wilson, M.A. (2003). A meta-analysis of job analysis reliability. *Journal of Applied Psychology, 88*(4), 635–646.

Digman, J. (1990). Personality structure: Emergence of the five-factor model. *Annual Review of Psychology, 41*, 417–440.

Fine, S.A. (1988). Functional job analysis. In S. Gael (Ed.), *The job analysis handbook for business, industry and government* (pp. 1019–1035). New York: Wiley.

Flanagan, J.C. (1954). The critical incident technique. *Psychological Bulletin, 51*, 327–358.

Gael, S. (1988). Interviews, questionnaires, and checklists. In S. Gael, *The job analysis handbook for business, industry and government* (pp. 391–414). New York: John Wiley & Sons.

García-Izquierdo, A.L., Ramos-Villagrasa, P.J., & Navarro, J. (2012). Dynamic criteria: A longitudinal analysis of professional basketball players' outcomes. *The Spanish Journal of Psychology, 15*(3), 1133–1146.

Gillan, D.J. (2012). Five questions concerning task analysis. In M.A. Wilson, W. Bennett, S.G. Gibson, & G.M. Alliger (Eds.), *The handbook of work analysis: Methods, systems, applications and science of work measurement in organizations* (pp. 201–213). New York: Routledge.

Goldstein, I.L., & Ford, J.K. (2002). *Training in organizations* (4th ed.). Belmont, CA: Wadsworth.
Guder, J.E. (2012). Identifying appropriate sources of work information. In M.A. Wilson, W. Bennett, S.G. Gibson, & G.M. Alliger (Eds.), *The handbook of work analysis: Methods, systems, applications and science of work measurement in organizations* (pp. 31–40). New York: Routledge.
Harvey, R.J. (2012). Analyzing work analysis data. In M.A. Wilson, W. Bennett, S.G. Gibson, & G.M. Alliger (Eds.), *The handbook of work analysis: Methods, systems, applications and science of work measurement in organizations* (pp. 93–126). New York: Routledge.
Hogan, J., & Rybicki, S. (1998). *Performance improvement characteristics job analysis manual.* Tulsa, OK: Hogan Assessment Systems.
Hogan, R., & Hogan, J. (2007). *Hogan Personality Inventory manual* (3rd ed.). Tulsa, OK: Hogan Assessment Systems.
Hurtz, G.M., & Wright, C.W. (2012). Designing work descriptions to maximize the utility of employee recruitment efforts. In M.A. Wilson, W. Bennett, S.G. Gibson, & G.M. Alliger (Eds.), *The handbook of work analysis: Methods, systems, applications and science of work measurement in organizations* (pp. 347–364). New York: Routledge.
Kristof-Brown, A.L., Zimmerman, R.D., & Johnson, E.C. (2005). Consequences of individual's fit at work: A meta-analysis of person-job, person-organization, person-group, and person-supervisor fit. *Personnel Psychology, 58*, 281–342.
Lawler, E.E. (1994). From job-based to competency-based organizations. *Journal of Organizational Behavior, 15*, 3–15.
Lievens, F., Highhouse, S., De Corte, W. (2005). The importance of traits and abilities in supervisors' hirability decisions as a function of method of assessment. *Journal of Occupational and Organizational Psychology, 78*, 435–470.
Lievens, F., Sánchez, J.I., Bartram, D., & Brown, A. (2010). Lack of consensus among competency ratings of the same occupation: Noise or substance? *Journal of Applied Psychology, 95*, 562–571.
Lofquist, L.H., & Dawis, R.V. (1969). *Adjustment to work.* New York: Appleton-Century-Crofts.
Management Research Institute. (2013). *Identifying the ability requirements of jobs.* Retrieved October 15, 2013, from MRI: http://www.managementresearchinstitute.com/f-jas.aspx
Martinko, M.J. (1988). Observing the work. In S. Gael, *The job analysis handbook for business, industry and government* (pp. 5419–5431). New York: John Wiley & Sons.
McClelland, D. (1973). Testing for competence rather than for intelligence. *The American Psychologist, 28*(1), 1–14.
McCormick, E.J., Mecham, R.C., & Jeanneret, P.R. (1977). *Position Analysis Questionnaire technical manual (System II).* Logan, UT: PAQ Services.
McPhail, S.M., Jeanneret, P.R., McCormick, E.J., & Mecham, R.C. (1989). *Position Analysis Questionnaire. Job analysis manual.* Palo Alto, CA: PAQ Services, Inc.
Mecham, R.C., McCormick, E.J., & Jeanneret, P.R. (1977). *Job analysis manual for the Position Analysis Questionnaire (PAQ).* Logan, UT: PAQ Services, Inc.
Morgeson, F.P., & Campion, M.A. (1997). Social and cognitive sources of potential inaccuracy in job analysis. *Journal of Applied Psychology, 82*(5), 627–655.
Motowidlo, S.J., Carter, G.W., Dunnette, M.D., Tippins, N., Werner, S., Burnett, J.R., & Vaughan, M.J. (1992). Studies of the structured behavioral interview. *Journal of Applied Psychology, 77*(5), 571–587.
Muchinsky, P.M., & Monahan, C.J. (1987). What is person-environment congruence? Supplementary versus complementary models of fit. *Journal of Vocational Behavior, 31*(3), 268–277.
Offermann, L.R., & Gowing, M.K. (1993). Personnel selection in the future: The impact of changing demographics and the nature of work. In N. Schmitt & W.C. Borman (Eds.), *Personnel selection in organizations* (pp. 385–417). San Francisco: Jossey Bass.

PAQ Services. (2013). *PAQ Services, Inc.* Retrieved October 15, 2013, from PAQ: http://enteract.paq.com

Pearlman K., & Sánchez, J.I. (2010). Work analysis. In J.L. Farr & N.T. Tippins (Eds.), *Handbook of employee selection* (pp. 73–98). New York: Routledge.

Peterson, N.G., Mumford, M.D., Borman, W.C., Jeanneret, P.R., & Fleishman, E.A. (1999). *An occupational information system for the 21st century: The development of O*NET*. Washington, DC: APA Books.

Ployhart, R.E., Schneider, B., & Schmitt, N. (2006). *Staffing organizations: Contemporary practice and theory* (3rd ed.). Mahwah, NJ: Lawrence Erlbaum Associates.

Raymark, P.H., Schmit, M.J., & Guion, R.M. (1997). Identifying potentially useful personality constructs for employee selection. *Personnel Psychology, 50,* 723–736.

Revelle, W. (2013, May 20). Classical test theory and the measurement of reliability. Retrieved October 1, 2013, from Personality Project, *An introduction to psychometric theory with applications in R*: http://www.personality-project.org/r/book/Chapter7.pdf

Revelle, W., & Zinbarg, R.E. (2009, March). Coefficients alpha, beta, omega, and the glb: Comments on Sijtsma. *Psychometrika, 74*(1), 145–154.

Salgado, J., Anderson, N., & Hülsheger, U.R. (2010). Psychotechnics and the forgotten history of modern scientific employee selection. In J.L. Farr & N. Tippins (Eds.), *Handbook of employee selection* (pp. 921–941). New York: Taylor & Francis.

Sánchez, J.I., & Levine, E.L. (1994). The impact of raters' cognition on judgment accuracy: An extension to the job analysis domain. *Journal of Business and Psychology, 9*(1), 47–57.

Sánchez, J.I., & Levine, E.L. (2001). The analysis of work in the 20th and 21st centuries. In N. Anderson, D.S. Ones, H.K. Sinangil, & C. Viswesvaran (Eds.), *Handbook of industrial, work, and organizational psychology* (pp. 71–89). Thousand Oaks, CA: Sage.

Sánchez, J.I., & Levine, E.L. (2009). What is (or should be) the difference between competency modeling and traditional job analysis? *Human Resources Management Review, 19,* 53–63.

Sánchez, J.I., & Levine, E.L. (2012). The rise and fall of job analysis and the future of work analysis. *Annual Review of Psychology, 63,* 397–425.

Sánchez, J.I., Zamora, A., & Viswesvaran, C. (1997). Moderators of agreement between incumbent and non-incumbent ratings of job characteristics. *Journal of Occupational and Organizational Psychology, 70,* 209–218.

Schippmann, J.S. (1999). *Strategic job modeling: Working at the core of integrated human resources.* Mahwah, NJ: Erlbaum.

Schippmann, J.S., Ash, R.A., Battista, M., Carr, L., Eyde, L.D., Hesketh, B., et al. (2000). The practice of competency modeling. *Personnel Psychology, 53,* 703–740.

Tims, M., Bakker, A.B., & Derks, D. (2014). Daily job crafting and the self-efficacy–performance relationship. *Journal of Managerial Psychology, 29,* 490–507.

U.S. Office of Personnel Management. (2008, September). *Structured interviews: A practical guide*. Retrieved October 29, 2013, from http://www.opm.gov/policy-data-oversight/assessment-and-selection/structured-interviews/guide.pdf

Viswesvaran, C., Ones, D., & Schmidt, F. (1996). Comparative analysis of the reliability of job performance ratings. *Journal of Applied Psychology, 81*(5), 557–574.

Voskuijl, O. (2005). Job analysis: Current and future perspectives. In A. Evers, N. Anderson, & O. Voskuijl (Eds.), *The Blackwell handbook of personnel selection* (pp. 27–46). Malden, MA: Blackwell Publishing.

Wernimont, P.F. (1988). Recruitment, selection, and placement. In S. Gael, *The job analysis handbook for business, industry, and government* (pp. 193–215). New York: John Wiley & Sons.

2
RECRUITMENT PROCESSES AND ORGANIZATIONAL ATTRACTION

Derek S. Chapman
UNIVERSITY OF CALGARY, CANADA

David Mayers
UNIVERSITY OF CALGARY, CANADA

Finding the right employees for any organization requires an intricate combination of systems working in tandem. You need effective systems to first attract a suitable and substantial pool of applicants. You need to screen and select the most appropriate candidates, and ultimately you need to convince those selected to accept the job offer (Barber, 1998; Rynes, 1989). Despite the interdependence of these systems, much of the literature on staffing organizations focuses on screening and selection, with far less attention being paid to the attraction functions. If an organization fails to attract sufficient quantities of candidates with the right qualities, the selection system will not be effective regardless of its sophistication (Boudreau & Rynes, 1985). In this chapter, we will focus on the front end of this series of systems – specifically, systems, processes, and strategies that are designed to maximize the size and quality of the applicant pool. Although our focus is on applicant attraction, many of these processes spill over into actual job choice, as the early impressions formed in the attraction stage tend to carry over into the job choice stage (Rynes, Bretz, & Gerhart, 1991). This makes the messages and strategies employed in the attraction stage all the more important.

Note that companies may have goals other than attraction for their recruiting processes, such as having an emphasis on retention (see Breaugh & Starke, 2000, for an excellent review of potential recruiting goals). We will focus on the most popular goal of recruiting – attracting high-quality job applicants in high quantities.

Job characteristics: building an attractive job

We know that job characteristics are important components of any recruiting effort (Schwab, Rynes, & Aldag, 1987). If a job was a product to be sold, job characteristics represent the features and capabilities of the product that you are trying to sell. Of course, one way to make your sales effort easier is to have a product that has highly desired features. One recruiting strategy, then, is to design jobs with recruiting in mind. Building in attractive features of the job can not only help retention efforts but can provide key information that can be used in recruiting messages ("our pay is the highest in the industry" or "you will get to use and develop a lot of skill sets in this position").

The challenge is to identify what job characteristics are likely to be universally attractive to job applicants and/or to engage in job design with the target audience in mind (e.g., what job characteristics would be most attractive to engineers?). A review of the literature provides us with some clues about how to design jobs that are more attractive to potential applicants.

Job design for recruiting

Here we draw upon two distinct literatures that examine the role of job characteristics and job design on applicant and employee attitudes respectively. As Morgeson and Campion (2003) describe, the job design literature has stagnated since the early 1990s. They suggest this was due, in part, to the predominance of Hackman and Oldham's (1975) Job Characteristics Model (JCM). Chapman and Borodenko (2006) suggested that if job characteristics have intrinsically motivating effects on employees, they should also have the potential to influence job applicants through a process of anticipating working in a job with those characteristics. This approach was also used recently in a study examining the role of fit information on attraction to organizations (Schmidt, Chapman, & Jones, in press). They found that employers who focus their recruiting advertisements on Needs/Supplies fit (fulfilling applicant needs) attracted more candidates and better-qualified candidates than those that focused on Demands/Abilities fit (requirements of the job). Minor changes in job advertisement wording related to employee fit was found to have an up to 23% increase in the effectiveness of real job advertisements (Schmidt et al., in press).

Increasing the components included in the conceptualization of job design, Humphrey, Nahrgang, and Morgeson (2007) describe three job design components that are likely to influence attitudes: Job Motivators (e.g., the traditional JCM components of Skill Variety, Task Identity, Autonomy, etc.), Social Components (including interdependence, feedback from others, and social support), and Work Context (e.g., physical demands). Their meta-analysis suggests that all three of these components predict unique variance in turnover-intentions (the attitudinal variable most closely aligned to attraction as the opposite side of the same coin). Increasingly, researchers are identifying the role of possible selves in applicant attraction. It has been argued that applicants can imagine themselves in the future working for the organization in a particular role (Markus & Nurius, 1986). They then test this potential future against their self-image or ideal image to determine whether it is a good fit for them. Using organizational image, Nolan and Harold (2010) found that applicants' perceptions of congruence between both actual and ideal self-images increased organizational attraction. We expect, then, that job characteristics that are known to increase employee satisfaction and intrinsic motivation will align well with an applicant's possible self and increase organizational attraction.

Pay and attraction

A review of the literature shows, not surprisingly, that there is a positive relationship between amount of pay and applicant attraction. A meta-analysis by Chapman, Uggerslev, Carroll, Piasentin, and Jones (2005) found this positive relationship to be strongest for early stages of attraction ($\rho = .27$), becoming less important in later stages such as actual job choice ($\rho = .12$). This finding is consistent with the theory that applicants use pay as a screening variable, and that once a reserve wage (the lowest wage considered acceptable by the applicant) is met, pay loses its status as a powerful attractant (Lippman & McCall, 1976).

When pay information is introduced in the recruiting process, its effectiveness is contingent upon the relative favorability of this information for candidates. A clear pay leader may wish to advertise this fact in job ads to attract the most applicants. However, if pay is not a strong point, introducing it later in the process may avoid self-selection early on and give the company an opportunity to convey other recruiting information more favorable to the applicant. Advertising relatively high pay, then, can be an effective recruiting strategy for attracting a larger pool of applicants, although it is not clear whether this affects the quality of the applicant pool. A high-pay strategy is also very easily copied by competitors, which can result in an escalating and expensive bidding war for skilled employees. Advertising the amount you pay can accelerate this bidding process, as competitors can more easily match or exceed your advertised pay.

Organizational characteristics: building an attractive company

Presumably, if we had detailed knowledge of what most employees are looking for in an employer, we could design and build organizations in ways that made them more attractive to the majority of potential employees. This would certainly make recruiting much less difficult. Unfortunately, there has been little work examining universal attractants of applicants on which to base this type of approach. Employee attraction is extraordinarily complex, and what might be attractive to one person (e.g., a remote location with great hunting and fishing) might prove to be highly unattractive to another (e.g., someone that prefers an urban environment). What organizational characteristics are desired by job applicants? A recent summary suggested that, over the years, not much has changed in the literature with respect to the organizational characteristics that applicants find attractive. Organizational characteristics such as organizational image, location, size, familiarity, reputation, industry, and profitability have all been shown to have a significant influence during the recruitment process (Darnold & Rynes, 2013).

In reviewing the literature, organizational image is the variable containing the greatest number of relevant effect size estimates for organizational characteristics (Chapman et al., 2005; Uggerslev, Fassina, & Kraichy, 2012). This is probably because organizational image can encompass individual perceptions related to various organizational characteristics simultaneously. Organizational image is defined as "the way the organization is perceived by an individual. It is a loose structure of knowledge, belief, and feelings about an organization" (Tom, 1971, p. 576). Based on the definition, the flexibility of the content domain is apparent. Many organizational characteristics have been used as a proxy for organizational image. For example, researchers have focused on corporate image as a combination of an individual's perception of product image, service image, citizenship image, and credibility image (Tsai & Yang, 2010). Other researchers have examined the overall image of the company as a suitable employer (i.e., employment image) based on hearsay, atmosphere, product image, and respectability (Highhouse, Zickar, Thornsteinson, Stierwalt, & Slaughter, 1999). Although there is some overlap between studies, given that the definition of organizational image is fairly loose, it is not surprising that researchers have incorporated a wide variety of dimensions as indicators of organizational image.

From a broad perspective, regardless of the ingredients that go into an organization's image, image has an influence on applicant behavior at all stages in the recruitment process (Chapman et al., 2005; Uggerslev et al., 2012) and becomes more important at later versus earlier stages (Uggerslev et al., 2012). However, based on the available research, it still remains unclear as to what organizational characteristics drive perceptions of organizational image at the different stages. Research aimed at determining the ingredients that go into perceptions of organizational image at the different stages of recruitment would represent a constructive contribution to the literature. One approach to do this would be to draw upon relevant theories that help explain why image is related to attraction in order to make specific directional hypotheses at each stage of the recruitment process. Another approach is using an inductive lexical decision task to identify the characteristics that are most commonly used in developing perceptions of organizational image, and when in the recruitment process these characteristics apply.

Two theories that are often used to explain the influence of image on attraction are signalling theory and social identity theory. Signalling theory (Rynes, 1991; Spence, 1973) suggests that in light of limited information, applicants or potential applicants use whatever information they have as a basis for their decision-making. Therefore, if individuals lack information regarding specific job characteristics, their overall image of the organization will be based on the information they do have. Before applicants start working for a new organization, it is likely that they will have incomplete information regarding all the characteristics relevant to their work. Thus, signalling theory helps us understand why organizational image is an important predictor of attraction at all stages in the recruitment process.

Social identity theory (Tajfel & Turner, 1985) suggests that an individual's self-concept is influenced by the group/s with whom the individual associates or belongs. Applying this to recruiting, particular aspects of the organization (i.e., familiarity, reputation, and image) will be positively related to organizational attraction because these characteristics are salient and viewed positively by those outside the organization (Cable & Turban, 2001). Similarly, recruiting researchers have begun to assess how employer branding can be leveraged to attract applicants to the organization (Ambler & Barrow, 1996; Cable & Turban, 2003; Cable & Yu, 2006; Lievens & Highhouse, 2003).

Organizational culture and attraction

When researchers examine organizational culture, they are generally referring to the intangible aspects of the organization that influence the behavior of individuals. Schein (1985) defined culture as the beliefs, values, and basic assumptions shared by organizational members. Although there are many possible ways to measure the culture of organizations and their members, a popular approach was proposed by O'Reilly (1989), who suggested that values are a suitable proxy for culture. Researchers have distinguished between environmental and interactionist perspectives, insofar as perceptions of the organization's culture can have a main effect on organizational attraction, or they can interact with the cultural values held by potential applicants (Ehrhart & Ziegert, 2005). In this section we examine the literature on organizational culture and its influence during the recruitment process.

Several studies have found a direct relationship between the organizational culture and applicant attraction. For example, Van Vianen and Fischer (2002) found that women prefer less competitive environments than men. Additionally, supportive environments were preferred more than competitive environments by both men and women. These results were replicated in a later study that found that supportive organizational cultures, compared to competitive cultures, led to increased pursuit intentions, organizational preferences, and job choice decisions (Catanzaro, Moore, & Marshall, 2010). Thus, organizational recruitment may benefit from an organizational culture that reflects support rather than competitiveness (Catanzaro et al., 2010).

The role of person–organization fit is also important when we think about the relationship between culture and attraction. Person–organization fit refers to the match between individual personality, values, and goals with that of the organization (Kristof, 1996). Early empirical research on this topic suggests that applicant perceptions of fit with regards to values, needs, and preferences are related to organizational attraction (Judge & Cable, 1997). Recent meta-analytic work on the predictors of applicant attraction does indeed support the relationship between person–organization fit and organizational attraction (Chapman et al., 2005). Furthermore, fit is an important driver of organizational attraction at all stages during the recruitment process (Uggerslev et al., 2012).

Understanding the role of person–organization fit during recruitment is important because it relates to attraction, but it is also important because it is related to a host of meaningful outcomes post-hire. Person–organization fit is related to job satisfaction, organizational commitment, turnover intentions, and eventual turnover (Arthur, Bell, Villado, & Doverspike, 2006; Chapman & Mayers, 2013; Kristof-Brown, Zimmerman, & Johnson, 2005). Thus, organizations will benefit by developing recruitment programs that provide information related to the fit between potential applicants and the organization.

Given the increased adoption of web-based job recruitment, it is important to note that Braddy, Meade, and Kroustalis (2006) found that website information can act as an indicator of the values present within the organization during the attraction stage of recruitment. Thus, providing signals that reflect a supportive culture and high corporate social responsibility should lead to larger applicant pools. Keep in mind, however, that the goal of recruitment is to attract a large and diverse applicant pool in order to be more selective in the hiring process. Therefore, job advertisements that are too narrow in their appeal to a specific applicant profile may turn off highly qualified applicants from applying because they perceive a low match between themselves and the organization. Therefore, care should be taken to identify meaningful dimensions on which potential applicants evaluate their fit with the organization. Organizations can increase the effectiveness of their recruitment procedures by understanding their organizational culture and using it to attract applicants.

Location, location, location

Chapman et al.'s (2005) meta-analysis found that the location of an organization was a significant predictor of attraction ($\rho = .32$), particularly for women. There are many reasons why location is important to job applicants. Proximity to family and friends, entertainment opportunities, lifestyle, spouse's job location, cost of living, school quality, crime rates, and so forth are all tied to where the organization is located. Open systems theory suggests that organizations consider their environment for the availability of resources, including human resources (Katz & Kahn, 1966). For example, high-tech firms may benefit from close physical proximity to universities with strong technical programs. Organizations should carefully consider what their employees are seeking in an attractive location and try to establish facilities in locations that provide those needs. This may require a company to develop offices or facilities in multiple locations to suit the needs of their target audiences. Surveys, focus groups, and interviews with current employees and prospective employees should assist in learning what makes a location attractive for them.

Recruiter effects: does it matter who does the selling?

Recruiting researchers have long been interested in how recruiters influence recruiting outcomes. A landmark study demonstrated that recruiter warmth and friendliness were key determinants of recruiter effectiveness (Taylor & Bergmann, 1987). This work has been replicated several times, and meta-analytic results support the overall conclusion that recruiters do matter when it comes to attracting employees (Chapman et al., 2005). The most common explanation for the positive effects of recruiter friendliness is a signalling effect (Rynes, 1991). Essentially, as representative agents of the organization, friendly recruiters signal to potential employees that the company is a warm and welcoming place to work. Conversely, cold and unfriendly recruiters signal that the workplace is likely to be unfriendly. Chapman, Uggerslev, and Webster (2003) further noted that these signals were most important when the employer was relatively unknown and when the applicant had several employment opportunities from which to choose.

Recruiter friendliness generates positive hiring expectations

A second mechanism by which recruiter friendliness influences applicants is in the generation of meta-perceptions of hiring expectations (Chapman & Webster, 2006). Interviewing research demonstrates that interviewers behave differently with highly desirable employees than with those considered to be less desirable (Macan & Dipboye, 1988). Recruiters interviewing desirable candidates spend more time talking about the company and opportunities for the applicant, whereas recruiters interviewing less desirable candidates tended to have shorter interviews, asked tougher questions, and allowed the applicant to do most of the talking (Macan & Dipboye, 1988). Applicants appear to be sensitive to this tendency and view friendly interviewer behavior as an indication of the likelihood of receiving a job offer (Chapman & Webster, 2006). These positive expectations were reciprocated such that when applicants expected a job offer, they bolstered those company attributes (Janis & Mann, 1977). Conversely, applicants inferred that unfriendly interviewers were unlikely to produce a job offer, and the bolstering effect worked against these companies, making them even less desirable (Chapman & Webster, 2006).

Recruiter demographics

Whereas friendly interviewers were found to be more effective, demographic differences in recruiters appears to yield either no or limited effects. Some have hypothesized that 'similar to me' effects could produce positive demographic benefits to having female or visible minority recruiters. However, empirical support for these benefits appears to be weak or nonexistent (Chapman et al., 2005). In the end it appears that who does the recruiting is less important than how they behave in the recruiting interview and the effectiveness of the recruiting message they are trying to convey.

Recruiting messages: what makes a recruiting message effective?

In essence, recruiting is a special case of persuasion. There is a vast literature on persuasion and the message attributes that are most effective in changing a potential applicants' attitude toward the organization. Recruiting researchers have begun to explore various message approaches and how they work. For example, Cromheecke, Van Hoye, and Lievens (2013) found that novelty is an important component of a recruiting message. Specifically, when potential applicants are surprised by the novelty of the recruiting message, they are more likely to apply for the job. Furthermore, novel recruitment mediums also have a positive effect on the quality of the applicant pools. Kraichy and Chapman (in press) found that focusing on the emotional or affective content of recruiting messages was more effective than focusing on the cognitive or factual aspects of a recruiting message, particularly for individuals with low need for cognition. Although one might expect that job seekers carefully weigh the pros and cons of job choices, most of the available evidence suggests that this is a difficult cognitive task and that heuristics and emotional responses are more influential. Image theory (Beach, 1990; Beach & Mitchell, 1987) predicts that job seekers engage in a two-stage process involving an initial appraisal of each choice in a limited way to screen out choices that are incongruent with the applicants' view of themselves, followed by a more reflective examination of a smaller subset of potential choices.

Other researchers have focused on the Elaboration Likelihood Model (ELM; Petty & Cacioppo, 1986) to describe when and how recruiting messages will be effective (Larsen & Phillips, 2002). The ELM predicts that job seekers will process recruiting messages peripherally, using heuristics such as length of the advertisement or attractive graphics when they have little time or constrained ability to process the messages (e.g., at a crowded job fair or when skimming advertisements online). Conversely, applicants who have time, motivation, and the ability to carefully examine the message content will process the information centrally and be more influenced by the quality of the message. Some support for the applicability of the ELM in a recruiting context has been found (e.g., Jones, Shultz, & Chapman, 2006), but more work is needed to define how ELM can be used to examine modern recruiting practices.

Branding: if you build it, they will come

In some respects, we can consider branding as a constant recruiting message broadcast to prospective employees. Branding relies on heuristics or cognitive laziness to shortcut applicants' thinking into making an automated judgment about the organization (Dutton & Dukerich, 1991; Maurer, Howe, & Lee, 1992). Past researchers have conceptualized employer brand as consisting of instrumental components (e.g., pay, location) and symbolic attributes (e.g., ruggedness or innovativeness) (Lievens & Highhouse, 2003). Although the research on the effects of employer branding on applicant attraction has been rare, preliminary research in this area suggests that employer branding can have a small but significant impact on applicant attraction (Cable & Turban, 2001; Lievens & Highhouse, 2003, Lievens, Van Hoye, & Schreurs, 2005). Furthermore, applicant familiarity with the company has been found to have a positive influence on attraction, which is consistent with the branding approach (Chapman et al., 2005). Clearly, there is much more work to be done on employer branding and how to leverage brand equity in a recruiting context.

Recruiting employed people: heads and the hunting of them

Ultimately, the market for talented employees is an open one where employees are somewhat free to move from one employer to the next. The very best potential employees for your organization are unlikely to be conveniently unemployed when you are recruiting for an available position. Rather, they are likely happily employed with a competitor, doing what they do best. The question then becomes how one can effectively source and attract talent away from their competitors. This process is colloquially described as 'headhunting' and describes a process that involves identifying, locating, and luring talent away from your competitors. Employing a headhunting strategy, in essence, is a double win for organizations, which not only acquire new talent for their company but simultaneously deny their competitors this same talent. A more contentious aspect of this is that these talented individuals also happen to have a lot of information on your competitors and their future plans. This aspect of headhunting is particularly problematic and has generated a whole legal industry around the sensitive issue of non-disclosure and non-compete clauses in contracts. History has shown that this is particularly difficult to police and, despite language in employment contracts designed to dissuade employees from allowing themselves to be headhunted, these provisions have lacked teeth in the courts.

There is little empirical or theoretical attention paid to the process of headhunting. We propose that the best way to understand the headhunting process is to understand the employee turnover processes. Since a successful headhunting recruiting strategy requires currently employed candidates to quit their job in the process of joining the new company, applying turnover theories to headhunting could prove useful.

Mobley's (1977) model of turnover represents one turnover model that could prove useful to understanding headhunting. Essentially, this model describes the turnover process as involving a series of appraisals regarding one's current employment position. Over time, low job satisfaction leads to thoughts of quitting, job search, appraisal of alternatives, and ultimately turnover if everything lines up. Headhunters effectively short-circuit this process by injecting thoughts of quitting with a viable alternative already available. These thoughts of quitting can introduce cognitive dissonance (Festinger, 1957) as the potential candidate, who may have been previously satisfied on the job, now reappraises the job in light of the new alternative.

The unfolding model of turnover (Lee & Mitchell, 1994) goes further to incorporate several turnover paths that employees may follow depending on the nature of their unhappiness with their company. The most relevant paths from this model from a headhunting perspective are the paths involving 'shocks' or significant events that cause employees to reevaluate their relationship with their employer. In the case of headhunting, a call from a recruiter offering an attractive alternative should create the conditions necessary for a shock to occur, thereby providing a catalyst for turnover. This shock should result in a reappraisal of the current job and ultimately turnover should the new alternative prove more attractive.

Mergers and acquisitions

One of the quickest ways to obtain a large body of skilled workers is to acquire them through a direct acquisition or merger with an organization that employs them. This approach is not without risk. For example, turnover is a common problem when companies merge, as many of the sought-after employees may leave to work with other competitors. For example, Daniel and Metcalf (2001) note that up to 42% of senior managers acquired through mergers leave within the first year of the merger. Many merger processes ignore the risks of clashing organizational cultures and focus solely on synergies and economies of scale. Paying closer attention to culture fit prior to merger should yield better results for retaining skilled personnel. Ultimately, if organizations are using mergers and acquisitions for recruitment purposes, they should plan retention strategies very carefully to maximize the benefits of bringing new talent into the organization in this manner.

Technology and new trends in recruiting

Recruiting practice has perhaps changed more in the past six years than it changed in several decades preceding. Technology shifts, demographic changes, and the explosive growth of social media have transformed the recruiting function from simply posting job advertisements or attending career fairs to an ongoing flexible activity involving multiple sources and technologies.

Online recruiting

Researchers have begun to investigate how the rapid shift to online recruiting is affecting the recruiting process. Early research has provided some clear guidance for certain aspects of attraction. For instance, website design appears to be an important determinant of applicant attraction. Specifically, empirical work has found that applicants show greater attraction toward websites that are aesthetically pleasing and easy to navigate (Cober, Brown, Levy, Cober, & Keeping, 2003) and provide information suggesting high levels of person-organization fit (Dineen, Ash, & Noe, 2002; Dineen & Noe, 2009). Others have found that tailoring online recruiting messages to individual differences such as need for cognition could prove useful (Kraichy & Chapman, in press).

The online medium also provides greater opportunities to include video-based recruiting materials such as employee testimonials, which have been found to be effective recruiting tools. Van Hoye and Lievens (2007) found that online employee testimonials were most effective and credible when they focused on the stories of specific employees rather than having employees simply espouse the benefits of the organization. There is nearly limitless potential to develop interactive online recruiting processes. Screening potential applicants with short online surveys could prove useful in tailoring online content that is relevant for the applicant and most likely to lead to attraction. Still, we know little about what information to tailor and how to tailor it.

Gamification of recruiting

Gamification refers to the use of games and game mechanics to facilitate various organizational functions. Little is known about the application of gamification in the recruiting process. Chow and Chapman (2013) proposed a theory illustrating the potential mechanisms for how gamification could influence applicant attraction. For example, game use could be as simple as branding the organization through exposure to the company through gameplay (e.g., a racing game with the company logo prominently displayed on billboards beside the virtual racetrack). At a more complex level, Chow and Chapman (2013) argue that games could influence attitudes toward companies and industries. Simulations involving gameplay, for instance, could provide centrally processed messages about how the company operates. For example, playing a game that requires the game player to assume the role of a manager in the company and make difficult decisions about how to allocate resources could influence how potential applicants feel about the company and the decisions made by its directors. There is a strong need for additional research addressing this emerging recruiting technology and its influence on both the size and quality of applicant pools.

Social media and recruiting

At the present time most adults of working age in North America and Western Europe have at least some access to or participation in social media networks. Popular sites such as Facebook and LinkedIn as well as Twitter feeds and other social media distribution sites connect millions of people around the world. This has led to an explosive growth in the use of social media to conduct recruiting (SHRM, 2011).

Practitioners need to exercise extreme caution when using social media information on candidates. Recent research shows that applicants tend to view a company's use of social networking in screening and selection of candidates to be an invasion of privacy, leading to negative reactions toward the company (Stoughton, Thompson, & Meade, in press). Given this potential negative reaction, recruiters should develop processes to inform candidates if and when they access their social media data and provide a cogent explanation for how and why they use this information to candidates. For example, it may be acceptable to locate and contact potential recruits through social media but unacceptable to search through social media information to screen out candidates. Given the growing popularity of this approach, research into the efficacy of social media recruiting practices and applicant reactions to these practices is highly desirable.

Methodological considerations in studying recruiting processes

A key concern when studying organizational recruiting is to ensure that some standardization exists in measuring important recruiting outcomes. Chapman et al. (2005) identified four major recruiting outcomes that have traditionally been measured in the recruiting literature. These outcomes include: Organizational Attraction, Job Pursuit Intentions, Acceptance Intentions, and Job Choice. Most of the empirical work in recruiting has focused on the first three outcomes, with far fewer studies examining actual job choices. Those that have measured job choice have typically examined student samples. Although students are a legitimate and important population to study, and despite the fact that meta-analytic findings show comparable results for student and applicant samples (Chapman et al., 2005), more studies need to focus on job applicants from nonstudent samples.

Additional qualitative work is also required to more fully understand the job search and recruiting processes. Limitations of self-reported preferences for various recruiting variables (e.g., pay, location) are well known and unreliable due to impression management and lack of self-knowledge. Qualitative work to uncover recruiting variables of importance is a key starting point, followed by policy capturing laboratory settings research and quasi-experimental designs in real-world settings.

Future research

With the combination of questions remaining, and shifts in the recruitment strategies being employed by organizations, there is a great need for more research that examines the systems, processes, and strategies that maximize the size and quality of the applicant pool. Most evidently, the majority of research that currently exists examines the effectiveness of traditional recruitment media. Therefore, future research is needed that attempts to replicate and extend previous findings using more modern methods of recruitment. Research into emerging technologies such as social media use, gamification, and branding in recruitment are sorely needed.

Second, researchers need to focus on the creation and development of new recruiting theory. The field needs researchers to engage in more qualitative research to help generate theories that can be tested empirically. Understanding recruiting theory should help practitioners create better recruiting strategies that draw upon research rather than relying on trial-and-error approaches that are common in the field. For example, there is practically no research on the effects of headhunting despite this being a common practice in recruiting. Understanding the combination of turnover and attraction that occurs in the headhunting function will contribute greatly to both research and practice. Testing existing theory in other areas of psychology such as persuasion (e.g., ELM) in a recruiting context could also prove useful.

Last, researchers need to employ more elaborate designs and statistical procedures in order to provide the ability to answer the interesting and novel questions outstanding. Recruiting is a longitudinal process, so researchers need to focus on techniques that examine this process as it unfolds. For example, many fields of research have begun to incorporate latent growth modeling into their designs. Traditionally, longitudinal recruitment research measures the relationship between the predictor(s) and dependent variable using simple correlations or a series of regressions or multiple regressions at different points in time. However, when multiple waves of data are collected, latent growth modeling is a more sophisticated approach. Latent growth modeling is capable of modeling change while also accounting for random between-person intercepts and random between-person slopes, as well as their combined effects. Applying this analytic strategy within recruitment research in general would be an excellent contribution to the literature.

Conclusion

The success of overall recruiting outcomes is highly contingent upon attracting sufficient quantity and quality of applicants to meet the needs of the organization. In this chapter we have proposed that effective recruiting can be accomplished through multiple approaches such as designing more attractive jobs and organizations and crafting persuasive recruiting messages that make the best of what you have to offer. There are significant unknowns regarding the efficacy of these practices that provide opportunities for future research. Creating and testing new and useful recruiting theories is critical if the field is to move forward with providing guidance to recruiting practitioners.

References

Ambler, T., & Barrow, S. (1996). The employer brand. *Journal of Brand Management, 4*, 185–206.

Arthur, W., Jr., Bell, S.T., Villado, A.J., & Doverspike, D. (2006). The use of person-organization fit in employment decision making: An assessment of its criterion-related validity. *Journal of Applied Psychology, 91*, 786–801.

Barber, A.E. (1998). *Recruiting employees: Individual and organizational perspectives.* Thousand Oaks, CA: Sage Publications, Inc.

Beach, L.R. (1990). *Image theory: Decision making in personal and organizational contexts.* Chichester, UK: Wiley.

Beach, L.R., & Mitchell, T.R. (1987). Image theory: Principles, goals, and plans in decision making. *Acta Psychologica, 66*, 201–220.

Boudreau, J.W., & Rynes, S.L. (1985). Role of recruitment in staffing utility analysis. *Journal of Applied Psychology, 70*, 354–366.

Braddy, P.W., Meade, A.W., & Kroustalis, C.M. (2006). Organizational recruitment website effects on viewers' perceptions of organizational culture. *Journal of Business and Psychology, 20*, 525–543.

Breaugh, J.A., & Starke, M. (2000). Research on employee recruitment: So many studies, so many remaining questions. *Journal of Management, 26*, 405–434.

Cable, D.M., & Turban, D.B. (2001). Establishing the dimensions, sources and value of job seekers' employer knowledge during recruitment. *Research in Personnel and Human Resources Management, 20*, 115–163.

Cable, D.M., & Turban, D.B. (2003). The value of organizational reputation in the recruitment context: A band-equity perspective. *Journal of Applied Social Psychology, 33*, 2244–2266.

Cable, D.M., & Yu, K.Y.T. (2006). Managing job seekers' organizational image beliefs: The role of media richness and media credibility. *Journal of Applied Psychology, 91*, 828–840.

Catanzaro, D., Moore, H., & Marshall, T.R. (2010). The impact of organizational culture on attraction and recruitment of job applicants. *Journal of Business and Psychology, 25*, 649–662.

Chapman, D.S., & Borodenko, N. (2006, April). Targeting recruiting efforts at the individual, occupational, or universal level. In C. Harold (Chair), *The rules of attraction: What, when, and why applicants choose.* Symposium presented at the annual meeting of the Society for Industrial & Organizational Psychology, Dallas, TX.

Chapman, D.S., & Mayers, D. (2013, August). *Predicting voluntary turnover with organizational culture, employee values and their congruence: A longitudinal analysis.* Paper presented at the 73rd Academy of Management Meeting, Lake Buena Vista, FL. Abstract retrieved from http://program.aomonline.org/2013/submission.asp?mode=ShowSession&SessionID=1547

Chapman, D.S., Uggerslev, K.L., Carroll, S.A., Piasentin, K.A., & Jones, D.A. (2005). Applicant attraction to organizations and job choice: A meta-analytic review of the correlates of recruiting outcomes. *Journal of Applied Psychology, 90,* 928–944.

Chapman, D.S., Uggerslev, K.L., & Webster, J. (2003). Applicant reactions to face-to-face and technology-mediated interviews: A field investigation. *Journal of Applied Psychology, 88,* 944–953.

Chapman, D.S., & Webster, J. (2006). Toward an integrated model of applicant reactions and job choice. *The International Journal of Human Resource Management, 17,* 1032–1057.

Chow, S., & Chapman, D.S. (2013, June). *Gamifying the employee recruitment process.* Paper presented at the First International Conference on Gameful Design, Research, and Applications, Waterloo, ON.

Cober, R.T., Brown, D.J., Levy, P.E., Cober, A.B., & Keeping, L.M. (2003). Organizational web sites: Web site content and style as determinants of organizational attraction. *International Journal of Selection and Assessment, 11,* 158–169.

Cromheecke, S., Van Hoye, G., & Lievens, F. (2013). Changing things up in recruitment: Effects of a 'strange' recruitment medium on applicant pool quantity and quality. *Journal of Occupational and Organizational Psychology, 86,* 410–416.

Daniel, T., & Metcalf, G. (2001). *Management of people in mergers and acquisitions.* Westport, CT: Greenwood Press.

Darnold, T.C., & Rynes, S.L. (2013). Recruitment and job choice research: Same as it ever was? In N.W. Schmitt, S. Highhouse, & I.B. Weiner (Eds.), *Handbook of Psychology: Vol. 12. Industrial and organizational psychology* (2nd ed., pp. 104–142). Hoboken, NJ: John Wiley & Sons Inc.

Dineen, B.R., Ash, S.R., & Noe, R.A. (2002). A web of applicant attraction: Person-organization fit in the context of web-based recruitment. *Journal of Applied Psychology, 92,* 356–372.

Dineen, B.R., & Noe, R.A. (2009). Effects of customization on application decisions and applicant pool characteristics in a web-based recruitment context. *Journal of Applied Psychology, 94*(1), 224.

Dutton, J.E., & Dukerich, J.M. (1991). Keeping an eye on the mirror: Image and identity in organizational adaptation. *Academy of Management Journal, 34*(3), 517–554.

Ehrhart, K.H., & Ziegert, J.C. (2005). Why are individuals attracted to organizations? *Journal of Management, 31,* 901–919.

Festinger, L. (1957). *A theory of cognitive dissonance.* Stanford, CA: Stanford University Press.

Hackman, J.R., & Oldham, G.R. (1975). Development of the job diagnostic survey. *Journal of Applied Psychology, 60,* 159–170.

Highhouse, S., Zickar, M.J., Thorsteinson, T.J., Stierwalt, S.L., & Slaughter, J.E. (1999). Assessing company employment image: An example in the fast food industry. *Personnel Psychology, 52,* 151–172.

Humphrey, S.E., Nahrgang, J.D., & Morgeson, F.P. (2007). Integrating motivational, social, and contextual work design features: A meta-analytic summary and theoretical extension of the work design literature. *Journal of Applied Psychology, 92,* 1332–1356.

Janis, I., & Mann, L. (1977). *Decision making: A psychological analysis of conflict, choice and commitment.* New York: Free Press.

Jones, D.A., Shultz, J., & Chapman, D.S. (2006). Recruiting through job advertisements: The effects of cognitive elaboration on decision making. *International Journal of Selection and Assessment, 14,* 167–179.

Judge, T.A., & Cable, D.M. (1997). Applicant personality, organizational culture, and organization attraction. *Personnel Psychology, 50,* 359–394.

Katz, D., & Kahn, R.L. (1966). *The social psychology of organizations.* New York: Wiley.

Kraichy, D., & Chapman, D.S. (in press). Tailoring web-based recruiting messages: Individual differences in the persuasiveness of affective and cognitive messages. *Journal of Business and Psychology*.

Kristof, A.L. (1996). Person-organization fit: An integrative review of its conceptualizations, measurement, and implications. *Personnel Psychology, 49*, 1–49.

Kristof-Brown, A.L., Zimmerman, R.D., & Johnson, E.C. (2005). Consequences of individuals' fit at work: A meta-analysis of person-job, person-organization, person-group, and person-supervisor fit. *Personnel Psychology, 58*, 281–342.

Larsen, D.A. & Phillips, J.I. (2002). Effect of recruiter on attraction to the firm: Implications of the Elaboration Likelihood Model. *Journal of Business and Psychology, 16*, 347–364.

Lee, T.W., & Mitchell, T.R. (1994). An alternative approach: The unfolding model of voluntary employee turnover. *Academy of Management Review, 19*, 51–89.

Lievens, F., & Highhouse, S. (2003). The relation of instrumental and symbolic attributes to a company's attractiveness as an employer. *Personnel Psychology, 56*, 75–102.

Lievens, F., Van Hoye, G., & Schreurs, B. (2005). Examining the relationship between employer knowledge dimensions and organizational attractiveness: An application in a military context. *Journal of Occupational and Organizational Psychology, 78*, 553–572.

Lippman, S.A., & McCall, J.J. (1976). The economics of job search: A survey. *Economic Inquiry, 14*, 155–189.

Macan, T.H. & Dipboye, R. L. (1988). The effects of interviewers' initial impressions on information gathering. *Organizational Behavior and Human Decision Processes, 42*, 364–387.

Markus, H., & Nurius, P. (1986). Possible selves. *American Psychologist, 41*, 954–969.

Maurer, S.D., Howe, V., & Lee, T.W. (1992). Organizational recruiting as marketing management: An interdisciplinary study of engineering graduates. *Personnel Psychology, 45*, 807–833.

Mobley, W.H. (1977). Intermediate linkages in the relationship between job satisfaction and employee turnover. *Journal of Applied Psychology, 62*, 237–240.

Morgeson, F.P., & Campion, M.A. (2003). Work design. In W.C. Borman, D.R. Ilgen, & R.J. Klimoski (Eds.), *Handbook of Psychology: Vol. 12. Industrial and organizational psychology* (pp. 423–452). New York: John Wiley.

Nolan, K.P., & Harold, C.M. (2010). Fit with what? The influence of multiple self-concept images on organizational attraction. *Journal of Occupational and Organizational Psychology, 83*, 645–662.

O'Reilly, C. (1989). Corporations, culture, and commitment: Motivation and social control in organizations. *California Management Review, 31*, 9–25.

Petty, R.E., & Cacioppo, J.T. (1986). *The Elaboration Likelihood Model of persuasion*. New York: Academic Press.

Rynes, S.L. (1989). The employment interview as a recruitment device. In R.W. Eder & G.R. Ferris (Eds.), *The employment interview: Research and practice* (pp. 127–141). Beverly Hills, CA: Sage.

Rynes, S.L. (1991). Recruitment, job choice, and post-hire consequences: A call for new research directions. In M.D. Dunnette & L.M. Hough (Eds.), *Handbook of industrial and organizational psychology* (2nd ed., Vol. 2, pp. 399–444). Palo Alto, CA: Consulting Psychologists Press.

Rynes, S.L., Bretz, R.D., & Gerhart, B. (1991). The importance of recruitment in job choice: A different way of looking. *Personnel Psychology, 44*, 487–521.

Schein, E. (1985). *Organizational culture and leadership*. London: Jossey-Bass Ltd.

Schmidt, J., Chapman, D.S., & Jones, D.A. (in press). Does emphasizing different types of person-environment fit in job ads influence application behavior and applicant quality? Evidence from a field experiment. *Journal of Business and Psychology*.

Schwab, D.P., Rynes, S.L., & Aldag, R.J. (1987). Theories and research on job search and choice. *Research in Personnel and Human Resources Management, 5*, 129–166.

SHRM. (2011, April). SHRM research spotlight: Social networking websites and staffing. Retrieved from www.shrm.org/research

Spence, M. (1973). Job market signaling. *The Quarterly Journal of Economics, 87*, 355–374. Retrieved from http://links.jstor.org/sici?sici=00335533%28197308%2987%3A3%3C355%3AJMS%3E2.0.CO%3B2-3

Stoughton, J.W., Thompson, L.F., & Meade, A.W. (in press). Examining applicant reactions to the use of social networking websites in pre-employment screening. *Journal of Business and Psychology*.

Tajfel, H., & Turner, J.C. (1985). The social identity theory of intergroup behaviour. In S. Worchel & W.G. Austin (Eds.), *Psychology of intergroup relations* (pp. 7–24). Chicago: Nelson Hall.

Taylor, M.S., & Bergmann, T.J. (1987). Organizational recruitment activities and applicants' reactions at different stages of the recruitment process. *Personnel Psychology, 40*, 261–285.

Tom, V.R. (1971). The role of personality and organizational images in the recruiting process. *Organizational Behavior and Human Performance, 6*, 573–592.

Tsai, W.C., & Yang, I.W.F. (2010). Does image matter to different job applicants? The influences of corporate image and applicant individual differences on organizational attractiveness. *International Journal of Selection and Assessment, 18*, 48–63.

Uggerslev, K.L., Fassina, N.E., & Kraichy, D. (2012). Recruiting through the stages: A meta-analytic test of predictors of applicant attraction at different stages of the recruiting process. *Personnel Psychology, 65*(3), 597–660.

Van Hoye, G., & Lievens, F. (2007). Investigating web-based recruitment sources: Employee testimonials vs word-of-mouse. *International Journal of Selection and Assessment, 15*, 372–382.

Van Vianen, A.E., & Fischer, A.H. (2002). Illuminating the glass ceiling: The role of organizational culture preferences. *Journal of Occupational and Organizational Psychology, 75*, 315–337.

PART B
The applicants' perspective

3

VIDEO RÉSUMÉS PORTRAYED

Findings and challenges

Annemarie M. F. Hiemstra

ERASMUS UNIVERSITY ROTTERDAM, THE NETHERLANDS

Eva Derous

GHENT UNIVERSITY, BELGIUM

The introduction of personal computers in the 1980s marked the onset of developments in computerized testing (Oostrom, 2010; Sands, Waters, & McBride, 1997). In the 1990s the use of the Internet started to spread. This development and the technological advancements in personal computers opened the door to the use of multimedia in selection procedures (Oostrom, 2010), such as video résumés (Doyle, 2010; Gissel, Thompson, & Pond, 2013; Hiemstra, Derous, Serlie, & Born, 2012). Video résumés have been described as short, videotaped messages in which applicants present themselves to potential employers on requested knowledge, skills, abilities, and other characteristics, such as motivation and career objectives (Hiemstra, Derous, et al., 2012). Typically, video résumés are uploaded to the Internet for potential employers to review (Doyle, 2010). Although the format of video résumés can vary (e.g., structure, multimedia usage), the common denominator is that auditory and visual information of the applicant is introduced in a short video clip (about one to two minutes), during the earliest screening phase, and in an asynchronous manner (i.e., the employer views the application at a later point in time). These characteristics differentiate the video résumé from a real-time, video-supported interview (e.g., via Skype).

Résumés are widely used for initial screening, but still little is known about new résumé formats like video résumés. With the increased use of multimedia applications such as video résumés, questions arise on their validity, fairness, and acceptability. This chapter describes the characteristics of video résumés, followed

---

Address for correspondence: Annemarie M.F. Hiemstra, Institute of Psychology, Erasmus University Rotterdam, PO Box 1738, 3000 DR Rotterdam, the Netherlands. E-mail: hiemstra@fsw.eurnl

by a review on what is currently known about video résumés, and an agenda for future research. The next section describes the characteristics of video résumés by means of a comparison with job interviews, being another popular and widely used screening method. Résumé screening and interview screening are typically considered as two different selection tools that are discussed separately in the literature (e.g., Guion, 2011). Multimedia applications, like the opportunity to post videotaped résumés on the Internet, may have altered the nature of résumé screening and may have made résumé screening in some aspects more comparable to face-to-face job interviews. Findings from the interview literature can help improve our understanding of the advantages and disadvantages of video résumés as a selection tool. Although video résumés and job interviews share some characteristics, they are not simply interchangeable. We aim to set the stage here by explaining the similarities and differences between video résumés and job interviews, thereby defining the video résumé as a selection instrument.

Setting the stage: characteristics of video résumés vis-à-vis job interviews

Arthur and Villado (2008) argue that one should distinguish comparisons made between predictor constructs (e.g., personality versus cognitive ability) from comparisons made between predictor methods (e.g., video résumés versus job interviews). This chapter focuses on the latter. However, without a clear construct-oriented approach, selection tools may be used in a rather intuitive way. For instance, interviews may merely serve the purpose of checking whether there is a 'click' between interviewer and interviewee. Without a clear construct-oriented approach, video résumés may result in invalid impressions about job candidates. Critics may add that a construct-oriented approach is not feasible for video résumés, contrary to structured interviews. After all, video résumés are self-presentational in nature, like paper résumés. But this can be refuted in the sense that requirements can be set by the hiring organization on the contents of the video résumé. We believe that the validity and reliability of constructs measured by video résumés can be improved in the same way that the validity and reliability of interviews can be improved: through various ways of structuring the content and the raters' evaluation of the applicant (Campion, Palmer, & Campion, 1997).

Having said that about the importance of distinguishing between constructs and methods, five comparable aspects are put forward here to compare video résumés and interviews as two methods for selection. Video résumés and job interviews can both be considered as general denominators for tools that vary in their *goal and content* (type of information exchanged), *format* (kind of communication code, administration duration, number of actors involved, direction of communication, degree of surveillance), *standardization/structure* (whether standardized procedures are maintained across applicants and whether tools are structured), *administration medium* (whether the information carrier is analogue or digital in nature), and *interactivity* (whether the tool allows for reciprocal information exchange and is synchronous or asynchronous in nature). Next, we will investigate these five basic features of tools for the video résumé, followed by the job interview. This chapter will not present an in-depth analysis of interview characteristics (the interested reader can find recent, more extensive reviews in Dipboye & Johnson, 2013; Levashina, Hartwell, Morgeson, & Campion, 2013; Macan, 2009). Instead, we will discuss the five abovementioned characteristics to compare video résumés to job interviews, thereby defining video résumés.

First, the *goal and content* of video résumés is to present personal information to potential employers. Video résumés typically include important educational and professional background information such as academic background, work experience, and extracurricular activities, comparable to paper résumés (Cole, Rubin, Feild, & Giles, 2007; Hiemstra, Derous, et al., 2012). In addition to bio data information, one's motivation to apply can be elucidated and relevant skills and knowledge can be presented, like software skills or communication skills. This information can be presented in a generic form (such as a résumé that is posted on a recruitment website) or can be tailored to fit a specific job profile that highlights specific skills as requested by the hiring organization (e.g., a résumé for a specific job).

Second, video résumés may vary widely in *format* characteristics because of new opportunities that arise with the use of multimedia. The format of video résumés may range from a verbal description of skills and accomplishments to a format in which a predefined set of questions are answered and/or requested work samples are provided that demonstrate job-relevant skills (e.g., for a ballet audition; Hamilton, 1998). Although there is no golden standard as to the length of the video résumé, video résumés are typically very short (i.e., lasting about one to two minutes; like an 'elevator pitch').

Third, *standardization*, or the degree that standardized procedures are maintained across all applicants/video résumés, may differ considerably. For instance, employers may offer applicants a free choice to use video résumés or not when applying. Additionally, employers may use a highly structured approach when they request all applicants apply with a video résumé. That is, the video résumé format can be *more or less structured* depending on whether applicants have to present the same type and amount of job-related information to potential employers and whether employers use a scoring protocol and numerical rating scales to evaluate video résumés, just like the structured interview (Campion et al., 1997; Guion, 2011). For instance, to apply for the YouTube Symphony Orchestra, musicians were requested by the YouTube organization and the London Symphony Orchestra to perform several preset audition pieces in a video résumé. As mentioned, when content requirements are lacking, the self-presentational nature of video résumés as initiated by the job applicant may result in a high variation of the amount, type, and degree of job-relevant information (Gissel et al., 2013). As with the individualized structured interview, the structure of video résumés might be unique for each candidate, specifically so when initiated by the job applicant.

Fourth, the *administration medium* of video résumés is digital (e.g., web-based), whereas interviews can be face-to-face, via phone, or via the Internet. Finally, and as consequence, the *interactivity* of video résumés is limited, meaning that the pace of feedback exchange is rather low. Video résumés are posted and can be consulted at any time from anywhere. Furthermore, communication is unidirectional, from the applicant to the recruiter. Other than with interviews or instant messaging through the Internet, video résumés are thus asynchronous in nature.

As will be further illustrated, job interviews may vary along the five aspects that were discussed here for video résumés. First, the content of job interviews may depend on the particular goal of the interview. Overall, four goals are distinguished in job interviews: information exchange between interviewer and interviewee, assessment of interviewees by interviewers, establishing personal contact between interviewers and interviewees, and providing a realistic job preview to interviewees (Lievens, 2011). That is, the interview allows interviewers to retrieve information about applicants' competencies in order to assess person–job fit. This face-to-face (or synchronous) encounter also allows interviewers to present the job and organization as well as to establish a relationship with the applicant (Dipboye & Johnson, 2013), which is not the case in video résumé applications. Second, the interview format is determined by factors such as interview duration, number of interviewers, or applied interview medium (e.g., videoconferencing or telephone interview). Third, the interview typically consists of three stages, namely a rapport building, information exchange, and evaluation stage. The degree of standardization and structure are largely determined by the level of structure in interview questions and evaluation forms, ranging from unstructured to highly structured (e.g., behavioral interviews), as well as the use of standard procedures across all interviews (see Table 3.1). Further, the administration medium of the classical face-to-face interview is analogue in nature, but current technological developments and globalization have opened the door to telephone and web-based interviews (Bauer, Truxillo, Paronto, Weekley, & Campion 2004; Dipboye & Johnson, 2013). Finally, as mentioned above, the interactivity in interviews is high, as they are synchronous in nature, unlike video résumés. The duration of interviews is also much longer than video résumés (with a typical interview lasting about 30 minutes; e.g., Dipboye & Johnson, 2013), thus allowing for more interaction between the applicant and the recruiter.

At least two facets make video résumés resemble the traditional interview. First, much like the traditional job interview, video résumés enable one to transmit more *dynamic information*, including both visual/nonverbal and auditory/verbal information (Potosky, 2008), in the earliest screening stage. Second, like the job interview, video résumés are self-reports that enable the applicant to actually convey knowledge, skills, and abilities to the recruiter instead of merely presenting biographic information such as in paper résumés (Hiemstra, Derous, et al., 2012). Depending on the degree of construct-oriented formalization (i.e., job requirements), the information exchanged through video résumés resembles more or less that of the traditional job interview (although asynchronous) compared to the paper résumé. That is, in addition to bio data information, applicants can elucidate their

TABLE 3.1 Comparison of two selection media: video résumé versus job interview

Features of both media		Video résumé	Job interview
Content	Type of information that is exchanged	Background information and KSAOs: past-oriented (e.g., biographic information) and present-oriented (e.g., demonstrating skills)	Background information and KSAOs: past-oriented (e.g., bio data; behavior description interview), present-oriented (e.g., skills demonstrated in the interview like in performance interviews), and future-oriented (e.g., situational and hypothetical questions)
Format	Format characteristics including the communication code (verbal vs. nonverbal), the administration duration, the number of actors involved, the direction of communication (one-way vs. two-way), and the degree of surveillance (actual security/invasiveness)	Spoken résumés that include both verbal and nonverbal information, short duration (typically less than two minutes), only one actor (applicant) involved, surveillance can vary from very low to high	Verbal and nonverbal communication, with varying duration from short to very long, two or more actors involved (one applicant and one or more recruiters), and typically high surveillance
Standardization	Degree of standardization, i.e., whether standardized procedures are maintained or not across all applicants and tests	Standardization fluctuates depending on the recruiters' policy (e.g., whether they request all applicants to send in a video résumé or not)	Typically, interviews are standardized across applicants (not necessarily across procedures)
Structure	Degree of structure, i.e., whether the tool is tailored to fit the work to be done, by whom it is structured, and whether a scoring protocol is used	Mostly structured by the applicant, but can also be structured by the recruiter. The video résumé can be tailored to fit the work to be done in several degrees. The video résumé can be scored according to a protocol.	Mostly structured by the recruiter. The interview structure (including rating scales) varies widely, from individualized structured interviews to comprehensive structured interviews.
Administration medium	Whether the information carrier is analogue or digital in nature	Digital (i.e., web-based)	Analogue (e.g., face-to-face interviews) and digital (e.g., web-based interviewing and videoconference interviews)
Interactivity	The extent to which the tool allows for reciprocal information exchange (i.e., turn taking) and, relatedly, whether the information exchange is asynchronous or synchronous in nature	Unidirectional, asynchronous	Bidirectional, synchronous

motivation to apply and present relevant skills and knowledge. Typically, this information is tailored to fit a specific job profile.

Yet, despite these two similarities in *dynamic information exchange* and *opportunity to demonstrate one's potential*, still notable differences exist between both tools that might affect their validity and fairness. First, both the content and form of video résumés are typically *structured by the applicant* with a *limited amount of time* allotted to impress the recruiter, whereas the job interview is typically longer and *structured by the recruiter* (to a greater or lesser extent). Second, video résumés are *asynchronous* in nature, thereby restricting the real-time two-way interaction/communication exchange between the applicant and the recruiter, whereas face-to-face interviews are *synchronous* in nature. Finally, and although the length of the job interview may vary considerably, there is typically more opportunity for applicants to *adjust* their behavior to the particular situation (e.g., what recruiters ask and also how they react in a nonverbal way) compared to video résumés. As a result, video résumés may restrict the amount of personalized/individuating information exchange about candidates as well as subtle impression management and adaptation on the part of the applicant when compared to more traditional face-to-face encounters in the job interview setting (e.g., Bangerter, Roulin, & König, 2012).

Review of video résumé research: what we know about video résumés

Exact numbers on the frequency of use of video résumés in current selection practices are still lacking. A study in 2009 among 176 HR professionals at medium- and small-sized enterprises in the Netherlands showed that 70% were aware of the existence of video résumés. Yet, only 8% actually used the video résumé, whereas about 40% were willing to consider it (Hiemstra, 2013). As with traditional résumés, popular media coverage on video résumés in conventional written media sources and on the Internet is abundant (Gissel et al., 2013). As described by Gissel et al. (2013), both practitioners and researchers have gained interest in video résumés. For instance, in 2012 one of the first symposia on video résumés was organized at the 27th annual conference of the Society for Industrial and Organizational Psychology (Derous, Buijsrogge, Gissel, Schmitt, Thompson, Hiemstra, et al., 2012).

Before that date, scholarly publications on the topic were scarce, however, as indicated by the limited amount of hits (three) on Web of Science after a search in 2012 (Derous, Taveirne, & Hiemstra, 2012). The three publications in Web of Science furthermore dated from the 1980s and 1990s (Hamilton, 1998; Kelly & O'Brien, 1992; Warshawski, 1987). The publications by Hamilton (1998) and Warshawski (1987) were about dance auditions through videotaped applications. For dancers and musicians it has been common practice for a longer period of time to send in tapes for audition. Kelly and O'Brien (1992) used the video résumé to teach job search skills to deaf students, helping them to present themselves to potential employers. Light (1993) also described the development of video résumés for persons with disabilities. One of the first scientific publications of video résumés for 'mainstream' applicants seems to stem from 1993 (Rolls & Strenkowski, 1993), in a pilot among education students. The authors stated that the distribution of video résumés may supply prospective employers with additional nonverbal and interpersonal information that may benefit all stakeholders.

More recently, the increased use of Internet and social media is starting to find its reflection in recruitment practices (Roth, Bobko, Van Iddekinge, & Thatcher, 2013; Stoughton, Thompson, & Meade, 2014), also with video résumés. For instance, in 2009 a worldwide recruitment program was launched by the Queensland Tourist Board in Australia, inviting applicants to send a 60-second video message to demonstrate their suitability for a marketing job. An impressive number of 34,000 applicants from around the world responded to this call (Queensland Tourist Board Australia, 2009). More and more examples exist of actual selection procedures in which applicants are invited to apply through a video résumé, both in Europe and in the United States (Hiemstra, Oostrom, Derous, Serlie, & Born, 2012; Silverman, 2012). Additionally, a growing number of companies are offering services that range from online hosting of video résumés in search databases for recruiters to the full production of résumés for applicants (Gissel et al., 2013).

As developments are moving fast, we conducted a new search of Web of Science and of conference proceedings in December 2013. This resulted in six recent scientific studies that specifically target video résumés (Derous, Taveirne, & Hiemstra, 2012; Gissel et al., 2013; Hiemstra, Derous, et al., 2012; Hiemstra, Oostrom, et al., 2012; Waung, Beatty, Hymes, & McAuslan, 2010; Waung, Hymes, Beatty, & McAuslan, 2012). The studies by Gissel et al. (2013) and Hiemstra, Derous, et al. (2012) focused on the applicants' perspective. Specifically, these authors studied applicants' intentions to apply with a video résumé and applicants' fairness perceptions of video résumés. The studies by Derous, Taveirne, & Hiemstra (2012) and Waung et al. (2010; 2012) focused more on the tool/recruiters' side, namely judgmental accuracy and potential biases. Each of these studies will be discussed here.

Gissel and colleagues (2013) studied video résumés from the applicants' perspective. They researched in a lab experiment among 154 students why some potential job seekers may choose to submit a video résumé, while others may not. The researchers used Ajzen's (1991) theory of planned behavior as a theoretical framework to assess applicant intentions to apply with a video résumé. The study showed support for the theory of planned behavior in intentions to create a video résumé among entry-level applicants (student participants): a positive attitude towards video résumés, applicants' perceived social pressure to submit video résumés (i.e., social norms), and their self-assessed ability to create/submit video résumés (i.e., perceived behavioral control) all related positively to applicants' intentions to submit video résumés to prospective employers. Attitudes and subjective norms were especially important factors when compared to perceived behavioral control.

Hiemstra, Derous, et al. (2012) and Hiemstra, Oostrom, et al. (2012) also investigated video résumés from the applicant perspective. These papers differ from the Gissel et al. (2013) paper in that they assessed actual applicants' fairness perceptions of video résumés compared to paper résumés. In the first study (Hiemstra, Derous, et al., 2012), applicant perspectives were investigated among 445 unemployed job seekers (both ethnic minorities and majorities). They were enrolled in a subsidized training by the Dutch government, which resulted in a personal video résumé. The study showed that, despite potential discriminatory concerns, ethnic minority applicants perceived the fairness of video résumés equally or more positively when compared to ethnic majority applicants, and when compared to paper résumés. Furthermore, language proficiency was a significant moderator: higher proficiency in the host country language (Dutch) was related to higher fairness perceptions of paper résumés. The implication was suggested that applicants with a relatively weak labor market position (e.g., those low on host country language skills, ethnic minority applicants) may prefer a more personalized way of applying (video résumé), instead of less personalized ways (e.g., with paper résumés).

The second study (Hiemstra, Oostrom, et al., 2012) investigated 103 higher-educated applicants for a legislative traineeship position who were obliged by the hiring organization to submit a videotaped application. Contrary to the findings among the unemployed job seekers, the highly educated traineeship applicants in the second study preferred paper résumés over video résumés in terms of fairness and procedural justice ($1.59 < d < 2.18$). This study also explored the role of applicants' personality and cognitive ability in explaining their preferences for paper versus video résumés: extraverted applicants perceived more opportunity to perform with video résumés compared to introverted applicants. Extraversion was also positively related to face validity perceptions of video résumés. Cognitive ability, on the other hand, related negatively to videotaped application fairness perceptions. The negative finding on cognitive ability pertains to the idea that video résumés may be preferred by applicants with a weaker labor market position (e.g., those with lower general mental ability or educational level, such as the unemployed job seekers in the Hiemstra, Derous, et al. [2012] study).

To summarize, the three available studies on the applicants' perspective showed individual differences in intentions to submit a video résumé, which seemed to be especially related to applicants' attitudes towards video résumés and the perceived social pressure to apply with a video résumé (subjective norm). Also, mixed findings in fairness perceptions of video résumés were shown, depending on applicants' ethnicity, language proficiency, cognitive ability, and extraversion.

The other three studies that we found in our search on Web of Science and in conference proceedings were on the equivalence, validity, and the possible discriminating nature of video résumés vis-à-vis paper résumés (Derous, Taveirne, & Hiemstra, 2012; Waung et al., 2010; Waung et al., 2012). Two of those three studies particularly focused on stigmatized applicants: age and attractiveness were studied by Derous, Taveirne, & Hiemstra (2012), and gender was studied by Waung et al. (2012).

As regards equivalence, Waung et al. (2010) studied the effect of résumé format on candidate evaluation and résumé outcomes among a group of MBA students. When mock applicants (MBA students) were evaluated based on their video résumés, they were rated as less open, extraverted, physically attractive, socially skilled, and mentally capable and more neurotic than when the same applicants were evaluated based on their paper résumés. Those who were rated as more socially skilled and more conscientious had a higher probability of positive résumé outcomes. Using two field experiments, Derous, Taveirne, & Hiemstra (2012) also examined the equivalence of video versus paper résumés on applicants' personality and job suitability ratings, as made by actual recruiters. They concluded that résumé type did not clearly affect applicant ratings. For instance, personality inferences from video résumés appeared as valid or invalid as those from paper résumés. As regards the possible discriminating nature of video résumés, applicants' stigma (age, physical attractiveness) was also manipulated in the two field experiments by Derous and colleagues. The results showed that résumé type did moderate the effect of applicants' stigma on personality and job suitability ratings, but that this depended on type of stigma.

Waung and colleagues (2012) further investigated the role of gender in video résumé screening. This was done among students in a laboratory experiment in which applicant gender and the frequency and intensity of self-promotion statements used in a video résumé were manipulated to examine their effects on applicant evaluation. In this way, differential effects of self-presentation tactics for men and women were hypothesized. It was found that gender role incongruence in the video résumé (i.e., a female using high levels of self-promotion tactics, or a male using low levels of self-promotion tactics) resulted in harsher ratings, especially for female applicants compared to male applicants. The female applicant in this study was evaluated more harshly on social skills, credentials, organizational fit, and résumé outcomes when she engaged in high-intensity self-promotion compared to low-intensity self-promotion. The male applicant received lower organizational fit and credential ratings when he used lower-intensity self-promotion. Notably, these effects were found only when evaluators were male.

The six studies described in this section provide an interesting first insight into the characteristics of video résumés from both the applicants' and recruiters' perspective. Building further on these findings, an agenda for future research is presented next.

Agenda for future research: what we want to know about video résumés

Although the screening of résumés is a ubiquitous procedure in the first selection stage of many hiring organizations, it has received less research attention compared to other selection instruments. This accounts especially for video résumé screening, which has hardly been researched at all. Suggestions for future research can therefore be made that build on the studies described in the previous section. In addition, new areas of research on video résumé screening that were not yet addressed in existing studies can be identified. These topics include research on the validity, reliability, cost-effectiveness, and ease of use of paper and video résumés. Furthermore, studies on the fairness of video résumés for a broader array of subgroups (e.g., disabled applicants) and issues regarding privacy and invasiveness deserve our research attention. Each of these topics will be dealt with here, and suggestions for future research are made.

In the 1970s it was already estimated that over one billion résumés were screened each year in the United States. Résumés are usually the first medium through which information is exchanged between the applicant and the hiring organization. The suggestion has been made that biographical information deduced from paper résumés, such as education and work experiences, can be used to draw inferences about underlying attributes, such as personality and intelligence (Brown & Campion, 1994; Levine & Flory, 1975). However, the *validity* in terms of accuracy and added value of this practice compared to other selection instruments is debatable (Cole, Feild, Giles, & Harris, 2009; Schmidt & Hunter, 1998), as was also shown in the experiments by Derous, Taveirne, & Hiemstra (2012). Despite this, résumés are still among the most widely used and best accepted instruments to screen applicants (Anderson, Salgado, & Hülsheger, 2010; Piotrowski & Armstrong, 2006). Although some cultural differences have been reported regarding selection practices (e.g., Huo, Huang, & Napier, 2002; Ryan, McFarland, Baron, & Page, 1999), selection in many countries follows a fairly similar pattern, starting with résumés as a form of prescreening.

Even less is known about the psychometric properties of video résumés. As with preemployment screening through social media (e.g., Stoughton et al., 2014), practitioners often introduce and use new selection tools that are not yet thoroughly investigated by scientists (like the use of social media for recruitment purposes; Roth et al., 2013) or that appear to be invalid (like the use of unstructured job interviews for selection purposes; Levashina et al., 2013). Studies on reasons for this science-practitioner gap are scarce (König, Joeri & Knuesel, 2011). An interesting exception is a study by König, Klehe, Berchtold, and Kleinmann (2010) among 506 HR professionals. Reasons to adopt selection procedures were assessed by these authors, and the main drivers for choice of selection instruments were applicant perceptions, costs, and diffusion in the field of the selection instrument. Though the predictive validity of selection instruments was deemed important, it only played a modest role in the actual adoption of a selection procedure, as did organizational self-promotion (i.e., using the selection situation to promote one's organization) and perceived legality. Future research may therefore focus on the validity and measurement equivalence of video résumés compared to other commonly used selection instruments. As regards measurement equivalence, video résumés may be too narrow a term, because the instrument does not necessarily imply a literal translation of the paper version to a video version, as is the case with some computerized tests. As was shown in this chapter, characteristics of the interview can be found in the video résumé. Additionally, characteristics of the paper résumé, work sample test, and letters of motivation are also identifiable in the video résumé.

As argued earlier, the reliability and validity of the video résumé can probably be improved in the same way as the reliability and validity of the interview and other selection tools (like the assessment center) can be improved, namely through various ways of structuring the content and the raters' evaluation of the applicant (Campion et al., 1997). Even more so, some factors that can reduce the reliability and validity from interviews – namely, unplanned prompting and taking questions from the candidate – are absent in video résumés (Campion et al., 1997), thereby reducing pitfalls associated with real-time interaction.

There is a fair amount of research on the validity of personality and cognitive ability impressions based on interviews (Macan, 2009) and some evidence of impression formation based on paper résumés (Brown & Campion, 1994; Cole et al., 2009). A video résumé that is created according to the construct requirements of the hiring organization may approach the validity of structured interviews to assess personality, in less time and with more opportunities for multiple raters to review the content (i.e., no real-time panel is needed and all materials remain available online for evaluation per default). Furthermore, research has shown that interviews are stressors and applicant anxiety can impair the validity of interview ratings (Macan, 2009; McCarthy & Goffin, 2004). Applicant training and coaching can improve the applicants' performance and thereby improve the validity of the interview. The good thing about video résumés is that both anxiety and training can be controlled. If an applicant knows his or her strong points and knows how to present them (i.e., the desired result of applicant training and coaching), without the anxiety that is associated with the typical selection situation, it can be implied that video résumés actually may allow for a more accurate person evaluation than the traditional face-to-face interview. Of course, these implications need to be tested using a rigorous construct-oriented approach.

As regards the *cost-effectiveness* and *ease of use*, some practitioners mention that it may be very time-consuming to screen video résumés, especially when compared to paper résumés. We are not aware of automated coding software, as is the case for paper résumés. Hence, further research is needed on this issue. On the other hand, if video résumé screening ensures more effective selection in the first round (i.e., improved predictive validity), its use may be more cost-effective in terms of reduced interview time. Of the participants from the survey on video résumé use in the Netherlands (Hiemstra, 2013), about 43% thought that the use of video résumés could actually speed up the selection process. For instance, video résumés would allow one to quickly assess the representativeness of the applicant before inviting him or her to the job interview. One HR manager who used video résumés in the selection procedure stated that he preferred spending a few more minutes on screening video résumés in order not to invite 'false positives' to the interview based on screening paper résumés only. Cost-effectiveness probably also depends on the size of the applicant pool and the selection ratio. We hypothesize a curvilinear effect here. That is, when the applicant pool is small and the selection ratio is high, most applicants will be invited for an interview, thereby limiting the added value of a video résumé in addition to the traditional paper résumé. The tradeoff may be better when the selection ratio is low and the number of applicants is higher but still manageable. Recruitment campaigns that result in thousands of applicants, on the other hand, may be more effective when using automated screening of the paper résumé in the first phase. The video résumés of those selected based on the automatic screening can then be viewed. In this way, the paper résumé is the first hurdle and the video résumé the second hurdle in the prescreening of applicants because viewing all individual video résumés in the first place may not be cost-effective. Cost-effectiveness may also be higher in global recruitment, when opportunities for face-to-face interactions are limited due to time and distance. Future research may address these claims. Caution is warranted, though, because the above claims on cost-effectiveness are based on adding video résumés to current, mainstream selection practices (i.e., starting the procedure with résumé screening). The practice of résumé screening itself, in terms of predictive validity, is despite its widespread use still debatable compared to other selection instruments, such as cognitive ability tests.

The *ease of use* of multimedia in selection has increased drastically the past few years, for both recruiters and applicants. Technological developments and software allow for web-based interviews, as well as video résumé creation, sending, and online hosting. As for the applicants, they may find it more convenient and up to date to use a video-based application instead of, or in addition to, a paper-based application (i.e., application form, paper résumé, motivational letter). End-user software and webcams are now readily available to all users of the Internet, making the creation and sending of a video résumé accessible to most applicants. Some authors warn of an increased 'digital divide' (Roth et al., 2013), pointing out the trend of less computer/Internet access for Blacks and Hispanics, and the trend for lack of use of social media by older individuals. This may raise possible differences between various groups on the basis of possibilities and ability (or interest) to create and send an online video message. Thus, the ease of use may differ per subgroup of applicants, which also taps into fairness issues.

As regards *fairness* and justice, future research could build on the studies that were already published to be able to disentangle the influence of the format (e.g., a highly structured, predefined format with content requirements vs. an unstructured format in which the content is determined by the applicant), the medium (paper vs. video vs. interview), and individual differences (e.g., educational level, ethnicity, personality) on applicant and recruiter perceptions. The role of ethnicity, gender, attractiveness, and age was considered in both lab and field studies, yielding some mixed findings (Derous, Taveirne, & Hiemstra, 2012; Hiemstra, 2013; Waung et al., 2012). More research is needed among actual applicants and actual recruiters. Moreover, the role of other stigmas, such as religious attire, disabilities, and disfigurements can be studied (e.g., Madera & Hebl, 2012). Another question is whether the results from the interview literature on the role that stigma plays in recruiters' judgments and decision making can be transferred to video résumés. As mentioned, video résumés and interviews share several characteristics, yet they are also distinct on several key features (e.g., synchronicity, duration, opportunities for impression management). The studies by Waung et al. (2010; 2012) and Derous, Taveirne, & Hiemstra (2012), showed a differential effect for different kinds of stigma that may be associated with the kinds of stereotypes that are associated with the stigma. More research is needed to disentangle the influence of medium (video résumé / paper résumé / interview) and type of stigma on impression formation and hiring decision making.

In addition to research on stigma and stereotypes as a source of judgmental bias, future research may also focus on impression formation and biases due to auditory factors in personnel selection. Auditory information covaries with visual information in both video résumés and interviews. Effects of auditory information on hiring decisions remained relatively under researched until now (Gluszek & Dovidio, 2010). Among these auditory factors are vocal cues like voice pitch (DeGroot &

Motowidlo, 1999), recruiters' language attitudes, and their relation with perceived accent understandability. These attitudes turned out to be related to job suitability ratings for interviews (DeGroot & Kluemper, 2007; Purkiss, Perrewé, Gillespie, Mayes, & Ferris, 2006). Future research may also focus on contextual conditions under which it is beneficial to apply with a video résumé and/or a paper résumé. For example, differences in impression formation may occur for types of occupations for which different job qualifications are required (e.g., a marketing versus an administrative position), or for different job types (e.g., a back-office versus front-office position).

Finally, with the emergence of video résumés and other Internet-based technologies, issues arise on *privacy* (compared to paper résumés). An infamous example of privacy breach is a student who applied with a video résumé, but the content did not match the corporate standards of the hiring organization (De la Merced, 2006). An employee forwarded the application to other recruiters, who put it on the Internet. The clip went viral and was parodied (Cera, 2006). The video résumé became famous, thereby making the applicant infamous. Thus, the increased social cue exchange in video résumés when compared to the 'paper person' in paper résumés, the digital and asynchronous nature of video résumés, and the lack of standardization of video résumé requirements may result in higher invasiveness and privacy intrusions for video résumé applications compared to traditional written applications and to face-to-face interviews. This may have negative consequences for the applicant in a particular selection procedure but also for his or her future applications, as was the case with the student in the example, because the video résumé remained visible on the Internet. Future research may focus on privacy issues in video résumé screening, and more broadly on the use of social media in selection (Roth et al., 2013).

Conclusion

In this chapter we have introduced the video résumé as a relatively new instrument that is being used for the early screening of job applicants. Though popular media coverage on video résumés is abundant, research on the topic is still scarce. Because the notion of the 'video résumé' might still be unclear, we started this chapter by comparing video résumés to job interviews, being another widely used selection instrument.

Like with any selection tool, video résumés have benefits and disadvantages too. We believe that video résumés may potentially be used for selection if the measurement intentions are clearly defined. Furthermore, video résumés can be considered when it is desirable to provide applicants a more personalized opportunity to apply, thereby appealing more to those with a weaker labor market position, as well as to more extraverted applicants. At the same time, the workplace in Western countries is rapidly becoming more diverse, and differential job access persists. Video résumés also have the potential to instigate discriminatory hiring practices; therefore, caution is also warranted when using video résumés. The growing use of multimedia instruments for selection, such as video résumés, needs to be continuously scrutinized, in research and in the field, to ensure fair and accurate application and evaluation procedures. We hope this chapter adds to this goal.

References

Ajzen, I. (1991). The theory of planned behavior. *Organizational Behavior and Human Decision Processes, 50*(2), 179–211.
Anderson, N., Salgado, J., & Hülsheger, U.R., (2010). Applicant reactions in selection: Comprehensive meta-analysis into reaction generalization versus situational specificity. *International Journal of Selection and Assessment, 18*(3), 291–304.
Arthur, W., & Villado, A.J. (2008). The importance of distinguishing between constructs and methods when comparing predictors in personnel selection research and practice. *Journal of Applied Psychology, 93*(2), 435–442.
Bangerter, A., Roulin, N., & König, C.J. (2012). Personnel selection as a signaling game. *Journal of Applied Psychology, 97*(4), 719–738.
Bauer, T.N., Truxillo, D.M., Paronto, M.E., Weekley, J.A., & Campion, M.A. (2004). Applicant reactions to different selection technology: Face-to-face, interactive voice response, and computer-assisted telephone screening interviews. *International Journal of Selection and Assessment, 12*(1), 135–148.
Brown, B.K., & Campion, M.A. (1994). Bio data phenomenology – recruiters perceptions and use of biographical information in résumé screening. *Journal of Applied Psychology, 79*(6), 897–908.
Campion, M.A., Palmer, D.K., & Campion, J.E. (1997). A review of structure in the selection interview. *Personnel Psychology, 50*(3), 655–702.
Cera, M. (2006, December 20). *Impossible is the opposite of possible*. Retrieved from http://www.youtube.com/watch?v=nAV0sxwx9rY
Cole, M.S., Feild, H.S., Giles, W.F., & Harris, S.G. (2009). Recruiters' inferences of applicant personality based on résumé screening: Do paper people have a personality? *Journal of Business and Psychology, 24*(1), 5–18.
Cole, M.S., Rubin, R.S., Feild, H.S., & Giles, W.F. (2007). Recruiters' perceptions and use of applicant résumé information: Screening the recent graduate. *Applied Psychology: An International Review, 56*(2), 319–343.
DeGroot, T., & Kluemper, D. (2007). Evidence of predictive and incremental validity of personality factors, vocal attractiveness and the situational interview. *International Journal of Selection and Assessment, 15*(1), 30–39.
DeGroot, T., & Motowidlo, S.J. (1999). Why visual and vocal interview cues can affect interviewers' judgments and predict job performance. *Journal of Applied Psychology, 84*(6), 986–993.
De la Merced, M.J. (2006, 19 October). The résumé mocked around the world. *The New York Times DealBook*. Retrieved from http://dealbook.blogs.nytimes.com/2006/10/19/the-resume-mocked-round-the-world-vayner-speaks/
Derous, E., Buijsrogge, A., Gissel, A., Schmitt, N., Thompson, L., Hiemstra, A.M.F., et al. (2012, April). Differential effects of video versus paper résumés on personality ratings. In E. Derous (Chair), *Assessing Video Résumés: Valuable and/or Vulnerable to Biased Decision Making?* Symposium conducted at the annual meeting of the Society for Industrial and Organization Psychology, San Diego, CA.
Derous, E., Taveirne, A., & Hiemstra, A.M.F., (2012, April). *Résumé-résumé on the video-wall: Who's the most hirable of all?* Interactive poster presented at the 27th annual conference of the Society for Industrial and Organizational Psychology, San Diego, CA.

Dipboye, R.L., & Johnson, S.K. (2013). Understanding and improving employee selection interviews. In K.F. Geisinger, B.A. Bracken, J.F. Carlson, J.-I.C. Hansen, N.R. Kuncel, S.P. Reise, & M.C. Rodriguez (Eds.), *APA Handbook of Testing and Assessment: Vol. 1. Test Theory and Testing and Assessment in Industrial and Organizational Psychology* (pp. 479–499). Washington, DC: American Psychological Association.

Doyle, A. (2010). *Video resume – video resumes for job seekers*. Retrieved from http://jobsearch.about.com/od/resumes/g/videoresume.htm

Gissel, A.L., Thompson, L.F., & Pond, S.B. (2013). A theory-driven investigation of prospective applicants' intentions to submit video résumés. *Journal of Applied Social Psychology, 43*(12), 2449–2461.

Gluszek, A., & Dovidio, J.F. (2010). Speaking with a nonnative accent: Perceptions of bias, communication difficulties, and belonging in the United States. *Journal of Language and Social Psychology, 29*(2), 224–234.

Guion, R.M. (2011). *Assessment, measurement and prediction for personnel decisions* (2nd ed.). New York: Lawrence Erlbaum.

Hamilton, L. (1998). Your first move – how to prepare a winning audition package (the dance résumé, photos and video). *Dance Magazine, 72*(2), 140.

Hiemstra, A.M.F. (2013). *Fairness in paper and video résumé screening.* (Doctoral dissertation). Retrieved from http://repub.eur.nl/pub/50432/

Hiemstra, A.M.F., Derous, E., Serlie, A.W., & Born, M. Ph. (2012). Fairness perceptions of video résumés among ethnically diverse applicants. *International Journal of Selection and Assessment, 20*(4), 423–433.

Hiemstra, A.M.F., Oostrom, J.K., Derous, E., Serlie, A.W., & Born, M. Ph. (2012, July). *Video and paper résumés: Exploring applicants' preferences based on personality and cognitive ability.* Paper presented at the 8th conference of the International Test Commission (ITC), Amsterdam, the Netherlands.

Huo, Y., Huang, H., & Napier, N. (2002). Divergence or convergence: A cross-national comparison of personnel selection practices. *Human Resource Management, 41*(1), 31–44.

Kelly, J., & O'Brien, E. (1992). Using video résumés to teach deaf college-students job search skills and improve their communication. *American Annals of the Deaf, 137*, 404–410. Retrieved from http://gupress.gallaudet.edu/annals/92volume.htm

König, C.J., Joeri, E., & Knuesel, P. (2011). The amazing diversity of thought: A qualitative study on how human resource practitioners perceive selection procedures. *Journal of Business and Psychology, 26*(4), 437–452.

König, C.J., Klehe, U., Berchtold, M., & Kleinmann, M. (2010). Reasons for being selective when choosing personnel selection procedures. *International Journal of Selection and Assessment, 18*(1), 17–27.

Levashina, J., Hartwell, C.J., Morgeson, F.P., & Campion, M.A. (2013). The structured employment interview: Narrative and quantitative review of the research literature. *Personnel Psychology.* Advance online publication. doi:10.1111/peps.12052

Levine, E., & Flory, A. (1975). Evaluation of job applications – conceptual framework. *Public Personnel Management, 4*(6), 378–385.

Lievens, F. (2011). *Handbook human resource management.* Leuven, Belgium: Lannoo Campus.

Light, L. (1993). *Video résumé: An application of technology for persons with severe disabilities.* Retrieved from ERIC database. (EJ459595).

Macan, T. (2009). The employment interview: A review of current studies and directions for future research. *Human Resource Management Review, 19*(3), 203–218.

Madera, J.M., & Hebl, M.R. (2012). Discrimination against facially stigmatized applicants in interviews: An eye-tracking and face-to-face investigation. *Journal of Applied Psychology, 97*(2), 317–330.

McCarthy, J., & Goffin, R. (2004). Measuring job interview anxiety: Beyond weak knees and sweaty palms. *Personnel Psychology, 57*(3), 607–637.

Oostrom, J.K. (2010). *New technology in personnel selection: The validity and acceptability of multimedia tests.* (Doctoral dissertation). Retrieved from http://repub.eur.nl/res/pub/20866/

Piotrowski, C., & Armstrong, T. (2006). Current recruitment and selection practices: A national survey of Fortune 1000 firms. *North American Journal of Psychology, 8*(3), 489–496.

Potosky, D. (2008). A conceptual framework for the role of the administration medium in the personnel assessment process. *Academy of Management Review, 33*(3), 629–648.

Purkiss, S.L.S., Perrewé, P.L., Gillespie, T.L., Mayes, B.T., & Ferris, G.R. (2006). Implicit sources of bias in employment interview judgments and decisions. *Organizational Behavior and Human Decision Processes, 101*(2), 152–167.

Queensland Tourist Board Australia. (2009). About the best job. Retrieved from: http://islandreefjob.com/about-the-best-job/

Rolls, J.A. & Strenkowski, R.A. (1993, August). *Video technology: Résumés of the future.* Retrieved from ERIC database. (ED362934).

Roth, P.L., Bobko, P., Van Iddekinge, C.H., & Thatcher, J.B. (2013). Social media in employee-selection-related decisions: A research agenda for uncharted territory. *Journal of Management.* Advance online publication.

Ryan, A.M., McFarland, L., Baron, H., & Page, R. (1999). An international look at selection practices: Nation and culture as explanations for variability in practice. *Personnel Psychology, 52*(2), 359–391.

Sands, W.A., Waters, B.K., & McBride, J.R. (Eds.). (1997). *Computerized adaptive testing: From inquiry to operation.* Washington, DC: American Psychological Association.

Schmidt, F.L., & Hunter, J.E. (1998). The validity and utility of selection methods in personnel psychology: Practical and theoretical implications of 85 years of research findings. *Psychological Bulletin, 124*(2), 262–274.

Silverman, R.E. (2012, January 24). No more résumés, say some firms. *Wall Street Journal.* Retrieved from http://online.wsj.com

Stoughton, J.W., Thompson, L.F., Meade, A.W. (2014). Examining applicant reactions to the use of social networking websites in pre-employment screening. *Journal of Business and Psychology.* Advance online publication.

Warshawski, E. (1987). Video résumés, sharpening the competitive edge for dancers, choreographers and dance-companies. *Dance Magazine, 61*(3), 40–41.

Waung, M., Beatty, J., Hymes, R., & McAuslan, P. (2010, April). *The effects of video and paper résumés on candidate evaluation.* Poster presented at the 25th annual conference of the Society for Industrial and Organizational Psychology, Atlanta, GA.

Waung, M., Hymes, R., Beatty, J., & McAuslan, P. (2012, April). Video résumé self-promotion tactics and gender. In E. Derous (chair), *Assessing Video Résumés: Valuable and/or Vulnerable to Biased Decision-making?* Symposium conducted at the 27th annual conference of the Society for Industrial and Organizational Psychology, San Diego, CA.

4

SOCIAL NETWORKING WEBSITES AND PERSONNEL SELECTION

A call for academic research

Donald H. Kluemper
UNIVERSITY OF ILLINOIS AT CHICAGO, USA

H. Kristl Davison
UNIVERSITY OF MISSISSIPPI, USA

Xiaoyun Cao
UNIVERSITY OF ILLINOIS AT CHICAGO, USA

Bingqing Wu
UNIVERSITY OF ILLINOIS AT CHICAGO, USA

Due to the rapid evolution of social media, scientific study of social networking websites (SNWs) has been substantially outpaced by organizational practice. A recent article in the *Journal of Management* sums up our sentiment: "Overall, we believe this is a somewhat *rare moment in staffing research* when a new assessment method arrives on the scene. The advent of this approach to hiring provides an important opportunity (and need) for new research." (Roth, Bobko, Van Iddekinge, & Thatcher, in press, p. 37).

SNWs are defined as "web-based services that allow individuals to (1) construct a public or semi-public profile within a bounded system, (2) articulate a list of other users with whom they share a connection, and (3) view and traverse their list of connections and those made by others within the system" (Boyd & Ellison, 2007, p. 3). It is unclear how common the use of SNWs for screening is, as surveys assessing the prevalence of SNW screening by those responsible for hiring range from 33% (SHRM, 2011) to 91% (The Reppler Effect, 2011), with screeners both accepting and rejecting candidates based on SNW information. Additionally, the prevalence of SNW screening appears to differ by country. Of four countries in one study, the percentage of hiring managers using online information for screening was highest in the United States (79%), followed by Germany (59%), the United Kingdom (47%), and France (23%) (Cross-Tab Marketing Services, 2010). Further, SNW screening prevalence may depend on the type of job and/or industry. Information technology and professional and business services are the most prevalent industries (CareerBuilder.com, 2009), and private firms screen via SNWs more than public entities (SHRM, 2011). Additionally, whereas Facebook was previously the most widely used SNW for screening, LinkedIn is now the most common among those using SNWs (85%), followed by Facebook (78%), MySpace (13%), and Twitter (11%) (SHRM, 2011). Thus, although most existing research relates specifically to Facebook, studies using SNWs such as Twitter and LinkedIn are emerging.

Given the growing use of SNW screening, it is clear that more extensive academic study is warranted. In this chapter we provide an overview of the state of the research on SNW screening and offer suggestions for future research directions. In particular, we discuss traditional psychometric issues (i.e., reliability, validity), along with issues regarding the fairness of SNW screening (i.e., discrimination, privacy). Whereas many of these issues are of interest to practitioners, our approach here is to provide a more academically oriented treatment of these issues to help guide researcher investigations, which can ultimately inform practice.

What is SNW screening?

Prior to discussing research on SNW screening, it may be valuable to provide an operational definition of SNW screening. As the "social networking" part of SNW implies, we are referring explicitly to screening of SNWs, not Internet searches in general (e.g., "googling", Gatewood, Feild, & Barrick, 2008). There is likely to be substantial overlap between using SNWs versus googling for screening applicants, particularly in terms of psychometric issues (e.g., reliability, validity). However, SNWs have particular issues with respect to impression management, discrimination, privacy, and applicant reactions that may not apply to googling. For example, given that SNWs have limitations on accessibility to the site and to applicant profiles, this represents a different standard of privacy than a broad Internet search of publicly available information.

We should also clarify which websites are the focus of this chapter. SNWs fall into a few categories (McCorvey, 2010): general SNWs such as Facebook, MySpace, Twitter, Ning, and Friendster; professional SNWs including LinkedIn, FastPitch, and Plaxo; and industry-specific SNWs like I-Meet and ResearchGate. The nature of SNW platforms greatly impacts the information available for screening and therefore may have implications regarding a wide range of SNW screening issues. To date, much of the research discussion has focused on the use of Facebook (e.g., Kluemper & Rosen, 2009; Kluemper, Rosen, & Mossholder, 2012), with more recent research emerging on the use of LinkedIn for screening (e.g., Kluemper, McLarty, & Rosen, 2013; McLarty, Kluemper, & Rosen, 2013; Sinar, 2013). Other widely used SNWs of potential interest are Twitter and MySpace. However, Wikipedia lists over 200 SNWs in regular use, including those that target specific countries (Wikipedia, 2013). Other websites that may warrant attention include

Classmates.com and Google+. However, as most of the research to date on SNWs has focused on Facebook, LinkedIn, and Twitter, those will be our primary focus.

We should also note that we are focusing here on using SNWs for screening (i.e., personnel selection). SNWs have been used for other human resource (HR) activities, in particular for recruitment (e.g., Davison, Maraist, & Bing, 2011; Karl & Peluchette, 2013) and terminations (e.g., Genova, 2009; Hidy & McDonald, 2013), but these HR activities are beyond the scope of this chapter. Given the widespread use of SNWs for screening, with limited scientific research on their psychometric properties and legality, we believe significant research should be directed toward addressing these issues.

Finally, although SNW screening is a relatively new development in selection, it has similarities with other kinds of selection techniques, and thus many issues regarding SNW screening will be common to established selection methods. For example, one issue is that of using personal (nonwork) information when hiring. Although applicants may not perceive such information as relevant, many established selection methods, such as background checks, biodata, interviews, and so forth, access personal information. Similarly, research on adverse impact, which has been studied extensively with respect to devices such as cognitive ability tests, physical ability tests, and so forth, may be informative for addressing this issue in SNW screening. Furthermore, both interviewing and SNW screening involve subjective evaluation of a large volume of information (Kluemper, 2013). The literature on the benefits of using structured employment interviews (see Campion, Palmer, & Campion, 1997; Kluemper, 2013) may inform issues of subjectivity in SNW screening. We present these few examples to illustrate that while SNW screening may involve a new selection technology, we are not dealing with entirely novel concerns.

In the remainder of this chapter, we address traditional selection issues regarding psychometric evidence of using SNW screening as a predictor. Specifically, we focus on issues of reliability and standardization, validity, and impression management or faking. We also address issues of fairness in using SNW screening, focusing on discrimination and privacy concerns. Further, we suggest a research agenda for future investigations on SNW screening.

SNW screening as a predictor

When evaluating any selection technique, various factors should be considered, including a theoretical rationale for why the predictor may be relevant to the job, the predictor's standardization, ability to be quantified, consistency of scoring, reliability, construct validity, and potential for discrimination, among others (Gatewood et al., 2008). We contend that by and large, SNWs have been used for screening with little consideration of these factors. Here we examine what is known about the psychometric properties of SNW screening.

Standardization

Standardization refers to whether the content, administration, and scoring of the selection measure are consistent across applicants, locations, and administrators

(Gatewood et al., 2008). SNW screening particularly lacks standardization, as much screening is often performed in a haphazard manner. Specifically, a single screener (e.g., an individual manager) typically reviews the applicant's SNW webpage *without* using a list of criteria for evaluating the page's content. Different screeners may be looking for different information, and using their own unwritten standards for evaluating applicants. Thus, scoring is not standardized, and quantification of the applicant's SNW is lacking, thus preventing any meaningful quantitative evaluation of an applicant's SNW. In this respect, SNW screening is similar to a holistic approach to evaluating application forms, which has been criticized for lack of standardization and scientific soundness (Gatewood et al., 2008; Highhouse, 2002).

Moreover, as SNWs differ from applicant to applicant, SNW content is also unstandardized. Users present what content they choose, with few limits or guidelines. Although sites such as Facebook and LinkedIn, for example, have templates that help new users prepare their webpages, these are very flexible, and users do not need to complete all sections. Twitter has no restrictions, except in terms of the character limit of 140 characters per "tweet". Thus, missing information is of particular concern.

Another standardization concern in SNW screening is that some users will not have SNWs. For example, if a screener examines applicants' Facebook pages, some applicants may not have Facebook accounts. Alternatively, a screener may examine various SNWs for the applicants, viewing LinkedIn pages for some applicants, Facebook for others, Twitter for still others, and so forth, leading to further inconsistency in content across applicants. This is also legally problematic if there are demographic differences in users across SNW platforms. This concern will be discussed later in more detail.

In sum, the lack of standardization, quantification, and scoring in SNW screening makes it particularly problematic for selection. Research on exactly what aspects of SNWs screeners attend to would be useful. Future research on SNWs could be directed at developing more effective ways to score content on SNWs. For example, the literature on training and experience evaluations could be informative for determining ways to quantify and score SNWs. Additionally, although SNW platforms share common elements and functional building blocks (Kietzmann, Hermkens, McCarthy, & Silvestre, 2011; Mayfield, 2008) such as conversations, user presence, and connectedness, they vary in user identity, social motivations, openness, community, and the platforms' reputation. Future research about user demographics (e.g., gender, ethnicity, cultural background, socioeconomic status), behavioral differences (e.g., information disclosure, identity presentation), and social network patterns across different SNW platforms may contribute to our understanding of the amount and quality of information available on SNWs.

Reliability

Reliability represents various ways to demonstrate that a measure is consistent and free from errors. Three methods of estimating reliability are germane to SNW screening: interrater reliability (consistency of test scores when measurements are taken by different evaluators), test-retest reliability (consistency of scores from one test administration to the next), and internal consistency reliability (consistency of results across independent pieces of information within a test).[1] Here we should note that in order to estimate reliability, some kind of quantification or scoring of SNWs is necessary.

Interrater reliability in SNW screening could be evaluated by comparing two or more raters' evaluations of a set of SNWs. Although such comparison could be based on the raters' holistic judgments (e.g., "acceptable" vs. "unacceptable"), more precise scoring is preferred. Such comparisons are rare, however, as typically only one screener conducts the screening, and without any standardized scoring system. Thus, we know little about the interrater reliability of SNW screening. Kluemper and Rosen (2009) conducted an interrater reliability study in which 63 raters from an undergraduate employment selection course assessed the personality traits and cognitive ability of six Facebook profiles by spending 10 minutes evaluating all aspects of the Facebook profile. Intra-class correlation coefficients (ICCs) ranged from .93 for extraversion, to .99 for conscientiousness. Further, the raters were generally able to distinguish those with high versus those with low levels of academic success. Finally, more intelligent and emotionally stable raters were shown to be more accurate when evaluating SNW profiles than their less intelligent and neurotic counterparts. These results demonstrate that IQ and the Big Five personality traits can be reliably assessed via Facebook.

A major problem with interrater reliability is that ratings are affected by the raters' characteristics (e.g., similarity with the ratee; see Turban & Jones, 1988) as well as what is being rated, producing two separate sources of potential error. Moreover, incomplete information and inconsistencies across SNW profiles may lead to differences in rater attributions and evaluations. For example, if an applicant has a sparse SNW profile, one rater may attribute that to the applicant's private nature, another might believe the applicant is hiding something, and another might assume the applicant is too lazy to complete the profile. Regardless of the rater's attribution, it is likely that the rater will evaluate the applicant with incomplete information more harshly (Jaccard & Wood, 1988). Clearly, more extensive research in this area is warranted.

Test-retest reliability involves the administration of a test at two different points in time, which assesses the temporal consistency of the test. Test-retest reliability could be evaluated by examining applicants' SNWs at different points in time and determining whether applicant characteristics rated based on their social networking profiles remain consistent. However, one issue is what constitutes a time interval? With traditional tests, applicants take the same test on two different occasions. With SNWs, a time interval can be based on examining applicants' SNWs at two different times. However, the SNW content would likely have changed over time, and the content may reflect more than the time interval that has elapsed. For example, imagine the same SNWs were examined on two occasions, one month apart. The content posted on those SNWs could include pictures that were *taken* during that one-month period. However, it could also contain pictures taken years ago but *posted* during that one-month period. In this latter case, changes in behaviors across phases in one's life (Slovensky & Ross, 2012) could lead to inconsistent SNW screening results over time, potentially harming test-retest reliability. No SNW studies, to our knowledge, address test-retest reliability.

Internal consistency reliability could be addressed by examining the consistency of information contained within a SNW profile. Evaluating internal consistency reliability with SNWs is more complex than with traditional tests, in which answers on different test items (measuring the same construct) can be compared. Kluemper and Rosen (2009) and Kluemper et al. (2012) demonstrate adequate internal consistency reliability for personality traits assessed via SNWs using standard observer ratings of personality (i.e., a self-rated personality test was reworded so that the observer conducts ratings after viewing a SNW profile) after comprehensively viewing all aspects of a user's profile. However, a variety of characteristics could be assessed within and across posts. Researchers might consider providing raters with a list of traits for use in evaluating different parts of SNW profiles, and evaluate internal consistency reliability for each trait separately. However, as not every part will relate to a particular trait, missing data would be a problem.

There are other sources of measurement error to be considered when using SNWs for screening. SNW information can be inconsistent (Smith & Kidder, 2010) when that information is false (Davison, Maraist, Hamilton, & Bing, 2012), such as with mistaken identities, differences in information across multiple accounts, and the creation of imitation accounts (Slovensky & Ross, 2012). Relying on third-party postings can also be a source of error, as when "friends" jokingly post altered pictures or false information. Such sources of measurement error and problems with reliability must be considered when screening SNWs.

In sum, there are various problems with assessing reliability in SNW ratings. There is some initial evidence that personality can be assessed reliably (i.e., interrater and internal consistency reliability). However, reliability has only been examined for a few personality traits, and whether other characteristics can be measured reliably needs investigating. Also, much of the work on reliability has been performed using students, and research using actual job applicants or employees is needed.

Validity of SNW screening

Validity in personnel selection is "the degree to which available evidence supports inferences made from scores on selection measures" (Gatewood et al., 2008). Based on this definition, it is apparent that the current state of SNW screening lacks validity, insofar as (1) SNW screening is performed without appropriate scoring (at least beyond a holistic "pass/no pass" decision), and (2) little evidence on the inferences made exists. Clearly, work needs to be done to establish the validity of SNW screening.

There are several approaches for validating selection devices. Assuming that screeners attempt to measure a particular set of constructs, the question becomes whether this operationalization (i.e., the measurement of such constructs in the SNW) actually measures what it claims to (i.e., construct validity). One approach to demonstrating construct validity is to demonstrate that the measure correlates with other measures that it is theoretically predicted to correlate with (i.e., convergent validity), and that it fails to correlate with theoretically distinct measures (i.e., discriminant validity). Another approach addresses whether the operationalization comprehensively covers all aspects of the construct (i.e., content validity). Whether the operationalization correlates significantly with a job performance criterion is a third approach (i.e., criterion-related validity). Though each of these validation approaches is important, in the context of SNW screening criterion-related validity is perhaps most critical. Criterion-related validity establishes that a selection test is job-related, and it can provide a greater degree of legal defensibility of the selection device as well as demonstrating the usefulness of the device (i.e., applicants who score well on the device do better on the job). Next we address each of these approaches to validation with respect to SNW screening.

Construct validity

When considering construct validity, we are asking whether the constructs measured in SNWs are the constructs that we claim to be measuring. However, screeners may not have specific constructs in mind when screening SNWs but are instead casually scanning profiles to make a pass/no pass decision. Thus, the first issue is to identify what constructs might be measured in SNW profiles. The second issue is to show that what screeners are measuring is what they think they are measuring (assuming they do have constructs in mind). A number of qualifications might be measured in SNW profiles, such as job-relevant knowledge, skills, abilities, and other characteristics (KSAOs). Empirical evidence has begun to emerge that suggests that traits such as the Big Five personality dimensions (Kluemper & Rosen, 2009; Kluemper et al., 2012), narcissism (Buffardi & Campell, 2008), and cognitive ability (Kluemper & Rosen, 2009) can be productively measured in SNWs. Further, the potential to assess a wide range of additional KSAOs has been suggested in the literature, including job-relevant background information such as education, work history, and professional memberships (Davison et al., 2012), language fluency, certain technical proficiencies, creative outlets, teamwork skills (Smith & Kidder, 2010), network ability and social capital (e.g., Steinfield, Ellison, & Lampe, 2008), creativity (Davison et al., 2012), communication, interpersonal skills, leadership, persuasion, and negotiation skills (Roth et al., in press). However, empirical work is needed to demonstrate that these characteristics can be assessed via SNWs.

Hiring managers may also try to measure person-organization (P-O) fit via SNW screening (Slovensky & Ross, 2012; Roth et al., in press). In this case, employers may search for similarities (i.e., complementary fit; Kristof, 1996) in terms of interests, goals, values, attitudes, and so forth, that indicate the applicant will be a good fit with the organization. However, screeners may not have a list of specific P-O fit characteristics in mind when screening profiles.

Finally, probably the most common current approach is to screen SNWs for disqualifying information, as a type of background check. SNW information pertaining to drug use, discriminatory comments, misrepresented qualifications, or shared confidential information about a current employer (CareerBuilder.com, 2009) might provide a strong basis to reject an applicant. However, little is known about the accuracy of using SNW screening in this manner.

In sum, it is apparent that various constructs might be measured via SNW screening, but work needs to establish whether they can be measured validly. Evidence is accumulating that certain personality traits might be measured successfully. For example, all of the Facebook-rated Big Five personality traits have been shown to demonstrate convergent validity with self-rated personality traits (Kluemper et al., 2012). Beyond personality, little is known about whether other KSAOs, P-O fit, or qualifications and disqualifications can be measured accurately in SNWs. Research could involve administering established measures of relevant KSAOs to participants and then using standardized scoring forms for screening the SNW profiles of those participants, to establish the convergent and discriminant validity of SNW screening. It might be beneficial to examine other selection techniques that are similarly rich in content and complexity to devise strategies for establishing the construct validity of SNW screening. For example, biodata shares some similarities with SNW screening (Davison et al., 2012), and research on biodata could inform SNW screening (Slovensky & Ross, 2012). SNWs may also share some similarities with assessment centers. Given the complex and likely multidimensional nature of SNW profiles, examining the assessment center literature for ways to improve construct validity (e.g., Lievens, 1998) might be informative for SNW screening.

Content validity

Content validity assesses whether the content of the test is a representative sample of job content. It is typically used with new test construction (Gatewood et al., 2008). When SNWs are screened without a job analysis and consideration of the constructs being measured, the link between job content and SNW content is tenuous. Finally, the Equal Employment Opportunity Commission (EEOC, 1978) has indicated in the Uniform Guidelines on Employee Selection Procedures that content validation is inappropriate when measuring abstract mental processes (e.g., intelligence, personality, judgment); thus, relying on a content validity strategy to infer such traits from SNW profiles may be inappropriate. Nonetheless, content validation may be appropriate when assessing observable job behaviors via SNWs, such as when searching for particular skills (e.g., foreign language fluency, specific computer experience). Similarly, searching for deviant behaviors that would be counterproductive on the job, such as illegal drug use and lying about absences, might also be defensible via content validity. However, research on the veracity of both positive and negative behaviors is needed.

Criterion-related validity

Criterion-related validity assesses whether scores on a test are correlated with scores on a job-relevant criterion. Limited research has examined whether ratings of traits from SNW profiles correlate with job performance. Kluemper et al. (2012) provided evidence that Facebook-rated personality traits correlate with supervisor ratings of job performance (Study 1) and provide incremental prediction of academic performance beyond what was obtained from self-rated personality and intelligence tests combined (for a critical assessment of these studies, see Roth et al., in press). However, a more recent study by Van Iddekinge, Lanivich, Roth, and Junco (in press) found that Facebook ratings of KSAOs largely did not predict job performance. Although this study used college recruiters to rate student Facebook profiles and obtained supervisor ratings of job performance one year later in a true predictive validation, this study utilized only one untrained rater per profile. Further, the raters were not subject matter experts on the job in question, and the 10 KSAOs measured were not necessarily germane to the wide range of student occupations. As the structured interview (e.g., Campion et al., 1997) and SNW (e.g., Kluemper, 2013) literatures advocate for multiple raters, using the same rater across ratings, basing KSAO questions on job analysis, and providing rater training, further work is needed to evaluate Van Iddekinge et al.'s (in press) approach to SNW screening. Taken together, these studies provide initial evidence that Facebook information based on personality (but perhaps not KSAOs) can be used to identify individuals who are more successful in college and on the job, and thus SNW screening has some evidence of criterion-related validity.

Future research

More research on personality as well as on other job-relevant characteristics is needed to further support the use of SNW screening. Moreover, as many employers are using SNW profiles to screen out applicants based on negative information, examining the validity of such negative information is warranted. The criterion-related validity of SNWs should also be assessed in relation to other variables beyond task performance, such as organizational citizenship behaviors, workplace deviance, and withdrawal behaviors (Roth et al., in press).

SNW screening should also demonstrate incremental validity beyond tests such as application blanks, biodata, personality tests, and so forth. (Roth et al., in press) to be considered value-added (Cronbach & Gleser, 1957). Finally, other psychometric issues that may harm the validity of a selection method or limit its usefulness need to be considered, such as low generalizability, low utility, or applicant impression management.

Other psychometric issues

Generalizability

Generalizability deals with the issue of whether what is found in one context remains so in another. There are numerous SNWs with divergent purposes, user demographics, access limits, volume and type of information provided, and so forth. For example, Facebook and LinkedIn differ substantially in terms of number of users, amount of information, focus on "friends" versus "professional" connections, and so forth. The platforms may also differ in demographic characteristics (e.g., age; Duggan & Brenner, 2013) and occupations of their users. Therefore, issues regarding

Facebook may not be germane to LinkedIn or Twitter, and establishing reliability or validity with one SNW platform does not mean that such psychometric properties will hold for others. A potential research area could actually capitalize on this – what traits are measured most accurately using which platform? For example, personality and negative traits might be accurately measured via Facebook, which has a very flexible format that may be conducive to expressing such traits (Blackman & Funder, 2002). Alternatively, more traditional KSAOs might be better assessed via the more structured and work-oriented LinkedIn.

Utility

Utility is defined as "methods that provide economic value greater than the cost of using them" (Noe, Hollenbeck, Gerhart, & Wright, 2011). SNWs are used because they are quick and cheap (Davison et al., 2012; Slovensky & Ross, 2012) and take little time and effort (SHRM, 2011). As such, SNWs may be seen as a goldmine of discoverable information (Hornberger, 2011). SNW screening is convenient for HR departments that wish to obtain as much information as possible about applicants to avoid negligent hiring (Woska, 2007). Moreover, SNW screening is one way for HR selection practices to incorporate the digital environment and trends regarding potential employees. Younger generations are increasingly reliant on SNWs to fulfill their needs to belong (Ellison, Steinfield, & Lampe, 2006), build their social networks (Steinfield et al., 2008), and conduct active job searches (Hermeier & Seng, 2009). However, quick and inexpensive approaches to SNW screening are likely unreliable and invalid. Thus, the cost-to-benefit ratio of SNW screening needs to be assessed more thoroughly. SNW screening may be more practical for higher-level or more visible positions because the cost for turnover is more expensive and the risks are greater. The utility of SNW screening may also depend on available organizational resources allocated to selection, such as number of recruiters, financial resources, formal organizational policies, and the number of available selection tools (Madera, 2012). It is also important to take into account the legal risks of using SNWs for screening when determining its utility. Davison et al. (2012) suggested that organizations conduct a risk-benefit analysis for screening using SNWs. The least risk involves searching professional networking sites such as LinkedIn, whereas searching SNWs such as Facebook and Twitter involves more risk, given that applicants may consider information on those sites to be private, especially third-party postings. Thus, depending on the specific SNW platforms, utility might be very low given legal risks.

Online identity/impression management

Vice President of HR at CareerBuilder.com Rosemary Haefner advises applicants to "make sure you are using this resource to your advantage by conveying a professional image and underscoring your qualifications" (CareerBuilder.com, 2009). This advice implies that applicants should engage in personal branding or impression management in their SNW profiles, and indeed, employers respond positively to such presentations. Pike (2011) found that the more value a user places on self-presentation via SNWs, the more suitable the candidate will be perceived by a hiring manager. Bohnert and Ross (2010) found that individuals with positive SNW profiles that were more family-oriented or professional were seen as more suitable for employment than those with party-oriented profiles.

When users attempt to portray themselves positively on their profiles, this limits the profile's usefulness for screeners. Users can manipulate or clean up content to present themselves in a more favorable manner (Davison et al., 2012; Kluemper et al., 2012), or even hire firms to help manage SNW information (Shiller, 2010). In contrast, screeners are attempting to obtain an accurate picture of the whole applicant, including negative information. When users only present positive information or post false information, they are engaging in impression management and/or faking. As faking harms criterion-related validity (e.g., Bing, Kluemper, Davison, Taylor, & Novicevic, 2011) and construct validity of personality tests (e.g., Stark, Chernyshenko, Chan, Lee, & Drasgow, 2001), and changes hiring decisions (e.g., Mueller-Hanson, Heggestad, & Thornton, 2003), it is reasonable to conclude that faking on SNW profiles would also have similar undesirable effects. However, research has yet to examine the impact of faking on SNW screening.

Alternatively, types of information (i.e., job-relevant or personal information) and SNW platforms may interact to affect the validity of SNW screening. Job-relevant information might be more accurate on certain SNWs because one's connections can contradict inaccuracies (Davison et al., 2011). Certain SNWs also might be less susceptible to socially desirable responding regarding personal information (Kluemper & Rosen, 2009), as faking runs counter to the purpose of SNWs (i.e., sharing information), and some information may be difficult to fake, such as third-party postings, number of friends, and content of photos (Kluemper et al., 2012). Thus, some hiring managers may focus on SNW information written by the applicant's "friends," as such information may be less subject to impression management (Slovensky & Ross, 2012).

Another issue is that SNW distortions may depend on the intended viewer (Davison et al., 2011), such that users may be creating SNWs for specific audiences or blurring personal, family, and professional aspects (Pike, 2011). SNW users may engage in impression management with the intent of impressing others with their negative, rather than positive, characteristics (Davison et al., 2012). Thus, both "faking good" directed at employers, and "faking bad" directed at one's peer group, may be present in SNW profiles. Nonetheless, SNW users may not be entirely successful at distorting their profiles. Back et al. (2010) found that ratings of personality from SNWs were more closely aligned with actual personality than with ideal-self ratings of personality. Similarly, Pike (2011) found a strong correlation between SNW users' online and offline identities, but a weak relationship between SNW identities and self-presentation on a résumé. Consequently, although SNW users may attempt to engage in impression management and self-presentation, they may be misdirected or insufficient in their efforts. Moreover, type and degree of faking may differ across SNW platforms, insofar as identities presented may differ across the platforms.

Finally, it is worth noting that users may not be the only ones "faking" on SNWs, but others who post information about the user may fake good or bad. For example, a connection of a user on LinkedIn might intentionally or unintentionally endorse the user's expertise in an area with which the user is unfamiliar. Alternatively, a Facebook friend might post negative information about the user in an attempt to be funny. Thus, the postings from others on SNWs are suspect, but little is known about the prevalence of such distortions.

Future research

Given the existing and extensive literatures in faking/social desirability, impression management, and identity, these areas may be the ripest for the development of theoretical advancement on SNW screening. Individual self-disclosure on SNWs and SNW screening are two sides of the same coin. While research has been conducted on how people present themselves online versus in-person, little has been done on screening using online information. For instance, one recent study suggested that individuals disclose differently online versus in-person, such that they disclose more intentional, less honest, and more negative information online (Chen & Marcus, 2012). Additionally, the identity and self-presentation literature (Goffman, 2002) has addressed the critical role of audiences in shaping motivations and enabling unconscious self-expression or conscious self-promotion. Indeed, studies have demonstrated that individuals reveal more audience-oriented information online versus in-person (Gibbs, Ellison, & Heino, 2006; Hew, 2011).

The availability of SNW profiles and multiple forces contributing to individual information disclosure on SNWs is underemphasized in current SNW screening studies. Beyond addressing issues of observable self-disclosure behaviors, the identity and impression management literatures may also shed light on our understanding of SNW users' internal motivations. As noted previously, not all SNW platforms are created for the same purposes. On the one hand, individuals who are managing multiple SNW profiles may face the challenge of maintaining consistency across multiple identities. On the other hand, the possible multiplicity of SNW profiles challenges HR managers to distinguish among relevant sources and identify useful information for their selection decisions. Together, these issues further suggest that the information available from SNWs may not only quantitatively but also qualitatively differ from that acquired from traditional selection methods. Future research may be productive in bridging the gap between the employers' role as social audience and the possible strategies for SNW screening by merging traditional HR literature with literature in impression management, identity, and self-presentation.

Fairness issues in SNW screening

In addition to research on the properties of SNW screening as a predictor, research also needs to address fairness of SNW screening. First, SNW screening has significant potential for discrimination (i.e., disparate treatment and adverse impact). For example, SNW screening creates a greater possibility of disparate treatment due to the availability of protected class status information on SNWs, such as religion or disabilities, not revealed in a résumé or in-person interview (Davison et al., 2012). Adverse impact can also occur when certain age or racial groups have less access to SNWs (Davison et al., 2012; Smith & Kidder, 2010), or when there are racial or gender differences in which SNWs a user is likely to adopt (Pike, 2011). Finally, recruiters may unfairly make negative attributions (without proof) about individuals because the people they associate with engage in dubious behaviors (Davison et al., 2012). Clearly, more research on discrimination using SNWs is needed, but as these issues are discussed extensively elsewhere (e.g., Kluemper & Rosen, 2009; Kluemper, 2013; Van Iddekinge et al., in press), we only briefly mention them here.

A second major issue of fairness in SNW screening is that of privacy. It is unclear whether SNW users have a reasonable expectation of privacy that affords legal protection (Brandenburg, 2008), particularly from private-sector employers. There is also disagreement as to what is private and public with SNWs. Applicants may view SNW screening as an invasion of privacy, whereas organizations may view SNWs as legitimate public information (Gustafson, 2012) and a valuable source for attempting to prevent negligent hiring (Woska, 2007). Indeed, failing to screen SNWs might incur legal liability, particularly for companies in certain industries (Slovensky & Ross, 2012). Nonetheless, a number of laws may restrict such screening for privacy reasons (e.g., Fair Credit Reporting Act, Stored Communications Act).

Clearly related to the issues of discrimination and privacy is how applicants view SNW screening as a selection device. Applicants have been shown to have more favorable views of certain selection approaches (e.g., job interviews, job knowledge tests, work sample tests) than others (e.g., cognitive ability tests, personality tests, college transcripts) (Reeve & Schultz, 2004). Importantly, applicants who view the hiring process as intrusive or invalid are more likely to perceive the process as unfair and potentially remove themselves from the applicant pool or even file a lawsuit (Wallace, Page, & Lippstreu, 2006). Some initial research has been conducted on applicant reactions to SNW screening. Black, Johnson, Takach, and Stone (2012) suggested that informational, procedural, sociocultural, and individual factors can result in negative organizational consequences such as fewer job acceptances, applicant lawsuits, and damage to company reputation from SNW screening.

Empirical research in this area is also emerging. Gustafson (2012) found that undergraduate students view Facebook screening as unfair, but these negative perceptions were reduced when applicants were asked permission to access the SNW. Siebert, Downes, and Christopher (2012) found that the use of SNW screening did not impact organizational attractiveness or application intentions but did negatively impact applicant attitudes toward the selection procedure. Further, more invasive SNW screening (i.e., requiring acceptance of a friend request from hiring managers) harmed applicant reactions. Stoughton, Thompson, and Meade (2013) found that applicants felt their privacy was invaded by SNW screening, resulting in lower organizational attraction. Importantly, the hiring decision did not affect perceptions of procedural justice of SNW screening. In contrast, Sanchez, Roberts, Freeman, and Clayton (2012) found no negative effects of SNW screening on perceptions of SNW checks, organizational attractiveness, job pursuit intentions, procedural justice, and informational justice. In fact, participants' perceptions of SNW checks were positively related to applicant reactions.

Together, these findings suggest that applicants might not always react negatively to SNW screening, depending on the screening approach. Clearly, more theoretical development and empirical studies are needed. In particular, future research should examine differences in perceptions across demographic groups, as well as differences across SNW platforms. Applicants may view searches of professional SNWs like LinkedIn as more acceptable, for example, versus personal SNWs like Facebook.

Nonetheless, societal culture may have a great impact on privacy perceptions. Chen and Marcus (2012) argue that SNWs lead to collectivist norms among users due to high levels of individual accountability. Taken a step further, it stands to reason that individuals with collectivistic culture norms are more likely to adjust their privacy settings and monitor their personal information. As such, national culture also may play a more prominent role in shaping individuals' fairness perceptions, by providing norms for exchanging information. Unfortunately, cross-cultural research with SNWs has been limited. Future research should explore differences in privacy and fairness perceptions and the norms for online information-disclosure between countries and across demographic groups.

Theoretical perspectives

Much work is needed to demonstrate the potential value and hazards of SNW screening. Key to this is the development of theoretical perspectives that help to better explain a wide range of relevant phenomena. These potential theoretical perspectives fall into two categories. The first is the development of new theoretical perspectives specific to the domain of social networking websites. We are aware of no such theories, but encourage theoretical development in this domain. Within the second category, existing theoretical perspectives are adopted from the existing literature and applied to the social networking context. In essence, this perspective allows for the testing of boundary conditions for a range of existing theories.

As an example, one such relevant theoretical perspective relates to the evaluation of personality via Facebook. Kluemper et al. (2012) incorporate the Realistic Accuracy Model (RAM; Funder, 1995) using the Big Five personality framework. RAM posits that rating accuracy is enhanced with an array of cues that are relevant, available, detectable, and utilized. Relevance requires the environment to enable the target (SNW user) to display personality-relevant behavior. These relevant cues consist of physical traces of activities conducted in the environment (behavioral residue) and behaviors individuals engage in to reinforce their personal preferences or to display their identities to others (identity claims) (Gosling, Ko, Mannarelli, & Morris, 2002) as guided by their personality characteristics (Kluemper et al., 2012). For example, extraverts are more social, leaving traces of such social behavior in their photos and posts. Availability requires an appropriate context in which the rater has sufficient information with which to perceive the personality trait of the target. Despite the inconsistent nature of the information available on SNWs, a high volume of moderately relevant cues may manifest themselves across a wide range of observable behaviors available via SNWs, making meaningful assessment of personality traits possible. For example, evaluating the full array of information available on a Facebook profile may provide a large number of cues that may be ambiguous and even meaningless when viewed in isolation, but when viewed in the context of other similarly ambiguous information, a pattern may emerge that represents the personality trait of the user. Raters must then detect this relevant information by accessing and evaluating the target's Facebook profile (which requires that the rater is trained to do so). Finally, the rater must utilize this information by correctly piecing together these cues to produce an accurate evaluation. In the context of Big Five personality assessment, this entails the rater completing a validated (other-oriented) personality measure. Although this theoretical perspective has been supported by preliminary research, many questions remain unanswered regarding the boundary conditions of RAM vis-à-vis social networking websites.

Like RAM, a wide range of cross-disciplinary theoretical perspectives may be applied to social networking websites, for which we provide three possibilities. First, the complex network structures of social media make social network theories (e.g., Granovetter, 1973) potentially useful. Second, information technology adoption has been a central concern of information systems research and practice. Substantial theoretical and empirical support has accumulated in favor of the technology acceptance model (TAM, Davis, 1989), which consistently explains substantial variance in usage intentions and behaviors regarding certain technologies (e.g., googling, job searching using social media). Finally, social media provides a place to exhibit our identities and enable us to express ourselves by constantly and selectively connecting with others. Actor-Network Theory (ANT; Latour, 2005), for example, may help to explain how social media are affected by individual identities, which could further shed light on our understanding of the effects of online impression/identity management. Once again, future research and theoretical advancements are essential if the field is to move forward.

Conclusions

It is clear from the literature that the use of SNWs by practitioners for selection purposes has been on the rise, yet academic efforts to inform practice are lacking and sorely needed. Precious little empirical evidence exists. In fact, the few empirical studies on this practice provide initial evidence in two general areas: that personality characteristics measured via Facebook are somewhat reliable and valid (Kluemper & Rosen, 2009; Kluemper et al., 2012) and that applicant reactions toward SNW screening are mixed (Gustafson, 2012; Sanchez et al., 2012; Siebert et al., 2012; Stoughton et al., 2013). More work in these areas is sorely needed. Further, no empirical evidence yet exists regarding issues of discrimination and applicant privacy, as well as impression management and online identities of applicants. Due to the nascent state of this research paradigm, perhaps more important is the application and development of sound theoretical approaches to these wide-ranging issues. Only after rigorous theoretical development and empirical testing will academicians be able to provide well-needed guidance to practitioners regarding this dynamic phenomenon.

Note

1. Parallel forms reliability is likely inappropriate for SNW screening, as it is typically assessed using two tests constructed to be equivalent in number and type of items, difficulty, and other psychometric properties. Clearly, two different SNW platforms (e.g., LinkedIn and Twitter) are not parallel, nor are they intended to be parallel.

References

Back, M.D., Stopfer, J.M., Vazire, S., Gaddis, S., Schuukle, S.C., Egloff, B., & Gosling, S.D. (2010). Facebook profiles reflect actual personality, not self-idealization. *Psychological Science, 21*, 372–374.

Bing, M.N., Kluemper, D.H., Davison, H.K., Taylor, S., & Novicevic, M. (2011). Overclaiming as a measure of faking. *Organizational Behavior and Human Decision Processes, 116*, 148–162.

Black, S.L., Johnson, A.F., Takach, S.E., & Stone, D.L. (2012, August). *Factors affecting applicants' reactions to the collection of data in social network websites*. Presented at the Academy of Management Annual Conference, Philadelphia, PA.

Blackman, M.C., & Funder, D.C. (2002). Effective interview practices for accurately assessing counterproductive traits. *International Journal of Selection and Assessment, 10*, 109–116.

Bohnert, D., & Ross, W.H. (2010). The influence of social networking websites on the evaluation of job candidates. *Cyberpsychology, Behavior, and Social Networking, 13*, 341–347.

Boyd, D.M., & Ellison, N.B. (2007). Social network sites: Definition, history and scholarship. *Journal of Computer Mediated Education, 13*, article 11. Retrieved July 31, 2013, from http://jcmc.indiana.edu/vol13/issue1/boyd.ellison.html

Brandenburg, C. (2008). The newest way to screen job applicants: A social networking nightmare. *Federal Communications Law Journal, 60*, 598–614.

Buffardi, L.E., & Campbell, W.K. (2008). Narcissism and social networking web sites. *Personality and Social Psychology Bulletin, 34*, 1303–1314.

Campion, M.A., Palmer, D.K., & Campion, J.E. (1997). A review of structure in the selection interview. *Personnel Psychology, 50*, 655–702.

CareerBuilder.com (2009). *Forty-five percent of employers use social networking sites to research job candidates, CareerBuilder survey finds: Career expert provides dos and don'ts for job seekers on social networking*. Retrieved October 16, 2013, from http://www.careerbuilder.com/share/aboutus/pressreleasesdetail.aspx?id=pr519&sd=8/19/2009&ed=12/31/2009

Chen, B., & Marcus, J. (2012). Students' self-presentation on Facebook: An examination of personality and self-construal factors. *Computers in Human Behavior, 28*, 2091–2099.

Cronbach, L.J., & Gleser, G.C. (1957). *Psychological tests and personnel decisions*. Urbana: University of Illinois Press.

Cross-Tab Marketing Services. (2010). *Online reputation in a connected world*. Retrieved September 26, 2012, from source download.microsoft.com/download/C/D/2/CD233E13-A600-482F-9C97-545BB4AE93B1/DPD_Online%20Reputation%20Research_overview.pdf

Davis, F.D. (1989). Perceived usefulness, perceived ease of use, and user acceptance of information technology. *MIS Quarterly*, 13, 319–340.

Davison, H.K., Maraist, C., & Bing, M.N. (2011). Friend or foe? The promise and pitfalls of using social networking sites for HR decisions. *Journal of Business and Psychology, 26*, 153–159.

Davison, H.K., Maraist, C.C., Hamilton, R.H., & Bing, M.N. (2012). To screen or not to screen? Using the Internet for selection decisions. *Employee Responsibility and Rights Journal, 24*, 1–21.

Duggan, M., & Brenner, J. (2013). The demographics of social media users – 2012. *Pew Internet, a project of the Pew Research Center*. Retrieved October 16, 2013, from http://pewinternet.org/Reports/2013/Social-media-users.aspx

Ellison, N., Steinfield, C., & Lampe, C. (2006). Spatially bounded online social networks and social capital. *International Communication Association, 36*(1–37).

Equal Employment Opportunity Commission, Civil Service Commission, Department of Labor, & Department of Justice. (1978). Uniform guidelines on employee selection procedures. *Federal Register, 43*(166), 38290–38315.

Funder, D.C. (1995). On the accuracy of personality judgment: A realistic approach. *Psychological Review, 4*, 652–670.

Gatewood, R.D., Feild, H.S., & Barrick, M. (2008). *Human resource selection* (6th ed.). Mason, OH: South-Western.

Genova, G.L. (2009). No place to play: Current employee privacy rights in social networking sites. *Business Communication Quarterly, 72*, 97–101.

Gibbs, J.L., Ellison, N.B., & Heino, R.D. (2006). Self-presentation in online personals: The role of anticipated future interaction, self-disclosure, and perceived success in Internet dating. *Communication Research, 33*, 152–177.

Goffman, E. (2002). *The presentation of self in everyday life*. Garden City, NY: Anchor.

Gosling, S.D., Ko, S.J., Mannarelli, T., & Morris, M.E. (2002). A room with a cue: Personality judgments based on offices and bedrooms. *Journal of Personality and Social Psychology, 82*, 379–398.

Granovetter, M. (1973). The strength of weak ties. *American Journal of Sociology, 78*, 1360–1380.

Gustafson, D.A. (2012). *Perceived fairness in the use of Facebook in the selection process*. (Unpublished master's thesis). University of Texas at Arlington.

Hermeier, B., & Seng, A. (2009). *Ergebnisbericht FOM Netzwerkumfrage 2009 – Relevanz von internetbasierten Netzwerken für die berufliche Entwicklung*. Retrieved October 16, 2013, from http://www.fom.de/fileadmin/fom/downloads/forschungsberichte/Tabellenband_Netzwerkumfrage2009.pdf

Hew, K.F. (2011). Students' and teachers' use of Facebook. *Computers in Human Behavior, 27*, 662–676.

Hidy, K.M., & McDonald, M.S.E. (2013). Risky business: The legal implications of social media's increasing role in employment decisions. *Journal of Legal Studies in Business, 18*, 69–107.

Highhouse, S. (2002). Assessing the candidate as a whole: A historical and critical analysis of individual psychological assessment for personnel decision making. *Personnel Psychology, 55*, 363–396.

Hornberger, S. (2011). Social networking websites: Impact on litigation and the legal profession in ethics, discovery, and evidence. *Touro Law Review, 27*, 279.

Jaccard, J., & Wood, G. (1988). The effects of incomplete information on the formation of attitudes toward behavioral alternatives. *Journal of Personality and Social Psychology, 54*, 580–591.

Karl, K.A., & Peluchette, J.V. (2013). Possibilities and pitfalls of using online social networking in human resource management. In M.A. Paludi (Ed.), *Psychology for Business Success:*

Vol. 4. *Implementing best practices in human resources* (pp. 119–139). Santa Barbara, CA: Praeger/ABC-CLIO.

Kietzmann, J.H., Hermkens, K., McCarthy, I.P., & Silvestre, B.S. (2011). Social media? Get serious! Understanding the functional building blocks of social media. *Business Horizons, 54,* 241–251.

Kluemper, D.H. (2013). Social network screening: Pitfalls, possibilities, and parallels in employment selection. In T. Bondarouk and M. Olivas-Lujan (Eds.), *Advanced Series in Management: Volume 12. Social media in human resource management* (pp. 1–21). Bingly, UK: Emerald Group Publishing Ltd.

Kluemper, D.H., McLarty, B., & Rosen, P. (2013). Exploring the relationship between individual characteristics and LinkedIn use. In R.F. Miguel (Chair), *The promise and perils of social media data for selection.* Symposium presented at the Society for Industrial and Organizational Psychology, Houston, TX.

Kluemper, D.H., & Rosen, P. (2009). Future employment selection methods: Evaluating social networking websites. *Journal of Managerial Psychology, 24,* 567–580.

Kluemper, D.H., Rosen, P., & Mossholder, K. (2012). Social networking websites, personality ratings, and the organizational context: More than meets the eye? *Journal of Applied Social Psychology, 42,* 1143–1172.

Kristof, A.L. (1996). Person-organization fit: An integrative review of its conceptualizations, measurement, and implications. *Personnel Psychology, 49,* 1–49.

Latour, B. (2005). *Reassembling the social: An introduction to actor-network theory.* Oxford, UK: Oxford University Press.

Lievens, F. (1998). Factors which improve the construct validity of assessment centers: A review. *International Journal of Selection and Assessment, 6,* 141–152.

Madera, J.M. (2012). Using social networking websites as a selection tool: The role of selection process fairness and job pursuit intentions. *International Journal of Hospitality Management, 31,* 1276–1282.

Mayfield, A. (2008). *What is social media?* Retrieved October 16, 2013, from http://www.icrossing.com/sites/default/files/what-is-social-media-uk.pdf

McCorvey, J.J. (2010). How to use social networking sites to drive business. Retrieved October 16, 2013, from http://www.inc.com/guides/using-social-networking-sites.html

McLarty, B., Kluemper, D.H., & Rosen, P. (2013). *Social networking websites and organizational relevance: Exploring relationships with LinkedIn adoption and use.* Presented at the Southern Management Association Annual Meeting, New Orleans, LA.

Mueller-Hanson, R., Heggestad, E.D., & Thornton, G.C. (2003). Faking and selection: Considering the use of personality from select-in and select-out perspectives. *Journal of Applied Psychology, 88,* 348–355.

Noe, R.A., Hollenbeck, J.R., Gerhart, B., & Wright, P. (2011). *Fundamentals of human resource management* (5th edition). New York: McGraw-Hill.

Pike, J.C. (2011). *The impact of boundary-blurring social networking websites: Self-presentation, impression formation, and publicness.* (Unpublished doctoral dissertation). University of Pittsburgh.

Reeve, C.L., & Schultz, L. (2004). Job-seeker reactions to selection process information in job ads. *International Journal of Selection and Assessment, 12,* 343–355.

Roth, P.L., Bobko, P., Van Iddekinge, C.H., & Thatcher, J.B. (in press). Social media in employment-related selection decisions: A research agenda for uncharged territory. *Journal of Management.*

Sanchez, R.J., Roberts, K., Freeman, M., & Clayton, A.C. (2012, August). *Do they care? Applicant reactions to on-line social networking presence checks.* Paper presented at the Academy of Management Annual Conference, Boston, MA.

Shiller, K. (2010). Getting a grip on reputation. *Information Today, 27,* 1–44.

SHRM. (2011). *SHRM survey findings: The use of social networking websites and online search engines in screening job candidates.* Retrieved October 16, 2013, from http://www.shrm.org/research/surveyfindings/articles/pages/theuseofsocialnetworkingwebsitesandonline-searchenginesinscreeningjobcandidates.aspx

Siebert, S., Downes, P.E., & Christopher, J. (2012, August). *Applicant reactions to online background checks: Welcome to a brave new world.* Paper presented at the Academy of Management Annual Conference, Boston, MA.

Sinar, E.F. (2013). What LinkedIn links to: Connecting virtual profiles to actual performance. In R.F. Miguel (Chair), *The promise and perils of social media data for selection.* Symposium presented at the Society for Industrial and Organizational Psychology, Houston, TX.

Slovensky, R., & Ross, W.H. (2012). Should human resource managers use social media to screen job applicants? Managerial and legal issues in the USA. *Info, 14,* 55–69.

Smith, W.P., & Kidder, D.L. (2010). You've been tagged! (Then again, maybe not): Employers and Facebook. *Business Horizons, 53,* 491–499.

Stark, S., Chernyshenko, O.S., Chan, K.-Y., Lee, W.C., & Drasgow, F. (2001). Effects of the testing situation on item responding: Cause for concern. *Journal of Applied Psychology, 86,* 943–953.

Steinfield, C., Ellison, N.B., & Lampe, C. (2008). Social capital, self-esteem, and use of online social network sites: A longitudinal analysis. *Journal of Applied Developmental Psychology, 29,* 434–445.

Stoughton, J.W., Thompson, L., & Meade, A. (2015). Examining Applicant Reactions to the Use of Social Networking Websites in Pre-Employment Screening. *Journal of Business and Psychology, 30*(1), 73–88.

The Reppler Effect. (2011, September 27). *Re: Managing your online image across social networks.* [Web log post]. Retrieved October 16, 2013, from http://blog.reppler.com/2011/09/27/managing-your-online-image-across-social-networks/

Turban, D.B., & Jones, A.P. (1988). Supervisor-subordinate similarity: Types, effects, and mechanisms. *Journal of Applied Psychology, 73,* 228–234.

Van Iddekinge, C.H., Lanivich, S.E., Roth, P.L., & Junco, E. (in press). Social media for selection? Validity and adverse impact potential of a Facebook-based assessment. *Journal of Management.*

Wallace, J.C., Page, E.E., & Lippstreu, M. (2006). Applicant reactions to pre-employment application blanks: A legal and procedural justice perspective. *Journal of Business and Psychology, 20,* 467–488.

Wikipedia. (2013). *List of social networking websites.* Retrieved October 16, 2013, from http://en.wikipedia.org/wiki/List_of_social_networking_websites

Woska, W.J. (2007). Legal issues for HR professionals: Reference checking/background investigations. *Public Personnel Management, 36,* 79–89.

5

APPLICANT REACTIONS TO SELECTION METHODS

An overview of recent research and suggestions for the future

Ioannis Nikolaou
ATHENS UNIVERSITY OF ECONOMICS AND BUSINESS, GREECE

Talya N. Bauer
PORTLAND STATE UNIVERSITY, USA

Donald M. Truxillo
PORTLAND STATE UNIVERSITY, USA

Employee recruitment and selection has changed and continues to evolve rapidly at the beginning of the twenty-first century. New recruitment and selection methods have appeared and attracted increased attention, both in research and practice, whereas traditional or "settled" questions remain (Ryan & Ployhart, 2014). Within the broader area of employee selection and assessment, applicant reactions research has become an important topic of study. It has been a fruitful and highly productive stream of research since the mid-1980s, when the first highly influential empirical study on this topic was published by Harris and Fink (1987). Gilliland and Steiner (2012) suggest, and our analysis of the literature confirms, that one to two dozen papers, on average, have been published annually on this topic since the research took off in the late 1990s (see Figure 5.1 for more detailed counts). However, this is only one of the main reasons why this chapter is important and a part of the current book. We also believe that in the future, applicant reactions research and practice will continue to evolve and take on a different focus, considering the changing nature of staffing practices in the twenty-first century.

The current chapter will focus on research published since the most recent reviews on the topic of applicant reactions (Gilliland & Steiner, 2012; Hausknecht, 2013). Therefore, we will briefly review and present the most important theoretical frameworks pertaining to applicant reactions research, and the most recent empirical

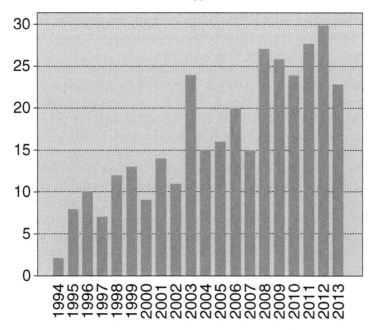

FIGURE 5.1 Number of published journal articles each year as reported in Web of Science using the search term "applicant reactions" from 1994–2013.

studies not covered in these reviews, with reference to a few earlier studies that are relevant to our current work. However, we will mainly focus on a number of issues we consider important and that have not been covered extensively in these reviews, such as the role of social networking websites (SNWs) and their impact on applicants' reactions. Finally, we will put emphasis on the future of applicant reactions research in an attempt to propose new avenues for research in the field.

Theoretical perspectives

The leading theoretical framework behind the majority of the research conducted in the field of applicant reactions is Gilliland's (1993) organizational justice framework. Although this is the most dominant approach, it is not the only one. Test-taking motivation, social psychological models, and invasion of privacy theories have also been studied in relation to applicant reactions research.

One of the first who tried to theoretically explore fairness reactions was Schuler (1993), who discussed the notion of "social validity." Schuler described a four-component model influencing the acceptability of the selection process to candidates, that is, the information provided to candidates regarding the position and the organization, the degree of the candidates' active involvement in the selection process, the transparency of the process so that they can understand its objective and its relevance to organizational requirements, and finally the provision of acceptable feedback in terms of content and form. Although this model has not been studied extensively, it is obvious that it has a significant impact on the way of thinking of other theorists in fairness reactions.

Gilliland's (1993) *organizational justice* framework has probably been the most influential in the study of applicant reactions (Truxillo, Bauer, & McCarthy, in press). In his model, selection practices, policies, and decisions all influence perceptions of organizational justice, which, in turn, have an impact on individual perceptions of fairness. Subsequently, the latter should influence a variety of pre-hire and post-hire outcomes. Gilliland also put increased emphasis on the role of procedural as opposed to distributive organizational justice. He developed 10 procedural rules, grouped into three categories: formal characteristics (job relatedness, opportunity to perform, reconsideration opportunity, and consistency), explanation (feedback, selection information, and honesty), and interpersonal treatment (interpersonal effectiveness, two-way communication, and propriety of questions). It is suggested that the invasiveness of questions and "fakeability" of responses might also influence the shaping of procedural justice perceptions. This model was further refined by Bauer et al. (2001), who confirmed and expanded the model while creating psychometrically sound items to tap the justice rules. Steiner and Gilliland (1996) added that, in addition to these procedural dimensions, a selection method may be considered as more acceptable by candidates when it is widely used, since they claim "people make an implicit judgment that a widely used technique must be valid" (p. 134). Thus, they developed a model of eight procedural justice dimensions, which formed the basis of considerable research on applicant reactions, especially in cross-cultural settings (e.g., Anderson, Ahmed, & Costa, 2012; Bilgic & Acarlar, 2010; Hoang, Truxillo, Erdogan, & Bauer, 2012; Ispas, Ilie, Iliescu, Johnson, & Harris, 2010; Moscoso & Salgado, 2004; Nikolaou & Judge, 2007).

Another widely used theoretical approach in applicant reactions research has been the *test-taking motivation* model developed by Arvey, Strickland, Drauden, and Martin (1990). The authors explored the impact of job applicants' motivation during the selection process and how this affects both their own performance and test validity. They developed the Test Attitude Scale, which measures nine different dimensions, with test motivation being the most important since it was accounting for the majority of the variance in the scale (Gilliland & Steiner, 2012). *Test anxiety* has also been studied as a potential cause of applicants' varying perceptions of the different selection methods, especially in relation to job interviews and psychometric tests. The meta-analysis by Hausknecht, Day, and Thomas (2004) has indicated a negative relationship between test anxiety and test performance, but this does not seem to extend and have an impact on actual job performance (McCarthy et al., 2013). The *self-serving bias* mechanism, defined as the extent to which preservation of a positive self-image has an impact on applicants' perceptions of the different selection methods, has also been studied in the area of test-taking motivation. In other words, rejected or poorly performing applicants, in an attempt to maintain a positive self-image, attribute their poor test performance to beliefs that the method is not valid or is irrelevant. Gilliland and Steiner (2012) highlight issues of causality in exploring the role of self-serving biases in applicant reactions research. This is an area calling for future research in the field of applicant reactions.

A third, relatively old approach in applicant reactions research was first explored in the late 1980s by Peter Herriot (1989). The *social psychological* theories focus on the perceptual processes that underlie these reactions and the two-way interaction occurring between applicants and the organizations during the selection process. More recently, Herriot (2004) extended his approach by exploring the role of applicants' personal-social identities and how these are associated with organizational identities, referring to applicants' perceived characteristics of an organization's culture. A congruence (or incongruence) between those two might influence applicants' perceptions of both the selection methods employed and the organization as a potential employer.

One final, more recent approach is the *invasion of privacy* model, developed by Bauer et al. (2006). Although the origins of this model were grounded in justice theory, the authors explored, in one of the very few studies in the field, the role of privacy invasion in selection. Specifically, they emphasized the negative consequences of invading applicants' personal lives through selection methods such as drug and integrity testing, and maybe personality testing as well. Gilliland and Steiner (2012) suggest, however, that the invasion of privacy model can be incorporated into the organizational justice perspective, since it is associated with justice perceptions, such as job relatedness and opportunity to perform.

Gilliland and Steiner (2012) provide an interesting theoretical integration of the main theoretical approaches in applicant reactions research. They emphasized three main domains: *self-interest, group-values motives*, and *deontic outrage*. The first deals with the conscious or unconscious attempt people make to maximize the likelihood of favorable outcomes, leading thus to positive reactions, if treated fairly on an individual level. Consistent with the test-taking model of motivation, self-interest emphasizes the role of self-serving biases in the development of applicant reactions (Gilliland & Steiner, 2012). The group-values motive, although it has attracted limited research attention, is based on a common assumption applicants often make during the selection process: that if they succeed in getting the job, as employees they will be treated in a similar way as they have been treated during the selection process. Job applicants, as "outsiders", make assumptions about the organization they want to join and the subsequent social identity of its employees. Finally, the third domain, of deontic outrage, deals with the impact of mistreatment to third parties, not the applicants themselves. As Gilliland and Steiner (2012) illustrate: ". . . when we see or hear about other applicants being treated poorly, do we form negative impressions (about the company) that shape our own reactions and decision making?" (p. 648). Gilliland and Steiner (2012), however, argue that deontic outrage is not a strong motivating force among job applicants, or at least not as important as the other two. Instead, they have emphasized the first two domains in future applicant reactions research. Later in this chapter we will discuss how deontic outrage might be an important perspective in the era of SNWs.

Another issue, which has not yet attracted increased interest in applicant reactions research, is the role of trust and trustworthiness. Klotz, da Motta Veiga, Buckley, and Gavin (2013) discussed the role of trustworthiness in the pre-entry period. They claim, that as a result of the "inability by potential employees and employers to supply proof that they will always fulfill the expectations of the other party when future contingencies arise, the trustworthiness that job applicants and recruiting organizations perceive in one another during pre-entry processes becomes potentially relevant as a proxy for such certainty and likely plays an influential role in applicants' job choice decisions and in organizations' job offer decisions" (p. 105). Organizational reputation has been shown to influence job applicants' initial perceptions of organizational trustworthiness, but the extent to which aspects of candidates' trustworthiness, such as benevolence, integrity, and ability, have an impact, especially at the early stages of the recruitment process, remains unclear. On the other hand, Klotz et al. (2013) emphasize the role that Internet job sites and SNWs play on influencing organizations' initial perceptions of applicants' trustworthiness.

On an issue related to trust and trustworthiness, Walker et al. (2013) have explored how job seekers react to recruitment activities following the application submission process. Walker and his colleagues have drawn from three management theories (signaling, uncertainty reduction, and uncertainty management theories) to develop a conceptual model exploring the relationships between recruitment interactions of the job applicants with the recruiter/company and organizational attraction. They conducted three studies showing that justice perceptions influence organizational attraction via positive relational certainty (i.e., reducing the uncertainty applicants feel regarding relations at work following organizational entry). They also provided additional evidence of the relational certainty mechanism through which justice signals influence organizational attraction, and they demonstrated that this relationship is dynamic, suggesting that organizations should pay increased attention to their communication process and policies during the recruitment and selection process, as they do matter to applicants a great deal.

Predictors of applicant reactions

One of the most widely studied issues in applicant reactions research has been the characteristics of the selection methods that seem to lead to positive or negative applicant reactions. Anderson, Salgado, and Hülsheger (2010) have summarized the cross-cultural research on the procedural dimensions of the different selection methods, as mentioned earlier. Their findings supported the *reaction generalizability* hypothesis, that is, the fact that candidates across very different countries seem to have very similar reactions towards the different selection methods, with work samples and interviews as the most preferred and honesty-integrity tests, personal contacts, and graphology as the least preferred selection methods. Interviews and work samples score very high in most procedural dimensions and especially on opportunity to perform and interpersonal warmth. Their major advantage is that through these methods, the applicants have the opportunity to meet in person with the assessors, as opposed to other methods, which might be more valid (e.g., cognitive tests) or more widely used (e.g., resumes) (Nikolaou & Judge, 2007).

Another well-studied predictor of applicant reactions has been the explanations given to candidates during the selection process. In a meta-analysis conducted by Truxillo, Bodner, Bertolino, Bauer, and Yonce (2009), the authors made the distinction between "structure" and "social fairness", with the former emphasizing the job-related and procedural characteristics of the selection method, whereas the latter focuses on issues such as the interpersonal sensitivity and the justification provided before or after selection decisions are made. The meta-analytic evidence demonstrated the existence of positive associations between explanations and most applicant reactions outcomes (perceived fairness, organizational perceptions, test performance, test-taking motivation), but no relationship was found with self-perceptions. Also, there were no differences between the structure and the social fairness types of explanations.

Personality has also been studied as a potential predictor of applicant reactions, but the small number of studies today has only shown minimal effect sizes. Truxillo, Bauer, Campion, and Paronto (2006) explored the relationship between the Five-Factor Model of personality measured before a written test and applicants' post-test fairness perceptions, perceptions of themselves, and perceptions of the hiring organization using a sample of actual law enforcement applicants ($N=120$). Personality accounted for significant variance in self-perceptions and perceptions of the hiring organization beyond that accounted for by fairness perceptions. Neuroticism and agreeableness were the most consistent predictors of applicant perceptions. Nikolaou and Judge (2007), in a study conducted in Greece, found only weak positive associations between core self-evaluations and fairness reactions across different popular selection methods. More recently, Honkaniemi, Feldt, Metsapelto, and Tolvanen (2013) explored in their study the role of personality types in a real-life selection setting. Although published research using personality types in selection research is scarce, Honkaniemi et al. (2013) showed that personality types explained applicants' fairness perceptions, when controlling for gender, but they were not associated with the face validity perceptions or predictive validity perceptions. They also briefly summarized the studies that have explored the relationship between the Five-Factor Model of personality and applicant reactions (see Honkaniemi et al., 2013, Table 1, p. 33). A quick look in this table will show that the associations identified in previous studies are only a few and relatively weak. In conclusion, the evidence seems to show that personality has a very weak effect, if any, on applicants' perceptions of the selection process, despite the small number of studies conducted today.

The effects of applicant reactions

Probably the most interesting aspect of applicant reactions research, mainly from a practical perspective, is the impact reactions might have on applicants' subsequent attitudes, behaviors, personal beliefs, and/or even the selection results and outcomes themselves. Truxillo and Bauer (2011) summarized the empirical literature on the relationship between applicant reactions and a number of different outcomes. Similarly to Gilliland and Steiner (2012), they suggested that applicant perceptions seem to have a much stronger association with applicants' attitudes, as opposed to their actual behaviors. Unfortunately, most of this research has been carried out in a pre-hire stage, using self-report measures, and thus faces problems with common method variance effects. Many of these studies are also carried out using students, in "experimental", non-selection settings.

Earlier research has shown that the impact of applicant reactions on applicants' attitudes is quite considerable, especially in a pre-hire condition, that is, when the applicants are not aware of the hiring decision. This relationship, though, is far weaker when the hiring outcome is known, suggesting the existence of a strong self-serving bias in applicant reactions (Gilliland & Steiner, 2012). In the pre-hire condition, researchers have explored a number of attitudes, such as satisfaction with the selection process, organizational attractiveness, organizational commitment, intentions to recommend the organization, to accept a job offer, or to purchase the organization's products and services, and intentions to pursue legal actions. On the other hand, limited research has explored the relationship between applicant reactions during the selection process and their post-hire attitudes, if selected, such as job satisfaction and organizational commitment, calling for further research on this matter (Hausknecht et al., 2004).

Similarly, it is worth exploring the impact of applicant reactions on their actual behaviors. This is another fundamental issue of applicant reactions research, if we assume that applicant reactions have a real impact on organizational life. However, this is yet another area of limited research in this field, especially in the post-hire condition. In one of the very few studies exploring this topic, McCarthy et al. (2013) recently conducted a large-scale research with four studies, six selection methods (personality tests, job knowledge tests, cognitive ability tests, work samples, situational judgment tests, and a selection inventory), five candidate reactions (anxiety, motivation, belief in tests, self-efficacy, and procedural justice), two contexts (industry and education), two study designs (predictive and concurrent), and four occupational areas (medical, sales, customer service, and technological), across three continents (North America, South America, and Europe). In summary, they showed that applicant reactions were related to test scores, and test scores were related to job performance. Further, there was some evidence that reactions affected performance indirectly through their influence on test scores. However, they found no evidence on the predictive validity of applicant reactions for actual job performance. In another recent study, Schinkel, Van Vianen, and Van Dierendonck (2013) demonstrated that successful applicants reported both the highest well-being and organizational attractiveness when they perceived the selection outcome as fair. On the other hand, rejected applicants reported higher well-being when they thought the outcome was unfair. Selection outcome and procedural fairness interacted with organizational attractiveness, with higher procedural fairness leading to higher attractiveness for rejected applicants. These outcomes demonstrate that the impact of applicant reactions on actual behavior and performance is probably minimal, although more studies are required on this topic, but their effect on employee attitudes, even in the post-hire condition, remain considerable.

One final, important result of applicant reactions concerns the impact of the selection process on applicants' self-perceptions, and especially on their self-efficacy and self-esteem levels. Earlier research has shown that the selection process can have a negative impact on applicants' self-concept, and this is especially the case for self-esteem rather than self-efficacy (Hausknecht et al., 2004). However, similar to the relationship between applicant reactions and applicants' attitudes, this relationship seems to be moderated by the hiring outcome. Thus, job relatedness of the selection process positively influences selected applicants' self-efficacy levels, and negatively for rejected candidates (Gilliland, 1994). It is obvious that rejected job applicants tend to attribute their failure to other, external factors, rather than themselves, in order to retain a positive self-image of themselves and also increased psychological well-being, as recently demonstrated by Schinkel et al. (2013).

Future research on applicant reactions

Ryan and Ployhart (2014), in the most recent review of the recruitment and selection research published in the *Annual Review of Psychology*, have discussed the role of applicant reactions in staffing research, especially in relation to negative word of mouth, consumer behavior, and organizational image/reputation. This is especially the case for new selection approaches, not widely employed yet and therefore still relatively unfamiliar between job seekers, such as situational judgment tests and the role of technology/social media on applicants' reactions. Moreover, both Gilliland and Steiner (2012) and Hausknecht (2013) in their reviews present a number of issues that applicant reactions researchers should focus on in the future. Our objective is not to repeat their suggestions here but to extend them further by incorporating a number of potential research areas not covered extensively in their work, such as the role of the Internet and the impact of SNWs in applicant reactions.

The role of the Internet regarding applicant reactions

Since the early 2000s, when one of the first papers on Internet recruitment and selection appeared in the *International Journal of Selection and Assessment* (Bartram, 2000), many things have changed in the field, impacting dramatically on both research and practice in staffing. Many of the issues raised then, such as security, confidentiality, authentication, control of assessment conditions, and equality of access, remain important, but many others have also surfaced, most of them as a result of the advent and increased use of Web 2.0 technologies, such as blogging, micro-blogging (e.g., Twitter), and more recently SNWs (e.g., Facebook, LinkedIn). The main characteristic of these technological developments, as applied to recruitment, selection, and applicant reactions, is the high degree of interaction allowed between parties, namely, companies, interviewers, job applicants themselves, and/or potential intermediaries, such as third-party vendors that are strongly involved in online assessment these days.

One of the theoretical approaches we could use in order to explore the impact of the Internet on applicant reactions is the *deontic outrage*, which, as mentioned earlier, deals with the impact of applicants' mistreatment on third parties, not on the applicants themselves. As we will discuss below, this approach might be very useful today, in the era of SNWs, when the selection process is not an isolated and "behind closed doors" process, as it used to be in the past. More than 18 million people now use Glassdoor.com (http://expandedramblings.com), a website providing for free "company reviews, CEO approval ratings, salary reports, interview reviews and questions, office photos and more" (Glassdoor.com, 2013). Word of mouth can have a powerful impact on organizational attraction, as demonstrated by a number of studies (e.g., Van Hoye, 2014), but much less is known about the individual characteristics of people most likely to spread and receive word of mouth, what organizations can do to stimulate word of mouth, what mechanisms explain the effects of word of mouth, and the conditions under which word of mouth is less or more influential (Van Hoye, 2014). Also, despite its independent nature, only a few studies have considered negative word of mouth (Van Hoye, 2014). In particular, the latter is associated with applicant reactions and could also be part of the deontic outrage approach. Applicants sharing their negative experiences during the recruitment and selection process in SNWs and other websites, such as Glassdoor.com, are quite likely to generate a negative word of mouth and create a respective image of potential employers. Thus, this information might affect candidates' job search activities and/or create negative word of mouth between potential job seekers, even without immediate experience of the organization's recruitment and selection process. Taking this even further, it is also possible that such negative word of mouth might ultimately influence the valuation of a company, thus affecting its bottom line.

Future research on this area could explore the interplay between candidates' preconceptions of an employer, as influenced by other applicants' reactions/perceptions and the impact those have on current applicants' attitudinal, emotional, and behavioral intentions. For instance, are candidates discouraged from applying for positions in companies that they have read or heard do not treat applicants/employees well? Or where the working conditions or salaries are poorly evaluated by current or past employees? How is this information assessed and evaluated by candidates when they make a decision to apply or when they are invited to participate in an interview?

SNWs and applicant reactions

The extensive usage of SNWs in employee screening and selection in recent years will also create an obvious effect on applicant reactions research and practice in the foreseeable future. As mentioned by Roth, Bobko, Van Iddekinge, and Thatcher (in press) in a recent review article and also by Kluemper and his colleagues in their respective chapter of this book (Chapter 4), the use of SNWs demonstrate a relatively rare moment in staffing research, where a new assessment method arrives raising the need for new research on this topic.

Only a handful of studies have explored the role of SNWs in applicant reactions. In the most recent published research, Stoughton, Thompson, and Meade (2013) conducted two studies exploring this topic. In their first study, they explored whether perceptions of privacy influence procedural justice and selection system perceptions. In addition, they tested whether employers' use of SNWs for screening purposes affects applicants' perceptions of organizational attractiveness in a realistic hiring scenario. Finally, they explored the moderating influence of agreeableness on applicant reactions to SNW screening. Participants in this study were undergraduate psychology students, and the researchers only focused on Facebook and not on other, work-oriented SNWs such as LinkedIn. The results demonstrated that preemployment SNW screening increases applicants' perceptions of invasion of privacy, decreases perceptions of organizational justice, and lowers organizational attraction. Perceptions of privacy partially mediated the relationship between screening and justice perceptions. Also, justice perceptions partially mediated the relationship between perceptions of invasion of privacy and organizational attraction. Finally, agreeableness moderated the effect of SNW screening on procedural justice perceptions, with participants low in agreeableness demonstrating very negative reactions when informed that their SNW profiles had been screened. In their second study, Stoughton et al. (2013) used a non-student (but also non-applicant) sample to further explore their previous hypotheses on a simulated selection scenario. They explored the impact privacy invasion might have on litigation intentions and also the role of the hiring decision on the relationship between SNW screening and procedural justice. Their results showed that applicants' negative perceptions of organizational justice lowered organizational attraction and increased litigation intentions. Also, the hiring decision of the organization had no effect on applicant perceptions of procedural justice. This was an interesting finding, demonstrating that SNW screening practices affect privacy outcomes (e.g., organizational attractiveness, intentions to litigate, etc.) irrespective of the hiring decision.

As evidenced by the Stoughton et al. (2013) study, the use of undergraduate students, instead of actual job applicants, is a common theme in applicant reactions research. These scholars propose, and we agree with them, that in the future, researchers should seek to explore the moderating effect of the type of SNW – for example, Facebook as opposed to LinkedIn. These two SNWs have different identities and characteristics, with the former used mainly for personal purposes and the latter used almost exclusively as a professional SNW. Therefore, we would expect them to be perceived differently by job applicants, who will also react differently when future employers use those as a screening tool, even without their explicit permission. Stoughton et al. (2013) further propose that future research should explore other moderators, such as making screening practices known to job candidates in advance of the screening process. Also, future research could examine the content of applicants' SNWs. Thus, researchers can determine whether the effects of screening practices depend on factors such as the degree to which the applicant's sites contain information generally regarded as inappropriate or unprofessional and whether the applicant has attempted to make his or her social media profile inaccessible to the general public. In a similar vein, future research needs to explore the impact of applicants' impression management on creating and maintaining SNWs. Since more companies use SNWs for screening purposes, active job seekers are now more aware of these tactics; therefore, it is quite likely that they will actively seek to improve or even amend their SNW profiles accordingly in order to increase the chance of attracting recruiters' interest.

Stoughton et al. (2013) have also demonstrated that SNW screening without the applicant's consent influences a number of outcomes, such as procedural justice, organizational attractiveness, and litigation intentions. They propose that an array of additional outcomes should also be explored, such as devaluation of the self and successful candidates' decreased organizational citizenship behaviors (OCBs) or even a decrease in current employees' OCBs if SNW screening takes place in a selection/promotion context. Researchers could also explore the impact that privacy violations have on successful candidates' psychological contract type, employee engagement, and/or counterproductive work behaviors, along with more "traditional" outcomes, such as job performance, job satisfaction, and organizational commitment.

Two more studies (Black, Johnson, Takach, & Stone, 2012; Sanchez, Roberts, Freeman, & Clayton, 2012) have explored the interaction between SNWs and applicant reactions. Black et al. (2012) presented a conceptual model, extending earlier research on privacy models, and consider a number of factors that may affect applicant reactions to the use of SNWs. They propose a number of questions for researchers to explore in the future. In their model, they suggested that informational, procedural, social, cultural, and individual factors may influence applicants' beliefs and attitudes and subsequently lead to behavioral intentions, such as job acceptance and litigation. Sanchez et al. (2102), in an empirical/experimental study among undergraduate students, explored the impact of checking applicants' SNW profiles in a simulated selection process. Controlling for age, gender, and time spent on SNWs, there were no differences between the experimental and control groups. The members of the former group reported lower organizational attractiveness and job pursuit intentions following the SNWs' manipulation. Moreover, experimental group participants reported lower job pursuit intentions and fairness perceptions following the SNWs' check manipulation than after the other selection methods (personality test, skills inventory).

Kluemper and his colleagues (2014; Chapter 4) claim that SNW screening does not have an impact on organizational attractiveness or application intentions but does negatively impact applicant attitudes towards the selection procedure (Siebert, Downes, & Christopher, 2012). However, these findings remain inconclusive, with authors calling for further research on this topic. As mentioned before, Stoughton et al. (2013) found that applicants felt their privacy was invaded by SNW screening, resulting in lower organizational attraction. In contrast, Sanchez et al. (2012) found no negative effects of SNW screening on perceptions of SNW checks, organizational attractiveness, job pursuit intentions, procedural justice, and informational justice. In fact, participants' perceptions of SNW checks were positively related to applicant reactions. Moreover, Van Iddekinge, Lanivich, Roth, and Junco (in press) have recently shown that screening of job applicants' Facebook profiles has very limited, if any at all, predictive validity and on the contrary is highly likely to lead to adverse impact in favor of females and White applicants.

Another area of research is the existence of cross-cultural differences in the use of SNWs among employers and job seekers. Employers use SNWs as a recruiting tool and also for screening job applicants' information, and job seekers use SNWs as another way of looking for a job and contacting potential employers. Nikolaou (2014) conducted two studies in Greece, exploring the use of SNWs among employees-job seekers and recruiters-human resource (HR) professionals in one of the very few studies conducted in a non-English country. His results demonstrated that job boards (e.g., careerbuilder.com or monster.com) are perceived as more effective job searching tools among active job seekers. However, it was interesting to note that the association between SNW usage and effectiveness is stronger for "passive" candidates, demonstrating the important role of SNWs for "poaching" – that is, the process of attracting "passive" candidates – a major advantage of the use of SNWs for HR professionals. Roulin (2014) also proposed that the use of SNWs as a screening tool by employers may vary from one country to another, potentially leading to different applicant reactions. Future studies should explore the evolution of employers' strategies and applicant reactions to the use of SNWs across different countries. More studies should also explore the intersection of SNWs with other established job search methods, such as job boards and the traditional personal networking, and how the use of SNWs in employee screening interacts with the existing and well-established recruitment and selection methods.

Methodological advances in future applicant reactions research

Most of the current research in applicant reactions has used non-applicants samples, with relatively simple research designs. There are a few withstanding exceptions published recently (e.g., McCarthy et al., 2013; Schinkel et al., 2013), but future studies should conduct more elaborative (e.g., multiple measures with multiple sources of data) and, ideally, longitudinal studies in order to explore the effects of applicant reactions on later recruitment and selection outcomes. Thus, the actual usefulness of applicant reactions among job seekers and recruiters will be demonstrated more accurately, avoiding common errors such as common-method variance effects or noncausal research designs. The use of active job seekers and longitudinal designs will also allow researchers to explore causal relationships. More longitudinal designs are also needed in order to explore the interplay between applicant reactions research and perceptions/usage of SNWs in job search and employee screening.

Another potentially fruitful avenue of future research, from a methodological point of view, is the use of multilevel research designs. We are not aware of any studies using this design in applicant reactions research. A few studies have adopted this methodology recently in the job search literature (e.g., Georgiou, Nikolaou,

Tomprou, & Rafailidou, 2012; Wanberg, Zhu, Kanfer, & Zhang, 2012; Zhaoli, Uy, Shuhua, & Kan, 2009), but we couldn't find any studies applying a multilevel perspective in applicant reactions research. For example, active job seekers could be asked to complete daily or weekly diaries assessing their reactions to different employers, recruiters, organizations, and/or different selection methods (e.g., psychometric test, interviews).

Hausknecht (2013) summarizes the potential methodological issues in future applicant reactions research as follows: (1) differentiating constructs from methods of assessment, that is, distinguishing the construct assessed from the method used to assess it; (2) collecting reactions data at multiple (more than two) time points; (3) designing studies to capture behavioral outcomes; (4) studying perceptions of candidates who have actually completed the assessment(s) of interest; (5) measuring attributes of various administration media. Applicant reaction researchers should pay increased attention in the future in the adoption of elaborative, well-designed research designs employing active job seekers during their job search activities, thus avoiding convenient samples (e.g., students).

Practical implications

The impact of fairness reactions on candidates' attitudinal, emotional, and behavioral intentions and their association with organizational attractiveness and, potentially, other important personal and organizational outcomes, demonstrates their importance for organizations and HR departments. HR professionals need to take the impact of applicant and fairness reactions in the selection process more seriously into consideration. This is especially the case today with the widespread use of SNWs in job search, screening, and selection.

A first, significant, practical implication is directly associated with the increased use of SNWs by applicants during the job search process. The selection process is no longer an isolated and "behind closed doors" process, as mentioned earlier. Applicants today are very often looking for more than just the mailing address of potential employers. They have, for example, the means to search for inside information about a company, to connect with recruiters and interviewers, to read about employees' and candidates' experiences and share their own. The impact these actions can have on a company's recruitment and organizational image can often be dramatic. This probably means that HR specialists will need to acquire a new skill set in order to use SNWs effectively.

Moreover, companies also need to adapt their recruitment and attraction policies in order to attract high-caliber candidates, who might only use SNWs in order to look for job opportunities. These candidates are very often the ones who can have a major impact on small communities (e.g., colleges and student clubs) and are often keen to share their experiences with others through SNWs. This is especially the case in specific sectors of the economy, such as the technology sector or in start-up companies, where people are accustomed to the extensive use of social media. Therefore, HR professionals should pay increased attention to how they deal with applicants in these sectors and the impact of their actions with job seekers.

Another important practical implication is associated with the actions companies themselves should take in order to manage applicant reactions. Following Van Hoye's (2014) perspective, organizations could take the role of observer, moderator, mediator, or participant in managing applicant reactions. As an observer, they should be aware of what is being said about them, by whom, to whom, and through which media, both for themselves and for competitors. As a moderator, companies could, for example, actively disseminate information extracted from employee or applicant surveys on the effective use of recruitment/selection tools. As a mediator, they should more actively manage and/or even take control of applicant reactions, if possible. For example, most companies are now actively managing their Twitter and Facebook accounts, dealing with both customers' and applicants' issues and/or complaints – a very effective tool, since applicant reactions are mostly subjective in nature. Finally, as a participant, Van Hoye (2014) proposes that recruiters could "create" their own word of mouth by participating actively in social interactions with applicants and potential applicants. Similarly, with regard to applicant reactions, recruiters should explain the rationale behind the selection methods employed and the selection decision made by providing feedback and explanations for the selection process, especially to rejected applicants.

Conclusions

The area of recruitment and selection has now reached an increased level of maturity (Ryan & Ployhart, 2014). Similarly, applicant reactions research has now progressed well throughout the years, but there are still many things to be done in the future. The focus of our chapter has been to review the most recent research appearing since the most recent reviews of this topic (Gilliland & Steiner, 2012; Hausknecht, 2013), but mainly we sought to emphasize a number of issues we consider important in future applicant reactions research, such as the role of SNWs and their interplay and impact on applicant reactions, both from a research and a practical perspective.

References

Anderson, N., Ahmed, S., & Costa, A.C. (2012). Applicant reactions in Saudi Arabia: Organizational attractiveness and core-self evaluation. *International Journal of Selection and Assessment, 20*, 197–208.

Anderson, N., Salgado, J.F., & Hülsheger, U.R. (2010). Applicant reactions in selection: Comprehensive meta-analysis into reaction generalization versus situational specificity. *International Journal of Selection and Assessment, 18*, 291–304.

Arvey, R.D., Strickland, W., Drauden, G., & Martin, C. (1990). Motivational components of test taking. *Personnel Psychology, 43*, 695–716.

Bartram, D. (2000). Internet recruitment and selection: Kissing frogs to find princes. *International Journal of Selection and Assessment, 8*, 261–274.

Bauer, T.N., Truxillo, D.M., Sanchez, R.J., Craig, J.M., Ferrara, P., & Campion, M.A. (2001). Applicant reactions to selection: Development of the selection procedural justice scale (SPJS). *Personnel Psychology, 54*, 387–419.

Bauer, T.N., Truxillo, D.M., Tucker, J.S., Weathers, V., Bertolino, M., Erdogan, B., & Campion, M.A. (2006). Selection in the information age: The impact of privacy concerns and computer experience on applicant reactions. *Journal of Management, 32,* 601–621.

Bilgic, R., & Acarlar, G. (2010). Fairness perceptions of selection instruments used in Turkey. *International Journal of Selection and Assessment, 18,* 208–214.

Black, S.L., Johnson, A.F., Takach, S.E., & Stone, D.L. (2012, August). *Factors affecting applicants' reactions to the collection of data in social network websites.* Presented at the Academy of Management Annual Conference, Philadelphia, PA.

Georgiou, K., Nikolaou, I., Tomprou, M., & Rafailidou, M. (2012). The role of job seekers' individual characteristics on job seeking behavior and psychological well-being. *International Journal of Selection and Assessment, 20,* 414–422.

Gilliland, S.W. (1993). The perceived fairness of selection systems: An organizational justice perspective. *Academy of Management Review, 18,* 694.

Gilliland, S.W. (1994). Effects of procedural and distributive justice on reactions to a selection system. *Journal of Applied Psychology, 79,* 691–701.

Gilliland, S.W., & Steiner, D.D. (2012). Applicant reactions to testing and selection. In N. Schmitt (Ed.), *The Oxford handbook of personnel assessment and selection* (pp. 629–666). Oxford, UK: Oxford University Press.

Glassdoor.com (2013). Glassdoor – an inside look at jobs and companies. Retrieved December 15, 2013, from http://www.glassdoor.com/index.htm

Harris, M., & Fink, L. (1987). A field study of applicant reactions to employment opportunities: Does the recruiter make a difference? *Personnel Psychology, 40,* 765–784.

Hausknecht, J.P. (2013). Applicant reactions. In K.Y.T. Yu & D.M. Cable (Eds.), *The Oxford handbook of recruitment* (pp. 35–46). Oxford, UK: Oxford University Press.

Hausknecht, J.P., Day, D.V., & Thomas, S.C. (2004). Applicant reactions to selection procedures: An updated model and meta-analysis. *Personnel Psychology, 57,* 639–683.

Herriot, P. (1989). Selection as a social process. In M. Smith & I. Robertson (Eds.), *Advances in selection and assessment* (pp. 171–187). Chichester, UK: Wiley.

Herriot, P. (2004). Social identities and applicant reactions. *International Journal of Selection and Assessment, 12,* 75–83.

Hoang, T.G., Truxillo, D.M., Erdogan, B., & Bauer, T.N. (2012). Cross-cultural examination of applicant reactions to selection methods: United States and Vietnam. *International Journal of Selection and Assessment, 20,* 209–219.

Honkaniemi, L., Feldt, T., Metsapelto, R.L., & Tolvanen, A. (2013). Personality types and applicant reactions in real-life selection. *International Journal of Selection and Assessment, 21,* 32–45.

Ispas, D., Ilie, A., Iliescu, D., Johnson, R.E., & Harris, M.M. (2010). Fairness reactions to selection methods: A Romanian study. *International Journal of Selection and Assessment, 18,* 102–110.

Klotz, A.C., da Motta Veiga, S.P., Buckley, M.R., & Gavin, M.B. (2013). The role of trustworthiness in recruitment and selection: A review and guide for future research. *Journal of Organizational Behavior, 34,* 104–119.

Kluemper, D.H., Davison, H.K., Cao, X, & Wu, B. (in press). Social networking websites and personnel selection: A call for academic research. In I. Nikolaou & J.K. Oostrom (Eds.), *Employee recruitment, selection, and assessment: Contemporary issues for theory and practice.* Hove, East Sussex: Routledge.

McCarthy, J.M., Van Iddekinge, C.H., Lievens, F., Kung, M.C., Sinar, E.F., & Campion, M.A. (2013). Do candidate reactions relate to job performance or affect criterion-related validity? A multistudy investigation of relations among reactions, selection test scores, and job performance. *Journal of Applied Psychology, 98,* 701–719.

Moscoso, S., & Salgado, J.F. (2004). Fairness reactions to personnel selection techniques in Spain and Portugal. *International Journal of Selection and Assessment, 12*, 187–196.

Nikolaou, I. (2014). Social networking web sites in job search and employee recruitment. *International Journal of Selection and Assessment, 22*(2), 179–189.

Nikolaou, I., & Judge, T.A. (2007). Fairness reactions to personnel selection techniques in Greece: The role of core self-evaluations. *International Journal of Selection and Assessment, 15*, 206–219.

Roth, P.L., Bobko, P., Van Iddekinge, C.H., & Thatcher, J.B. (in press). Social media in employee-selection-related decisions: A research agenda for uncharted territory. *Journal of Management*.

Roulin, N. (2014). The influence of employers' use of social networking websites in selection, online self-promotion, and personality on the likelihood of faux pas postings. *International Journal of Selection and Assessment, 22*, 80–87.

Ryan, A.M., & Ployhart, R.E. (2014). A century of selection. *Annual Review of Psychology, 65*, 693–717.

Sanchez, R.J., Roberts, K., Freeman, M., & Clayton, A.C. (2012, August). *Do they care? Applicant reactions to on-line social networking presence checks*. Paper presented at the Academy of Management Annual Conference, Boston, MA.

Schinkel, S., Van Vianen, A., & Van Dierendonck, D. (2013). Selection fairness and outcomes: A field study of interactive effects on applicant reactions. *International Journal of Selection and Assessment, 21*, 22–31.

Schuler, H. (1993). Social validity of selection situations: A concept and some empirical results. In H. Schuler, J.L. Farr, & M. Smith (Eds.), *Personnel selection and assessment: Individual and organizational perspectives* (pp. 11–26). Hillsdale, NJ: Lawrence Erlbaum.

Siebert, S., Downes, P.E., & Christopher, J. (2012, August). *Applicant reactions to online background checks: Welcome to a brave new world*. Paper presented at the Academy of Management Annual Conference, Boston, MA.

Steiner, D.D., & Gilliland, S.W. (1996). Fairness reactions to personnel selection techniques in France and the United States. *Journal of Applied Psychology, 81*, 134–141.

Stoughton, J.W., Thompson, L., & Meade, A. (2015). Examining Applicant Reactions to the Use of Social Networking Websites in Pre-Employment Screening. *Journal of Business and Psychology, 30*(1), 73–88.

Truxillo, D.M., & Bauer, T.N. (2011). Applicant reactions to organizations and selection systems. In S. Zedeck (Ed.), *APA handbook of industrial and organizational psychology* (pp. 379–398). Washington, DC: American Psychological Association.

Truxillo, D.M., Bauer, T.N., Campion, M.A., & Paronto, M.E. (2006). A field study of the role of Big Five personality in applicant perceptions of selection fairness, self, and the hiring organization. *International Journal of Selection and Assessment, 14*, 269–277.

Truxillo, D.M., Bauer, T.N., & McCarthy, J. (in press). Perceived fairness of hiring practices. In R. Cropanzano & M. Ambrose (Eds.), *The Oxford handbook of justice in work organizations*. Oxford, UK: Oxford University Press.

Truxillo, D.M., Bodner, T.E., Bertolino, M., Bauer, T.N., & Yonce, C.A. (2009). Effects of explanations on applicant reactions: A meta-analytic review. *International Journal of Selection and Assessment, 17*, 346–361.

Van Hoye, G. (2014). Word-of-mouth as a recruitment source: An integrative model. In K.Y.T. Yu & D.M. Cable (Eds.), *The Oxford handbook of recruitment* (pp. 251–268). New York: Oxford University Press.

Van Iddekinge, C.H., Lanivich, S.E., Roth, P.L., & Junco, E. (in press). Social media for selection? Validity and adverse impact potential of a Facebook-based assessment. *Journal of Management*.

Walker, H.J., Bauer, T., Cole, M., Bernerth, J., Feild, H., & Short, J. (2013). Is this how I will be treated? Reducing uncertainty through recruitment interactions. *Academy of Management Journal, 56*, 1325–1347.

Wanberg, C.R., Zhu, J., Kanfer, R., & Zhang, Z. (2012). After the pink slip: Applying dynamic motivation frameworks to the job search experience. *Academy of Management Journal, 55*, 261–284.

Zhaoli, S., Uy, M.A., Shuhua, Z., & Kan, S. (2009). Daily job search and psychological distress: Evidence from China. *Human Relations, 62*, 1171–1197.

PART C
Advances in predictors' research

6
NEW DEVELOPMENTS IN INTELLIGENCE THEORY AND ASSESSMENT

Implications for personnel selection

Charles Scherbaum

BARUCH COLLEGE, CITY UNIVERSITY OF NEW YORK, USA

Harold Goldstein

BARUCH COLLEGE, CITY UNIVERSITY OF NEW YORK, USA

Rachel Ryan

BARUCH COLLEGE, CITY UNIVERSITY OF NEW YORK, USA

Paul Agnello

BARUCH COLLEGE, CITY UNIVERSITY OF NEW YORK, USA

Ken Yusko

MARYMOUNT UNIVERSITY, USA

Paul Hanges

UNIVERSITY OF MARYLAND, USA

Intelligence is an individual difference that is arguably more important than ever for success in the constantly changing and increasingly complex modern business world. Despite its importance and the dramatic changes that have occurred in the nature of work, the conceptualization and use of intelligence in personnel selection has changed very little over the past seventy years (Scherbaum, Goldstein, Yusko, Ryan, & Hanges, 2012). Although the field of personnel selection has only incrementally evolved in its thinking about intelligence, many other fields (e.g., clinical and cognitive psychology, developmental and educational research, and the neurosciences) have been very active in conducting modern intelligence research

(Goldstein, Scherbaum, & Yusko, 2009). These fields have made considerable progress in understanding the intelligence construct, its role in the modern world, and how it can be measured. However, the field of personnel selection has yet to take advantage of these developments. As some have argued, the tests that we commonly use have not substantially evolved since their inception (Thorndike, 1997). As a result, a great opportunity to better understand, measure, and use intelligence in personnel selection is being missed.

This chapter reviews some of the innovations and developments in the conceptualization and measurement of intelligence that have the potential to impact personnel selection. Specifically, we review the developments in modern conceptualizations of psychometric approaches to intelligence (e.g., CHC model, XBA), cognitive approaches to intelligence (e.g., neuropsychological approaches, PASS model), and modern intelligence test design principles as well as the implications of these developments for personnel selection.

Intelligence and personnel selection

Researchers have studied intelligence and various aspects of it (e.g., cognitive ability, general mental ability, g) and its impact on a wide array of criteria for over a century (Schmidt & Hunter, 1998). In this research, the psychometric approach based on Spearman's (1927) work (i.e., psychometric g) has been the dominant way of operationalizing and understanding intelligence in applied psychology (Neisser et al., 1996; Scherbaum et al., 2012). The dominance of this approach is not surprising given that tests measuring this cognitive ability are related to performance in academic and work contexts (Herrnstein & Murray, 1994; Schmidt & Hunter, 1998). However, these tests are also associated with large test score differences between particular racial/ethnic groups (Hough, Oswald, & Ployhart, 2001; Roth, Bevier, Bobko, Switzer, & Tyler, 2001). These group differences in test scores can create disparities on important outcomes such as school admissions and employment decisions.

Despite the dominance of Spearman's (1927) psychometric approach, researchers are increasingly recognizing the limitations of this approach, including how well it captures the full construct space of intelligence, that the measures based on it may be partly responsible for the observed score differences between groups, and that improved prediction may be possible with modern theoretical conceptualizations and measures (Fagan & Holland, 2007; Goldstein et al., 2009; Nisbett, Aronson, Blair, Dickens, Flynn, Halpern, & Turkheimer, 2012; Scherbaum et al., 2012; van der Maas et al., 2006). In the subsequent sections of this chapter, we describe some of the modern research on intelligence and its measurement that has the potential to address some of these limitations and contribute to our understanding of intelligent behavior in the workplace.

Modern conceptualization of psychometric approaches to intelligence

In the early days of intelligence research, the development of theoretical models of intelligence was a vibrant area of activity. As Wechsler (1975) noted, as far back as 1921 there were as many theories and definitions of intelligence as there were theorists. Over a relatively short period of time, the applied areas of psychology coalesced around the Spearman (1927) model of psychometric *g*. In Spearman's theory, there is only a single latent construct (i.e., *g*) that is needed to account for variation in performance on tests designed to assess cognitive abilities. In the area of personnel selection, the tenets of this model still guide most thinking on the theory and measurement of intelligence (Goldstein et al., 2009).

Contemporary thinking on intelligence in other areas of psychology and research has long postulated that intelligence is a network of different cognitive constructs rather than a single entity (Gottfredson, 2009; Horn & Blankson, 2012; Jensen, 1998; Reeve & Bonaccio, 2011; Schneider & McGrew, 2012). Modern theories have focused on developing hierarchically arranged taxonomies of these abilities. The most supported, accepted, and influential of these models is the Cattell–Horn–Carroll (CHC) model of intelligence (McGrew, 1997; Schneider & McGrew, 2012). The CHC model represents the integration of Carroll's (1993) three-stratum theory of intelligence with Horn and Cattell's (1966) theory of fluid and crystalized intelligence.

This theory describes the key dimensions of intelligence at three hierarchical levels of specificity. At the highest and broadest level of this theory is a single general ability (stratum III). The next level (stratum II) includes a number of broad cognitive abilities including fluid reasoning, short-term memory, long-term memory, processing speed, reaction and decision speed, psychomotor speed, comprehension/knowledge (i.e., crystalized intelligence), domain-specific knowledge, reading and writing, quantitative knowledge, visual processing, auditory processing, and three other abilities related to sensory functioning (see Schneider & McGrew, 2012, or Schneider & Newman, in press, for detailed reviews). As Schneider and McGrew (2012) note, the factors at the second level can be organized into abilities related to acquired knowledge, abilities that are independent of a specific domain, and those related to sensory-motor domains. At the lowest and most specific level (stratum I) are sixty-four narrow cognitive abilities (e.g., induction, sequential reasoning, perceptual speed).

The CHC model has served as the theoretical foundation for the revision of many existing tests of intelligence (e.g., Stanford-Binet 5th edition, Woodcock-Johnson III) and the development of some new tests (Keith & Reynolds, 2010). Also, a substantial amount of research has focused on operationalizing this theory into measurement practices. For example, the cross-battery assessment approach (XBA) of Flanagan and colleagues (Flanagan & McGrew, 1997; Flanagan, Ortiz, & Alfonso, 2007) can be used to create theory-driven and comprehensive assessments of cognitive abilities. At the core of this approach is the alignment between the broad abilities (stratum II or III) that one wishes to measure and the abilities that are actually measured by the tests that one wishes to use. This alignment process can identify where there are deficiencies in measuring the desired broad abilities. Additional tests can then be incorporated to ensure that the abilities of interest are adequately measured.

Although the XBA approach has primarily focused on tests more commonly used in non-employment settings (e.g., Wechsler tests), the principles on which the

XBA and the CHC theory are based have a number of implications for current practice of using psychometric tests. First, the XBA approach requires that one starts with a theory of intelligence and then aligns the tests to the desired broader abilities from that theory. As has been argued elsewhere (Kaufman, 2000; Scherbaum et al., 2012; Thorndike, 1997), many cognitive ability tests used in personnel assessment are not linked to any theory of intelligence. Moreover, they are not well aligned to the broad abilities that they seek to measure. Consider the distinction described above of organizing broad abilities into those that represent acquired knowledge and those that represent abilities that are independent of a specific domain. A cursory examination of the types of cognitive ability tests that are commonly used in employment contexts would reveal that many of them most closely align with abilities related to acquired knowledge. For example, the Wonderlic Personnel Test consists primarily of items reflecting acquired knowledge in the verbal and quantitative domains. However, many of these tests and the scores obtained from them are described and interpreted as if they assess abilities that are independent of a specific domain. There is often a misalignment between what is measured and the desired broader abilities. This is not to suggest that measuring abilities related to acquired knowledge is unimportant. Such abilities clearly are important, and we would argue that they are potentially becoming increasingly important as the complexity of the workplace grows. However, if one needs an acquired set of knowledge to perform a job, it should be specified and a test of that knowledge should be used rather than testing for general capabilities in a manner that is contaminated with specific acquired knowledge that might not be relevant to the job.

We do suggest that there is an opportunity to better measure intelligence and possibly improve prediction by basing our tests on theory and aligning the measure with the desired construct by following test development principles such as those in the XBA approach. Although these types of suggestions are not new to personnel selection (e.g., Binning & Barrett, 1989), they have yet to substantially impact the development of cognitive ability tests that are used in work settings.

Second, a key principle of the XBA approach is that a wide range of tests are needed to adequately assess broader cognitive abilities. The notion that a wide range of tests are needed is not unique to XBA and has been acknowledged by many intelligence theorists and researchers (e.g., Jensen, 1998). However, many tests of cognitive ability used in personnel selection capture a very small number of the factors in the CHC model and would fall far short on the 'wide range' criteria. By this standard, one could argue that a number of the cognitive ability tests used in employment contexts are deficient assessments of the targeted broad cognitive abilities that they aim at capturing. There appears to be some recognition and agreement in the field that there is more to intelligence than what is measured by typical standardized ability tests, but there is also the belief that the standardized tests we use measure cognitive ability reasonably well (Murphy, Cronin, & Tam, 2003). Based on modern psychometric intelligence theory and the associated approaches for measuring intelligence, it may be time to revisit these beliefs and take advantage of the modern developments. The XBA approach represents a reasonable starting point in these efforts. By clearly articulating the desired broad cognitive abilities one seeks to measure and then aligning tests to those cognitive abilities, it may well be possible to improve the measurement and prediction of the most important individual difference in personnel selection. This approach, however, would require an increased use of more narrow ability tests than is currently common practice, although there are several prominent examples from employment and occupational contexts, such as Project A and the Armed Services Vocational Aptitude Battery (McHenry, Hough, Toquam, Hanson, & Ashworth, 1990), that demonstrate how this approach can be effectively used.

We believe that the need to use narrow ability tests will be a barrier to the acceptance and application of these theoretical models and measurement practices in personnel selection. There is the obvious issue that this approach will lead to increased test length and testing time, which will run counter to the constant pressure to create and use shorter and less time-intensive tests. Also, many of those who work in personnel selection have had little opportunity for training in intelligence theory and the more narrow abilities (Aiken, West, Sechrest, & Reno, 1990; Schmidt, 2002). In addition, and perhaps most importantly, the field has tended to accept without question the research that suggests narrow cognitive abilities are not useful (e.g., Ree & Carretta, 2002; Ree & Earles, 1991). We speculate that these research findings have discouraged personnel selection researchers and practitioners from measuring narrow abilities. More recently, personnel researchers have begun to reevaluate this conclusion and the research supporting it (e.g., Lang, Kersting, Hülsheger, & Lang, 2010; Reeve, 2004; Reeve, Scherbaum, & Goldstein, in press; Schneider & Newman, in press).

They are also beginning to explore non-Spearman psychometric models of intelligence as well as expanded conceptualizations of the role of narrow cognitive abilities in the manifestation of intelligent behavior at work. For example, Lang and Bliese (2012) discuss the utility of the nested-factor conceptualizations of intelligence. In the nested-factor models, it is not necessary to assume g causes the cognitive abilities at lower levels of the intelligence hierarchy. Instead, they can be viewed as cognitive abilities that are parallel to g, but differ in their scope. Thus, they can be equally if not more useful for predicting important criteria. Lang et al. (2010) found that when modern analytical techniques are used to examine the contribution of narrow abilities, g can account for much less of the explainable variance in job performance than previously believed (only 10% to 28% of the variance in job performance). In fact, in some cases the narrow abilities were more important than g for predicting job performance. In a similar spirit, Reeve et al. (in press) discuss a number of theoretical advancements focused on the utility of constellations of narrow abilities for understanding the manifestation of intelligence at work. For example, Snow's (1992; 1994; Shavelson et al., 2002) comprehensive theory of aptitude, Ackerman's (1996) PPIK theory, and Chamorro-Premuzic and Furnham's (2005) model of intellectual competence provide rigorous and well-developed explanations of the coordination of cognitive abilities, noncognitive individual differences, and motivational and social processes that give rise to intelligent behavior.

Despite the static way in which psychometric theory and measurement has been treated in personnel research and practice, it is actually a dynamic area with many important developments (Deary, 2012; Hunt, 2011). There are well-established modern psychometric theories of intelligence and measurement approaches based on them that can facilitate the development of comprehensive, modern, and theoretically based measures of intelligence. Given the consequences associated with using intelligence tests in personnel decisions, researchers should proceed cautiously in utilizing the modern developments in application when there is yet to be a larger body of research examining their use in employment contexts (Oswald & Hough, 2012). To aid in this effort, we strongly encourage personnel researchers to actively pursue these research questions to advance the state of our professional practice.

Cognitive approaches to intelligence

In addition to improving the conceptualization and measurement of intelligence within the psychometric tradition, researchers are exploring other approaches to intelligence, especially those that leverage the theory and research from cognitive psychology and the neurosciences. Two areas that have the potential to impact the assessment of intelligence in employment contexts are the neuropsychological approaches to intelligence and Naglieri and colleagues' (Naglieri, 2005; Naglieri & Das, 1997; Naglieri, Rojahn, Matto, & Aquilino, 2005) Planning, Attention-Arousal, Simultaneous and Successive (PASS) theory of intelligence. Although these developments may be less readily and immediately applied to personnel selection than the developments related to psychometric theory, their description here is intended to introduce them to those working in personnel selection and hopefully spur personnel selection research examining these developments.

Neuropsychological approaches in intelligence

Neuropsychology can be defined as the study of how the brain relates to behavior. Neuropsychological conceptualizations and measures of intelligence are beginning to garner the attention of applied researchers (e.g., Higgins, Peterson, Pihl, & Lee, 2007; Miller & Maricle, 2012; Sabet, Scherbaum, & Goldstein, 2013). Neuropsychological tests consist of tasks that when performed activate the parts of the frontal lobes in the brain responsible for working memory and executive attention (Conway, Kane, & Engle, 2003; Kane & Engle, 2002). That is, these assessments include tasks where performance differences are associated with differences in functioning and activity in the frontal lobes of the brain.

Neuropsychological intelligence tests can include a variety of verbal and nonverbal tasks. For example, Higgins et al.'s (2007) neuropsychological intelligence test included seven tasks. There are three conditional associative learning tasks (i.e., spatial conditional associative task, nonspatial conditional associative task, and go/no-go task). Conditional associative learning tasks require the participant to learn behavioral rules (e.g., If Prompt A, then Respond with Behavior Y; if Prompt B, then Respond with Behavior Z). The basic rules are the same for spatial and nonspatial conditional associative tasks, but they feature different stimuli (i.e., nonspatial tasks typically have a verbal element and spatial tasks frequently use shapes). The go/no-go task is also a conditional task (e.g., If Prompt A, then Respond with Go; if Prompt B, then Respond with No-Go). There are three working memory tasks (i.e., self-ordered pointing task, randomization task, and recency task). The last task is a verbal fluency task. Verbal fluency tasks typically require the participant to generate words based on a given rule (e.g., words that start with the letter M). Typically, each task is repeated over several trials.

The neuropsychological approach to intelligence relies heavily on a variety of biologically based methods, including studying individuals with ablations and lesions or other forms of damage to the brain and neuroimaging techniques (e.g., fMRI and EEG) to establish construct validity evidence. That is, research supporting neuropsychological assessments focuses on establishing the links between the functioning of specific areas of the brain and performance on neuropsychological tasks (Choi et al., 2008; Conway et al., 2003). Much of the recent research has used neuroimaging techniques (e.g., EEG, PET, and fMRI) to determine what areas of the prefrontal cortex are activated during neuropsychological tasks.

Although the construct validity evidence for these tests relies on biological and neuroimaging methods, neuropsychological tests do not require the use of biological or physiological measurement methods in their administration and use. Neuropsychological tests can be individually or group administered using a computer, similar to most ability tests. This approach to intelligence is not new, with its long history in clinical settings, but its application to other applied areas has been more limited. Given the close connection between scores on these assessments and executive functioning in the brain, neuropsychological measures may provide unique insights into the intelligence construct, the prediction of outcomes, and score differences between racial/ethnic groups. The results from the little research that does exist indicate that neuropsychological intelligence tests can contribute to our understanding of these three concerns (e.g., Allen & Bosco, 2010; Higgins et al., 2007; Sabet et al., 2013).

Some intelligence researchers have already laid the theoretical groundwork for integrating psychometric approaches into broader models of neuropsychological constructs (e.g., Flanagan, Alfonso, Ortiz, & Dynda, 2010; Flanagan & McGrew, 1997; Miller, 2007; 2010; Miller & Maricle, 2012). The initial work comparing psychometric and neuropsychological intelligence tests indicates that they are strongly related but not redundant (e.g., Higgins et al., 2007; Sabet et al., 2013). Research is also beginning to explore the utility of neuropsychological intelligence tests in educational and work contexts in terms of prediction and score differences. For example, Higgins et al. (2007) examined the predictive validities of neuropsychological and psychometric intelligence tests for academic and workplace performance. They found that a neuropsychological intelligence test was able to predict academic performance and job performance (in the form of supervisory ratings), and in some cases the neuropsychological test was better able to predict academic performance than a psychometric intelligence test.

Specifically, Higgins et al. (2007) found uncorrected correlations of $r = .37$ (study 1) and $r = .33$ (study 2) between the scores on the neuropsychological intelligence test and academic performance; correlations between the scores on the psychometric intelligence test and academic performance were $r = .24$ (study 1) and $r = .37$ (study 2). The scores on the neuropsychological test predicted academic performance even after controlling for the scores on the psychometric intelligence test. In the work domain, they found uncorrected correlations between the scores on the neuropsychological intelligence test and supervisor ratings of job performance ranging from $r = .42$ (sample with less than one year of work experience) to $r = .57$ (sample with three or more years' work experience) on a set of jobs with medium to high job complexity. However, they found a correlation of only $r = .12$ on a low complexity job. Using a different version of the measure used by Higgins et al. (2007), Sabet et al. (2013) found that a neuropsychological intelligence test was a stronger predictor of academic performance compared to a psychometric intelligence test. Sabet et al. reported an uncorrected correlation with academic performance of $r = .14$ for the neuropsychological intelligence test and $r = .11$ for a psychometric test.

Similarly, Allen and Bosco (2010) reported that measures of executive attention, an underlying mechanism of neuropsychological intelligence related to the allocation of resources, were a slightly better predictor of performance on managerial simulations compared to a psychometric intelligence test. Specifically, in their first study, using an undergraduate student sample, they reported correlations of $r = .57$ for the Wonderlic Personnel Test and $r = .51$ for executive attention measure with performance on a managerial simulation. In their second study, using a graduate student sample, they reported correlations of $r = .27$ for the Wonderlic Personnel Test and $r = .19$ for executive attention measure with performance on a managerial in-basket exercise. In their third study, they reported a correlation of $r = .26$ for executive attention and $r = .20$ for the Wonderlic with performance on the simulation.

Although the research is limited, the initial results suggest that group differences on neuropsychological intelligence tests are smaller compared to what has been reported in the literature for psychometric tests (e.g., Allen & Bosco, 2010; Sabet et al., 2013). Together, these studies indicate that these tests may have the potential to increase our understanding and prediction of the outcomes that are typically of interest to personnel researchers as well as to minimize group differences. Additional research is clearly needed to further explore and replicate these findings. Although we have focused on the potential advantages of neuropsychological intelligence tests, there are potential disadvantages that need to be considered and given research attention. Given that these tests depart from the look of psychometric intelligence tests and may appear more abstract, we would also encourage research that examines applicant reactions to these assessments. In some ways these types of tests may evoke more positive reactions, but they certainly could also evoke negative reactions. Also, most researchers and practitioners in personnel selection are not trained in these methods. Therefore, a substantial amount of education and training may be needed to ensure that these tests are used and interpreted appropriately.

Planning, attention-arousal, simultaneous and successive (pass) theory of intelligence

The Planning, Attention-Arousal, Simultaneous and Successive (PASS) theory of intelligence (Naglieri, 2005; Naglieri & Das, 1997; Naglieri et al., 2005) is rooted in research and theory from both cognitive psychology (Das, 2002) and neuropsychology (e.g., Luria, 1980; 1982). The focus of this theory is information processing and the cognitive processes involved. The cognitive processes emphasized by the model focus on performance and delineate four main factors as the cognitive building blocks of human intellectual functioning (Naglieri, 2005). The first is planning. Planning includes problem-solving, goal striving, strategy formation, utilization of knowledge, and control of the other three processes. The second is attention. Attention includes focus, selective attention, and continuation of attention to specific stimuli in the environment. The third is simultaneous processing. Simultaneous processing includes organizing stimuli into coherent patterns and perceiving the relationships between stimuli. The fourth is successive processing. Successive processing includes integrating information into a sequential order as well as the use of sequential information. The major difference between the PASS theory and psychometric theories is that PASS conceptualizes ability within a cognitive processing framework that is built from different functions in the brain.

From this theory, the Cognitive Assessment System (CAS; Naglieri & Otero, 2012) has been developed. The CAS is an individually administered test designed for children and adolescents; it consists of twelve subtests organized into the four scales that represent the planning, attention, simultaneous, and successive dimensions of the model. A number of the subtests focus on having test takers make decisions when facing novel tasks, and other subtests aim at measuring very specific cognitive functions, such as closely examining the features of stimuli and making decisions based on what is observed, performing tasks involving speech, and using memory when examining various geometric objects. A key distinction of the CAS compared to psychometric tests is that it does not contain the typical verbal tasks and test items. It instead uses a number of novel tasks to focus on specific cognitive functions, such as decision making, attention, memory, and processing of information.

Although research on the CAS is still in the early stages, results thus far have shown predictive validity for achievement in school settings that is similar to existing tests of intelligence (Naglieri, 2005; Naglieri, Das, & Goldstein, 2012). In addition, the CAS shows much lower race-based score differences than what is typically found with other tests of intelligence (Naglieri et al., 2005). For instance, Naglieri (2005) reported a Black-White score difference of only 0.26 *SD*. While it may not currently be appropriate for personnel selection, its structure and design could possibly be leveraged to create tests that are appropriate for a work setting. In particular, tests could be designed that more specifically target the dimensions of intelligence pinpointed by cognitive theory (as is also the case for the XBA approach). Similar to the CAS, such tests may show strong validity and reduced score differences. We encourage researchers to explore the potential applications of this theory to determine its utility in personnel selection contexts.

Modern intelligence test design principles

In addition to theoretical developments, fields outside of personnel selection have devoted substantial attention to aspects of the measurement of intelligence. In particular, they have explored how the design of intelligence test items may lead to construct deficiency and construct contamination, with a particular emphasis on how the design of intelligence test items may contribute to the score differences between groups. Based on this work, many intelligence researchers have recommended that modern intelligence tests be designed using some different principles. Although there are many specific modern test design principles (see Flanagan & Harrison, 2012, for a detailed review), we focus on three principles that we believe have the potential to benefit research and professional practice in personnel selection. Specifically, we consider the practices of developing theory-based tests, reduced use of non-domain-relevant and cultural content, and the inclusion of non-entrenched tasks.

Create theory-driven cognitive ability tests

Historically, most tests designed to measure intelligence lack a solid theoretical foundation for their development (Kaufman, 2000). Tests were designed by combining various subtests to generate a composite without much thought given to creating a battery of subtests that comprehensively reflected the diverse nature of the intelligence domain. As previously noted, researchers have begun to build intelligence tests that reflect modern theories of intelligence from the psychometric perspective and other perspectives (e.g., Flanagan et al. 2007; Kaufman & Kaufman, 1983; Naglieri & Das, 1997; Thorndike, Hagen, & Sattler, 1986; Woodcock & Johnson, 1989). This theory-driven approach has led to the revision of existing tests (e.g., WAIS, version 3) as well as the development of new tests (e.g., Cognitive Assessment System) and test development approaches (e.g., XBA).

Research has also focused on understanding the cognitive processes involved in solving test problems (e.g., Embretson, 1983). This research attempts to identify the knowledge structures, cognitive processes, and cognitive strategies that are required to solve test items as well as understand how these processes lead to items being more or less difficult for test takers. On a related note, theoretical work has also been devoted to understanding how stimulus features of items contribute to item difficulty and impact item performance (e.g., Irvine, 2002; Lievens & Sackett, 2007).

Collectively, this research aims to build better intelligence tests that are firmly rooted in theories of intelligence and the cognitive processes involved in successfully completing intelligence test items. There is a lot that can be learned from this research. Unfortunately, these new developments have yet to substantially impact the research or practice related to intelligence testing in personnel selection. We argue that it is time to begin drawing on these developments to understand how we can improve our tests and build a stronger theoretical basis for them. Given that other areas have updated their high-stakes tests to incorporate these principles (e.g., Stanford-Binet 5, Woodcock-Johnson III, WISC-IV, WAIS-IV, DAS-II), it is clearly possible to build theoretically based intelligence tests that will be useful for making consequential decisions.

Reduced reliance on non-domain-relevant and cultural content

Researchers have recommended that intelligence tests be designed to reduce non-domain-relevant and cultural content in the test items (e.g., Fagan, 2000; Fagan & Holland, 2002, 2007; 2009; Helms-Lorenz, van de Vijver, & Poortinga, 2003; Malda, van de Vijver, & Temane, 2010; van de Vijver, 1997). These researchers have argued that items requiring knowledge of non-domain-relevant and cultural content serve to create a source of contamination in intelligence tests. Moreover, it is argued that knowledge of and familiarity with this content may vary by background, country of origin, race, gender, culture, economic standing, or experience. Therefore, it may contribute to the observed score differences on cognitive ability tests (Fagan, 2000; Fagan & Holland, 2002; Goldstein et al., 2009).

One line of this research has focused on the impact of cultural-specific content on cognitive ability test performance (e.g., Freedle, 2003; Freedle & Kostin, 1997; Helms-Lorenz et al., 2003; Malda et al., 2010; van de Vijver, 1997; van de Vijver, 2008). This line of research has found that test performance suffers when the cultural content embedded in a test is different than the cultural content the test taker is familiar with. For example, Malda et al. (2010) experimentally manipulated the cultural content embedded in measures of short-term memory, attention, working memory, and figural and verbal fluid reasoning to be consistent with White South African culture or Black South African culture. In this study, they created test items that were equivalent, but they manipulated the cultural content so that it was more familiar for one culture than the other. They found test performance was better on the test versions that were consistent with the test taker's culture. The cultural content of the test moderated the relationship between race and test performance.

Also, Freedle and colleagues (Freedle, 2003; Freedle & Kostin, 1997) have found that cultural differences in the use and interpretation of common words can lead to differential item functioning that serves to disadvantage the cultural minority test taker. Common to both of these programs of research is that the linguistic demands of tests may be confounded with the cultural content embedded in tests (Ortiz & Ochoa, 2005). As described by Helms-Lorenz et al. (2003), "differential mastery of the testing language by cultural groups creates a spurious correlation between *g* and intergroup performance differences, if complex tests require more linguistic skills than do simple tests" (p. 13). Hence, many researchers have suggested that tests should reduce their linguistic demands and utilize more nonverbal stimuli (Naglieri, 2005).

Another line of this research has focused on how content requiring previously acquired knowledge impacts performance on tests of information processing. For tests that purport to measure information processing, the use of previously acquired knowledge should not be needed to successfully complete the test items. For example, Fagan and Holland (2002, 2007, 2009) have conducted many studies to examine if race-based score differences on cognitive ability tests could be attributed to differences in the ability to process information or differences in prior exposure to the acquired knowledge that test items use. They found that test performance was equal across groups of White and Black test takers when knowledge required by the test items was unfamiliar and there was an equal opportunity to learn it. However, when the knowledge required by the test items was such that it was believed to be common and previously acquired by all test takers, the typical score differences emerged. Thus, Fagan and Holland argue that test developers need to pay close attention to their assumptions about what is considered to be common previously acquired knowledge and need to reconsider the use of these types of test items to assess the information processing aspects of intelligence.

In general, these lines of research point to the need to understand the degree to which intelligence tests contain culturally specific or non-domain-relevant content, particularly as it relates to linguistic content. The inclusion of this content considerably raises the likelihood of introducing a source of contamination into the measurement process. In the domain of personnel selection, this is particularly important, given that cognitive tests may be used on a global scale and used with culturally diverse populations within a country. In these cases, a lack of familiarity with content that is not related to the construct of interest can create some substantial problems for accurately assessing individuals and interpreting test scores. Although best practice recommendations cover many aspects of test content when applied to the development or adaptation of tests for use globally (e.g., Byrne et al., 2009; Ryan & Tippins, 2009), these same recommendations are much less frequently applied when tests are developed for domestic use with globally diverse populations.

Use of novel or non-entrenched tasks

In addition to the research focusing on the role of non-domain-relevant and cultural content, there has been work exploring the use of test items containing non-entrenched tasks (e.g., Bokhorst, 1989; Sternberg, 1981a; 1981b; 1982b; Sternberg & Gastel, 1989; Tetewsky & Sternberg, 1986). Non-entrenched tasks are those that use novel or abnormal stimuli or concepts to solve problems. The core feature of non-entrenched items is that they do not represent the natural state of problems or stimuli in everyday life (Sternberg, 1982a). For example, Sternberg (1981a) describes a number of non-entrenched tasks including one where individuals need to determine the physical state of an object (e.g., liquid or solid) and the object's fictional name (e.g., plin, kwef) as it moves from north to south or south to north on the fictional planet Kryon from a set of rules presented at the start of the task.

The logic for the use of non-entrenched items is that they remove acquired knowledge from the assessment of non-domain-specific broad and narrow abilities such as fluid reasoning or induction. Similar to the work of Fagan and Holland (2002; 2007; 2009), these types of items put all examinees on equal footing from an acquired knowledge perspective and remove previously acquired knowledge as a potential source of contamination in the assessment of non-domain-specific broad and narrow abilities. Sternberg and colleagues (Sternberg, 1982b; Sternberg & Gastel, 1989) have found that performance on non-entrenched tasks shows strong correlations with tests of fluid reasoning, supporting such tasks' usefulness in assessing non-domain-specific broad and narrow abilities.

The initial work on non-entrenchment was less focused on the issues that are most critical in personnel selection, such as predictive validity or score differences between groups. However, later research drawing on the principles of non-entrenchment has found that tests made of non-entrenched items correlate with existing ability tests, predict academic and job performance criteria, and show lower score differences between racial/ethnic groups (Sternberg, 2006; Yusko, Goldstein, Scherbaum, & Hanges, 2012). For example, Yusko et al. (2012) report a mean uncorrected correlation of $r = .33$ for a cognitive ability test using entrenched items, with supervisory ratings of job performance and score differences that range between $d = 0.18$ and $d = 0.43$ (compared to $d = 1.00$ that is typically reported; Roth et al., 2001).

It is also interesting to consider the promising results of the neuropsychological intelligence tests from the perspective of non-entrenchment, as many of the tasks on these tests could be considered non-entrenched. Additional research is certainly needed on the use of non-entrenched tasks in tests and assessments used for personnel selection, but the initial findings seem promising. Moreover, the use of non-entrenched tasks may be particularly useful when ability tests are used with culturally diverse groups, as these items are likely to decrease the cultural and non-domain-relevant content in test items.

Conclusions

Intelligence has been and will continue to be one of the most important individual difference variables in personnel selection. However, it has been our observation that the field of personnel selection has stood still while the science of intelligence has raced ahead. Given its role as one of the most important individual difference variables in the field, it is time to reengage in modern and cutting-edge research as is common in many other areas of psychology. Our aim for this chapter is to help start this process by highlighting several advancements in psychometric theory, cognitive perspectives on intelligence, and techniques for improving the measurement of intelligence that we believe have potential to impact personnel selection research and practice. Clearly, much more research on many of these developments is needed to support and explore their use in employment contexts. Nevertheless, it is time for the field to collectively launch a new and modern research agenda on the construct of intelligence to answer these questions.

References

Ackerman, P.L. (1996). A theory of adult intellectual development: Process, personality, interests, and knowledge. *Intelligence, 22*(2), 227–257.

Aiken, L.S., West, S.G., Sechrest, L., & Reno, R.R. (1990). Graduate training in statistics, methodology, and measurement in psychology. *American Psychologist, 45*(6), 721–734.

Allen, D., & Bosco, F. (2010). *Executive attention as a predictor of employee performance: Reconsidering the relationship between cognitive ability and adverse impact potential* (Technical report). Alexandria, VA: SHRM Foundation.

Binning, J., & Barrett, G. (1989). Validity of personnel decisions: A conceptual analysis of the inferential and evidential bases. *Journal of Applied Psychology, 74*, 478–494.

Bokhorst, F. (1989). Intelligence and creative thinking ability in learning to perform a non-entrenched colour-naming task. *South African Journal of Psychology, 19*, 28–33.

Byrne, B., Oakland, T., Leong, F., van de Vijver, F., Hambleton, R., Cheung, F.M., & Bartram, D. (2009). A critical analysis of cross-cultural research and testing practices: Implications for improved education and training in psychology. *Training and Education in Professional Psychology, 3*(2), 94–105.

Carroll, J. (1993). *Human cognitive abilities: A survey of factor analytic studies.* New York: Cambridge University Press.

Chamorro-Premuzic, T., & Furnham, A. (2005). Intellectual competence. *The Psychologist, 18*(6), 352–354.

Choi, Y., Shamosh, N., Cho, S., DeYoung, C., Lee, M., Lee, J., Kim, S., Cho, Z., Kim, K., Gray, J., & Lee, K. (2008). Multiple bases of human intelligence revealed by cortical thickness and neural activation. *Journal of Neuroscience, 28*, 10323–10329.

Conway, A., Kane, M., & Engle, R. (2003). Working memory capacity and its relation to general intelligence. *Trends in Cognitive Sciences, 7*, 547–552.

Das, J. (2002). A better look at intelligence. *Current Directions in Psychology, 11*(1), 28–32.

Deary, I. (2012). Intelligence. *Annual Review of Psychology, 63*, 453–482.

Embretson, S. (1983). Construct validity: Construct representation versus nomothetic span. *Psychological Bulletin, 93*, 179–197.

Fagan, J. (2000). A theory of intelligence as processing: Implications for society. *Psychology, Public Policy, and Law, 6*, 168–179.

Fagan, J., & Holland, C. (2002). Equal opportunity and racial differences in IQ. *Intelligence, 30*, 361–387.

Fagan, J., & Holland, C. (2007). Racial equality in intelligence: Predictions from a theory of intelligence as processing. *Intelligence, 35*, 319–334.

Fagan, J., & Holland, C. (2009). Culture-fair prediction of academic achievement. *Intelligence, 37*, 62–67.

Flanagan, D., Alfonso, V., Ortiz, S., & Dynda, A. (2010). Integrating cognitive assessment in school neuropsychological evaluations. In D. Miller (Ed.), *Best practices in school neuropsychology: Guidelines for effective practice, assessment, and evidence-based intervention* (pp. 101–140). Hoboken, NJ: Wiley.

Flanagan, D., & Harrison, P. (Eds.). (2012). *Contemporary intellectual assessment: Theories, tests, and issues* (3rd ed., pp. 73–98). New York: Guilford Press.

Flanagan, D., & McGrew, K. (1997). A cross-battery approach to assessing and interpreting cognitive abilities: Narrowing the gap between practice and cognitive science. In D. Flanagan, J. Genshaft, and P. Harrison (Eds.), *Contemporary intellectual assessment: Theories, tests, and issues.* New York: Guilford.

Flanagan, D., Ortiz, S., & Alfonso, V. (2007). *Essentials of cross-battery assessment* (2nd ed.). New York: Wiley.

Freedle, R. (2003). Correcting the SAT's ethnic and social-class bias: A method for reestimating SAT scores. *Harvard Educational Review, 73*, 1–42.

Freedle, R., & Kostin, I. (1997). Predicting Black and White differential item functioning in verbal analogy performance. *Intelligence, 24*, 417–444.

Goldstein, H., Scherbaum, C., & Yusko, K. (2009). Adverse impact and measuring cognitive ability. In J. Outtz's (Ed.), *Adverse impact: Implications for organizational staffing and high stakes testing* (pp. 95–134). New York: Psychology Press.

Gottfredson, L. (2009). Logical fallacies used to dismiss the evidence on intelligence testing. In R. Phelps (Ed.), *Correcting fallacies about educational and psychological testing* (pp. 11–65). Washington, DC: American Psychological Association.

Helms-Lorenz, M., van de Vijver, F., & Poortinga, Y. (2003). Cross-cultural differences in cognitive performance and Spearman's hypothesis: g or c? *Intelligence, 31*, 9–29.

Herrnstein, R., & Murray, C. (1994). *The bell curve: Intelligence and class structure in American life*. New York: Free Press.

Higgins, D., Peterson, J., Pihl, R., & Lee, A. (2007). Prefrontal cognitive ability, intelligence, Big Five personality, and the prediction of advanced academic and workplace performance. *Journal of Personality and Social Psychology, 93*, 298–319.

Horn, J., & Blankson, N. (2012). Foundations for better understanding of cognitive abilities. In D.P. Flanagan & P.L. Harrison (Eds.), *Contemporary intellectual assessment: Theories, tests, and issues* (3rd ed., pp. 73–98). New York: Guilford Press.

Horn, J., & Cattell, R. (1966). Refinement of the theory of fluid and crystalized general intelligences. *Journal of Educational Psychology, 57*, 253–270.

Hough, L., Oswald, F., & Ployhart, R. (2001). Determinants, detection and amelioration of adverse impact in personnel selection procedures: Issues, evidence and lessons learned. *International Journal of Selection and Assessment, 9*, 152–194.

Hunt, E. (2011). *Human intelligence*. Cambridge, UK: Cambridge University Press.

Irvine, S. (2002). The foundation of item generation for mass testing. In S.H. Irvine & P.C. Kyllonen (Eds.), *Item generation for test development*. Mahwah, NJ: Lawrence Erlbaum Associates, Inc.

Jensen, A. (1998). *The g factor: The science of mental ability*. Westport, CT: Praeger.

Kane, M.J., & Engle, R.W. (2002). The role of prefrontal cortex in working-memory capacity, executive attention, and general fluid intelligence: An individual-differences perspective. *Psychonomic Bulletin and Review, 9*, 637–671.

Kaufman, A. (2000). Tests of intelligence. In R.J. Sternberg (Ed.), *Handbook of intelligence* (pp. 445–476). New York: Cambridge University Press.

Kaufman, A.S., & Kaufman, N.L. (1983). *Kaufman Assessment Battery for Children*. Circle Pines, MN: American Guidance Service.

Keith, T.Z., & Reynolds, M.R. (2010). CHC theory and cognitive abilities: What we've learned from 20 years of research. *Psychology in the Schools, 47*, 635–650.

Lang, J., & Bliese, P. (2012). I–O psychology and progressive research programs on intelligence. *Industrial and Organizational Psychology: Perspectives on Science and Practice, 5*, 161–168.

Lang, J., Kersting, M., Hülsheger, U., & Lang, J. (2010). General mental ability, narrower cognitive abilities, and job performance: The perspective of the nested-factors model of cognitive abilities. *Personnel Psychology, 63*, 595–640.

Lievens, F., & Sackett, P. (2007). Situational judgment in tests in high-stakes settings: Issues and strategies with generating alternate forms. *Journal of Applied Psychology, 92*, 1043–1055.

Luria, A. (1980). *Higher cortical functions in man* (2nd ed.). New York: Basic Books.

Luria, A. (1982). *Language and cognition*. New York: Wiley.

Malda, M., van de Vijver, F., & Temane, M. (2010). Rugby versus soccer in South Africa: Content familiarity explains most cross-cultural differences in cognitive test scores. *Intelligence, 38*, 582–595.

McGrew, K. (1997). Analysis of the major intelligence batteries according to a proposed comprehensive Gf-Gc framework. In D.P. Flanagan, J.L. Genshaft, & P.L. Harrison (Eds.), *Contemporary intellectual assessment: Theories, tests, and issues* (pp. 151–179). New York: Guilford.

McHenry, J., Hough, L., Toquam, J., Hanson, M., and Ashworth, S. (1990). Project A validity results: The relationship between predictor and criterion domains. *Personnel Psychology, 43*, 335–354.

Miller, D. (2007). *Essentials of school neuropsychological assessment.* Hoboken, NJ: Wiley.

Miller, D. (2010). School neuropsychological assessment and intervention. In D.C. Miller (Ed.), *Best practices in school neuropsychology: Guidelines for effective practice, assessment, and evidence-based intervention* (pp. 599–640). Hoboken, NJ: Wiley.

Miller, D., & Maricle, D. (2012). The emergence of neuropsychological constructs into tests of intelligence and cognitive abilities. In D. Flanagan & P. Harrison (Eds.), *Contemporary intellectual assessment: Theories, tests, and issues* (3rd ed., pp. 800–819). New York: Guilford.

Murphy, K., Cronin, B., & Tam, A. (2003). Controversy and consensus regarding the use of cognitive ability testing in organizations. *Journal of Applied Psychology, 88*(4), 660–671.

Naglieri, J. (2005). The cognitive assessment system. In D.P. Flanagan & P.L. Harrison (Eds.), *Contemporary intellectual assessment* (2nd ed., pp. 441–460). New York: Guilford.

Naglieri, J., & Das, J. (1997). Intelligence revised. In R. Dillon (Ed.), *Handbook on testing* (pp. 136–163). Westport, CT: Greenwood Press.

Naglieri, J., Das, J., & Goldstein, S. (2012). Planning, attention, simultaneous, successive: A cognitive-processing-based theory. In D. Flanagan & P. Harrison (Eds.), *Contemporary intellectual assessment: Theories, tests, and issues* (3rd ed., pp. 178–194). New York: Guilford Press.

Naglieri, J.A., & Otero, T. (2012). The cognitive assessment system: From theory to practice. In D.P. Flanagan & P.L. Harrison (Eds.), *Contemporary intellectual assessment: Theories, tests, and issues* (3rd ed., pp. 376–399). New York: Guilford Press.

Naglieri, J., Rojahn, J., Matto, H., & Aquilino, S. (2005). Black-White differences in intelligence: A study of the PASS theory and Cognitive Assessment System. *Journal of Psychoeducational Assessment, 23*, 146–160.

Neisser, U., Boodoo, G., Bouchard, T., Boykin, A., Brody, N., Ceci, S., Halpern, D., Loehlin, J.C., Perloff, R., Sternberg, R., & Urbina, S. (1996). Intelligence: Knowns and unknowns. *American Psychologist, 51*, 77–101.

Nisbett, R., Aronson, J., Blair, C., Dickens, W., Flynn, J., Halpern, D., & Turkheimer, E. (2012). Intelligence: New findings and theoretical developments. *American Psychologist, 67*, 130–159.

Ortiz, S., & Ochoa, S. (2005). Advances in cognitive assessment of culturally and linguistically diverse individuals. In D. Flanagan & P. Harrison (Eds.), *Contemporary intellectual assessment: Theories, tests, and issues* (2nd ed., pp. 234–250). New York: Guilford Press.

Oswald, F., & Hough, L. (2012). I–O 2.0 from intelligence 1.5: Staying (just) behind the cutting edge of intelligence theories. *Industrial and Organizational Psychology: Perspectives on Science and Practice, 5*, 174–177.

Ree, M., & Carretta, T. (2002). g2K. *Human Performance, 15*, 3–23.

Ree, M., & Earles, J. (1991). Predicting training success: Not much more than g. *Personnel Psychology, 44*, 321–332.

Reeve, C. (2004). Differential ability antecedents of general and specific dimensions of declarative knowledge: More than g. *Intelligence, 32*, 621–652.

Reeve, C., & Bonaccio, S. (2011). The nature and structure of "intelligence". In T. Chamorro-Premuzic, A. Furnham, & S. von Stumm (Eds.), *Handbook of individual differences* (pp. 187–216). Oxford, UK: Wiley-Blackwell.

Reeve, C., Scherbaum, C., & Goldstein, H. (in press). Manifestations of intelligence: Expanding the measurement space to reconsider specific cognitive abilities. *Human Resource Management Review.*

Roth, P., Bevier, C., Bobko, P., Switzer, F., & Tyler, P. (2001). Ethnic group differences in cognitive ability in employment and educational settings: A meta-analysis. *Personnel Psychology, 54*, 297–330.

Ryan, A.M., & Tippins, N. (2009). *Designing and implementing global selection systems.* Malden, MA: Wiley-Blackwell.

Sabet, J., Scherbaum, C., & Goldstein, H. (2013). Examining the potential of neuropsychological intelligence tests for predicting academic performance and reducing racial/ethnic test scores differences. In F. Metzger (Ed.), *Neuropsychology: New Research* (pp. 1–24). New York: Nova Publishers.

Scherbaum, C., Goldstein, H., Yusko, K., Ryan, R., & Hanges, P. (2012). Intelligence 2.0: Reestablishing a research program on *g* in I-O psychology. *Industrial and Organizational Psychology: Perspectives on Science and Practice, 5,* 128–148.

Schmidt, F. (2002). The role of general cognitive ability and job performance: Why there cannot be a debate. *Human Performance, 15,* 187–210.

Schmidt, F.L., & Hunter, J.E. (1998). The validity and utility of selection methods in personnel psychology: Practical and theoretical implications of 85 years of research findings. *Psychological Bulletin, 124,* 262–274.

Schneider, W.J., & McGrew, K. (2012). The Cattell-Horn-Carroll model of intelligence. In D. Flanagan & P. Harrison (Eds.), *Contemporary intellectual assessment: Theories, tests, and issues* (3rd ed., pp. 99–144). New York: Guilford Press.

Schneider, W.J., & Newman, D.A. (in press). Intelligence is multidimensional: Theoretical review and implications of specific cognitive abilities. *Human Resource Management Review.*

Shavelson, R.J., Kupermintz, H., Ayala, C., Roeser, R.W., Lau, S., Haydel, A., Schultz, S., Gallagher, L., & Quihuis, G. (2002). Richard E. Snow's remaking of the concept of aptitude and multidimensional test validity: Introduction to the special issue. *Educational Assessment, 8*(2), 77–99.

Snow, R.E. (1992). Aptitude theory: Yesterday, today, and tomorrow. *Educational Psychologist, 27,* 5–32.

Snow, R.E. (1994). Abilities in academic tasks. In R.J. Sternberg & R.K. Wagner (Eds.), *Mind in context: Interactionist perspectives on human intelligence* (pp. 3–37). Cambridge, UK: Cambridge University Press.

Spearman, C. (1927). *The abilities of man, their nature and measurement.* New York: Macmillan.

Sternberg, R. (1981a). Intelligence and non-entrenchment. *Journal of Educational Psychology, 73,* 1–16.

Sternberg, R. (1981b). Testing and cognitive psychology. *American Psychologist, 36,* 1181–1189.

Sternberg, R. (1982a). Natural, unnatural, and supernatural concepts. *Cognitive Psychology, 14,* 451–488.

Sternberg, R. (1982b). Nonentrenchment in the assessment of intellectual giftedness. *Gifted Child Quarterly, 26,* 63–67.

Sternberg, R. (2006). The Rainbow Project: Enhancing the SAT through assessments of analytical, practical, and creative skills. *Intelligence, 34,* 321–350.

Sternberg, R., & Gastel, J. (1989). If dancers ate their shoes: Inductive reasoning with factual and counterfactual premises. *Memory and Cognition, 17,* 1–10.

Tetewsky, S., & Sternberg, R. (1986). Conceptual and lexical determinants of nonentrenched thinking. *Journal of Memory and Language, 25,* 202–225.

Thorndike, R. (1997). *Measurement and evaluation in psychology and education.* Upper Saddle River, NJ: Merrill.

Thorndike, R., Hagen, E., & Sattler, J. (1986). *The Stanford-Binet Intelligence Scale: Fourth Edition. Guide for administering and scoring.* Chicago: Riverside.

van der Maas, H., Dolan, C., Grasman, R., Wicherts, J., Huizenga, H., & Raijmakers, M. (2006). A dynamical model of general intelligence: The positive manifold of intelligence by mutualism. *Psychological Bulletin, 113,* 842–861.

van de Vijver, F. (1997). Meta-analysis of cross-cultural comparisons of cognitive test performance. *Journal of Cross-Cultural Psychology, 28*, 678–709.
van de Vijver, F. (2008). On the meaning of cross-cultural differences in simple cognitive measures. *Educational Research and Evaluation, 14*(3), 215–234.
Wechsler, D. (1975). Intelligence defined and undefined: A relativistic appraisal. *American Psychologist, 30*, 135–139.
Woodcock, R.W., & Johnson, M.B. (1989). *Woodcock-Johnson Psycho-Educational Battery Revised Tests of Achievement: Standard and supplemental batteries*. Itasca, IL: Riverside.
Yusko, K., Goldstein, H., Scherbaum, C., & Hanges, P. (2012, April). *Siena Reasoning Test: Measuring intelligence with reduced adverse impact*. Invited M. Scott Myers Award talk at the 27th annual conference of the Society for Industrial and Organizational Psychology, San Diego.

7

PERSONALITY TESTING IN PERSONNEL SELECTION

Love it? Leave it? Understand it!

Janina Diekmann

UNIVERSITÄT DES SAARLANDES, GERMANY

Cornelius J. König

UNIVERSITÄT DES SAARLANDES, GERMANY

The quality of selection procedures is judged primarily by looking at predictive validity results, as the prediction of performance at work is clearly the most important issue for the practice of personnel selection. Based on these results, researchers have made recommendations to improve methods such as the interview (Kepes, Banks, McDaniel, & Whetzel, 2012; McDaniel, Whetzel, Schmidt, & Maurer, 1994) or have contributed to the abandonment of methods with no predictive quality, such as graphology (Driver, Buckley, & Frink, 1996).

Although most established selection methods such as mental ability tests or assessment centers have been found to be valid, the situation is significantly different with regard to personality testing. Discussions about whether personality tests are valid instruments began 60 years ago, with studies finding moderate but profession-dependent results at best (Ghiselli & Barthol, 1953), and generally troubling results at worst (Guion & Gottier, 1965). This discussion was intensified when, in their Big Five meta-analysis, Barrick and Mount (1991) found conscientiousness to be the only trait that was generally and at least moderately predictive of work performance, whereas the other four Big Five traits showed only small correlations that varied between different occupations. Currently, the debate about whether or not one should use personality tests in personnel selection procedures is dominated by two perspectives, both of which are supported by good arguments.

On the one hand, there are those advocators of personality tests who "love it" (e.g., Bartram, 2004; Ones, Viswesvaran, & Dilchert, 2005): the findings of Barrick and Mount (1991) as well as further meta-analyses (Hurtz & Donovan, 2000;

Salgado, 1997) and a second-order meta-analysis (Barrick, Mount, & Judge, 2001) are used to argue that there are consistent correlations and to support the central role of conscientiousness and (in part) of emotional stability in predicting job performance. Although the other Big Five traits were not related to overall work performance, they were able to predict performance in specific professions or criteria. Numerous studies and meta-analyses explored the personality-performance relationship. For example, a number of researchers examined the longitudinal impact of the Big Five on career success (Judge, Higgins, Thoresen, & Barrick, 1999) using specific criteria such as job satisfaction (Judge, Heller, & Mount, 2002), or specific occupations or roles such as social professions (Blickle & Kramer, 2012) or leadership roles (Judge, Bono, Ilies, & Gerhardt, 2002). In these studies and meta-analyses, researchers frequently found high criterion-related validities (for a detailed overview of research, see Rothstein & Goffin, 2006). Moreover, advocates of personality measures in personnel selection argue that personality traits particularly predict typical performance, whereas general mental ability particularly predicts maximum performance (e.g., Marcus, Goffin, Johnston, & Rothstein, 2007).

Some debate within the "love it" group concerns the preference for broad or narrow personality traits: while some researchers recommend using all relevant personality traits together to maximize validity (Barrick & Mount, 2005) or using so-called compound personality traits (Ones et al., 2005; Ones & Viswesvaran, 1996) to predict overall job performance, others believe that narrow traits (and specific criteria) with well-considered theoretical assumptions of the trait-performance relationship will lead to better predictions (Dudley, Orvis, Lebiecki, & Cortina, 2006; Hogan & Holland, 2003; Tett, Steele, & Beauregard, 2003). Nevertheless, there is a group of advocates of personality testing who feel that "personality matters" (Barrick & Mount, 2005, p. 359).

On the other hand, there are researchers (e.g., Murphy & Dzieweczynski, 2005) who are more drawn to a "leave it" position. They argue that the correlations found in the above-mentioned meta-analyses are quite small and that there is a lack of convincing general theories that relate personality constructs to job performance (Murphy & Dzieweczynski, 2005). Even those who see themselves as more or less impartial (Morgeson et al., 2007) are concerned about the low validity, which is sometimes "pimped" by corrections for predictor unreliability (Campion in Morgeson et al., 2007). They therefore advise against the use of most personality tests in personnel selection contexts or recommend the additional use of tests of general mental ability. In addition to this validity issue, critics often also point to the problem of faking. There is little doubt that applicants can, and actually do, fake answers when completing a personality test (e.g., Birkeland, Manson, Kisamore, Brannick, & Smith, 2006). Although some researchers consider this to be unproblematic (e.g., Hogan, Barrett, & Hogan, 2007), faking does seem to change rank orders and therefore affects actual selection decisions (Stewart, Darnold, Zimmerman, Parks, & Dustin, 2010). Common correction methods such as lie scales do not provide a satisfactory solution to the problem either (e.g., Campion, Dipboye, and Schmitt in Morgeson et al., 2007), although assessors believe that they do (Robie, Tuzinski, & Bly, 2006).

As this "love it or leave it" debate continues, so, too, does the use of personality tests (Bartram, 2004). Research clearly shows that organizations use personality tests: personality testing is quite popular in Belgium, Britain, France, Greece, Ireland, the Netherlands, Portugal, and Spain (Bruchon-Schweitzer & Ferrieux, 1991; Eleftheriou & Robertson, 1999; Hodgkinson, Daley, & Payne, 1995; Hodgkinson & Payne, 1998; Ryan, McFarland, Baron, & Page, 1999; Schuler, Frier, & Kauffmann, 1993; Shackleton & Newell, 1994; Williams, 1992; Zibarras & Woods, 2010). It is also known to be a regularly used instrument in several other countries such as Germany, Italy, Scotland, and the USA (Harris, Dworkin, & Park, 1990; Piotrowski & Armstrong, 2006; Ryan et al., 1999; Rynes, Orlitzky, & Bretz, 1997; Scholarios & Lockyer, 1999; Schuler et al., 1993; Schuler, Hell, Trapmann, Schaar, & Boramir, 2007; Shackleton & Newell, 1994).

Understand it: the practice of personality test use

Against this background, we believe that it is time to set out on a new research path that concentrates on the practice of personality test use in organizational settings. Apart from the highly important questions of validity and faking, research should find out which tests are being used in which ways and for what reasons in order to optimize our recommendations to practitioners.

To our knowledge, only a few authors have been interested in which tests are actually used by organizations or (industrial and organizational) psychologists in general (e.g., Brown, 1999; Evers et al., 2012; Furnham, 2008; Muñiz & Fernández-Hermida, 2010; Muñiz, Prieto, Almeida, & Bartram, 1999; Ryan & Sackett, 1987, 1992; Sneath, Thakur, & Madjuck, 1976; Steck, 1997). Even fewer have explored which tests are used for personnel selection in particular (Berchtold, 2005; Di Milia, 2004), even though the criticism has been raised that personality tests are "poorly chosen" (Murphy & Dzieweczynski, 2005, p. 343).

First, we will have a look on general test use in business contexts. Taking into account those studies which survey general test use in organizations and those conducted by industrial and organizational psychologists without a specific focus on selection (Berchtold, 2005; Brown, 1999; Di Milia, 2004; Furnham, 2008; Muñiz & Fernández-Hermida, 2010; Ryan & Sackett, 1987, 1992), the evidence so far shows that the tests most frequently mentioned across studies are the 16 Personality Factor Questionnaire (16PF), the Myers-Briggs Type Indicator (MBTI), the Occupational Personality Questionnaire (OPQ), the Minnesota Multiphasic Personality Inventory (MMPI), the Big Five Personality Inventory (NEO), the California Psychological Inventory (CPI), and the Thomas Assessment/Personal Profile Analysis (PPA). This is in line with information from job websites or free personality test websites listing the supposed main personality tests (Donston-Miller, n.d.; Free Personality Test, n.d.). However, many more tests are mentioned in these studies, reflecting the huge variety of tests that exist (there are an estimated 2,500 publishers in the United States alone, see Hogan, 2005; Hough & Oswald, 2005; Psychometric Success, 2013), operating in a $500 million industry (Psychometric Success, 2013).

A closer look at the two studies that exclusively considered tests used in personnel selection procedures (Berchtold, 2005; Di Milia, 2004) reveals that there may be differences in test use that could be due to regional preferences or the fact that some tests have only a national range. Examining personality test use in selection procedures of Australian organizations, Di Milia (2004) found not only the OPQ, MBTI, NEO, and 16PF to be frequently used, but also questionnaires such as the Personal Characteristics Inventory (PCI), the Fifteen Factor Questionnaire, the Occupational Personality Profile (OPP), and the DISC (standing for Dominance, Influence, Steadiness, and Conscientiousness). Swiss organizations (Berchtold, 2005) also use the MBTI, 16PF, Thomas Assessment, OPQ, and NEO, supplemented by tests like the Master Person Analysis (MPA), Insights Discovery or MDI, the Bochum Inventory for profession-related personality description (BIP), the DISG (the German version of the DISC), or the Herrmann Brain Dominance Instrument (HBDI). All in all, 173 companies were found to use 52 different personality tests for selection purposes in Switzerland.

To complement the existing studies and to survey the current state of personality testing in Germany, we conducted our own study, questioning HR practitioners in companies of all sizes across Germany.[1] We found that personality tests were used in 15.1% of the surveyed companies (see Figure 7.1 for the application frequency of all selection methods). This is slightly less than the 20% that has usually been found in Germany over the last 20 years (Schuler et al., 2007) but can probably be explained by the fact that we also had smaller companies in our sample (41.6% had fewer than 500 employees). Respondents found personality tests to be moderately useful for promotion, planning of personnel development activities, assistance in team development activities, and for personnel selection at the employee level, and to be somewhat more useful for personnel selection at the management level (see Figure 7.2). Actual test users found personality tests to be significantly more useful for all purposes than did non-test users. Concerning the question of which personality tests were used, in accordance with the studies mentioned above, we found a huge variety of different methods, including Insights Discovery or MDI, the BIP, the PPA, the 16PF, the DISC, the Hogan Personality Inventory (HPI), and the Predictive Index (PI). For an overview of all mentioned tests, see Figure 7.3.

This study and the two previous ones (Berchtold, 2005; Di Milia, 2004) provide a first impression of the world of selection by personality testing. The MBTI is clearly one of the most frequently used personality tests; it is not only mentioned in various different studies, but is also high in the rank order of frequently used tests within these studies. Although the NEO personality inventory is also used in several countries, it generally ranks (far) below the MBTI (Berchtold, 2005; Di Milia, 2004; Furnham, 2008). This points towards the so-called research-practice gap in personnel selection, which describes the fact that research contents and recommendations of researchers are not always in line with the current implementation practice (e.g., Rynes, Giluk, & Brown, 2007): while we as researchers focus very much on the Big Five and instruments measuring these personality traits, practitioners seem to prefer other instruments like the MBTI although there is great doubt about its validity

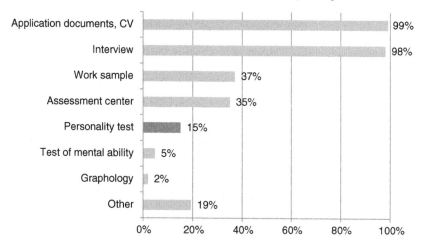

FIGURE 7.1 Frequency of selection methods used in percent ($N = 166$ German companies).

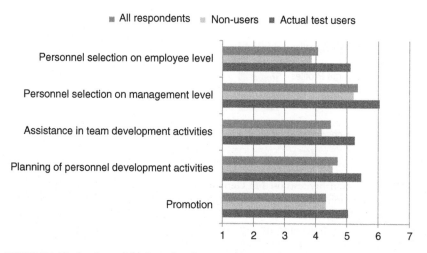

FIGURE 7.2 Evaluation of the benefit of personality tests for different purposes. Agreement regarding usefulness was given on a seven-point scale (1 = no agreement to 7 = full agreement). All differences between users and non-users were significant ($p < 0.01$, all t's < -2.6).

(e.g., Ones et al., 2005). Moreover, the three studies concentrating on selection (Berchtold, 2005; Di Milia, 2004; and our own study) clearly show that there is much more to personality testing than the MBTI and NEO (surprisingly, neither the MBTI nor the NEO are among the tests used in Germany). These three studies demonstrate the huge variety of personality tests in existence and use, some of which are restricted to certain countries/languages (for example, the BIP, which

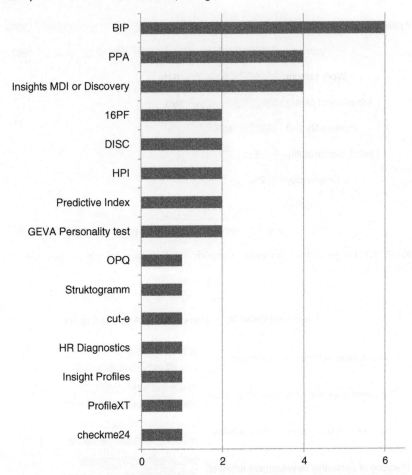

FIGURE 7.3 Personality tests used in Germany (in frequencies). (BIP = Bochum Inventory for profession-related personality description; PPA = Thomas Assessment / Personal Profile Analysis; HPI = Hogan Personality Inventory; GEVA = the Geva Institute is a German consulting company specialized in behavioral analysis and evaluation tools; OPQ = Occupational Personality Questionnaire).

was developed in Germany) and some of which are probably not appropriate in selection procedures.

Personality tests by comparison: what's it all about?

Let's take a closer look at the above-mentioned personality questionnaires. In the following section, we describe and discuss several important criteria beyond standard criteria such as reliability and validity (because previous research has shown that these criteria are not the only criteria important to practitioners; see, e.g.,

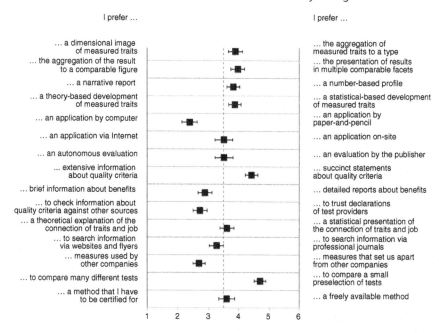

FIGURE 7.4 Preferences for different criteria that distinguish personality tests. Error bars indicate 95% confidence interval. Preferences were rated on a six-point semantic differential scale.

König, Klehe, Berchtold, & Kleinmann, 2010) that concern characteristics of the personality test and its presentation of results, aspects of application, description of quality criteria, and the process of finding a personality test that might influence the allure of often-used personality tests for practitioners.

Test characteristics and presentation of results

A first distinguishing criterion is whether the test results in a personality type (e.g., MBTI, DISC, HBDI) or in a dimensional personality profile (e.g., 16PF, NEO, BIP, MPA). Whereas dimensions reflect the idea that a person usually shows all traits to a certain degree on a continuous scale, types group people into discrete classes (Gangestad & Snyder, 1985). The measurement of dimensions is widespread in psychological research, but there seems to be a nagging distrust of types, which are often seen as an (over)simplification, a trigger of stereotyped thinking, or even pure invention (e.g., Gangestad & Snyder, 1985). Moreover, it is often difficult to decide where to set theoretically or empirically meaningful cutoff points that assign a person to one type or the other without misclassification, and there is the general question of whether a person can exclusively be assigned to one type

(Robins, John, & Caspi, 1998; York & John, 1992). Even defenders of the MBTI believe that people can belong to more than one type and that the test alone will not find the "right" type, but that one needs to talk to the test taker (Bayne, 2005). At the same time, type tests may have advantages over dimensional personality tests. For example, the reduction of information and complexity into one type may be easier to interpret and therefore more appealing. Whereas a dimension-based test reports many scales with a person varying on all of these scales, a type includes all information in an economical manner and makes it easier to differentiate between applicants. A schema-like categorization system may also better match the human knowledge structure of cognitive schemata (Smith & Queller, 2008) and limitations of cognitive capacity (Tversky & Kahneman, 1974).

Both approaches to personality testing may thus have their advantages and disadvantages (and may not only coexist but even benefit from each other; Robins & Tracy, 2003). In our survey, we also asked the practitioners whether they preferred dimension-based personality tests or type tests and whether they preferred the results to be aggregated into one comparable value or to be presented in multiple comparable facets[2] (see Figure 7.4). Results of one-sample t-tests, testing for differences to the scale middle of 3.5, showed a significant[3] preference for types rather than dimensions ($M = 3.89$, $SD = 1.53$) on the one hand and a significant preference for facets rather than an aggregation to one value ($M = 3.97$, $SD = 1.51$) on the other. This indicates that a mixture of both types of results may be most attractive. Interestingly, actual test users ($n = 28$, $M = 3.21$, $SD = 1.62$) preferred dimensions, whereas those who did not use personality tests ($n = 138$, $M = 4.03$, $SD = 1.48$) showed a strong preference for types. This suggests that a certain expertise concerning personality tests leads to a difference in preferences (but given the small sample of test users, this result should be treated with caution).

A second criterion concerns the report. The user is confronted with a type or a profile that he or she needs to interpret and compare with an ideal type or profile and/or other applicants. On the one hand, this compact alternative has the advantage that the user does not have to read a long report but can focus on the aspects that are important to him or her. On the other hand, if a practitioner is interested in an interpretation, he or she is left alone with this task. That can be a considerable problem if he or she is not a psychologist with appropriate training in test interpretation. A manual can be very helpful, but may not always be easy to understand. The other option, which is usually provided automatically with online test versions, consists of detailed narrative reports, which offer the advantage of an extensive, easy-to-understand, and quick evaluation that is less prone to mistakes regarding subjectivity and the difficult task of simultaneously processing several variables (Bartram, 1995; Snyder, 2000). So-called computer-based test interpretations have been used and discussed for decades now, especially in clinical psychology (e.g., Butcher, Perry, & Dean, 2009; Fowler, 1985). They are almost standard in reports of commercial test publishers as well as in science-based personality tests like the NEO (at least in some versions: in Germany, a narrative report is available for the NEO-PI R+, but not for the NEO FFI) and the BIP. These narrative reports can differ in terms of various aspects, for example, the extent to which text and graphs are integrated, the involvement of interpretation of configurations and interactions, or the possibility to adapt a test to the context (e.g., development or selection; Bartram, 1995).

The gain of being provided with an interpretation is often bought with the uncertainty about accuracy and validity of these interpretations, and narrative reports of different tests probably differ in their accuracy (Kellett, McCahon, & James, 1991). Especially in the case of tests from commercial publishers, it is often difficult to evaluate how these interpretations are generated, which statistical methods and which interpretive rules or algorithms are used to combine test results and text modules, or how these text modules were developed. Frequently, the report cannot be modified or adapted to the current test context (Bartram, 1995), and even if this were the case, it is questionable whether non-trained personnel staff would be able to do so appropriately. Some reports may even take advantage (knowingly or not) of the Barnum effect: they make such broad statements that people usually feel that the report is accurate, scientifically precise, and offers good reasons for decisions, but it is actually too general for a practitioner to make well-grounded judgments (Guastello, Guastello, & Craft, 1989; Guastello & Rieke, 1990; Snyder, 2000). Unfortunately, there is barely any research concerning the issue of narrative reports in an organizational context or addressing the huge variety of tests in use. Our survey found a significant preference for a profile ($M = 3.82, SD = 1.41$) rather than a narrative report. Perhaps there is a stronger need for quick comparisons in selection procedures, making narrative reports less important than, for example, consulting and development activities.

Another criterion concerns the development and background of a test. Although test development can have different backgrounds, there seem to be two major variations: A personality test can be based on a personality theory or on a statistical approach. The MBTI, for instance, is an example of the theory-based approach. It was developed by Katherine Briggs and her daughter Isabel Briggs Myers, under the influence of C. G. Jung's typology (Briggs Myers & Myers, 1993; Jung, 1960). Another influential theory concerns William Marston's (1979) behavioral types – originally called Dominance (D), Inducement (I), Submission (S), and Compliance (C). This led not only to the DISC assessment but also to the development of other personality tests such as the Personal Profile Analysis. Usually, these tests use an adapted version of Marston's original types, called Dominance (D), Influence (I), Steadiness (S), and Conscientiousness (C). Insights MDI used both models as a background (Euteneier & Scheelen, 2010). The HBDI, by contrast, was developed by Ned Herrmann (1989), taking into account brain hemispheres theory (e.g., Mintzberg, 1976) and MacLean's (1985) theory of the "triune brain." It results in four thinking styles, reflected by a four-quadrant brain model. Another (main) way of developing a test, which is favored by most scientists, is based on a statistical approach. The NEO, for example, has such a statistical, nontheoretical background. It is based on the so-called lexical approach, and the Five Factors measured in this test were developed through factor analytical methods (e.g., McCrae & Costa, 1997).

There are good reasons why practitioners might be attracted by both approaches. On the one hand, the statistical, factor analytical method is an empirical one. This alone may give a personality test a serious appearance, meeting needs of legal security. On the other hand, people have a strong need for explanations, in particular explanations of human behavior (Keil, 2006; Lombrozo, 2006; Malle, 2004), and although the above-mentioned theories probably do not deliver such an explanation, they may serve as compensation. At least they suggest that there is more to a test than just a description of traits, and people may usually not require a scientifically tested theory (Keil, 2003, 2006; Rozenblit & Keil, 2002; Wilson & Keil, 1998). Moreover, such a general structure as derived in the NEO may not meet practitioners' requirements, as it does not refer to work-related applications such as personnel selection (Hough & Oswald, 2005). In our study, we also asked practitioners whether they preferred a theory-based or statistically based development of traits. Results indicate that practitioners significantly favored a statistically based development ($M = 3.87$, $SD = 1.32$). It thus appears that practitioners do understand the importance of a scientific approach.

Mode of delivery

The most apparent point of application concerns the presentation of the test: the "classic" paper-and-pencil form and the application at the computer with a local test system or via the Internet. The advantages of an electronic application are obvious: the testing material as well as test and response time can be controlled, items can be easily adapted, application and evaluation of results are highly objective, printing costs and unwieldy paper copies are eliminated, and feedback is available in an instant (Bartram, 2000; Lievens & Harris, 2003). What is more, the Internet provides a high flexibility, as applicants can be tested independently of place and time (Lievens & Harris, 2003). At the same time, there are some difficulties that have to be faced, which have been discussed to different degrees in the literature: problems such as connection troubles during Internet testing or a lack of computer or Internet access are likely not as serious as they were a couple of years ago, but are probably still an issue. Moreover, practitioners should keep in mind that people have different levels of affinity to computers and the Internet, which might lead to discrimination of some groups such as older people or ethnic minorities (Bartram, 2000). The ethical question of security of data transfer and confidential management of test results also remains important. A further question concerns the transferability of paper-and-pencil tests to the computer format. Currently, computer-based tests are usually still the same as their paper-and-pencil predecessors (Bartram, 2000). However, it is necessary to ensure that the psychometric properties are the same for two reasons: first, companies may use both versions and compare applicants undergoing paper-and-pencil and computer-based assessments, and second, equivalent scores are required in order to use the norms traditionally gleaned from the paper-and-pencil version (Meade, Michels, & Lautenschlager, 2007). Most studies found encouraging results (Bartram & Brown, 2004; Chuah,

Drasgow, & Roberts, 2006; Salgado & Moscoso, 2003) and even some benefits of web-based testing (e.g., more normal distribution or higher reliabilities, Ployhart, Weekley, Holtz, & Kemp, 2003). Nevertheless, there are differences (e.g., concerning means, Ployhart et al., 2003), and Meade et al. (2007) warn that comparability cannot be taken for granted. Practitioners in our sample strongly preferred a computer application over a paper-and-pencil application ($M = 2.38$, $SD = 1.62$) but were indifferent as to whether the test should be applied via the Internet or on-site ($M = 3.51$, $SD = 1.93$). Moreover, there is no preference regarding who (the company/the practitioner or the test publisher) evaluates test results ($M = 3.51$, $SD = 1.97$), meaning that the focus seems to be on an automated process and not on the way in which this automation is delivered (by an external provider, on-site, or via the Internet). On the other hand, actual test users do prefer an application by Internet ($n = 28, M = 2.61, SD = 1.77$) compared to non-users ($n = 138, M = 3.70$, $SD = 1.87$), meaning that people who already use personality tests seem to perceive the advantages of this medium.

Declaration and description of quality criteria

Quality criteria, especially measures of reliability and validity (which we will subsume with the term *quality criteria* in the following), are very important to researchers, who consequently present these measures in extensive test manuals, as do some commercial test publishers. However, considering the huge number of personality tests available, the extent to which publishers are interested in measuring and providing quality criteria likely varies. Besides, the existence of quality criteria does not mean that practitioners have access to such information before buying a test. There is a huge variety of ways in which quality criteria can be reported. According to our experience, information on publishers' or distributors' websites is (a) seldom extensive, (b) often only brief, (c) sometimes only available on demand or by buying the manual, or (d) not available at all. A brief description of quality criteria may be an alternative that is more convenient to practitioners, as they probably do not have the time to read long manuals. In our study, practitioners significantly preferred succinct statements about quality criteria rather than extensive information ($M = 4.42$, $SD = 1.36$), and brief information about benefits rather than detailed reports ($M = 2.88$, $SD = 1.49$). Nevertheless, they do not seem to be naïve in terms of believing these statements, as they strongly prefer to check this information rather than trusting the declarations of the author ($M = 2.72$, $SD = 1.49$). At the same time, actual test users significantly preferred more detailed reports about the benefits of a certain test ($n = 28, M = 3.57, SD = 1.69$) compared to non-users ($n = 138, M = 2.74, SD = 1.41$), whereas there was no difference concerning the length of quality criteria information. Consequently, there is perhaps more to selling personality tests than numerical criteria. Moreover, no significant results were found regarding the question of whether practitioners would prefer a theoretical explanation of why the measured traits should be important for their employees' professional performance compared to statistical measures ($M = 3.61$, $SD = 1.53$).

Once again, this indicates that both kinds of information are needed, and more is needed to convince practitioners of the benefit of personality tests in personnel selection than the scientists' mere focus on proving validity data.

Finding a personality test

An additional criterion that distinguishes personality tests is where and how practitioners can find information about them. In our survey, practitioners significantly preferred to inform themselves by searching websites and flyers rather than professional journals and magazines[4] ($M = 3.26$, $SD = 1.56$). Answers to an open question concerning sources revealed that most used the Internet (35.5%), information and recommendations from their personal network (12.7%), and professional (HR-related) magazines (12.0%). They strongly favored tests used by many companies rather than tests that set them apart from other companies ($M = 2.69$, $SD = 1.29$), a confirmation of the finding of König et al. (2010). Most commercial publishers seem to take advantage of this practice of using recommendations, by citing referees who predominantly work in well-known companies on their websites. These references do not necessarily contain any information about the frequency and reason of use in the respective company. Moreover, our sample preferred to compare a small preselection of tests rather than many different tests ($M = 4.70$, $SD = 1.28$), even more so when they were not currently using a personality test ($n = 138$, $M = 4.80$, $SD = 1.22$) than when they were already using one ($n = 28$, $M = 4.21$, $SD = 1.45$), which might not be too surprising considering the huge number of tests available.

Another criterion that may affect the selection of a personality test is whether practitioners have to gain a certificate to use a special test (i.e., some publishers do not sell their inventories or at least part of them to people who are not trained and certified, and others offer training as an additional service, e.g., the MBTI and the HBDI certification). Practitioners in our sample did not have a particular preference for or against certification ($M = 3.60$, $SD = 1.72$), although actual test users prefer certification ($n = 28$, $M = 2.89$, $SD = 1.77$) compared to non-users ($n = 138$, $M = 3.74$, $SD = 1.68$). Offering training seems reasonable, at least for non-psychologists, who have probably not had such training during their education, because otherwise, there is no guarantee that users are really informed about the proper application and interpretation of results.

An additional factor that is important in the decision-making process but is not covered in our survey[5] concerns the promotion of personality tests. Promotion strategies may differ to various extents: for example, there is "classic" advertisement in HR journals or stands at HR fairs. In addition, some may rely on a factual strategy, while others may (consciously or unconsciously) emphasize special characteristics of their tests in the sense of a unique or emotional selling proposition (e.g., the HBDI stresses a metaphorical connection to the brain; Herrmann International, n.d.) or point out the model of personality upon which the test is based (i.e., they can highlight that their tests rely on well-established models, for instance, the MBTI on Jungian theory). Whatever their strategy, commercial test publishers probably invest a lot in their promotion strategies in order to stand out from the crowd of personality tests.

Future prospects and conclusions

We were able to show that – at least in Germany – there is definitely more to personality testing than just the Big Five or MBTI, and we believe that it is necessary to gain a broader overview, an international appraisal of actual personality test use, rather than to focus solely on particular single measures. Not only is there a large range of personality tests offered to practitioners, but many of them are also in use in the context of personnel selection. We discussed the influence of different criteria on the decision-making process, such as certain test characteristics, the different ways of presenting results, or aspects of application. We believe that a deeper understanding needs to be gained of this decision-making process, the requirements and needs of practitioners, and the advantages and disadvantages of the manifold alternatives. For instance, we know nothing about the quality and actual handling of narrative reports in the selection process. Moreover, we concentrate strongly on dimension-based tests without even considering whether types might somehow meet practitioners' needs. Although the development of the Big Five certainly has great advantages in terms of comparability, it may not fit with categories of practitioners in personnel selection. Other traits or competencies may be more important to them because they are meaningful in terms of showing an intuitive theoretical relation to job performance. We need to find out a lot more about how personality tests are actually used, what may influence the decision for implementing personality tests in the selection process, and how attitudes to personality tests may change before and after this implementation. Our survey was only a first attempt to learn something about practitioners' needs and requirements concerning the use of personality testing in personnel selection, and to initiate a change in perspectives – away from believing that reliability and validity are the only criteria important to practitioners, towards an understanding of the existence of multiple influences. There may be many more criteria according to which personality tests can be differentiated (e.g., whether items relate to organizational contexts, to clinical contexts, or neither; the costs of one or several applications; the number of dimensions or types measured; item format; how dimensions and types are named; whether they are special tests for different roles like leaders or salesmen; etc.). It will be the task of future research to use this new perspective to develop arguments for propositions and specific hypotheses concerning the influence of different criteria to the decision-making process of practitioners. Moreover, it is not enough merely to survey practitioners, as questionnaires are prone to socially desirable responding (as probably happened in our question whether practitioners would prefer to check quality information or trust declarations of the author). Rather, practitioners' decision making needs to be experimentally analyzed. In addition, it may be necessary to take a step away from pure research and to try to diminish the research-practice gap in personnel selection. One such step may be to simplify the search and comparison of different personality tests by setting up national websites that list personality tests categorized according to their benefit for different purposes (e.g., development, selection, general assessment of personality, etc.) and provide the most important information and professional and independent evaluations of common tests. Another step may be to develop training programs for different personality tests in different organizational contexts in order to improve actual test use.

As personality tests continue to be used – no matter how scientists evaluate this – it is important to understand this use and make adequate recommendations and offers to practitioners. Thus, not only do scientists need to be better in explaining validity to inform practitioners about its value, they should also not ignore the needs and requirements of practitioners and should therefore try to adapt their research priorities accordingly.

Notes

1. We randomly called 769 companies; in 605, we were able to talk to employees or managers who worked in conducting the selection process. Of these, 403 people were interested in participating in the study and were invited to take part in the online survey by e-mail. A total of 166 persons (37.3% male, 56.6% female, 6.0% did not specify their gender) actually completed the whole survey (237 dropped out). Respondents had been in their current jobs for an average of 12.7 years ($SD = 8.8$) and most (71.7%) had a university education, with the majority being trained in business administration (58.0%) and only 5.0% in psychology. On average, they had been involved in 41.3 selection procedures during the last year ($SD = 111.9$), and a total of 77.1% had decision-making rights concerning the choice of selection methods. Companies had approximately 904.4 ($SD = 1608.9$) employees (7.8% had up to 50 employees, 16.3% between 51 and 250, 24.1% between 251 and 500 and 39.2% had over 500 employees; 12.7% did not answer this question), 72.3% were operating internationally, mostly in manufacturing, wholesale and the retail trade, financial and insurance activities, or personnel services. The survey consisted of three main parts. First, we wanted to know which selection methods the companies used. Second, we asked participants about the purposes for which they found personality tests to be useful. Third, we concentrated on personality test use in personnel selection and asked for preferences of 15 different criteria that can be used to distinguish these tests.
2. Each preference item had two poles on a one- to six-point scale, e.g., "Would you prefer . . ." and ". . . a dimensional representation of measured traits" on one pole and ". . . the aggregation of measured traits in types" on the other pole.
3. Whenever we speak of significance, we mean at least $p < .05$.
4. In our survey we used the German word "Fachzeitschrift" that includes professional and peer-reviewed journals as well as magazines.
5. Practitioners probably do not know anything about promotion strategies and they cannot consciously evaluate the effect of promotion on their decision.

References

Barrick, M.R., & Mount, M.K. (1991). The Big Five personality dimensions and job performance: A meta-analysis. *Personnel Psychology, 44*, 1–26.

Barrick, M.R., & Mount, M.K. (2005). Yes, personality matters: Moving on to more important matters. *Human Performance, 18*, 359–372.

Barrick, M.R., Mount, M.K., & Judge, T.A. (2001). Personality and performance at the beginning of the new millennium: What do we know and where do we go next? *International Journal of Selection and Assessment, 9*, 9–30.

Bartram, D. (1995). The role of computer-based test interpretation (CBTI) in occupational assessment. *International Journal of Selection and Assessment, 3*, 178–185.

Bartram, D. (2000). Internet recruitment and selection: Kissing frogs to find princes. *International Journal of Selection and Assessment, 8*, 261–274.

Bartram, D. (2004). Assessment in organisations. *Applied Psychology: An International Review, 53*, 237–259.

Bartram, D., & Brown, A. (2004). Online testing: Mode of administration and the stability of OPQ 32i scores. *International Journal of Selection and Assessment, 12*, 278–284.

Bayne, R. (2005). *Ideas and evidence: Critical reflections on MBTI theory and practice.* Gainesville, FL: CAPT.

Berchtold, M. (2005). Häufigste Auswahlverfahren in der Personalselektion [Most frequently used selection methods in personnel selection]. *HR Today, 12/2005*, 37–39.

Birkeland, S.A., Manson, T.M., Kisamore, J.L., Brannick, M.T., & Smith, M.A. (2006). A meta-analytic investigation of job applicant faking on personality measures. *International Journal of Selection and Assessment, 14*, 317–335.

Blickle, G., & Kramer, J. (2012). Intelligenz, Persönlichkeit, Einkommen und Fremdbeurteilungen der Leistung in sozialen Berufen [Intelligence, personality, income, and job performance assessments by others in social welfare jobs: A validation study]. *Zeitschrift für Arbeits- und Organisationspsychologie, 56*, 14–23.

Briggs Myers, I., & Myers, P.B. (1993). *Gifts differing: Understanding personality type.* Palo Alto, CA: Consulting Psychologists Press.

Brown, R. (1999). The use of personality tests: A survey of usage and practice in the UK. *Selection and Development Review, 15*, 3–8.

Bruchon-Schweitzer, M., & Ferrieux, D. (1991). Une enquête sur le recrutement en France [An inquiry on personnel recruitment in France]. *European Review of Applied Psychology, 41*, 9–17.

Butcher, J.N., Perry, J.N., & Dean, B.L. (2009). How to use computer-based reports. In J.N. Butcher (Ed.), *Oxford handbook of personality assessment* (pp. 693–706). Oxford, UK: Oxford University Press.

Chuah, S.C., Drasgow, F., & Roberts, B.W. (2006). Personality assessment: Does the medium matter? No. *Journal of Research in Personality, 40*, 359–376.

Di Milia, L. (2004). Australian management selection practices: Closing the gap between research findings and practice. *Asia Pacific Journal of Human Resources, 42*, 214–228.

Donston-Miller, D. (n.d.). Top personality tests used in hiring. *The Ladders*. Retrieved August 26, 2013, from http://www.theladders.com/career-advice/top-personality-tests-hiring

Driver, R.W., Buckley, M.R., & Frink, D.D. (1996). Should we write off graphology? *International Journal of Selection and Assessment, 4*, 78–86.

Dudley, N.M., Orvis, K.A., Lebiecki, J.E., & Cortina, J.M. (2006). A meta-analytic investigation of conscientiousness in the prediction of job performance: Examining the intercorrelations and the incremental validity of narrow traits. *Journal of Applied Psychology, 91*, 40–57.

Eleftheriou, A., & Robertson, I. (1999). A survey of management selection practices in Greece. *International Journal of Selection and Assessment, 7*, 203–208.

Euteneier, R.J., & Scheelen, F.M. (2010). INSIGHTS MDI® by Scheelen – Verhalten, Werte, Fertigkeiten [INSIGHTS MDI® by Scheelen – behavior, values, skills]. In W. Simon

(Ed.), *Persönlichkeitsmodelle und Persönlichkeitstests [Models of personality and personality tests]* (pp. 19–36). Offenbach, Germany: GABAL.

Evers, A., Muñiz, J., Bartram, D., Boben, D., Egeland, J., Fernández-Hermida, J. R., . . . Urbánek, T. (2012). Testing practices in the 21st century. *European Psychologist, 17,* 300–319.

Fowler, R. D. (1985). Landmarks in computer-assisted psychological assessment. *Journal of Consulting and Clinical Psychology, 53,* 748–759.

Free Personality Test. (n.d.). Personality tests: The main personality tests (Myers Briggs, Big 5, 16PF . . .). *Personality test free.* Retrieved August 26, 2013, from http://www.personalitytestfree.net/personality-tests.php

Furnham, A. (2008). HR professionals' beliefs about, and knowledge of, assessment techniques and psychometric tests. *International Journal of Selection and Assessment, 16,* 300–305.

Gangestad, S., & Snyder, M. (1985). "To carve nature at its joints": On the existence of discrete classes in personality. *Psychological Review, 92,* 317–349.

Ghiselli, E. E., & Barthol, R. P. (1953). The validity of personality inventories in the selection of employees. *Journal of Applied Psychology, 37,* 18–20.

Guastello, S. J., Guastello, D. D., & Craft, L. L. (1989). Assessment of the Barnum effect in computer-based test interpretations. *Journal of Psychology, 123,* 477.

Guastello, S. J., & Rieke, M. L. (1990). The Barnum effect and validity of computer-based test interpretations: The Human Resource Development Report. *Psychological Assessment: A Journal of Consulting and Clinical Psychology, 2,* 186–190.

Guion, R. M., & Gottier, R. F. (1965). Validity of personality measures in personnel selection. *Personnel Psychology, 18,* 135–164.

Harris, M. M., Dworkin, J. B., & Park, J. (1990). Preemployment screening procedures: How human resource managers perceive them. *Journal of Business and Psychology, 4,* 279–292.

Herrmann, N. (1989). *The creative brain.* Lake Lure, NC: Brain Books.

Herrmann International. (n.d.). A history of innovation in business. Retrieved December 30, 2013, from http://www.herrmannsolutions.com/our-foundation/

Hodgkinson, G. P., Daley, N., & Payne, R. L. (1995). Knowledge of, and attitudes towards, the demographic time bomb: A survey of its impact on graduate recruitment in the UK. *International Journal of Manpower, 16,* 59–76.

Hodgkinson, G. P., & Payne, R. L. (1998). Graduate selection in three European countries. *Journal of Occupational and Organizational Psychology, 71,* 359–365.

Hogan, J., Barrett, P., & Hogan, R. (2007). Personality measurement, faking, and employment selection. *Journal of Applied Psychology, 92,* 1270–1285.

Hogan, J., & Holland, B. (2003). Using theory to evaluate personality and job-performance relations: A socioanalytic perspective. *Journal of Applied Psychology, 88,* 100–112.

Hogan, R. (2005). In defense of personality measurement: New wine for old whiners. *Human Performance, 18,* 331–341.

Hough, L. M., & Oswald, F. L. (2005). They're right, well . . . mostly right: Research evidence and an agenda to rescue personality testing from 1960s insights. *Human Performance, 18,* 373–387.

Hurtz, G. M., & Donovan, J. J. (2000). Personality and job performance: The Big Five revisited. *Journal of Applied Psychology, 85,* 869–879.

Judge, T. A., Bono, J. E., Ilies, R., & Gerhardt, M. W. (2002). Personality and leadership: A qualitative and quantitative review. *Journal of Applied Psychology, 87,* 765–780.

Judge, T. A., Heller, D., & Mount, M. K. (2002). Five-factor model of personality and job satisfaction: A meta-analysis. *Journal of Applied Psychology, 87,* 530–541.

Judge, T. A., Higgins, C. A., Thoresen, C. J., & Barrick, M. R. (1999). The Big Five personality traits, general mental ability, and career success across the life span. *Personnel Psychology, 52,* 621–652.

Jung, C. G. (1960). *Psychologische Typen [Psychological types]* (9th ed.). Zürich, Switzerland: Rascher.

Keil, F.C. (2003). Folkscience: Coarse interpretations of a complex reality. *Trends in Cognitive Sciences, 7*, 368.
Keil, F.C. (2006). Explanation and understanding. *Annual Review of Psychology, 57*, 227–254.
Kellett, D., McCahon, S., & James, J. (1991). Preliminary evaluation of five computer-generated narrative reports derived from four different personality questionnaires. *European Work and Organizational Psychologist, 1*, 196–210.
Kepes, S., Banks, G.C., McDaniel, M., & Whetzel, D.L. (2012). Publication bias in the organizational sciences. *Organizational Research Methods, 15*, 624–662.
König, C.J., Klehe, U., Berchtold, M., & Kleinmann, M. (2010). Reasons for being selective when choosing personnel selection procedures. *International Journal of Selection and Assessment, 18*, 17–27.
Lievens, F., & Harris, M.M. (2003). Research on Internet recruiting and testing: Current status and future directions. In C.L. Cooper & I.T. Robertson (Eds.), *International review of industrial and organizational psychology* (Vol. 18). New York: Wiley.
Lombrozo, T. (2006). The structure and function of explanations. *Trends in Cognitive Sciences, 10*, 464–470.
MacLean, P.D. (1985). Evolutionary psychiatry and the triune brain. *Psychological Medicine, 15*, 219–221.
Malle, B.F. (2004). *How the mind explains behavior: Folk explanations, meaning, and social interaction.* Cambridge, MA: MIT Press.
Marcus, B., Goffin, R.D., Johnston, N.G., & Rothstein, M.G. (2007). Personality and cognitive ability as predictors of typical and maximum managerial performance. *Human Performance, 20*, 275–285.
Marston, W.M. (1979). *Emotions of normal people.* Minneapolis: Persona Press.
McCrae, R.R., & Costa, P.T.J. (1997). Personality trait structure as a human universal. *American Psychologist, 52*, 509–516.
McDaniel, M.A., Whetzel, D.L., Schmidt, F.L., & Maurer, S.D. (1994). The validity of employment interviews: A comprehensive review and meta-analysis. *Journal of Applied Psychology, 79*, 599–616.
Meade, A.W., Michels, L.C., & Lautenschlager, G.J. (2007). Are Internet and paper-and-pencil personality tests truly comparable? An experimental design measurement invariance study. *Organizational Research Methods, 10*, 322–345.
Mintzberg, H. (1976). Planning on the left side and managing on the right. *Harvard Business Review, 54*, 49–58.
Morgeson, F.P., Campion, M.A., Dipboye, R.L., Hollenbeck, J.R., Murphy, K.R., & Schmitt, N. (2007). Reconsidering the use of personality tests in personnel selection contexts. *Personnel Psychology, 60*, 683–729.
Muñiz, J., & Fernández-Hermida, J.R. (2010). La opinión de los psicólogos españoles sobre el uso de los tests [Spanish psychologists' opinions on test use]. *Papeles Del Psicólogo, 31*, 108–121.
Muñiz, J., Prieto, G., Almeida, L., & Bartram, D. (1999). Test use in Spain, Portugal and Latin American countries. *European Journal of Psychological Assessment, 15*, 151–157.
Murphy, K.R., & Dzieweczynski, J.L. (2005). Why don't measures of broad dimensions of personality perform better as predictors of job performance? *Human Performance, 18*, 343–357.
Ones, D.S., & Viswesvaran, C. (1996). Bandwidth–fidelity dilemma in personality measurement for personnel selection. *Journal of Organizational Behavior, 17*, 609–626.
Ones, D.S., Viswesvaran, C., & Dilchert, S. (2005). Personality at work: Raising awareness and correcting misconceptions. *Human Performance, 18*, 389–404.
Piotrowski, C., & Armstrong, T. (2006). Current recruitment and selection practices: A national survey of Fortune 1000 firms. *North American Journal of Psychology, 8*, 489–496.

Ployhart, R.E., Weekley, J.A., Holtz, B.C., & Kemp, C. (2003). Web-based and paper-and-pencil testing of applicants in a proctored setting: Are personality, biodata, and situational judgment tests comparable? *Personnel Psychology, 56*, 733–752.

Psychometric Success. (2013). Understanding the personality test industry. *Psychometric Success*. Retrieved August 26, 2013, from http://www.psychometric-success.com/personality-tests/personality-tests-understanding-industry.htm

Robie, C., Tuzinski, K.A., & Bly, P.R. (2006). A survey of assessor beliefs and practices related to faking. *Journal of Managerial Psychology, 21*, 669–681.

Robins, R.W., John, O.P., & Caspi, A. (1998). The typological approach to studying personality. In R.B. Cairns, L.R. Bergman, & J. Kagan (Eds.), *Methods and models for studying the individual* (pp. 135–160). Thousand Oaks, CA: Sage.

Robins, R.W., & Tracy, J.L. (2003). Setting an agenda for a person-centered approach to personality development. *Monographs of the Society for Research in Child Development, 68*, 110–122.

Rothstein, M.G., & Goffin, R.D. (2006). The use of personality measures in personnel selection: What does current research support? *Human Resource Management Review, 16*, 155–180.

Rozenblit, L., & Keil, F.C. (2002). The misunderstood limits of folk science: An illusion of explanatory depth. *Cognitive Science, 26*, 521–562.

Ryan, A.M., McFarland, L., Baron, H., & Page, R. (1999). An international look at selection practices: Nation and culture as explanations for variability in practice. *Personnel Psychology, 52*, 359–391.

Ryan, A.M., & Sackett, P.R. (1987). A survey of individual assessment practices by I/O psychologists. *Personnel Psychology, 40*, 455–488.

Ryan, A.M., & Sackett, P.R. (1992). Relationships between graduate training, professional affiliation, and individual psychological assessment practices for personnel decisions. *Personnel Psychology, 45*, 363–387.

Rynes, S.L., Giluk, T.L., & Brown, K.G. (2007). The very separate worlds of academic and practitioner periodicals in human resource management: Implications for evidence-based management. *Academy of Management Journal, 50*, 987–1008.

Rynes, S.L., Orlitzky, M.O., & Bretz, R.D. (1997). Experienced hiring versus college recruiting: Practices and emerging trends. *Personnel Psychology, 50*, 309–339.

Salgado, J.F. (1997). The Five Factor model of personality and job performance in the European Community. *Journal of Applied Psychology, 82*, 30–43.

Salgado, J.F., & Moscoso, S. (2003). Internet-based personality testing: Equivalence of measures and assesses' perceptions and reactions. *International Journal of Selection and Assessment, 11*, 194–205.

Scholarios, D., & Lockyer, C. (1999). Recruiting and selecting professionals: Context, qualities and methods. *International Journal of Selection and Assessment, 7*, 142–156.

Schuler, H., Frier, D., & Kauffmann, M. (1993). *Personalauswahl im europäischen Vergleich [Personnel selection in a European comparison]*. Göttingen, Germany: Verlag für Angewandte Psychologie.

Schuler, H., Hell, B., Trapmann, S., Schaar, H., & Boramir, I. (2007). Die Nutzung psychologischer Verfahren der externen Personalauswahl in deutschen Unternehmen: Ein Vergleich über 20 Jahre [Use of personnel selection instruments in German organizations during the last 20 years]. *Zeitschrift für Personalpsychologie, 6*, 60–70.

Shackleton, V., & Newell, S. (1994). European management selection methods: A comparison of five countries. *International Journal of Selection and Assessment, 2*, 91–102.

Smith, E.R., & Queller, S. (2008). Mental representations. In A. Tesser & N. Schwarz (Eds.), *Blackwell handbook of social psychology: Intraindividual processes* (pp. 111–133). New York: Wiley.

Sneath, F., Thakur, M., & Madjuck, B. (1976). *Testing people at work* (Information Report No. 24). London: Institute of Personnel Management.

Snyder, D.K. (2000). Computer-assisted judgment: Defining strengths and liabilities. *Psychological Assessment, 12*, 52–60.

Steck, P. (1997). Psychologische Testverfahren in der Praxis: Ergebnisse einer Umfrage unter Testanwendern [Psychological tests in practice: A survey among test users]. *Diagnostica, 43*, 267–284.

Stewart, G.L., Darnold, T.C., Zimmerman, R.D., Parks, L., & Dustin, S.L. (2010). Exploring how response distortion of personality measures affects individuals. *Personality and Individual Differences, 49*, 622–628.

Tett, R.P., Steele, J.R., & Beauregard, R.S. (2003). Broad and narrow measures on both sides of the personality–job performance relationship. *Journal of Organizational Behavior, 24*, 335–356.

Tversky, A., & Kahneman, D. (1974). Judgment under uncertainty: Heuristics and biases. *Science, 185*, 1124–1131.

Williams, R.S. (1992). Management selection in local government: A survey of practice in England and Wales. *Human Resource Management Journal, 3*, 63–73.

Wilson, R.A., & Keil, F.C. (1998). The shadows and shallows of explanation. *Minds and Machines: Journal for Artificial Intelligence, Philosophy, and Cognitive Science, 8*, 137–159.

York, K.L., & John, O.P. (1992). The four faces of Eve: A typological analysis of women's personality at midlife. *Journal of Personality and Social Psychology, 63*, 494–508.

Zibarras, L.D., & Woods, S.A. (2010). A survey of UK selection practices across different organization sizes and industry sectors. *Journal of Occupational and Organizational Psychology, 83*, 499–511.

8
TRENDS IN TESTING
Highlights of a global survey

Ann Marie Ryan
MICHIGAN STATE UNIVERSITY, USA

Ilke Inceoglu
SURREY BUSINESS SCHOOL, UNIVERSITY OF SURREY, UK

Dave Bartram
CEB'S SHL TALENT MEASUREMENT SOLUTIONS, AND UNIVERSITY OF PRETORIA, SOUTH AFRICA

Juliya Golubovich
EDUCATIONAL TESTING SERVICE ETS, USA

James Grand
UNIVERSITY OF AKRON, USA

Matthew Reeder
APT METRICS, USA

Eva Derous
GHENT UNIVERSITY, BELGIUM

Ioannis Nikolaou
ATHENS UNIVERSITY OF ECONOMICS AND BUSINESS, GREECE

Xiang Yao
PEKING UNIVERSITY, CHINA

In the mid-1990s, Ryan, McFarland, Baron, and Page (1999) conducted a survey of selection practices globally. Because their study is one of the few published surveys

Trends in testing **137**

of employer practices, it garnered significant citations in the years that followed. Even though much time has passed since that data collection, a comparable, comprehensive examination of employer practices has not surfaced in the selection area. This chapter provides an overview of a more recent effort to capture trends in testing.

On the surface, hiring practices may have changed dramatically since the mid-1990s due to a number of social, economic, and technological trends. Skill and demographic shifts among labor market occupants and changes in job and occupational requirements have led employers to source applicants for jobs in wider markets (and even globally). Technological developments have facilitated and accelerated staffing processes (Scott & Lezotte, 2012). Greater use of computer- and particularly Internet-based testing has provided organizations with greater efficiency in resource allocation, quicker processing of applicants, and access to a larger pool of potential applicants. Technology has allowed for new and varied ways of presenting assessment content to applicants, but has also heightened concerns regarding test security and potential cheating.

Given that these trends have reshaped hiring and staffing over the past 20 years, this chapter provides an updated description of the practices and policies used by organizations around the world. A 54-item survey on selection practices was translated into 15 languages, and data was collected from HR professionals in more than 25 countries. This chapter focuses on trends in test use around the globe; specific country differences are not detailed, as sample sizes varied across countries, with many too small to make specific inferences about trends in individual countries.[1]

Survey respondents

A total of 1,197 HR professionals completed an online questionnaire about testing practices and policies. Respondents were sourced via a number of methods targeted specifically at reaching HR professionals. Note that we sought to include HR managers/directors/executives within organizations, not HR consultants or lower-level HR employees, and thus our sampling strategy aimed to capture that. Professional associations and in particular selection-related groups were contacted in all the countries selected for inclusion in the study (based on coverage of countries in different clusters in the GLOBE study, House, Hanges, Javidan, Dorfman, & Gupta, 2004, as well as practical constraints regarding translation capabilities) and were asked to either email a survey announcement to their mailing lists or to post a notification of the survey on their websites. LinkedIn groups of HR professionals in each targeted country were identified, and we posted survey notices in those groups. We also accessed the email list for marketing for a major test publisher and culled HR manager/director/executive emails from that list for a direct mailing about the survey. Finally, collaborators in several countries had contacts within professional associations and assisted us by distributing the survey link. Thus, it is impossible to calculate a response rate, as the true population of HR professionals with internal responsibilities for selection systems is not known.

The largest representation in the sample was from the United States (22.9%), Belgium (19.4%), and China (15.4%), with others from Sweden (8.2%), the Netherlands (6.5%), Greece (4.3%), Portugal (3.4%), France (3.0%), and the United Kingdom (2.0%). Other countries with respondents (less than 2% of total sample) included Italy, Russia, Australia, India, Germany, Hong Kong, Indonesia, Turkey, Brazil, New Zealand, Saudi Arabia, Singapore, Spain, Denmark, and South Africa. Most survey respondents were professionals in the private sector (81%), including professional services (21.2%), manufacturing (17.9%), financial (8.4%), retail (7.1%), health care (6.5%), telecommunications (3.8%), and transportation (3.0%), with smaller numbers in construction, information, utilities, insurance, educational services, hospitality, business consulting, chemical, pharmaceutical, mining, and energy. Most respondents were in an HR function in their organizations but held different types of roles (e.g., HR manager [29.8%], HR executive such as director or vice president [26.3%], HR consultant [8.7%]).

Overview of survey content

Questions addressed several areas:

1. **Decisions to use tests and future plans**: Reasons why organizations elect to use or not use tests, and plans for developing, purchasing, or implementing tests in the future.
2. **Test program description**: How tests are created and used in the hiring process, and characteristics assessed by tests.
3. **Use of technology**: Use of adaptive testing, use of supervision and other security measures when testing applicants, reasons for choosing to administer tests without supervision, differences in supervision practices by test type, estimates of cheating and of disqualification of applicants for cheating, and security and data protection practices.
4. **Test policies and practices**: Frequency and type of feedback provided to applicants, reasons for not providing feedback, retesting policies, global testing practices such as use of standardized testing practices across countries and practices associated with administering tests in multiple languages (e.g., translation, psychometric adequacy, evaluation), and metrics used to monitor the effectiveness of tests (e.g., job performance, attrition, hiring process efficiency, return on investment).

Note that we focused specifically on testing rather than other aspects of a hiring process (e.g., interviewing, recruiting, applicant tracking) in the interest of keeping the survey at a reasonable length while gathering sufficient detail on specific current trends. We defined *test* for respondents as "any standardized assessment instrument other than an interview or resume review that is designed to evaluate whether a job applicant possesses certain qualities and characteristics (e.g., knowledge, skill, traits)."

In the following sections we detail key findings in each of these areas.

Decisions to use tests and future plans

Researchers have long been interested in understanding why employers decide to use or not use different selection tools (Terpstra & Rozell, 1997; Wilk & Cappelli, 2003). About 60% of respondents said their organizations typically use tests for selecting entry-level management employees. Of particular interest is why organizations choose not to use tests (see Table 8.1). Consistent with earlier research on the predictors of selection tool use (König, Klehe, Berchtold & Kleinmann, 2010), cost and the extent to which use of tests is common practice for targeted jobs or locations were of relatively greater concern than legal considerations. But, in contrast to the earlier research (König et al., 2010), which had found perceived tool validity to have modest importance, many of the reasons for not using standardized assessments indicated by our respondents seem to represent a lack of belief in or knowledge about the value of tests (e.g., preferences for other methods, inability to obtain buy-in, unable to assess return on investment [ROI]). Thus, continued concerted efforts by testing professionals to educate and inform HR managers about the value of tests seem warranted. Klehe (2004) provides a framework that outlines the many institutional pressures (internal markets, industry norms) that affect organizations' willingness to adopt selection procedures; analyzing these factors might enable testing professionals to garner a better understanding of when and why organizations may not respond to efforts to educate decision makers on the value of testing in particular contexts.

TABLE 8.1 Reasons for not using tests

	Percentage of respondents
Prefer own methods of testing (e.g., interviewing, resume or CV sifting)	60.4%
Too expensive	37.7%
Too uncommon a practice for this type of job	30.3%
Inability to obtain internal buy-in or support to use testing	30.3%
Unable to effectively implement (e.g., lack technology or personnel to administer)	28.4%
Unaware of tests that would assess what we are looking for	27.0%
Not enough candidates to justify cost	26.8%
Adds too much to total time-to-hire	25.1%
Unable to calculate ROI of using tests	23.5%
Too uncommon a practice in locations where we hire	19.9%
Overlaps too much with other methods of assessing candidates	15.0%
Prior negative experiences with testing	13.4%
Applicants can cheat or fake answers too easily	11.7%
Poses too great a legal risk to use	10.4%
Insufficient support/training from vendor/provider	5.2%
Other	18.3%

Respondents = 366
Note: Respondents could select more than one answer

The literature also suggests that some types of tests may not be adopted because of tool-specific concerns, such as faking on personality tests (Rothstein & Goffin, 2006) and resources needed for building and administering simulations (Whetzel, McDaniel, & Pollack, 2012), so we also asked about reasons for not using specific assessment types (e.g., cognitive ability, personality, simulations). In most cases, top reasons were beliefs that the particular skill/ability assessed was not needed for the job or that the test would overlap with other parts of the hiring process (e.g., interview). While it is true that an interview can be used to assess many things (Huffcutt, Conway, Roth, & Stone, 2001), traditional (unstructured) interviews have low validity (e.g., Conway, Jako, & Goodman, 1995). Further, even when more valid, structured interviews are used, depending on the constructs they are designed to assess, additional assessments (e.g., personality or cognitive tests) may provide incremental validity (Berry, Sackett, & Landers, 2007). Providing practitioners with a clearer understanding of the intercorrelations of various testing tools and interviews in understandable language might enable individuals to better understand the degree of overlap; translating concepts such as incremental validity into language familiar to organizational stakeholders would also be valuable to increasing test adoption and selection system effectiveness (Boudreau, 2012).

Finally, among respondents whose companies do not currently use tests, approximately 40% indicated that they do plan on developing, purchasing, or implementing tests for hiring in the next three years. Based on this data, one might forecast an increased use of testing tools by organizations, as would fit with the trends noted earlier regarding technology and the ease of test use.

We also asked those who already used testing in some capacity why they had adopted tests in their hiring processes (see Table 8.2). Validity/effectiveness, fairness, and perceived value are the top three factors that influence companies' decisions to use tests. This again highlights how important persuading HR decision makers of the value of testing is to adoption. These findings are interesting, as König et al.

TABLE 8.2 Factors influencing decisions to test

	Very important
Validity/effectiveness	82.9%
Fairness	67.9%
Perceived value	61.7%
Ease of use by organization	55.5%
Prior positive experience	54.5%
Ease of use by applicants	34.5%
Ability to reduce applicant pool	32.6%
To reduce time required of hiring managers	31.4%
To reduce time to hire	30.4%
Reinforces employer brand	24.8%
Legal/political considerations	21.9%
To reduce time required of applicants	17.9%

Respondents = 725–738
Note: Respondents rated different reasons on importance

(2010) found that validity was only a modest consideration in adoption decisions; our broader sample and use of the term "effectiveness," which may encompass different types of evidence than formal evaluation, may explain the differences. Legal/political considerations, reducing time required of applicants, and reinforcing the employer brand were the top three reasons "not important" for decisions to test. König et al. (2010) had likewise found legal and organizational self-promotion to be modest predictors of test adoption. The rest of this chapter focuses on this subsample ($N = 766$) of test users and details how they use testing.

Test program descriptions

Tests in use were more commonly created by individuals external to the organization (50.8%) or through collaboration with external individuals (41.8%) than solely by those working within the organization (19.8%).[2] Companies used tests at different stages of the selection process (beginning [20.9%], intermediate [50.7%], end [23.3%]; total $N = 756$). Tests were typically used along with other tools to make selection decisions, as only 2% of respondents reported using tests as the only tool in selection. Personality, abilities, and leadership competencies were the most common characteristics assessed by tests. Interests were among the least commonly assessed (see Table 8.3).

Of particular interest is that although most companies use test scores in a relatively formal manner, either by combining test scores and interview ratings in a standardized manner to make decisions (43.1%; $N = 745$) or by using tests as screeners before interviews (25.1%), a substantial portion of respondents (27.1%) indicated that test scores and interpretive information are provided to hiring managers, who make decisions. It is important to consider how much bearing objective test scores have on managerial decisions when scores are used in this less formal way, particularly when a manager's subjective intuition about a candidate is at odds with

TABLE 8.3 Characteristics assessed by tests

	Percentage of respondents
Personality (e.g., conscientiousness, adaptability, work styles)	84.5%
Abilities (e.g., math, verbal, language)	81.6%
Leadership competencies	65.3%
Social skills (e.g., interpersonal skill, social perceptiveness)	59.6%
Motivation (e.g., achievement orientation)	57.7%
Administrative skills (e.g., planning, organizing)	53.8%
Knowledge (e.g., job-specific technical knowledge)	51.8%
Work values (e.g., autonomy)	48.9%
Experience (e.g., background)	22.5%
Interests	18.9%
Other	5.6%

Respondents = 755
Note: Respondents could select more than one answer

the individual's scores. Managers' implicit beliefs can inhibit their willingness to use test information in hiring (Highhouse, 2008), and some managers have explicit preferences for intuition-based hiring (Lodato, Highhouse, & Brooks, 2011). Providing hiring managers with some degree of control (e.g., you cannot hire a candidate with scores below a certain level and you are cautioned about hiring others in a "yellow" zone, but are free to choose those with a "green" test score) may lessen their resistance to additional structure in the hiring process. Considering ways to allow managers to feel their preference is met while simultaneously structuring elements of the process to ensure test information is appropriately weighed is an area in need of further research (Lievens & De Paepe, 2004).

Use of technology

Because the greatest changes in selection practice since the 1990s appear to be technology-linked, we focused much of our survey on questions on the use of technology in testing.

Assessment content

While the general trend is toward increased use of technology in the hiring process, there are differences across employers in the adoption of technology. Some methods of assessment were more likely to be computerized than paper and pencil (assessments of cognitive ability, language capability, personality [work styles], interests, integrity, and situational judgment) and others more likely to not be computerized (job knowledge test, simulation test [in-basket, role play]). Across the test types we asked about, an average of 14% of respondents indicated that their organizations test in *both* paper-and-pencil and computerized formats. Approximately 87% of respondents have considered or are currently considering using computerized tests in their organizations ($N = 542$).

Technology has been widely advocated as a means of expanding what is assessed and how it is assessed (e.g., new KSAs, new formats). As Table 8.4 indicates,

TABLE 8.4 Elements used in computerized testing

	Already use	Intend to use
Drag-and-drop items	46.3%	32.2%
Video/multimedia in test item content	44.2%	51.0%
Video/multimedia images in test instructions	41.7%	49.8%
Audio	30.4%	31.4%
Animation in test content	26.9%	32.9%
Interactive voice response	9.9%	25.5%
Avatars (computer-generated visual representation of the candidate)	8.1%	21.6%

Respondents = 283
Note: Respondents could select more than one answer

drag-and-drop items and video/multimedia are more commonly used elements in computerized testing than animation, interactive voice response, and avatars, despite how much the latter are touted as benefits of computerized assessments (Reynolds & Dickter, 2010; Scott & Lezotte, 2012).

Proctoring practices

Computerized tests can be administered in either a supervised or an unsupervised setting. Related to the latter, a major concern among organizational psychologists has been the use of unproctored tests (Tippins, 2009; Tippins et al., 2006). Among those whose companies use computerized testing, 40.2% ($N = 691$) indicated using unproctored testing for all their computerized testing, or using unsupervised testing depending on hiring process stage (23.6%) or geographic location of applicant/job (16.1%). A minority of respondents (20.1%) said that all computerized testing was supervised. As Tippins (2009) noted, "the UIT [unproctored Internet testing] train has left the station" (p. 4), and debate about the viability or ethicality of the practice needs to be replaced by research on how to improve practices. The primary reason driving decisions to administer computerized tests in unsupervised settings appears to be the desire to make the process convenient for applicants (65.9%; $N = 531$). Other frequently stated reasons are cost effectiveness (54.4%) and convenience for hiring managers (53.9%), easier assessment of a larger applicant pool (51.8%), and reduction in time-to-hire (51.8%). As this list shows, unproctored testing is adopted for efficiency reasons (see Scott & Lezotte, 2012); it is therefore incumbent upon psychologists to ensure that greater efficiency does not necessarily mean lower quality/effectiveness. This has been a particular concern of testing standards groups (see International Test Commission, 2006; Naglieri et al., 2004).

In response to calls for a better understanding of proctoring practices in employment testing (Arthur & Glaze, 2011; Drasgow, Nye, Guo, & Tay, 2009), we asked a number of more specific questions about how companies use unsupervised tests. As shown in Table 8.5, companies' practices of unsupervised testing vary somewhat by

TABLE 8.5 Use of unsupervised tests

	Unsupervised paper & pencil	Unsupervised computerized
Personality assessment (work styles)	40.2%	79.7%
Background data	49.4%	61.2%
Cognitive ability test	20.3%	59.8%
Interests assessment	36.7%	56.1%
Integrity test	33.3%	54.2%
Language capability test	26.4%	50.9%
Situational judgment test	23.7%	46.8%
Job knowledge test	25.8%	45.9%
Simulation test (in-basket, role play)	25.2%	40.5%

Respondents = 39–531
Note: Respondents could select more than one answer

type of test. Note that we asked about supervision for both paper-and-pencil and computerized tests. As Drasgow et al. (2009) have noted, it is wrong to automatically assume that proctoring occurs when testing is via paper and pencil, and our data support that. However, unsupervised testing is more likely when the tests are computerized.

Personality and background data assessments are most frequently administered unsupervised. Tests that evaluate candidates' cognitive ability, knowledge, and judgment are somewhat less frequently administered unsupervised but still used this way fairly often. Implications of administering cognitive tests, job knowledge tests, and other assessments on which a candidate could cheat (e.g., have a substitute take the test, use an advisor, share the test with others) unsupervised has been of greatest concern to researchers (Arthur & Glaze, 2011). These concerns were expressed by respondents in our study as well. Of those using *supervised* computerized testing ($N = 378$), 51.6% reported that the risk of cheating was too great and 36.5% reported concern over test content dissemination. Only 33.3% supervised because of concern over applicant comfort with technology and only 29.1% reported the Internet was not universally available for their applicant pool.

Table 8.6 shows that strategies for delivery of items are evolving. About 35% of respondents ($N = 666$) said their organizations use either adaptive computerized tests or randomly selected items from a larger pool (44% said they did not use adaptive tests and 20% said they did not know). Varying test content (e.g., using different items or different forms) is a relatively uncommon practice. About 54% of respondents indicated their companies use fixed tests. The promise of computerized testing is still to be delivered, as many organizations apparently simply have created page-turner versions of paper-and-pencil test items (Potosky & Bobko, 2004).

TABLE 8.6 Strategies used when administering unsupervised computerized tests

	Percentage of respondents
Use a fixed test that does not change	53.9%
Randomize order of items for each test administration	30.2%
Restrict when participants can take the computerized test (e.g., a specific date, time, place, etc.)	23.7%
Periodically refresh item content (i.e., replace items with similarly calibrated ones from an item bank, replace the entire test with an alternate version)	20.4%
Create a unique version of the test for each applicant based on responses to each item (computer adaptive testing)	17.6%
Create a unique version of the test for each applicant using randomly selected items from a large item bank	17.0%
Create a new version of the test for a job opening using randomly selected items from a large item bank	14.6%
Rotate among several different forms of the test across applicants	11.7%

Respondents = 460
Note: Respondents could select more than one answer

Security measures and data protection

We asked about companies' security measures to better understand the extent to which companies employ test administration practices that may minimize the chances of cheating and tests becoming compromised. The most frequently used security measure with unproctored computerized testing is adhering to time limits (see Table 8.7). Research indicates that administering speeded tests can help to minimize cheating, as time constraints limit opportunities for these behaviors (Arthur, Glaze, Villado, & Taylor, 2010). A substantial number of respondents (40%) also indicated that their companies use warnings, which have likewise been recommended in the research literature for minimizing intentional distortion (e.g., Hough, 1998). Although testing guidelines advocate the use of verification testing (i.e., administration of a proctored confirmation test to those initially assessed remotely to detect cheating; Naglieri et al., 2004; ITC, 2006), fewer than 20% of respondents indicated using verification testing; however, many companies may be using tests such as personality measures, where verification makes less sense. Finally, consistent with Arthur et al.'s (2010) recent observation, few companies seem to be using technological innovations for monitoring candidates (e.g., webcams, keystroke analyses). Of the technological tools we asked about, preventing backtracking and other computer applications from running were the most commonly used.

In addition to asking about security measures specific for unproctored computerized testing, we asked about security measures for paper-and-pencil testing as well as for supervised computerized testing. As Tables 8.8 and 8.9 indicate, the most frequently used security measure for both paper-and-pencil testing and supervised computerized testing is following test procedures and adhering to time limits for tests. Companies using paper-and-pencil tests seem least concerned with test materials going missing (only 31% count and keep track of test materials). In summary, Drasgow et al.'s (2009) assertion that test security is not necessarily strong for paper-and-pencil testing is supported by the survey results.

TABLE 8.7 Security measures used when administering unsupervised computerized tests

	Percentage of respondents
Strict time limits	59.3%
Use of warnings regarding cheating	40.0%
No backtracking	32.1%
Disabling other applications on the computer	19.5%
Use of supervised confirmation or verification testing	18.3%
Use of honesty certificates that require examinees to certify they will not cheat	13.6%
Use of webcams	6.7%
Use of keystroke analyses	4.7%
Other	7.7%

Respondents = 405
Note: Respondents could select more than one answer

TABLE 8.8 Security measures used when administering paper-and-pencil tests

	Percentage of respondents
Strictly follow test procedures and adhere to administration time limits	71.8%
Prohibit copying or reproducing test materials	59.8%
Allow access to tests only to personnel with a legitimate need	54.9%
Always use properly trained test administrators and proctors	53.1%
Never leave applicants unsupervised with access to secure test materials	49.6%
Provide testing accommodations only to those eligible to receive them	46.3%
Store test materials in a secure, locked area	44.1%
Count and keep track of the number of secure test materials	31.0%

Respondents = 510
Note: Respondents could select more than one answer

TABLE 8.9 Security measures used when administering supervised computerized tests

	Percentage of respondents
Strictly follow test procedures and adhere to administration time limits	65.9%
Password-protect test materials	57.7%
Always use properly trained test administrators and proctors	56.2%
Allow access to tests only to personnel with a legitimate need	55.1%
Prohibit copying or reproducing test materials	54.6%
Never leave applicants unsupervised with access to secure test materials	46.5%
None of the above/Other	3.1%

Respondents = 381
Note: Respondents could select more than one answer

Approximately half of the respondents believe that somewhere between 1 and 20% of applicants cheat or misrepresent themselves on their organizations' tests, regardless of the test format (paper and pencil, supervised computerized, unsupervised computerized; see Table 8.10). As Arthur and Glaze (2011) noted, the expectation is not that there is no cheating in proctored settings but that rates may increase in unproctored settings. Unsupervised computerized tests were associated with the highest uncertainty among respondents about the amount of cheating that happens, and this format is seen as presenting the most risk (only 9.3% of respondents thought applicants could not cheat).

Among those choosing to use unproctored computer tests, the risk that applicants may cheat and the uncertainty regarding the extent to which they actually do apparently does not outweigh the efficiency gained by administering computerized tests in an unsupervised setting (recall that efficiency considerations were the top drivers of the decision to adopt this method of testing). The majority of

TABLE 8.10 Beliefs about the percentage of applicants who engage in some form of cheating or misrepresentation on the organization's tests

	Paper-and-pencil tests	Supervised computerized tests	Unsupervised computerized tests
Do not know	24.6%	29.0%	35.1%
0% (Not possible for applicants to cheat)	16.4%	19.3%	9.3%
1–5%	25.5%	28.0%	31.4%
6–10%	14.9%	13.5%	12.3%
11–20%	10.2%	7.1%	7.3%
21–30%	6.9%	2.5%	3.7%
More than 30%	1.5%	0.5%	0.7%

Respondents = 393–549

respondents were willing to tolerate up to 20% of applicants cheating on an unsupervised computerized test (71.9% would not stop using the test for selection). Cheating on UITs may not be quite that high, however. For example, Arthur et al. (2009) estimate 7.7% of their sample cheated on a cognitive ability unproctored computerized test.

Interestingly, respondents actually indicated similar attitudes about cheating regardless of method of test administration. The majority of respondents were also willing to tolerate up to 20% of applicants cheating on a paper-and-pencil test (67.4% would not stop using) or a supervised computerized test (76.8% would not stop using) – compare to percentages cited above for unproctored computerized tests. However, Arthur and Glaze (2011) note, the real concern is not with the number of cheaters but with their distributional placement and relation to cut scores. That is, it matters less what total percent cheat and more what percentage of cheaters receive a passing score when they would not have otherwise or who end up ranking higher than honest test takers who they would not otherwise have surpassed. Further, the majority of respondents said that their organizations either never or very rarely had to disqualify applicants for cheating on paper-and-pencil tests (85%), supervised computerized tests (90%), or unsupervised computerized tests (93%).

The most common data protection strategy was allowing only relevant staff to access test data (93.1%; $N = 664–729$). Other strategies were to use firewalls and password protections (81.7%), to have physical security where data is stored (66.2%), to have regular data backups (65.8%), to ensure data is protected in electronic transit (e.g., by encryptions; 55.0%), and to have disaster recovery plans in place (37.8%). Respondents also seemed to be relatively less familiar with certain data protection strategies. For example, about 43% of respondents were not aware of whether their organizations have disaster recovery plans. This overall lack of attention to data protection is disconcerting, particularly given the European Union Privacy Directive (1998)[3] and the US Safe Harbor Provisions (2000), which attempt to set guidelines for the protection of personal data and test data (Reynolds & Dickter, 2010).

Test policies and practices

Researchers have been interested in the effects of test feedback (or lack thereof) on applicant perceptions (see London & McFarland, 2010, for summary of research). About half of the respondents (51.3%; $N = 745$) said their companies almost always or always provide applicants with feedback on test results. A minority (8.7%) of respondents indicated that their companies never provide feedback to applicants on test results. About 65% of respondents ($N = 676$) indicated that their companies explain to applicants how to interpret a test score and 50.7% at least provide applicants with their test scores, while 45.9% provide pass/fail feedback. Letting applicants know how they did relative to others is relatively uncommon (23.7%), as is providing other normative score information (33.1%). The most common reason for not providing feedback ($N = 59$) to applicants is time constraints (20.3%), followed by lack of benefit to the organization (18.6%) and concerns about legal liabilities (18.6%). Cost is typically not a factor (5.1%). Applicant complaints about not getting timely feedback are common (Gilliland, 1995), so one question is how quickly applicants receive this feedback. Another factor behind applicant concerns is that they may desire more specific feedback than is typically provided. Also, complaints about lack of feedback may be related more to interviewing than testing processes.

Retake policies have also been a focus of considerable research (Hausknecht, Halpert, Di Paolo, Moriarty, & Gerrard, 2007; Lievens, Buyse, & Sackett, 2005; Schleicher, van Iddekinge, Morgeson, & Campion, 2010), with studies indicating score increase upon retesting, which may affect validity in some cases. Surprisingly, 77% of respondents ($N = 739$) said their companies do not allow job applicants to retake assessments if they initially failed or were not hired. It may be that respondents interpreted our question to be about immediate retests rather than retesting after a set interval, which is part of many testing policies. Applicants are most often allowed to retake cognitive ability tests (58.2%; $N = 92$). Retesting is rare for integrity tests and interest assessments (less than 15% allow; $N = 22$). When companies allow retesting, applicants are more likely to take the same exact test than a different version of the test for assessments of background data, interests, personality, and situational judgment. Applicants are more likely to take a different version of the test than the same exact test for assessments of cognitive ability, integrity, and language capability. Applicants are about equally likely to take the same exact test or a different version of the test for job knowledge and simulation tests. While one can appreciate cost concerns of alternate forms (see, for example, Lievens & Sackett, 2007, on SJT alternate form development), fielding only one version has test security risks. Note, though, that few respondents actually answered the question about retesting opportunities (Ns from 17–81).

The majority (66%) of respondents ($N = 759$) said their organizations do not administer tests globally. The majority (71%) of respondents whose organizations do administer tests globally ($N = 250$) said they test in more than one language. It is typical for multinational testing practices ($N = 247$) to either be the same across

TABLE 8.11 Practices used when dealing with tests that are administered in multiple languages

	Percentage of respondents
Our assessment vendor handles all matters pertaining to translation	62.2%
Review by end users in countries of use	35.4%
Back translation procedures to ensure accuracy	29.3%
Development of separate norms for different country/language groups	29.3%
Revision beyond translation to accommodate cultural differences/nuances	24.4%
Psychometric assessments of measurement equivalence	21.3%
Separate validation studies for each translation	14.0%
Other	4.3%

Respondents = 164
Note: Respondents could select more than one answer

TABLE 8.12 Regularly monitored metrics

	Percentage of respondents
Job performance of those hired	70.6%
Attrition rates of those hired	45.3%
Opinions of key internal stakeholders on effectiveness of selection tools	41.7%
Process efficiency (e.g., cost pre-hire, time to hire)	39.0%
Views of applicants on our selection process	37.4%
Pass/fail rates	35.5%
Return on investment for testing (ROI)	19.2%
Other	2.7%

Respondents = 677
Note: Respondents could select more than one answer

countries (39.7%) or to include a combination of custom and standardized processes (39.3%), rather than use different processes across countries (21.1%). Most companies (62.2%) that administer tests in multiple languages let their assessment vendors handle matters pertaining to translation; indeed, in forecasting the future of selection, Ryan and Ployhart (2014) noted that the trend for outsourcing of selection tool development and research is likely to continue to grow. Table 8.11 details other practices when testing across languages; it is clear that not all recommended practices are being followed (International Test Commission, 2006).

Finally, we asked respondents about how they evaluated the effectiveness of testing programs. As Table 8.12 indicates, the most frequently monitored metric is job performance of those hired (70.6%). ROI for tests is calculated relatively infrequently (19.2%). Note that "monitoring" a metric does not necessarily mean that organizations are engaged in ongoing, rigorous validation studies.

Research implications

Throughout this chapter we have noted some of the practical implications of our findings, but there are also important implications for selection researchers. First, in relation to the practical implications, is the need for research on methods of "messaging" assessment practices so that they are more likely to be adopted. As noted earlier, researchers like Boudreau (2012) have suggested we retool in terms of how we try to communicate concepts like utility; further research in this area can only be helpful. The challenge for selection experts is how to improve the communication of this information so that it is readily available on a global basis to interested HR practitioners and managers and that it is in a format that is easily understood and used.

Second, research on the adoption of innovation and technology has been applied to some extent to selection contexts (König et al., 2010), but there is ample room for further theoretical development in this regard. Third, the security methods examined here were chosen based on what is considered good practice, but research as to the usefulness and effectiveness of their employment in deterring cheating is still limited.

Finally, in this paper we report findings on assessment use from a global sample. Research to tease apart what factors affect adoption, such as legal environment, unionization, country economic conditions, educational systems, and so forth, has not been particularly systematic, largely due to the challenges in obtaining adequate samples from different countries. It may behoove researchers to form consortia and to focus efforts on specific factors that vary globally as considerations in sampling, so as to better design studies that can adequately test the role of these factors in selection practice adoption.

Limitations

As with any effort, this survey was not without limitations. As noted earlier, we were challenged to identify appropriate respondents (HR managers and executives with responsibilities for selection programs), particularly in certain countries. This led us to use professional associations and web groups as a primary means of sourcing respondents, and it made response rates incalculable (i.e., we did not have access to total numbers of members, or total number of views of web pages). Further, those who do not test may be less likely to respond to such a survey. We were not able to access multiple respondents per organization to provide us with reliability information, although most questions were designed to be objective. Collecting data globally also presents challenges in that we did not have access to associations or contacts in certain locations, and we only possessed resources to have professional translations in 15 languages.

Summary recommendations

Based on the findings of this survey, we see a number of directions for organizational psychology research and practice:

1. Reasons for using or not using testing were tied to the value of testing, suggesting that continued work to document and especially to communicate the value of testing should be a focus of research and practice efforts. In particular, enhanced communication regarding the incremental validity of testing may be important to adoption decisions.
2. Companies have taken advantage of the availability of technology to move away from using a paper-and-pencil format for most types of tests. However, most do not seem to be using the capabilities provided by recent technological advancements to the extent possible, in that less than half of respondents indicated using various elements made feasible by computerized tests (e.g., video/multimedia, avatars, adaptive testing). Researchers and practitioners can focus efforts on enhancing these technological advances and promoting greater use.
3. Test security practices do not seem to be widely or fully employed for paper-and-pencil or supervised computerized testing, let alone for unproctored computerized tests. The value of a selection system can be completely degraded by poor security, so attention by practitioners to communicating the importance of security and data protection as well as attention to means of making security measures easy to implement may help. Development of alternate forms in cases where adaptive pools are not in use should also be a focus, given retesting policies. Note that this lack of attention to security may be due to beliefs that not many individuals cheat, willingness to tolerate a certain rate of cheating, and the rarity of detecting cheaters.
4. Global testing programs are likely to increase given the globalization of business, suggesting a need for greater attention to international testing standards. Many of the advocated practices for using testing worldwide did not appear to be followed.
5. Organizations increasingly track metrics that may be used to evaluate selection systems; further work to establish high-quality evaluation programs may even further support the value of test use in selection.

Notes

1. Analyses of the influence of cultural values on testing practices at a regional level are available from the first author on request.
2. Note that some respondents indicated more than one response for this question (e.g., some of the organization's tests were created externally while others were created collaboratively). Total N = 754.
3. The directive was published in 1995 but became effective in 1998.

References

Arthur, W., & Glaze, R.M. (2011). Cheating and response distortion on remotely delivered assessments. In N.T. Tippins & S. Adler (Eds.), *Technology-enhanced assessment of talent* (pp. 99–152). San Francisco: Jossey-Bass.

Arthur, W., Glaze, R.M., Villado, A.J., & Taylor, J.E. (2009). Unproctored Internet-based tests of cognitive ability and personality: Magnitude of cheating and response distortion. *Industrial and Organizational Psychology: Perspectives on Science and Practice, 2*, 39–45.

Arthur, W., Glaze, R.M., Villado, A.J., & Taylor, J.E. (2010). The magnitude and extent of cheating and response distortion effects on unproctored Internet-based tests of cognitive ability and personality. *International Journal of Selection and Assessment, 18*, 1–16.

Berry, C.M., Sackett, P.R., & Landers, R.N. (2007). Revisiting interview-cognitive ability relationships: Attending to specific range restriction mechanisms in meta-analysis. *Personnel Psychology, 60*, 837–874.

Boudreau, J.W. (2012). "Retooling" evidence-based staffing: Extending the validation paradigm using management mental models. In N. Schmitt (Ed.), *The Oxford handbook of personnel assessment and selection* (pp. 793–813). New York: Oxford University Press, Inc.

Conway, J.M., Jako, R.A., & Goodman, D.F. (1995). A meta-analysis of interrater and internal consistency reliability of selection interviews. *Journal of Applied Psychology, 80*(5), 565–579.

Drasgow, F., Nye, C.D., Guo, J., & Tay, L. (2009). Cheating on proctored tests: The other side of the unproctored debate. *Industrial and Organizational Psychology: Perspectives on Science and Practice, 2*(1), 46–48.

European Union Privacy Directive. (1998). Directive 95/46/EC of the European Parliament and of the Council of 24 October 1995 on the protection of individuals with regard to the processing of personal data and on the free movement of such data. Retrieved from http://eur-lex.europa.eu/legal-content/EN/TXT/?uri=CELEX:31995L0046

Gilliland, S.W. (1995). Fairness from the applicant's perspective: Reactions to employee selection procedures. *International Journal of Selection and Assessment, 3*(1), 11–19.

Hausknecht, J.P., Halpert, J.A., Di Paolo, N.T., Moriarty, N.T., & Gerrard, M.O. (2007). Retesting in selection: A meta-analysis of practice effects for tests of cognitive ability. *Journal of Applied Psychology, 92*(2), 373–385.

Highhouse, S. (2008). Stubborn reliance on intuition and subjectivity in employee selection. *Industrial and Organizational Psychology: Perspectives on Science and Practice, 1*(3), 333–342.

Hough, L.M. (1998). Effects of intentional distortion in personality measurement and evaluation of suggested palliative. *Human Performance, 11*, 209–244.

House, R.J., Hanges, P.J., Javidan, M., Dorfman, P.W., & Gupta, V. (2004). *Culture, leadership, and organizations: The GLOBE study of 62 societies*. Thousand Oaks, CA: Sage.

Huffcutt, A.I., Conway, J.M., Roth, P.L., & Stone, N.J. (2001). Identification and meta-analytic assessment of psychological constructs measured in employment interviews. *Journal of Applied Psychology, 86*, 897–913.

International Test Commission (2006). International guidelines on computer-based and Internet-delivered testing. *International Journal of Testing, 6*(2), 143–171.

Klehe, U.-C. (2004). Choosing how to choose: Institutional pressures affecting the adoption of personnel selection procedures. *International Journal of Selection and Assessment, 12*, 327–342.

König, C.J., Klehe, U.-C., Berchtold, M., & Kleinmann, M. (2010). Reasons for being selective when choosing personnel selection procedures. *International Journal of Selection and Assessment, 18*, 17–26.

Lievens, F., Buyse, T., & Sackett, P.R. (2005). Retest effects in operational selection settings: Development and test of a framework. *Personnel Psychology, 58*, 981–1007.

Lievens, F., & De Paepe, A. (2004). An empirical investigation of interviewer-related factors that discourage the use of high structure interviews. *Journal of Organizational Behavior, 25*, 29–46.

Lievens, F., & Sackett, P.R. (2007). Situational judgment tests in high-stakes settings: Issues and strategies with generating alternative forms. *Journal of Applied Psychology, 92*, 1043–1055.

Lodato, M.A., Highhouse, S., & Brooks, M.E. (2011). Predicting professional preferences for intuition-based hiring. *Journal of Managerial Psychology, 26*, 352–365.

London, M., & McFarland L.A. (2010). Assessment feedback. In J.L. Farr & N.T. Tippins (Eds.), *Handbook of employee selection* (pp. 417–438). New York: Routledge.

Naglieri, J.A., Drasgow, F., Schmit, M., Handler, L., Prifitera, A., Margolis, A., et al. (2004). Psychological testing on the Internet: New problems, old issues. *American Psychologist, 59*(3), 150–162.

Potosky, D., & Bobko, P. (2004). Selection testing via the Internet: Practical considerations and exploratory empirical findings. *Personnel Psychology, 57*, 1003–1034.

Reynolds, D.H., & Dickter, D.N. (2010). Technology and employee selection. In J.L. Farr & N.T. Tippins (Eds.), *Handbook of employee selection* (pp. 171–194). New York: Routledge.

Rothstein, M.G., & Goffin, R.D. (2006). The use of personality measures in personnel selection: What does current research support? *Human Resource Management Review, 16*(2), 155–180.

Ryan, A.M., McFarland, L., Baron, H., & Page, R. (1999). An international look at selection practices: Nation and culture as explanations for variability in practice. *Personnel Psychology, 52*(2), 359–391.

Ryan, A.M., & Ployhart, R.E. (2014). A century of selection. *Annual Review of Psychology, 65*(1), 693–717.

Schleicher, D.J., van Iddekinge, C.H., Morgeson, F.P., & Campion, M.A. (2010). If at first you don't succeed, try, try again: Understanding race, age, and gender differences in retesting score improvement. *Journal of Applied Psychology, 95*, 603–617.

Scott, J.C., & Lezotte, D.V. (2012). Web-based assessments. In N. Schmitt (Ed.), *The Oxford handbook of personnel assessment and selection* (pp. 485–516). New York: Oxford University Press.

Terpstra, D., & Rozell, E. (1997). Why some potentially effective staffing practices are seldom used. *Public Personnel Management, 26*, 483–495.

Tippins, N.T. (2009). Internet alternatives to traditional proctored testing: Where are we now? *Industrial and Organizational Psychology: Perspectives on Science and Practice, 2*, 2–10.

Tippins, N.T., Beaty, J., Drasgow, F., Gibson, W.M., Pearlman, K., Segall, D.O., & Shepherd, W. (2006). Unproctored Internet testing in employment settings. *Personnel Psychology, 59*, 189–225.

US Safe Harbor Provisions. (2000). Retrieved from http://www.export.gov/safeharbor/eu/eg_main_018365.asp

Whetzel, D.L., McDaniel, M.A., & Pollack, J.M. (2012). Work simulations. In M.A. Wilson, W. Bennett, S.G. Gibson, & G.M. Alliger (Eds.), *The handbook of work analysis: Methods, systems, applications and science of work measurement in organizations* (pp. 401–418). New York: Routledge.

Wilk, S.L., & Cappelli, P. (2003). Understanding the determinants of employer use of selection methods. *Personnel Psychology, 56*, 103–124.

9

BEYOND VALIDITY

Shedding light on the social situation in employment interviews

Klaus G. Melchers

UNIVERSITÄT ULM, GERMANY

Pia V. Ingold

UNIVERSITÄT ZÜRICH, SWITZERLAND

Annika Wilhelmy

UNIVERSITÄT ZÜRICH, SWITZERLAND

Martin Kleinmann

UNIVERSITÄT ZÜRICH, SWITZERLAND

For a long time, interview research mainly focused on ways to improve the psychometric properties of employment interviews. Thus, a large body of research has been accumulated concerning ways to improve the reliability and validity of interviews (Campion, Palmer, & Campion, 1997; Levashina, Hartwell, Morgeson, & Campion, in press; Macan, 2009). However, even structured interviews are not verbally administered selection tests but represent a very specific social interaction for both the interviewee and the interviewer (Anderson, 1992). Accordingly, recent definitions of employment interviews do not only capture the issue of determining "the qualifications of a given individual for a particular open position" (Huffcutt &

Author Note

Preparation of this chapter was partially supported by a grant from the Swiss National Science Foundation (Schweizerischer Nationalfonds; Grant 100014-124449).

Correspondence concerning this chapter should be addressed to Klaus G. Melchers, Institut für Psychologie und Pädagogik, Universität Ulm, Albert-Einstein-Allee 41, D-89069 Ulm, Germany, e-mail: klaus.melchers@uni-ulm.de

Youngcourt, 2007, p. 182) but also see the "interpersonal interaction and communication between the interviewer and interviewee" (Levashina et al., in press, p. 6) as a cornerstone of the interview. In line with this, over recent years research has given more weight to aspects related to the social situation, variables that influence the perception of this situation, and ways in which the two parties involved try to handle it.

A better understanding of the social situation in employment interviews and of effects related to it is important because this situation influences the behavior of both interviewers and interviewees. For example, the way interviewers present themselves and their organization may influence applicants' intentions towards the company, such as their willingness to accept a job offer or to recommend the company to others. Similarly, the way that interviewees try to present themselves in a favorable manner may affect evaluations of their interview performance and, as a consequence, also the prediction of future job performance on the basis of these evaluations. The potential effect on the criterion-related validity of interview ratings is also a reason for attempts to detect and reduce self-presentation behavior in the interview. However, to date only limited evidence is available on whether it is possible to detect the different kinds of self-presentation behavior that can be used in interviews and whether this behavior is in fact harmful for interview validity.

The aim of the present chapter is to give an overview of research that sheds light on this specific situation that has a social interaction at its core (Bangerter, Roulin, & König, 2012; Barrick, Swider, & Stewart, 2010). First, we will focus on the relevant theoretical background. We will then consider the interviewees' perspective and will review research that deals with the question of what interviewees do to influence the interview situation. Thus, we will discuss the role of interviewees' perception of the situation they face during an interview and the self-presentation behavior they use. Then, we will deal with the interviewers' perspective and will consider what interviewers do to create a specific impression and the potential effects of their impression management behavior. Finally, we will also look at technology-mediated interviews (e.g., telephone or videoconference interviews) and will discuss to what degree technology might influence the social situation and the interaction between interviewers and interviewees, as well as interviewee reactions to the interview.

Theoretical background

Signaling processes in the employment interview

As noted above, it has been more and more emphasized in the recent interview literature that employment interviews constitute a highly complex and competitive social endeavor (Dipboye, Macan, & Shahani-Denning, 2012). The interview involves selection decisions that are crucial for both interviewees and interviewers: a selection decision about interviewees (i.e., whether they get a job offer) and a selection decision about organizations (i.e., whether the interviewee decides to accept a potential job offer). Therefore, scholars have recognized that both interviewees and interviewers adapt their behaviors in a way that helps them reach their respective objectives (Macan, 2009).

As suggested by Bangerter et al. (2012), signaling theory (Connelly, Certo, Ireland, & Reutzel, 2011; Spence, 1973) is of great value in improving our understanding of why interviewees and interviewers try to adapt their behaviors to influence each other. Bangerter et al. (2012) have recently applied the principles of signaling theory to personnel selection while considering not only the interviewees' but also the interviewers' perspective. Their framework implies several important issues of how interviewees and interviewers interact and will therefore serve as a general theoretical underpinning for this chapter.

Signaling theory is helpful for describing and explaining behavior when two parties have access to dissimilar information, such as interviewers and interviewees (Spence, 1973). In more abstract words, signaling theory suggests that each social situation involves signaling systems consisting of a sender, a receiver, and a signal that is associated to a characteristic of the sender that is unobservable in that situation (Connelly et al., 2011). In the interview context, interviewees have information that is not directly available to interviewers, such as information about their skills and abilities, past failures, or personal goals (Bangerter et al., 2012). Similarly, interviewers are likely to have knowledge that is not available to interviewees, such as information about the job, the organization, and future colleagues. Consequently, both interviewees and interviewers are faced with incomplete information and thus use any information that is available in the interview process. For example, interviewees may interpret interviewers' behavior as signaling whether the company as a whole is a good place to work, and interviewers may interpret interviewees' behavior as signaling whether the interviewee provides a good fit to the job (Connelly et al., 2011).

In addition, to reduce information asymmetry, interviewees and interviewers are likely to communicate positive qualities to the other party when this other party lacks information (Bangerter et al., 2012). Whereas interviewees send signals to interviewers to increase their chances of being hired, interviewers are likely to send signals to interviewees to enhance the chances that interviewees accept a potential job offer. These signaling behaviors have mainly been studied in terms of self-presentation such as impression management (IM), which Schlenker (1980) defined as attempts to control information during a social interaction in order to favorably influence the impressions formed by others.

Furthermore, the employment interview can be seen as a network of dynamic, adaptive relationships between interviewees and interviewers (Bangerter et al., 2012); both interviewees and interviewers try to detect what their interaction partner is interested in and then to adapt their behaviors in order to send the right signals. In turn, the other party may counteradapt to these adaptations by changing the way signals are interpreted and used for making decisions. For example, interviewees may place less value on interviewers' signals of innovativeness if they find out that the reason why interviewers present their organizations as being innovative is their belief that most interviewees like innovativeness (Bangerter et al., 2012). Over time, these cycles of adaptation and counteradaptation between interviewees and interviewers determine which signals are sent and the stability of these signals (i.e., whether a certain signal is regularly used in employment interviews).

Models of interviewee performance

While signaling theory integrates both interviewees' and interviewers' perspectives, some recent models have focused on factors that influence interviewees' behavior and performance in interviews (Huffcutt, Van Iddekinge, & Roth, 2011; Levashina & Campion, 2006; Marcus, 2009). Among them, Huffcutt et al.'s (2011) model of interviewee performance supplements signaling theory as it also adopts the perspective of the interview as an interaction of the interviewer and the interviewee. Furthermore, this model also elaborates on the nomological network of interviewees' performance and stresses the importance of social effectiveness (e.g., self-presentation) and the influence of the situation (e.g., the level of structure or the interview medium).

In this recent model of interviewee performance, Huffcutt et al. (2011) define interviewee performance as what interviewees say and do, hence including the content of their answers, how they deliver these answers (e.g., pitch), and their nonverbal behavior (e.g., smiling). Furthermore, they highlight that individual differences between interviewees as well as interview design factors can influence interviewees' performance and, hence, interviewer ratings. According to this model, there are several factors that may affect interviewee performance: interviewer-interviewee dynamics, state variables like interviewee anxiety or motivation, supplemental preparation, interview design consideration, and interviewees' general attributes and core qualifications (Huffcutt et al., 2011).

With regard to the interpersonal nature of the interview, interviewer-interviewee dynamics are particularly important. These dynamics relate directly to the capability to deal with the interpersonal nature of the interview and to self-presentation in the interview. As such, interviewer-interviewee dynamics encompass interviewer's personality on the one hand and interviewees' social effectiveness including impression management and other forms such as self-monitoring on the other hand.

Interview design considerations relate to factors that determine the interview format – that is, the structure and the medium through which it is delivered (e.g., telephone, videoconference, or face-to-face). The underlying notion is that these two factors can influence interviewee performance. For instance, when participating in a highly structured interview, interviewees' amount of impression management might be limited, or when participating in a telephone interview, for example, they have fewer cues about the interviewers' reactions at hand than in a face-to-face interview.

What do interviewees do?

In the employment interview, applicants face a social situation that is ambiguous in many ways but in which they are motivated to make a good impression to increase their chances to get a job offer. Accordingly, the following sections deal with aspects like interviewees' perception of the situational requirements that they face in an interview, the strategies they use to make a good impression, factors that influence their IM attempts, consequences of IM, and finally the issue of faking in employment interviews.

Interviewees' perception of situational requirements in employment interviews

A first step for successful self-presentation in an interview lies in perceiving and understanding the social situation faced in this interview. This perception will then influence interviewees' behavior and the way in which they answer the different questions (Kleinmann et al., 2011; Melchers et al., 2009). Imagine, for example, a question that is asked during an interview that is intended to measure cooperation. An interviewee who identifies cooperation as the targeted dimension will respond differently than an interviewee who incorrectly assumes that the question is to assess leadership or assertiveness. The former interviewee will be more likely to present himself or herself in a cooperative manner than the other interviewee.

Furthermore, as a consequence of showing more relevant behavior and providing answers related to the targeted performance criteria (i.e., the targeted interview dimensions), it becomes more likely that interviewees who are better at identifying relevant performance criteria also receive more positive evaluations in an interview. In line with this, previous research found differences between interviewees concerning their ability to identify the criteria (ATIC) that were targeted in employment interviews (Melchers et al., 2009). This means that some interviewees were generally better than others in discerning and correctly understanding which criteria were targeted by the different questions in structured interviews. Furthermore, previous evidence also confirmed that interviewees who were better at identifying the targeted interview dimensions also received better performance evaluations by the interviewers (Ingold, Kleinmann, König, Melchers, & Van Iddekinge, in press; Melchers et al., 2009; Oostrom, Melchers, Ingold, & Kleinmann, 2013).

An important question related to these findings is whether tailoring one's answers to the discerned interview dimensions reflects a kind of misrepresentation on the side of the interviewee. The fear concerning this question is that potential misrepresentation might impair the quality of employment decisions based on the interview and thus the criterion-related validity of the interview. However, in contrast to such a fear, it has been argued that the ability to identify criteria does not reflect a factor that impairs criterion-related validity but that this ability represents an important aspect of social effectiveness that even contributes to the interview's good criterion-related validity (Kleinmann et al., 2011; Melchers et al., 2009).

The reason why applicants' ability to identify criteria in interviews (as well as in other selection procedures like assessment centers, e.g., Jansen et al., 2013) is relevant for predicting job performance is that the ability to understand social situations and to adapt one's behavior to better deal with the discerned performance criteria is important not only during selection situations but also later on the job (Kleinmann et al., 2011). Both during selection situations and during many situations encountered on the job, the actual requirements and the necessary steps of action that are required to successfully handle the respective situations are not entirely obvious. Thus, individuals who are better at reading social situations have an advantage in both kinds of situations. In line with this, there is evidence that the ability to identify criteria in an interview also predicts performance in other situations. Specifically, König et al. (2007) and Oostrom et al. (2013) found that scores for this ability from an interview significantly predicted performance in an assessment center and a job simulation, respectively.

In further support of the argument that a better understanding of the requirements faced in an interview represents a relevant social skill, there are also several findings with regard to other ability and social skill measures. First, the ability to identify criteria has consistently been found to correlate with cognitive ability (e.g., Melchers et al., 2009). Second, there is evidence that this ability mediates the relationship between cognitive ability and interview performance (Kleinmann et al., 2011). This finding supports earlier suggestions by Huffcutt, Roth, and McDaniel (1996), who suggested that the reason why cognitive ability and interview performance are correlated is that interviewees with higher cognitive ability are better at thinking through questions and therefore give more appropriate answers. And third, there is evidence that the ability to identify evaluation criteria is correlated to scores from a video-based social judgment test (Kleinmann, 1997) as well as with self-ratings of participants' political skill (Jansen, Melchers, & Kleinmann, 2011).

Interviewees' self-presentation behavior in employment interviews

Besides perceiving and understanding the social situation faced in the interview, interviewees can employ self-presentation behaviors to create a positive impression. Our focus in the present chapter is on verbal impression management tactics (e.g., flattering the interviewer or self-promoting one's accomplishments) to obtain higher ratings. However, we would like to mention that interviewees also use other behaviors like dressing up for the interview (e.g., by wearing suits) and nonverbal IM tactics (e.g., eye contact or smiling) to send out positive signals to interviewers. Furthermore, former research has found that especially professional appearance has a strong and positive relationship with interview scores (Barrick, Shaffer, & DeGrassi, 2009)

As noted above, impression management refers to attempts to influence the image interviewees convey in social interactions (Schlenker, 1980). Traditionally, selection research on verbal impression management distinguishes assertive tactics that aim at actively conveying a positive image and defensive tactics that aim at protecting or repairing threatened images by apologizing for, excusing, or justifying one's actions or attributes. Assertive tactics can further be differentiated into self-focused tactics and other-focused tactics (Kacmar, Delery, & Ferris, 1992). Self-focused tactics (alternatively termed *self-promotion*) are employed to convey a positive image of oneself, and other-focused tactics (alternatively termed *ingratiation*) aim at arousing sympathy in others or to make others feel better by flattering them (see, for example, Stevens & Kristof, 1995, or Van Iddekinge, McFarland, & Raymark, 2007, for details on further subcategories).

In addition, a category of deceptive IM tactics has also been introduced more recently (Levashina & Campion, 2007) that refers to IM that deviates from the truth (e.g., by telling about invented achievements). This category supplements the established IM tactics and has been contrasted with honest IM tactics (e.g., telling about real achievements). Deceptive IM includes slight image creation (embellishing prior experiences or skills) and extensive image creation (intentionally inventing experiences or skills) as self-focused tactics, deceptive ingratiation (dishonest praise of others) as other-focused tactics, and image protection (intentionally disguising relevant information) as a defensive tactic (Levashina & Campion, 2007; Roulin, Bangerter, & Levashina, in press).

Concerning the frequency of honest IM tactics, previous research has revealed that nearly all interviewees employ IM tactics in interviews and that this is true for structured as well as for unstructured interviews (Levashina et al., in press). For instance, in a field study including behavioral description interviews and also less structured interviews, all interviewees used self-focused tactics, about half of the interviewees used other-focused tactics, and one fifth used defensive tactics (Stevens & Kristof, 1995). Similarly, dishonest IM tactics were found to be frequently used by undergraduates, with more than 90% reported using this form of IM in mock interviews as well as in recent employment interviews when they applied for jobs or internships (Levashina & Campion, 2007). Additionally, 44% of the applicants surveyed by Roulin et al. (in press) reported employing slight image creation, and 21% reported employing extensive image creation.

What effects does interviewees' IM have on their interview performance?

Given that interviewees aim to maximize their chances of receiving a job offer by using IM in the interview, one of the key questions is to what degree IM tactics influence interviewers' performance ratings. Another question is whether the degree of interview structure also affects the relation of IM and interview performance. This might be the case, because structure might affect interviewees' opportunity to influence ratings such that interview structure lowers the impact of IM (e.g., as argued by Barrick et al., 2009).

Meta-analytic results help to answer these two questions. Across different interview types, IM is indeed moderately related to interview performance. This relationship is stronger for unstructured interviews than for highly structured interviews (Barrick et al., 2009). Furthermore, concerning the effects of the different IM tactics, meta-analytic results from Barrick et al. (2009) and Levashina et al. (in press) indicate that self-focused tactics have the largest impact on interviewer ratings, followed by other-focused tactics and defensive IM.

Which factors influence interviewees' impression management?

Through the lens of Huffcutt et al.'s model (2011), interviewees' dispositions and situational characteristics are supposed to influence IM. Furthermore, research on antecedents of IM has provided initial insights and hints at an interaction of dispositional and situational influences.

Concerning individual differences, Machiavellianism was positively related to all four deceptive IM categories reported by interviewees who participated in mock interviews in an applicant condition (i.e., when imagining applying for a job), whereas self-monitoring related positively to all deceptive IM categories except for extensive image creation (Levashina & Campion, 2007).

With regard to situational influences, a few studies (e.g., Peeters & Lievens, 2006; Van Iddekinge et al., 2007) investigated how the format of structured interviews, or more specifically, the use of situational versus past-behavior interviews, influences interviewees' use of IM tactics. Recently, Levashina et al. (in press) meta-analyzed these results and found that self-promotion and defensive tactics were used more often in past-behavior interviews, whereas other-focused IM tactics were used more often in situational interviews. A possible reason for this is that the respective interview format provides cues that influence the prevalence of different IM tactics (e.g., Peeters & Lievens, 2006). Hence, when interview questions request interviewees to focus on the past, it is more probable to defend personal actions and results and to self-promote to appear competent for the job. Questions that focus on hypothetical situations, in turn, provide different cues and may request interviewees to show their fit to the organization and the interviewers as representatives of the organization, so that other-focused tactics may occur more often. Concerning the generalizability of the results, however, one should note that only the results for self-focused IM had a confidence interval that did not contain zero.

Further insights on the interplay of dispositions and situations are provided by two studies that compared interviews conducted under applicant and honest conditions (Peeters & Lievens, 2006; Van Iddekinge et al., 2007) and that found that situational characteristics affect the relation of interviewees' dispositions and IM. In the study by Van Iddekinge et al. (2007), vulnerability predicted other-focused IM tactics and altruism predicted defensive tactics only in the honest condition that did not elicit impression motivation, but not in the applicant condition. Similarly, results from Peeters and Lievens (2006) showed that self-esteem was only related to self-focused IM in the honest condition but not in the applicant condition. In contrast to this, emotional stability or its facet vulnerability were only related to defensive tactics in the applicant condition in both studies.

Taken together, the findings reviewed here indicate that interviewees' individual differences can influence interviewees' self-presentation and that the format of structured interviews affects the use of self-promotion, but that it is also necessary to consider the joint influence of individual differences and situational influences on these relationships. Thus, future research needs to dig deeper into the interaction of dispositions and situational influences on IM to increase our understanding of why some dispositions relate to IM in honest conditions, whereas others relate to IM in applicant conditions.

Faking in employment interviews

Faking has mainly been investigated in the domain of personality testing (for reviews, see, e.g., Goffin & Boyd, 2009, or Tett et al., 2006), but applicants might also try to fake in other selection procedures. Thus, an obvious question concerns the issue of whether interviewees can fake in employment interviews – and if so, to what degree they do so. However, the answer to this question is difficult, because different people consider very different things as faking.

On the one hand, some researchers would consider anything as faking that goes beyond applicants' typical behavior (i.e., behavior that is representative of how they act in their everyday life, e.g., Levin & Zickar, 2002). Thus, they would even consider the honest IM tactics mentioned above as faking. On the other hand, it has been suggested to only consider those behaviors as faking that are deceptive or that represent conscious distortions of the truth (Levashina & Campion, 2006). Accordingly, the latter view would only consider behaviors that correspond to Levashina and Campion's (2007) category of deceptive IM as faking because, as noted above, only this category refers to IM that deviates from the truth.

Independent of a specific definition of faking, we want to briefly review evidence related to three questions that are relevant in the present context. First, to what degree can interviewees present themselves more positively in comparison to when they answer in a way that describes their typical behavior? Second, to what degree do these attempts to create a positive image include deviations from the truth, and how serious are those deviations? And third, are interviewers able to detect faking in employment interviews?

Concerning the first question, the limited available evidence suggests that it is more difficult to intentionally create a positive impression in an interview than in a personality test. For example, in a study with mock interviews and student participants, Van Iddekinge, Raymark, and Roth (2005) found that mean differences between an honest condition and an applicant condition were much smaller in comparison to a personality test that targeted the same dimensions (on average, effect sizes were less than a third in the interview compared to the personality test). Furthermore, in a similar study other researchers even failed to find significant differences between honest and applicant conditions (Allen, Facteau, & Facteau, 2004).

Concerning the second question, to what degree interviewees' answers deviate from the truth, several studies investigated the prevalence of things that interviewees do that might be considered as faking (e.g., Donovan, Dwight, & Hurtz, 2003; Jansen, König, Stadelmann, & Kleinmann, 2012). These studies found that many or even most applicants stress or overemphasize their positive attributes and de-emphasize potential negative attributes. However, only a few applicants claimed to have knowledge or experiences that they actually did not have or outright fabricated information about themselves. Thus, telling real lies does not seem to be as common as attempts to stretch the truth. Furthermore, the available evidence also suggests that the kind of self-presentation behavior that most applicants show is considered less severe by interviewers or is even explicitly expected by them in application contexts (Donovan et al., 2003; Jansen et al., 2012).

Finally, concerning the question of whether interviewers are able to detect interviewees' attempts at honest or dishonest IM, the available evidence suggests that this only seems possible to a rather limited degree. In a recent study, for example, Roulin et al. (in press) found little convergence between interviewer perceptions of several different types of IM and interviewees' self-reports of those behaviors. Specifically, although interviewers' perceptions of interviewees' use of several IM tactics were related to their evaluations of interviewees' performance, these perceptions were not related significantly to interviewees' reports of their actual IM. And even though more evidence is needed with regard to interviewers' ability to detect actual lies in employment interviews, these first results from Roulin et al. do not justify too much optimism in this regard. Finally, this skeptical view is also supported by meta-analytic evidence from studies that compared differences in people's actual behavior when they are lying versus when they are telling the truth (DePaulo et al., 2003). This evidence shows that most of the potential "cues to deception" did not differ between liars and truth tellers and that effect sizes were rather small for those cues for which systematic differences were found.

After having reviewed evidence concerning these three questions, another obvious question concerns the issue of whether faking affects the psychometric properties of employment interviews. However, we are not aware of any published research that has investigated actual consequences for the interview's criterion-related validity. Thus, even though faking in interviews is a topic that has attracted considerable recent attention, it is unclear to date to what degree it impairs the psychometric properties of these interviews.

What do interviewers do?

As noted above, the interview is characterized by social interaction and communication in which the interviewer also plays an important role (Dipboye et al., 2012). Below, we will review research on interviewers' aims in the interview to gain insights into the diverse intentions they may have. Furthermore, we will illustrate findings on what interviewers aim to signal during the interview, and what they actually do to create their intended impressions. Finally, we will review past research on the impact of interviewer IM on organizations' recruitment success and on psychometric properties of the interview.

Traditionally, the interviewer has mainly been seen as someone who is collecting and integrating information and making decisions. However, to remain viable in today's highly competitive business environments, it is crucial for organizations to attract, select, and retain top-talent applicants (Berkson, Ferris, & Harris, 2002; Dipboye & Johnson, 2013). Hence, interviewers usually have to balance their goal of selection (i.e., assessing applicants' job qualifications) with their goal of recruitment (i.e., attracting the most qualified applicants). This recruitment goal usually involves considering the interviewees' perspective, particularly the impressions interviewees form during the interview process, and how these impressions can be influenced (Dipboye et al., 2012).

As a consequence, recent theoretical models that focus on what interviewees say and do (Huffcutt et al., 2011) also consider the role of interviewer-interviewee dynamics such as positive reinforcements interviewers may provide to interviewees. While we still know surprisingly little about how interviewers intentionally send signals to interviewees in terms of IM (Koslowsky & Pindek, 2011), it is widely recognized that the way interviewers are perceived exerts a strong influence on the impressions interviewees form during the interview (Huffcutt & Culbertson, 2011). For example, meta-analytic findings show that applicants' impressions of organizational representatives such as interviewers strongly influence their subsequent steps in the selection process (Chapman, Uggerslev, Carroll, Piasentin, & Jones, 2005).

What interviewers intend to signal in employment interviews

More recently, studies have provided some insights into what impressions interviewers want to create when they interact with interviewees. Specifically, it has been found that interviewers usually intend to establish rapport with interviewees through friendly conversation and by making them feel comfortable (Chapman et al., 2005). In addition, interviewers often have the goal of creating an impression of objectivity and fairness (Derous, 2007; Lewis & Sherman, 2003). Furthermore, a qualitative field study (Wilhelmy, Kleinmann, Melchers, & König, 2012) revealed a wide range of different kinds of impressions that interviewers want to create that go beyond rapport building and objectivity. For instance, interviewers may also aim to signal authenticity, professionalism, and dominance.

Additionally, different aims or foci of interviewer IM should be taken into consideration. For example, Wilhelmy et al. (2012) found that interviewers try to influence applicant impressions not only regarding impressions of themselves (e.g., signaling their competence as an interviewer) but also regarding impressions of the organization as a whole (e.g., signaling their organization's staff-supportive organizational culture). Moreover, interviewers were found to apply IM not only to increase their organization's recruitment success but also to increase their own career opportunities (e.g., by enhancing their reputation).

Interviewers' impression management behaviors in employment interviews

In addition to recent findings on what interviewers intend to signal, there have been some insights into what behaviors interviewers actually use to create favorable impressions on interviewees. For example, interviewers may make interviewees wait longer to signal their higher status (Greenberg, 1989) or may harshly evaluate interviewees to demonstrate their competence (Amabile, 1983). Moreover, qualitative results (Wilhelmy et al., 2012) revealed that interviewers apply a broad range of additional signaling behaviors. Similar to interviewee IM, interviewers may use the content of what they say to influence interviewee impressions, such as self-promotion (e.g., talking about their own accomplishments) and ingratiation (e.g., paying compliments to interviewees). Furthermore, interviewers were found to modulate their voice to enhance interviewee impressions, such as speaking in an empathetic way.

In addition, interviewers were found to regularly apply nonverbal IM, such as smiling and nodding. Interestingly, in contrast to interviewee IM, a lack of nonverbal signals was also found to be intentionally used by interviewers, such as putting on a poker face (Wilhelmy et al., 2012). Additionally, these qualitative findings revealed that interviewers use status and aesthetic cues to create favorable impressions, for example, by adapting one's clothing or choosing a certain room for the interview. Another kind of interviewer IM refers to organizing the interview, such as timeliness of the interview start, or providing personal feedback to interviewees (Wilhelmy et al., 2012). Taken together, this evidence indicates that while some interviewer IM behaviors seem quite similar to strategies applied by interviewees, there is also a broad range of differences because interviewers tend to have multiple aims and thus may have diverse IM intentions.

What effects does interviewers' IM have on recruiting outcomes and interview validity?

In the interview literature, it has been stressed repeatedly that interviewer IM behaviors are a key factor for attracting applicants and thus for ensuring an organization's success (e.g., Macan, 2009; Rosenfeld, 1997). To examine interviewer IM effectiveness, Stevens, Mitchell, and Tripp (1990) conducted a laboratory study using videos of three different interviewers. Each of the interviewers applied a different IM strategy to present the same hypothetical study program. The authors found that interviewers using other-enhancement (i.e., statements flattering the interviewee) and opinion conformity (i.e., statements that were in line with attitudes of a hypothetical interviewee) were well-liked and perceived as being convincing, while interviewers using self-promotion (i.e., statements highlighting the program's prestige) were perceived as being less likeable and less convincing. However, only interviewer opinion conformity was found to have strong effects on participants' decision on which study program they would choose.

Furthermore, regarding the relative effectiveness of different IM strategies, Stevens et al. (1990) found an influence of the order in which these were used. Self-promotion was most persuasive when seen first, while opinion conformity was most persuasive when seen second or last. Other-enhancement was equally persuasive in all presentation orders. A potential reason for these order effects may be based on interviewees' attributions. For example, interviewees may interpret interviewer self-promotion as arrogant behavior, especially in contrast to other-enhancement, which is usually seen as "buttering the ego" (Stevens et al., 1990, p. 1087). Taken together, these findings suggest that interviewer IM can influence applicant attraction but that the context in which interviewer IM is used may play a major role.

Despite these positive effects on organizations' recruiting success, interviewer IM may negatively influence psychometric properties of the employment interview, such as interview reliability and validity. The main idea underlying this fear is that similar to interviewee IM, interviewer IM may be considered as a potential source of measurement bias (e.g., Anderson, 1992). For example, interviewers' behaviors and judgments may vary from interview to interview depending on perceived applicant fit and sympathy. In addition, interviewers' effort to create favorable impressions might require part of the interviewers' cognitive resources and thus prevent them from accurately assessing interviewees' performance (Dipboye et al., 2012).

A recent study by Marr and Cable (2013) provided initial evidence for these propositions. In a laboratory study, interviewers' selling orientation, which refers to their motivational inclination to attract an interviewee during the employment interview, was found to decrease accuracy of their judgments about interviewees' core self-evaluations. Furthermore, in a second study from a field context, Marr and Cable found that interviewers' selling orientation reduced the interviews' predictive validity. When selling orientation was low, interviewers' judgments more accurately predicted which interviewees would be highest regarding performance, organizational citizenship behavior, and fit when they started their job. In contrast, when selling orientation was high, interviewers' judgments no longer predicted these outcomes. Together, these results indicate that despite positive effects on recruiting success, interviewer IM may hinder the accuracy and predictive validity of employment interviews if performance evaluations happen at the same time as when interviewers strongly try to sell the job and the organization.

Does it matter whether interviews are conducted face-to-face?

If one considers Huffcutt et al.'s (2011) interview performance model, then using technology-mediated interviews is important in the present context because how an interview is administered is a design factor that can change the social situation and how the two parties involved in it interpret it and try to influence it. Traditionally, employment interviews represented a face-to-face interaction between an interviewee and an interviewer. However, with the advancement of telecommunication technology, interviews are no longer restricted to a face-to-face setting but might also be conducted via telephone or videoconference systems (e.g., Chapman, Uggerslev, & Webster, 2003). Furthermore, it is even possible to conduct an interview without an actual interviewer by using interactive voice responding technology, in which interviewees self-administer a screening interview via the phone and answer the questions either verbally or by pressing the indicated button on the phone (e.g., Bauer, Truxillo, Paronto, Weekley, & Campion, 2004).

Two important theories have been developed to account for preferences and suitability of different media that can be used to communicate with others: social presence theory (Short, Williams, & Christie, 1976) and media richness theory (Daft & Lengel, 1984). Regarding the former of these theories, social presence refers to the degree to which a communication medium conveys the actual presence of a communication partner. The perception of others as being present depends not only on the words that are exchanged between communication partners but also on various paraverbal and nonverbal cues. Similar to social presence theory, media richness theory assumes that media differ in the way in which they convey certain types of information, so that they provide cues that help to make information less ambiguous and to establish a common frame of reference between the communication partners.

Both theories consider face-to-face interactions as preferable to technology-mediated interactions in situations in which it is important to support social presence and to transmit rich information. The reason for this is that some of the cues that are available in face-to-face interactions (e.g., nonverbal cues like gestures or paraverbal cues like intonation) are no longer available in technology-mediated interactions, or their transmission and perception are impaired by the technology that is used.

In line with these theories, interviewees have a clear preference for face-to-face interviews in comparison to technology-mediated interviews and, in addition, face-to-face interviews are perceived as more fair (Chapman et al., 2003; Sears, Zhang, Wiesner, Hackett, & Yuan, 2013). Furthermore, there is also evidence that interviewees in technology-mediated interviews achieve lower performance ratings than in face-to-face interviews (Melchers, Petrig, & Sauer, 2013; Sears et al., 2013).

Concerning interviewee perceptions of technology-mediated interviews, evidence suggests that these interviews are perceived as offering less opportunity to show one's qualifications or even as impairing interpersonal treatment of the interviewee and two-way communication (Bauer et al., 2004; Sears et al., 2013). Nonetheless, the reasons why interviewees often receive lower performance evaluations in technology-mediated interviews are still relatively unclear.

However, given the lower media richness of these interviews, it seems likely that conducting interviews via telephone or videoconference systems can impair interviewees' interpretation of the social situation. Furthermore, the technological "barrier" (Short et al., 1976) between interviewers and interviewees also restricts or even prevents the use of certain IM strategies. Professional appearance, for example, is not relevant in telephone interviews, and physical closeness is not relevant in technology-mediated interviews.

Concluding remarks and lines for future research

Taken together, the research reviewed confirms that interviewees' perception of the interview situation matter, so that interviewees who are better at discerning the targeted evaluation criteria also perform better in the interview. Similarly, there is clear evidence that interviewees' use of IM tactics (particularly of self-focused tactics like self-promotion) is related to their performance, and that this is especially true for unstructured interviews. In addition, there is some initial evidence that interviewers also use various IM tactics. Furthermore, several studies found that interviewees can deliberately try to present an overly positive or even untrue image of themselves and lie. However, the extent of faking seems to be considerably smaller than in personality tests – and usually, interviewers are hardly able to detect faking. Finally, technology changes the interview situation so that interviewees experience some impairments of the interview situation and often perform worse in comparison to face-to-face interviews. However, it is unclear to what degree technological constraints that impede interviewees' self-presentation behavior contribute to this.

As noted in the introduction, much of the reviewed research was motivated by fears that attempts to present oneself in a favorable way might impair the psychometric properties of employment interviews. However, hardly any research directly speaks to these concerns – and in contrast to these concerns, the limited available evidence suggests that interviewees' correct understanding of the interview situation is not only paralleled by better interview ratings but also by better performance in work-related situations. Nevertheless, more research is needed that also considers questions such as how interviewees' IM is related to job performance or whether faking endangers the criterion-related validity of employment interviews.

Finally, in contrast to interviewee IM, research on interviewer IM still is in its infancy. Even though it is well known that impressions of organizational representatives play an important role for interviewees' perceptions of the selection process and the organization as well as for their subsequent behavior, little is known about the effects of specific IM tactics of the interviewers on interviewees as well as on the psychometric properties of the interview.

Given that the reviewed research has illustrated many fruitful insights on how interviewees and interviewers try to deal with the social situation that they face in interviews, we believe that further insights can be gained from following this line of research. Therefore, we advocate further research that continues examining the interactive nature of employment interviews to foster our understanding of the factors that are important in these interviews.

References

Allen, T.D., Facteau, J.D., & Facteau, C.L. (2004). Structured interviewing for OCB: Construct validity, faking, and the effects of question type. *Human Performance, 17*, 1–24.

Amabile, T.M. (1983). Brilliant but cruel: Perceptions of negative evaluators. *Journal of Experimental Social Psychology, 19*, 146–156.

Anderson, N.R. (1992). Eight decades of employment interview research: A retrospective meta-review and prospective commentary. *European Work and Organizational Psychologist, 2*, 1–32.

Bangerter, A., Roulin, N., & König, C.J. (2012). Personnel selection as a signaling game. *Journal of Applied Psychology, 94*, 719–738.

Barrick, M.R., Shaffer, J.A., & DeGrassi, S.W. (2009). What you see may not be what you get: Relationships among self-presentation tactics and ratings of interview and job performance. *Journal of Applied Psychology, 94*, 1394–1411.

Barrick, M.R., Swider, B.W., & Stewart, G.L. (2010). Initial evaluations in the interview: Relationships with subsequent interviewer evaluations and employment offers. *Journal of Applied Psychology, 95*, 1163–1172.

Bauer, T.N., Truxillo, D.M., Paronto, M.E., Weekley, J.A., & Campion, M.A. (2004). Applicant reactions to different selection technology: Face-to-face, interactive voice response, and computer-assisted telephone screening interviews. *International Journal of Selection and Assessment, 12*, 135–148.

Berkson, H.M., Ferris, G.R., & Harris, M.M. (2002). The recruitment interview process: Persuasion and organization reputation promotion in competitive labor markets. *Human Resource Management Review, 12*, 359–375.

Campion, M.A., Palmer, D.K., & Campion, J.E. (1997). A review of structure in the selection interview. *Personnel Psychology, 50*, 655–702.

Chapman, D.S., Uggerslev, K.L., Carroll, S.A., Piasentin, K.A., & Jones, D.A. (2005). Applicant attraction to organizations and job choice: A meta-analytic review of the correlates of recruiting outcomes. *Journal of Applied Psychology, 90*, 928–944.

Chapman, D.S., Uggerslev, K.L., & Webster, J. (2003). Applicant reactions to face-to-face and technology-mediated interviews: A field investigation. *Journal of Applied Psychology, 88*, 944–953.

Connelly, B.L., Certo, S.T., Ireland, R.D., & Reutzel, C.R. (2011). Signaling theory: A review and assessment. *Journal of Management, 37*, 39–67.

Daft, R.L., & Lengel, R.H. (1984). Information richness: A new approach to managerial behavior and organizational design. *Research in Organizational Behavior, 6*, 191–233.

DePaulo, B.M., Lindsay, J.J., Malone, B.E., Muhlenbruck, L., Charlton, K., & Cooper, H. (2003). Cues to deception. *Psychological Bulletin, 129*, 74–118.

Derous, E. (2007). Investigating personnel selection from a counseling perspective: Do applicants' and recruiters' perceptions correspond? *Journal of Employment Counseling, 44*, 60–72.

Dipboye, R.L., & Johnson, S.K. (2013). Understanding and improving employee selection interviews. In K.F. Geisinger (Ed.), *APA handbook of testing and assessment in psychology* (pp. 479–499). Washington, DC: American Psychological Association.

Dipboye, R.L., Macan, T.H., & Shahani-Denning, C. (2012). The selection interview from the interviewer and applicant perspectives: Can't have one without the other. In N. Schmitt (Ed.), *The Oxford handbook of personnel assessment and selection* (pp. 323–352). New York: Oxford University Press.

Donovan, J.J., Dwight, S.A., & Hurtz, G.M. (2003). An assessment of the prevalence, severity, and verifiability of entry-level applicant faking using the randomized response technique. *Human Performance, 16*, 81–106.

Goffin, R.D., & Boyd, A.C. (2009). Faking and personality assessment in personnel selection: Advancing models of faking. *Canadian Psychology/Psychologie Canadienne, 50*, 151–160.

Greenberg, J. (1989). The organizational waiting game: Delay as a status-asserting or status-neutralizing tactic. *Basic and Applied Social Psychology, 10*, 13–26.

Huffcutt, A.I., & Culbertson, S.S. (2011). Interviews. In S. Zedeck (Ed.), *APA handbook of industrial and organizational psychology* (pp. 185–203). Washington, DC: American Psychological Association.

Huffcutt, A.I., Roth, P.L., & McDaniel, M.A. (1996). A meta-analytic investigation of cognitive ability in employment interview evaluations: Moderating characteristics and implications for incremental validity. *Journal of Applied Psychology, 81*, 459–473.

Huffcutt, A.I., Van Iddekinge, C.H., & Roth, P.L. (2011). Understanding applicant behavior in employment interviews: A theoretical model of interviewee performance. *Human Resource Management Review, 21*, 353–367.

Huffcutt, A.I., & Youngcourt, S.S. (2007). Employment interviews. In D.L. Whetzel & G.R. Wheaton (Eds.), *Applied measurement: Industrial psychology in human resources management* (pp. 181–199). New York: Taylor & Francis.

Ingold, P. V., Kleinmann, M., König, C.J., Melchers, K.G., & Van Iddekinge, C.H. (in press). Why do situational interviews predict job performance: The role of interviewees' ability to identify criteria. *Journal of Business and Psychology*.

Jansen, A., König, C.J., Stadelmann, E.H., & Kleinmann, M. (2012). Applicants' self-presentational behavior: What do recruiters expect and what do they get? *Journal of Personnel Psychology, 11*, 77–85.

Jansen, A., Melchers, K.G., & Kleinmann, M. (2011, September). Beeinflusst soziale Kompetenz die Leistung im Assessment Center? Ein Vergleich verschiedener Maße sozialer Kompetenz [Does social skill influence assessment center performance? A comparison of different social skill measures]. Paper presented at the 7th conference of the German Society for Work, Organizational, and Business Psychology, Rostock, Germany.

Jansen, A., Melchers, K.G., Lievens, F., Kleinmann, M., Brändli, M., Fraefel, L., & König, C.J. (2013). Situation assessment as an ignored factor in the behavioral consistency paradigm underlying the validity of personnel selection procedures. *Journal of Applied Psychology, 98*, 326–341.

Kacmar, M.K., Delery, J.E., & Ferris, G.R. (1992). Differential effectiveness of applicant impression management tactics on employment interview decisions. *Journal of Applied Social Psychology, 22*, 1250–1272.

Kleinmann, M. (1997). Transparenz der Anforderungsdimensionen: Ein Moderator der Konstrukt- und Kriteriumsvalidität des Assessment-Centers [Transparency of the requirement dimensions: A moderator of assessment centers' construct and criterion validity]. *Zeitschrift für Arbeits- und Organisationspsychologie, 41*, 171–181.

Kleinmann, M., Ingold, P.V., Lievens, F., König, C.J., Melchers, K.G., & Jansen, A. (2011). A different look at why selection procedures work: The role of candidates' ability to identify criteria. *Organizational Psychology Review, 1*, 128–146.

König, C.J., Melchers, K.G., Richter, G.M., Kleinmann, M., & Klehe, U.-C. (2007). The ability to identify criteria in nontransparent selection procedures: Evidence from an assessment center and a structured interview. *International Journal of Selection and Assessment, 15*, 283–292.

Koslowsky, M., & Pindek, S. (2011). Impression management: Influencing perceptions of self. In D. Chadee (Ed.), *Theories in social psychology* (pp. 280–296). Chichester, UK: Wiley-Blackwell.

Levashina, J., & Campion, M.A. (2006). A model of faking likelihood in the employment interview. *International Journal of Selection and Assessment, 14*, 299–316.

Levashina, J., & Campion, M.A. (2007). Measuring faking in the employment interview: Development and validation of an interview faking behavior scale. *Journal of Applied Psychology, 92*, 1638–1656.

Levashina, J., Hartwell, C.J., Morgeson, F.P., & Campion, M.A. (in press). The structured employment interview: Narrative and quantitative review of the research literature. *Personnel Psychology*.

Levin, R.A., & Zickar, M.J. (2002). Investigating self-presentation, lies, and bullshit: Understanding faking and its effects on selection decisions using theory, field research, and simulation. In J.M. Brett & F. Drasgow (Eds.), *The psychology of work: Theoretically based empirical research* (pp. 253–276). Mahwah, NJ: Erlbaum.

Lewis, A.C., & Sherman, S.J. (2003). Hiring you makes me look bad: Social-identity based reversals of the ingroup favoritism effect. *Organizational Behavior and Human Decision Processes, 90*, 262–276.

Macan, T. (2009). The employment interview: A review of current studies and directions for future research. *Human Resource Management Review, 19*, 203–218.

Marcus, B. (2009). 'Faking' from the applicant's perspective: A theory of self-presentation in personnel selection settings. *International Journal of Selection and Assessment, 17*, 417–430.

Marr, J.C., & Cable, D.M. (2013). Do interviewers sell themselves short? The effects of selling orientation on interviewers' judgements. *Academy of Management Journal.* Advance online publication.

Melchers, K.G., Klehe, U.-C., Richter, G.M., Kleinmann, M., König, C.J., & Lievens, F. (2009). "I know what you want to know": The impact of interviewees' ability to identify criteria on interview performance and construct-related validity. *Human Performance, 22*, 355–374.

Melchers, K.G., Petrig, A., & Sauer, J. (2013). *A comparison of conventional and technology-mediated selection interviews with regard to interviewees' performance, affective reactions, and stress.* Manuscript in preparation.

Oostrom, J.K., Melchers, K.G., Ingold, P.V., & Kleinmann, M. (2013, May). *Exploring two explanations for the validity of situational interviews: Saying how you would behave or knowing how you should behave.* Paper presented at the 16th congress of the European Association of Work and Organizational Psychology, Münster, Germany.

Peeters, H., & Lievens, F. (2006). Verbal and nonverbal impression management tactics in behavior description and situational interviews. *International Journal of Selection and Assessment, 14*, 206–222.

Rosenfeld, P. (1997). Impression management, fairness, and the employment interview. *Journal of Business Ethics, 16*, 801–808.

Roulin, N., Bangerter, A., & Levashina, J. (in press). Interviewers' perceptions of impression management in employment interviews. *Journal of Managerial Psychology.*

Schlenker, B.R. (1980). *Impression management.* Monterey, CA: Brooks/Cole.

Sears, G.J., Zhang, H., Wiesner, W.H., Hackett, R.D., & Yuan, Y. (2013). A comparative assessment of videoconference and face-to-face employment interviews. *Management Decision, 51*, 1733–1752.

Short, J., Williams, E., & Christie, B. (1976). *The social psychology of telecommunications.* London: Wiley.

Spence, M. (1973). Job market signaling. *Quarterly Journal of Economics, 87*, 355–374.

Stevens, C.K., & Kristof, A. (1995). Making the right impression: A field study of applicant impression management during job interviews. *Journal of Applied Psychology, 80*, 587–606.

Stevens, C.K., Mitchell, T.R., & Tripp, T.M. (1990). Order of presentation and verbal recruitment strategy effectiveness. *Journal of Applied Social Psychology, 20*, 1076–1092.

Tett, R.P., Anderson, M.G., Ho, C.-L., Yang, T.S., Huang, L., & Hanvongse, A. (2006). Seven nested questions about faking on personality tests: An overview and interactionist model of item-level response distortion. In R.L. Griffith & M.H. Peterson (Eds.), *A closer examination of applicant faking behavior* (pp. 43–83). Greenwich, CT: Information Age Publishing.

Van Iddekinge, C.H., McFarland, L.A., & Raymark, P.H. (2007). Antecedents of impression management use and effectiveness in a structured interview. *Journal of Management, 33*, 752–773.

Van Iddekinge, C.H., Raymark, P.H., & Roth, P.L. (2005). Assessing personality with a structured employment interview: Construct-related validity and susceptibility to response inflation. *Journal of Applied Psychology, 90*, 536–552.

Wilhelmy, A., Kleinmann, M., Melchers, K.G., & König, C.J. (2012, April). *How interviewers try to make favorable impressions: A qualitative study.* Paper presented at the 27th annual conference of the Society for Industrial and Organizational Psychology, San Diego, CA.

10
SITUATIONAL JUDGMENT TESTING
A review and some new developments

Janneke K. Oostrom

VU UNIVERSITY AMSTERDAM, THE NETHERLANDS

Britt De Soete

GHENT UNIVERSITY, BELGIUM

Filip Lievens

GHENT UNIVERSITY, BELGIUM

Situational judgment tests (SJTs) have been used for employee selection for about 80 years (e.g., McDaniel, Morgeson, Finnegan, Campion, & Braverman, 2001; Moss, 1926). A typical SJT presents test takers with job-related dilemmas that require relevant knowledge, skills, abilities, or other characteristics to solve. The dilemmas are followed by alternative courses of action from which the test taker chooses the most appropriate response. SJTs were originally designed to sample behaviors (Motowidlo, Dunnette, & Carter, 1990). Samples or simulations are based on the assumption that one can predict how well an individual will perform on the job based on a simulation of the job (McDaniel & Nguyen, 2001). As a measurement method, SJTs can be used to assess a variety of constructs (Arthur & Villado, 2008). Christian, Edwards, and Bradley (2010) showed in a review of SJT research that a substantial number of SJTs (33%) measure heterogeneous composites. In some cases SJTs have been developed to assess specific constructs, most often leadership skills (38%) or interpersonal skills (13%).

This chapter will describe the traditional way of developing SJTs, followed by a literature review concerning how design considerations impact the quality of the SJT. First, we update the earlier reviews of Whetzel and McDaniel (2009) and Lievens, Peeters, and Schollaert (2008). Then, we focus on several promising new developments regarding the way SJTs are designed and scored.

SJT development

In this section, we describe current practices regarding the development of SJT items. Each item consists of a job-related dilemma, from here on named *item stem*, and several possible means of handling the dilemma, from here on named *response options*.

Development of the items

There are two popular methods for developing SJT items: critical incident and theory-based methods (Weekley, Ployhart, & Holtz, 2006). The critical incident method (Flanagan, 1954) is the most common approach used to identify the content of the items (Motowidlo, Hanson, & Crafts, 1997). The critical incidents can be collected from archival records or from interviews with subject matter experts (SMEs), for example, managers, incumbents, clients, or other key stakeholders, following a format known as the antecedent-behavior-consequence (A-B-C) method (Weekley et al., 2006). The antecedents, or situational descriptors of the context leading up to the incident, are used to develop the item stem while the subsequent behavior described is used in the development of one or more of the response options. Although the critical incident approach is time-consuming and expensive, the realism of the items that are generated using this approach is likely to be high. Kanning, Grewe, Hollenberg, and Hadouch (2006) provide an example of how critical incident interviews can be used to develop an SJT for police officers. Hunter (2003) provides an example of how archival records (i.e., a review of accident causal factors and anecdotes) can be used to develop an SJT for aviation pilots.

The second approach used to identify the content of the items is to use an underlying model (e.g., competencies identified via a job analysis, a theoretical model) and write items that reflect the dimensions of the model. If SMEs are not used to write the items, they should at least be used to review them for realism. Along these lines, Mumford, Van Iddekinge, Morgeson, and Campion (2008) provide an example of using an underlying model, in this case a team role typology, to develop an SJT measuring knowledge of team roles. Using an underlying model ensures the representativeness and job-relatedness of the SJT. However, a limitation of this approach is the lack of theory about work situations (Weekley et al., 2006).

In most cases, the items are presented by text (McDaniel & Nguyen, 2001), but it is also possible to use short video clips (Drasgow, Olson-Buchanan, & Moberg, 1999; Weekley & Jones, 1997, 1999). Apart from the higher development costs, the use of video clips has several advantages compared with texts. First, using video clips, richer information can be presented in the same time span because the test taker receives visual as well as auditory information (Paivio, 1986). Second, the use of video clips leads to a higher fidelity of the SJT items. The items become more realistic, making it easier for the test takers to imagine that they are actually part of the situational dilemma (Motowidlo et al., 1990). Third, the use of video clips has the advantage that test takers are not required to read lengthy texts (Chan & Schmitt, 1997).

Response instructions

After developing the SJT items, the response instructions have to be determined. There are two types of response instructions that can be used: knowledge-based and behavioral tendency instructions (McDaniel & Nguyen, 2001). Knowledge-based response instructions, also known as 'should-do' response instructions, ask the test taker to identify the best or correct course of action in the given situation. Behavioral tendency response instructions, also known as 'would-do' response instructions, ask the test taker to express how he or she would likely behave in the given situation (McDaniel, Hartman, & Whetzel, & Grubb, 2007). The two instruction types relate to the distinction between typical and maximal performance (Cronbach, 1984). Maximal performance tests assess test takers' performance when doing their best and are generally used to make inferences about ability. Typical performance tests assess how test takers typically behave and are generally used to make inferences about personality, attitudes, and other non-cognitive aspects. SJTs with knowledge response instructions are maximal performance tests, as test takers make judgments about what constitutes effective performance. SJTs with behavioral tendency response instructions are typical performance tests, as test takers report how they typically behave (McDaniel et al., 2007).

Scoring methods

A final aspect to consider when developing SJTs is how to score test takers' answers. At least three different methods for determining the effectiveness of the response options have been explored in the literature, that is, expert-based, empirical-based, and theory-based methods. Note that it is also possible to combine some of these methods. In that case, a hybrid scoring method is used.

The most common scoring approach in the SJT literature is asking SMEs to make judgments concerning the effectiveness of the response options (e.g., Lievens et al., 2008; McDaniel & Nguyen, 2001). These judgments are pooled subsequently either using consensus or actuarial methods (McDaniel & Nguyen, 2001). Although the results with the expert-based scoring method are generally positive (e.g., McDaniel et al., 2007; Krokos, Meade, Cantwell, Pond, & Wilson, 2004), this approach has several drawbacks (Lievens, 2000). When SJTs are scored by experts, the test taker's score represents the level of agreement with the judgments of the SMEs and therefore is dependent on the unique perspectives of the SME group (Krokos et al., 2004). It is likely that different groups of SMEs derive different keys. A final drawback is that it can be difficult to gain agreement among SMEs regarding the effectiveness of the response alternatives (McHenry & Schmitt, 1994).

There are two different empirical-based scoring methods, namely external and internal. When SJTs are externally scored, they usually are administered to a large pilot sample (Lievens et al., 2008). Based on the correlation with a criterion measure, items are selected and weighted. The crucial issue in external scoring is the quality of the criterion. If the criterion is deficient, contaminated, or biased, empirical keys will reflect these problems in the scoring structure (Mumford & Owens, 1987). External scoring approaches are rarely used for SJTs. Dalessio (1994) presents one of the few examples of an empirical scoring method for an SJT to predict turnover among insurance agents. The internal approach requires test items being scored in terms of their interrelationships. Factor analytic procedures are used to create subscales, which may then be combined for prediction in a multiple regression (Schoenfeldt & Mendoza, 1994). One of the advantages of this scoring approach is that the items can be scored and weighted taking account of their relationship with the other items and that the number of items can be reduced. A drawback is that the factors may be difficult to interpret, especially when heterogeneous item pools are used (Lievens, 2000). We were able to trace only one study on SJTs in which an internal scoring approach is used, namely the study of Lievens (2000), who developed and applied an empirically based scoring procedure based on a multiple correspondence analysis on an SJT for sales performance. Although empirical-based scoring methods often have high validity (e.g., Bergman, Drasgow, Donovan, Henning, & Juraska, 2006), the method is criticized for being atheoretical. Furthermore, the method is questioned regarding its generalizability and stability (Mumford & Owens, 1987), and capitalization on chance (Bergman et al., 2006).

The third and least frequently used method of developing scoring keys is to rely on an underlying model. This scoring method is often used when the response options are already constructed to reflect a theoretical model. Bergman et al. (2006) describe an SJT in which the response options reflect three graduated levels of delegation of decision-making to the team and that used Vroom's contingency model to score test takers' answers (Vroom & Jago, 1978). Theory-based scoring methods are more likely to generalize. Yet, the crucial issue in external scoring is the quality of the theory, which might be flawed or fundamentally incorrect (Bergman et al., 2006).

SJT characteristics and their impact on selection test criteria

As described above, many choices have to be made when developing SJTs. It is important to know how these design considerations impact the quality of the SJT as a tool in selecting new employees. In this section, we describe how these design considerations affect six important selection test criteria.

Reliability

Regarding SJTs, the most widely used measure of reliability is the internal consistency reliability as indexed by coefficient alpha. However, estimating the internal consistency of SJT scores is often problematic and not very relevant, because most SJTs – specifically those SJTs that are developed using the critical incident method – tend to assess multiple constructs (McDaniel & Whetzel, 2005). As a result, over the years many researchers have suggested that test-retest reliability is a better estimate of SJT score reliability (e.g., McDaniel et al., 2007; Motowidlo et al., 1990).

Ployhart, Campion, and MacKenzie (2012) have conducted a meta-analysis on SJT reliability coefficients and found a mean test-retest reliability of .61. However, they were able to trace only eight studies in which the rest-retest reliability coefficient was mentioned. Ployhart and Ehrhart (2003), who compared one SJT with six different response instructions, found significant differences in test-retest reliability coefficients; behavioral tendency response instructions showed higher test-retest reliabilities than knowledge-based response instructions. However, these results should be interpreted with caution, as the analyses were based on small samples ranging from 21 to 30.

SJTs that are developed based on an underlying theory are expected to show higher internal consistency, as the items are more likely to load highly on one or more factors (Ployhart et al., 2012). Yet, no systematic research exists wherein development procedures or different scoring methods are compared in terms of reliability.

Construct-related validity

The construct-related validity of SJTs remains hard to pin down. According to Stemler and Sternberg (2006), SJTs measure practical intelligence, which is the ability to adapt to, shape, and select everyday environments. However, most researchers argue that SJT performance can be determined by a number of constructs such as cognitive ability, personality, and job experience (Weekley & Jones, 1999). For SJTs that are developed based on an underlying theory, it should evidently be clearer which constructs they are measuring. However, most SJTs in which the item stems and/or response options reflect different dimensions failed to provide reliable subscores reflecting these dimensions (e.g., Weekley et al., 2006).

Almost all construct-related validity evidence until now has been restricted to paper-and-pencil SJTs. The test medium is expected to affect the construct-related validity (McDaniel, Whetzel, Hartman, Nguyen, & Grubb, 2006). For example, video-based SJTs are expected to reduce the cognitive load of an SJT primarily by reducing the reading demands. Chan and Schmitt (1997) demonstrated that reading comprehension correlated positively with performance on a paper-and-pencil SJT but was nearly uncorrelated with performance on a video-based version of the same SJT. Similarly, Lievens and Sackett (2006) found that cognitive ability correlated positively with performance on a paper-and-pencil SJT but not with performance on a video-based version of the same SJT.

The response instruction has also been found to affect the SJT's construct validity. The meta-analysis of McDaniel et al. (2007) showed that SJT scores with knowledge-based response instructions correlate more highly with cognitive ability scores than SJTs with behavioral tendency response instructions, whereas SJT scores with behavioral tendency response instructions correlate more highly with personality ratings. This is in line with the notion that SJTs with knowledge-based response instructions tap more into maximal performance and SJTs with behavioral tendency response instructions tap more into typical performance (McDaniel et al., 2007). Test developers should, therefore, choose the type of instructions on the basis of the type of performance they wish to emphasize in their assessment (Whetzel & McDaniel, 2009).

Criterion-related validity

In general, the literature has found SJT scores to have good predictive validities (e.g., Christian et al., 2010). McDaniel et al. (2007) demonstrated in their meta-analysis that SJT scores have an average observed validity of .20 and have incremental validity over cognitive ability scores and Big Five personality ratings. There is no systematic research in which the design procedures (critical incident and theory-based methods) are compared. Yet the effects of the other design features on SJT criterion-related validity have been examined.

Christian et al. (2010) meta-analytically showed that video-based SJTs have higher validity than paper-and-pencil SJTs for predicting interpersonal skills. That is, video-based SJT scores of interpersonal skills had an average validity of .47, which was significantly higher than the average validity of .27 for paper-and-pencil SJT scores of interpersonal skills.

The meta-analysis of McDaniel et al. (2007) showed that response instructions had little moderating effect on criterion-related validity. Note that most studies included in these meta-analyses are based on incumbent samples. More recently, Lievens, Sackett, and Buyse (2009) conducted a study on the moderating effect of response instructions on criterion-related validity in a large-scale high-stakes selection context. Their results corroborated the findings of McDaniel et al. (2007); no moderating effect of response instructions on criterion-related validity was found.

Several studies have shown that empirical-based scoring methods and expert-based scoring methods have similar levels of validity (e.g., Bergman et al., 2006; MacLane, Barton, Holloway-Lundy, & Nickles, 2001; Weekley & Jones, 1999). Criterion-related validity results regarding the theory-based scoring method are inconsistent (e.g., Bergman et al., 2006; Olson-Buchanan et al., 1998). Clearly more research is needed to better understand when theory-based scoring methods work best.

McDaniel, Psotka, Legree, Yost, and Weekley (2011) describe two adjustments to common scoring approaches that improve the criterion-related validity of the SJT. The first adjustment – which is only applicable to SJTs that use Likert scales – is to standardize scores using a within-person z transformation, so that all test takers have the same mean and SD across items. This transformation removes information related to elevation (i.e., the mean of the items for a test taker) and scatter (i.e., the magnitude of a test taker's score deviations from his or her own mean). Elevation and scatter are a source of systematic error, as they often reflect response tendencies, such as a preference for using extreme ends of the scale. McDaniel et al. (2011) demonstrated that controlling for elevation and scatter resulted in substantial improvements to item validity. The second adjustment is to drop response options with midrange means, because these response options tend to provide little information on whether the test taker is able to identify (in)effective behavior. McDaniel et al. showed that dropping midrange items permits the SJT to be shortened without harming validity.

Ethnic score differences

SJTs appear to display smaller ethnic score differences than cognitive ability tests, which makes them an attractive selection tool. Whetzel, McDaniel, and Nguyen (2008) reported in their meta-analysis a Black-White score difference of 0.38 SD

and a Hispanic-White score difference of 0.24 *SD*, in favor of Whites. Research on ethnic SJT score differences in Europe revealed comparable findings, with ethnic minorities obtaining systematically somewhat lower scores than majority test takers ($d = 0.38$; De Meijer, 2008).

Research on ethnic score differences on selection tools has repeatedly shown that the instrument's cognitive loading constitutes one of the most important drivers of ethnic score differences (e.g., Bobko, Roth, & Buster, 2005; Dean, Bobko, & Roth, 2008). In this context, SJTs with a higher cognitive loading have been found to display larger ethnic score differences than SJTs with a lower cognitive loading (Roth, Bobko, & Buster, 2013; Whetzel et al., 2008). A promising strategy to reduce ethnic score difference on SJTs is by using video-based items instead of paper-and-pencil items, as this results in lower reading demands and therefore a lower cognitive loading (Chan & Schmitt, 1997; Lievens & Sackett, 2006). Along these lines, Chan and Schmitt (1997) found that video-based SJTs displayed significantly smaller ethnic score differences than content-wise identical paper-and-pencil SJTs ($d = 0.21$ versus $d = 0.95$). Personality loading has also been found to influence the magnitude of ethnic score differences. Black-White score differences demonstrated to be larger when the SJT is characterized by a lower emotional stability loading, whereas Hispanic-White score differences tend to increase with lower agreeableness and conscientiousness loadings (Whetzel et al., 2008).

The type of response instructions has been found to influence the size of ethnic score differences (Nguyen & McDaniel, 2003; Whetzel et al., 2008). Whetzel et al. (2008) showed that SJTs with knowledge-based instructions consistently display larger differences than SJTs with behavioral tendency instructions for Black-White, Hispanic-White, and Asian-White score comparisons. This finding can in most cases be attributed to the larger cognitive loading of knowledge-based response instructions (Nguyen & McDaniel, 2003).

Finally, the scoring method has proven to influence ethnic score differences. As mentioned above, to increase the criterion-related validity of SJTs with Likert scales, McDaniel et al. (2011) suggested to control for elevation and scatter by using a within-person z transformation. An additional benefit of this adjustment is that score differences arising as a result of Black-White discrepancies in extreme responding are reduced. In a first study, Black-White ethnic score differences decreased from $d = 0.43$ to $d = 0.29$. A second study yielded similar results, with d decreasing from 0.56 to 0.36.

The effect of the development procedure, more specifically the influence of the cultural (dis)similarity of the SMEs involved in SJT developing and scoring, on the magnitude of ethnic score differences is still unknown. Additionally, as most studies on ethnic score differences are performed in a US context, systematic research incorporating other ethnic minority groups than Blacks and Hispanics is rather limited.

Fakability

Faking on a selection test can be defined as applicants' conscious distortion of their answers to score more favorably (e.g., McFarland & Ryan, 2000). Although there is an ongoing debate on whether faking influences a selection test's criterion-related validity (e.g., Hough, 1998; Ones & Viswesvaran, 1998), researchers do agree that faking can have a significant effect on who is hired.

As far as we know, there are no studies on the influence of the development procedure or scoring method of the SJT on its fakability. Nevertheless, it seems plausible that the constructs measured, the development of response options, and the scoring method affect an SJT's fakability. SJTs that tap into less fakable domains such as cognitive ability should be less susceptible to faking than those that tap into domains such as personality (Hooper, Cullen, & Sackett, 2006). When the response options reflect dimensions of an underlying model and the model is used to score test takers' answers, the SJT is expected to be more susceptible to faking due to its greater transparency (Hough & Paullin, 1994). Weekley et al. (2006) argue that test developers should be able to control the SJT's fakability by developing and selecting response options with comparable social desirability, so that test takers are not easily able to identify the correct response.

McDaniel et al. (2011) showed that standardizing SJT scores using a within-person z transformation – which is only applicable to SJTs that use Likert scales – reduces the coachability of SJTs. Like faking, coaching may lead to the hiring of individuals whose true score is less than what it appears to be. McDaniel et al. found that the coaching strategy of avoiding extreme responses, which is generally an effective strategy (Cullen, Sackett, & Lievens, 2006), is ineffective for the standardized scales and even lowered scores up to 1.07 SD.

A few studies have been conducted regarding the effects of response instruction on the SJT's fakability. Nguyen, Biderman, and McDaniel (2005) found that test takers could distort their answers on an SJT with behavioral tendency instructions such that on average they were able to elevate their scores with 0.15 or 0.34 SD, depending on whether they took the SJT in the honest or faking condition first. As it is difficult to fake knowledge, the results for the SJT with knowledge instructions were inconsistent; faking even lead to lower scores when test takers had to answer honestly first. Peeters and Lievens (2005) conducted a between-subjects study on the fakability of SJTs with behavioral tendency instructions and found that the test takers in the fake condition scored 0.89 SD higher than the test takers in the honest condition. Furthermore, they found that faking had a negative effect on the criterion-related validity of the SJT. Note that these effect sizes are derived from experimental faking research. The effect sizes are likely to be different in an applicant sample. Lievens et al. (2009) found that in such a context test takers respond similarly to an SJT with behavioral tendency instructions and an SJT with knowledge-based instructions.

Test taker perceptions

Previous studies have demonstrated that test takers' perceptions are related to numerous outcomes, such as intentions to accept the job, the likelihood of litigation against the outcome of the selection procedure, and perceived organizational attractiveness (e.g., Anderson, Lievens, Van Dam, & Ryan, 2004; Ryan & Ployhart, 2000). Systematic research on the effects of the development procedure, response instructions, and scoring method on test taker perceptions is lacking. However, a fair amount of research has been conducted on the effects of stimulus format on test taker perceptions. Video-based SJTs provide a realistic job preview and therefore are expected to be more attractive for test takers in terms of interest and motivation than paper-and-pencil SJTs. Richman-Hirsch, Olson-Buchanan, and Drasgow (2000) demonstrated that compared to a paper-and-pencil SJT, the video-based version with identical content indeed yielded more positive reactions. The video-based SJT was perceived as more content valid, more face valid, more enjoyable, and led to more satisfaction with the assessment process. Chan and Schmitt (1997) demonstrated that test takers rate the face validity of a video-based SJT significantly more positively than the face validity of a paper-and-pencil SJT. Kanning et al. (2006) examined reactions to SJT items that differed with regard to interactivity (non-interactive versus interactive) and medium (video versus paper-and-pencil). Video-based SJT items in which the response of the participants determines the further course of the item were perceived as the most favorable in terms of enjoyment, acceptance, and job relatedness.

Table 10.1 presents an overview of the research findings regarding the impact of design characteristics on the six key criteria for selection tests. As has become apparent, there are many gaps in the literature. More systematic research is needed to establish consensus regarding optimal SJT development methods.

New developments

Recently, there have been new developments in the way SJTs are developed and scored. In this section, we describe three important advancements that aim at improving the construct- and criterion-related validity of SJTs.

A construct-based approach

Based on their meta-analysis, Christian et al. (2010) argue that SJT research could benefit from a construct-based approach. So far, there has been a lack of attention to SJT constructs (Arthur & Villado, 2008; Schmitt & Chan, 2006). Many studies fail to report the constructs measured by SJTs (e.g., Cucina, Vasilopoulos, & Leaman, 2003; Pereira & Schmidt, 1999) and even when SJTs are developed to assess one or more specific constructs, overall scores rather than scores for specific constructs are reported (e.g., Chan & Schmitt, 2002; Weekley & Jones, 1997, 1999). A construct-based approach offers several theoretical and practical advantages: (1) the specification of the construct domain helps to reduce contamination due to the measurement of unintended, non-job-relevant constructs (Christian et al., 2010); (2) the items of the SJT will load highly on one (or more) factors and exhibit few item-specific variance SJTs, leading to higher reliability coefficients (Ployhart et al., 2012); (3) it provides insight into why the SJT is related to the criterion of interest (Arthur & Villado, 2008; Schmitt & Chan, 1998); and (4) it provides the opportunity to conceptually match the predictor and criterion domain (Paunonen, Rothstein, & Jackson, 1999).

TABLE 10.1 Impact of design characteristics on selection test criteria

Selection test criterion	Development method	Response instructions	Scoring method	Key references
Reliability	Unknown	Some evidence for higher test-retest reliability, behavioral tendency instructions	Unknown	Ployhart et al. (2012), Ployhart & Ehrhart (2003)
Construct-related validity	Video-based SJTs have lower cognitive loading than paper-and-pencil SJTs	Knowledge-based instructions capture maximal performance and behavioral tendency instructions capture typical performance	Unknown	Chan & Schmitt, (1997), Lievens & Sackett (2006), McDaniel et al. (2007)
Criterion-related validity	Video-based SJTs have higher validity for interpersonal skills than paper-and-pencil SJTs	No moderating effects	Some evidence that empirical-based methods and expert-based methods have higher validity than theory-based methods. Scoring adjustments (within-person z transformation and removing items with midrange means) lead to higher validity	Bergman et al. (2006), Christian et al. (2010), Lievens et al. (2009), McDaniel et al. (2007), McDaniel et al. (2011)
Ethnic score differences	Video-based SJTs show smaller ethnic score differences than paper-and-pencil SJTs	Behavioral tendency instructions lead to lower ethnic score differences than knowledge-based instructions	Scoring adjustments (within-person z transformation) lead to smaller ethnic score differences	Chan & Schmitt (1997), McDaniel et al. (2011), Whetzel et al. (2008)
Fakability	Unknown	Knowledge-based instructions are less fakable than behavioral tendency instructions	Some evidence that theory-based methods lead to higher susceptibility to faking than other scoring methods. Scoring adjustments (removing items with midrange means) reduces coachability	Hough & Paullin (1994), McDaniel et al. (2011), Nguyen et al. (2005), Peeters & Lievens (2005)
Acceptability	Video-based and interactive SJTs lead to more positive test taker perceptions	Unknown	Unknown	Chan & Schmitt (1997), Kanning et al. (2006), Richman-Hirsch et al. (2000)

De Meijer, Born, Van Zielst, and Van der Molen (2010) developed an SJT to measure the construct of integrity and Bledow and Frese (2009) developed an SJT to measure the construct of personal initiative. Both found support for the convergent and divergent validity of SJT scores. Furthermore, De Meijer et al. (2010) report an internal consistency coefficient of .69. These results demonstrate that it is possible to develop an SJT that assesses a specific construct. However, not all attempts have been successful (e.g., Pulakos & Schmitt, 1996). According to Ployhart, Porr, and Ryan (2004), this is because most recent studies have used minor variations of the method of developing SJT items described above. Ployhart et al. (2004) describe an alternative way of developing SJTs to assess specific constructs. The steps are: (1) defining the performance domain and identifying relevant criterion behaviors; (2) identifying situations that result in the maximal variability in behaviors such that the trait(s) of interest can be manifested; (3) linking the situations to the criterion behaviors; (4) constructing response options that lie on a continuum, with each response option reflecting a different level of the trait; and (5) asking experts to rate the situations and the response options for their relevance to the trait(s) of interest. Ployhart et al. used this approach to develop an SJT for neuroticism, agreeableness, and conscientiousness. Their results suggested that SJT items can be written to reflect personality traits and that such an SJT shows adequate criterion-related validity.

The use of alternative response formats

There are two recent developments regarding the response format of SJTs. The first development aims at increasing the fidelity of the SJT by using a constructed response format instead of a multiple-choice format. Although a multiple-choice format has several advantages over a constructed response format such as the possibility to administer the test to large groups at the same time and the cost-effectiveness in scoring test takers' answers (Edwards, Arthur, & Bruce, 2012; Motowidlo et al., 1990), the format does not correspond with real life. In addition, a multiple-choice format is susceptible to guessing and other test-taking strategies (Ellis & Ryan, 2003). In so-called constructed response SJTs, challenging job-related scenarios are presented by using video clips. After the scenario is presented, applicants are asked to act out their response, while being filmed by a webcam (Oostrom, Born, Serlie, & Van der Molen, 2010). Although such a format is less standardized and therefore more expensive and time-consuming to score as compared to a multiple-choice format, it invokes greater realism and fidelity than a multiple-choice response format. Subsequently, test takers typically perceive it more positively. Ethnic minority test takers, who might have negative experiences with multiple-choice tests, particularly seem to appreciate tests with constructed response formats (Edwards & Arthur, 2007; Ryan & Ployhart, 2000). Furthermore, constructed response SJTs have been found to be predictive of various criteria such as employment agents' job placement success (Oostrom et al., 2010), learning activities of students (Oostrom, Born, Serlie, & Van der Molen, 2011), training performance ratings of policemen

(Lievens, De Corte, & Westerveld, in press), and contextual job performance ratings of government employees (De Soete, Lievens, & Oostrom, 2013). Effects on ethnic score differences have been promising, with constructed response SJTs displaying ethnic score differences of 0.14 SD (De Soete, Lievens, Oostrom, & Westerveld, in press).

The second development regarding the response format of SJTs is presenting one response option instead of multiple, usually 3 to 12, response options per item. Motowidlo and colleagues (Crook et al., 2011; Martin & Motowidlo, 2010; Motowidlo, Crook, Kell, & Naemi, 2009) have developed several of these so-called single-response SJTs. They argue that the development and scoring of single-response SJTs is less labor intensive than the development of traditional SJTs as it eliminates the need for SMEs to generate behavioral responses to situations and minimizes the time needed to rate multiple response options for effectiveness. Moreover, with single-response SJTs the items can be more easily classified to a criterion dimension, which is likely to improve the construct-related validity of the SJT and allows for a better predictor-criterion alignment. Initial evidence is promising. Motowidlo et al. (2009) showed that a single-response SJT is able to predict the work effort of volunteers. Crook et al. (2011) showed that a single-response SJT is a valid predictor of tour guide performance at a children's museum.

Implicit trait policies

To explain why SJTs are often correlated with measures of personality traits, Motowidlo, Hooper, and Jackson (2006) developed the implicit trait policy (ITP) theory. ITPs are the implicit beliefs of individuals about the effectiveness of different levels of trait expression. For instance, an individual may believe that the expression of conscientiousness is generally very effective. ITPs are measured by correlating test takers' effectiveness ratings of SJT response options with the level of trait expression of these response options. The central proposition of the ITP theory is that individual differences in personality traits affect judgments of the effectiveness of SJT response options that express those personality traits. Motowidlo et al. (2006) found empirical support for their theory, as they were able to demonstrate that ITPs for agreeableness, conscientiousness, and extraversion are related to individual differences in these personality traits. Furthermore, Motowidlo and Beier (2010) demonstrated that ITPs are able to predict a performance composite based on supervisor ratings. Similarly, Oostrom, Born, Serlie, and Van der Molen (2012) demonstrated that an SJT for leadership skills can be used to measure individual differences in ITPs and that those ITPs are able to predict leadership behavior over and above leadership experience and personality traits.

The ITP theory also provides practitioners an alternative scoring method for SJTs, by which this general domain knowledge about the costs and benefits of expressing particular personality traits can be measured. There are several advantages of using this alternative scoring method. First, scoring keys for ITPs do not require experts with considerable domain-specific knowledge and experience. Second, as

ITPs tap general domain knowledge, the validity of ITPs for targeted traits may be more generalizable across job domains than the validity of traditionally scored SJTs.

Suggestions for future research

From our review of the literature on the development and scoring of SJTs, it has become clear that there are several pressing research needs. First of all, much more systematic studies are needed in which the different development methods, response instructions, and scoring methods are compared in terms of reliability, validity, ethnic score differences, and test taker reactions. Consensus regarding optimal SJT development methods is a prerequisite to establishing SJTs as a means to measure and predict specific constructs. These studies should consider using a construct-based approach. A construct-based approach offers several theoretical and practical advantages, such as the ability to generalize findings across time and jobs (Arthur & Villado, 2008; Schmitt & Chan, 1998).

We also presented several new developments that we believe will help improve SJTs. Yet, more research on these trends is welcomed. Ployhart et al. (2004) have presented an alternative way of developing construct-based SJTs, and Motowidlo et al. (2006) have presented an alternative scoring method for SJTs by which ITPs can be measured. Although researchers have called for a more construct-based approach in SJT research (e.g., Christian et al., 2010), these alternative development and scoring methods are not yet widespread. Studies are needed to compare the usability of alternative development and scoring methods to that of traditional methods. Future studies should also look into the boundary conditions of these alternative methods. For example, it might be that the alternative SJT development method of Ployhart et al. (2004) is more suited for the assessment of constructs that lie on a continuum, such as personality, than for other constructs. In addition, it might make the SJT more fakable.

Two promising alternative response formats have been presented, that is, the use of constructed response formats and single-response formats. Future studies should compare constructed response SJTs to traditional multiple-choice SJTs in terms of validity, ethnic score differences, and test taker perceptions. Motowidlo and colleagues (Crook et al., 2011; Martin & Motowidlo, 2010; Motowidlo et al., 2009) have developed so-called single-response SJTs that are less labor intensive to develop than traditional SJTs. So far, results have been promising, which should encourage future studies on the development of single-response SJTs.

Conclusion

In this chapter, we have reviewed the traditional way of developing and scoring SJTs and how different development and scoring procedures affect the SJT's reliability, validity, ethnic score differences, fakability, and acceptability. Clearly, more systematic research is needed in which the different development and scoring procedures are compared. Consensus regarding optimal SJT development methods is important to establish SJTs as a means to measure and predict specific constructs. We also presented several new developments, namely the use of a construct-based approach, constructed response formats, single-response formats, and ITPs. We believe these developments will help improve SJTs. Yet, more research-based evidence is needed to evaluate their viability.

References

Anderson, N.R., Lievens, F., Van Dam, K., & Ryan, A.M. (2004). Future perspectives on employee selection: Key directions for future research and practice. *Applied Psychology: An International Review, 53*, 487–501.

Arthur, W.J., & Villado, A. (2008). The importance of distinguishing between constructs and methods when comparing predictors in personnel selection research and practice. *Journal of Applied Psychology, 93*, 435–442.

Bergman, M.E., Drasgow, F., Donovan, M.A., Henning, J.B., & Juraska, S.E. (2006). Scoring situational judgment tests: Once you get the data, your troubles begin. *International Journal of Selection and Assessment, 14*, 223–235.

Bledow, R., & Frese, M. (2009). A situational judgment test of personal initiative and its relationship to performance. *Personnel Psychology, 62*, 229–258.

Bobko, P., Roth, P.L., & Buster, M.A. (2005). Work sample selection tests and expected reduction in adverse impact: A cautionary note. *International Journal of Selection and Assessment, 13*, 1–10.

Chan, D., & Schmitt, N. (1997). Video-based versus paper-and-pencil method of assessment in situational judgment tests: Subgroup differences in test performance and face validity perceptions. *Journal of Applied Psychology, 82*, 143–159.

Chan, D., & Schmitt, N. (2002). Situational judgment and job performance. *Human Performance, 15*, 233–254.

Christian, M.S., Edwards, J.C., & Bradley, J.C. (2010). Situational judgment tests: Constructs assessed and a meta-analysis of their criterion-related validities. *Personnel Psychology, 63*, 83–117.

Cronbach, L.J. (1984). *Essentials of psychological testing* (4th ed.). New York: Harper & Row.

Crook, A.E., Beier, M.E., Cox, C.B., Kell, H.J., Hanks, A.R., & Motowidlo, S.J. (2011). Measuring relationships between personality, knowledge, and performance using single-response situational judgment tests. *International Journal of Selection and Assessment, 19*, 363–373.

Cucina, J.M., Vasilopoulos, N.L., & Leaman, J.A. (2003, April). *The bandwidth-fidelity dilemma and situational judgment test validity*. Paper presented at the 18th annual conference of the Society for Industrial and Organizational Psychology, Orlando, FL.

Cullen, M.J., Sackett, P.R., & Lievens, F. (2006). Threats to the operational use of situational judgment tests in the college admission process. *International Journal of Selection and Assessment, 14*, 142–155.

Dalessio, A.T. (1994). Predicting insurance agent turnover using a video-based situational judgment test. *Journal of Business and Psychology, 9*, 23–32.

Dean, M.A., Bobko, P., & Roth, P.L. (2008). Ethnic and gender subgroup differences in assessment center ratings: A meta-analysis. *Journal of Applied Psychology, 93*, 685–691.

De Meijer, L.A.L. (2008). *Ethnicity effects in police officer selection: Applicant, assessor, and selection-method factors*. (Unpublished doctoral dissertation). Erasmus University, Rotterdam.

De Meijer, L.A.L., Born, M. Ph., Van Zielst, J., & Van der Molen, H.T. (2010). The construct-driven development of a video-based situational judgment test measuring integrity: A study in a multi-ethnic police setting. *European Psychologist, 15*, 229–236.

De Soete, B., Lievens, F., & Oostrom, J.K. (April, 2013). *The diversity-validity dilemma in selection: The role of response fidelity.* Poster presented at the 28th annual conference of the Society for Industrial and Organizational Psychology, Houston, TX.

De Soete, B., Lievens, F., Oostrom, J.K., & Westerveld, L. (in press). Alternative predictors for dealing with the diversity-validity dilemma in personnel selection: The constructed response multimedia test. *International Journal of Selection and Assessment.*

Drasgow, F., Olson-Buchanan, J.B., & Moberg, P.J. (1999). Development of interactive video assessments. In F. Drasgow & J.B. Olson-Buchanan (Eds.), *Innovations in computerized assessment* (pp. 177–196). Mahwah, NJ: Erlbaum.

Edwards, B.D., & Arthur, W.J. (2007). An examination of factors contributing to a reduction in subgroup differences on a constructed-response paper-and-pencil test of scholastic achievement. *Journal of Applied Psychology, 92,* 794–801.

Edwards, B.D., Arthur, W., & Bruce, L.L. (2012). The three-option format for knowledge and ability multiple-choice tests: A case for why it should be more commonly used in personnel testing. *International Journal of Selection and Assessment, 20,* 65–81.

Ellis, A.P.J., & Ryan, A.M. (2003). Race and cognitive-ability test performance: The mediating effects of test preparation, test-taking strategy use and self-efficacy. *Journal of Applied Social Psychology, 33,* 2607–2629.

Flanagan, J.C. (1954). The critical incident technique. *Psychological Bulletin, 51,* 327–358.

Hooper, A.C., Cullen, M.J., & Sackett, P.R. (2006). Operational threats to the use of SJTs: Faking, coaching, and retesting issues. In J.A. Weekley & R.E. Ployhart (Eds.), *Situational judgment tests: Theory, measurement, and application* (pp. 205–232). Mahwah, NJ: Lawrence Erlbaum.

Hough, L.M. (1998). Effects of intentional distortion in personality measurement and evaluation of suggested palliatives. *Human Performance, 11,* 209–244.

Hough, L. M, & Paullin, C. (1994). Construct-oriented scale construction: The rational approach. In G.S. Stokes, M.D. Mumford, & W.A. Owens (Eds.), *Biodata handbook: Theory, research, and use of biographical information in selection and performance prediction* (pp. 109–145). Palo Alto, CA: CPP Books.

Hunter, D.R. (2003). Measuring general aviation pilot judgment using a situational judgment technique. *The International Journal of Aviation Psychology, 13,* 373–386.

Kanning, U.P., Grewe, K., Hollenberg, S., & Hadouch, M. (2006). From the subjects' point of view: Reactions to different types of situational judgment items. *European Journal of Psychological Assessment, 23,* 168–176.

Krokos, K.J., Meade, A.W., Cantwell, A.R., Pond, S.B., & Wilson, M.A. (2004, April). *Empirical keying of situational judgment tests: Rationale and some examples.* Paper presented at the 19th annual conference of the Society for Industrial and Organizational Psychology, Chicago, IL.

Lievens, F. (2000). Development of an empirical scoring scheme for situational inventories. *European Review of Applied Psychology, 50,* 117–124.

Lievens, F., De Corte, W., & Westerveld, L. (in press). Understanding the building blocks of selection procedures: Effects of response fidelity on performance and validity. *Journal of Management.*

Lievens, F., Peeters, H., & Schollaert, E. (2008). Situational judgment tests: A review of recent research. *Personnel Review, 37,* 426–441.

Lievens, F., & Sackett, P.R. (2006). Video-based versus written situational judgment tests: A comparison in terms of predictive validity. *Journal of Applied Psychology, 91,* 1181–1188.

Lievens, F., Sackett, P.R., & Buyse, T. (2009). The effects of response instructions on situational judgment test performance and validity in a high-stakes context. *Journal of Applied Psychology, 94,* 1095–1101.

MacLane, C.N., Barton, M.G., Holloway-Lundy, A.E., & Nickles, B.J. (2001, April). *Keeping score: Expert weights on situational judgment responses.* Paper presented at the 16th annual conference of the Society for Industrial and Organizational Psychology, San Diego, CA.

Martin, M.P., & Motowidlo, S.J. (2010, April). *A single-response SJT for measuring procedural knowledge for human factors professionals.* Paper presented at the 25th annual conference of the Society for Industrial and Organizational Psychology, Atlanta, GA.

McDaniel, M.A., Hartman, N.S., Whetzel, D.L., & Grubb, W.L., III. (2007). Situational judgment tests, response instructions, and validity: A meta-analysis. *Personnel Psychology, 60,* 63–91.

McDaniel, M.A., Morgeson, F.P., Finnegan, E.B., Campion, M.A., & Braverman, E.P. (2001). Use of situational judgment tests to predict job performance: A clarification of the literature. *Journal of Applied Psychology, 86,* 730–740.

McDaniel, M.A., & Nguyen, N.T. (2001). Situational judgment tests: A review of practice and constructs assessed. *International Journal of Selection and Assessment, 9,* 103–113.

McDaniel, M.A., Psotka, J., Legree, P.J., Yost, A.P., & Weekley, J.A. (2011). Toward an understanding of situational judgment item validity and group differences. *Journal of Applied Psychology, 96,* 327–336.

McDaniel, M.A., & Whetzel, D.L. (2005). Situational judgment test research: Informing the debate on practical intelligence theory. *Intelligence, 33,* 515–525.

McDaniel, M.A., Whetzel, D.L., Hartman, N.S., Nguyen, N.T., & Grubb, W.L., III. (2006). Situational judgment tests: Validity and an integrative model. In J.A. Weekley & R.E. Ployhart (Eds.), *Situational judgment tests: Theory, measurement, and application* (pp. 183–204). Mahwah, NJ: Lawrence Erlbaum.

McFarland, L.A., & Ryan, A.M. (2000). Variance in faking across noncognitive measures. *Journal of Applied Psychology, 85,* 812–821.

McHenry, J.J., & Schmitt, N. (1994). Multimedia testing. In M.G. Rumsey, C.B. Walker, & J.H. Harris (Eds.), *Personnel selection and classification* (pp. 193–232). Hillsdale, NJ: Lawrence Erlbaum.

Moss, F.A. (1926). Do you know how to get along with people? *Scientific American, 135,* 26–27.

Motowidlo, S.J., & Beier, M.E. (2010). Differentiating specific job knowledge from implicit trait policies in procedural knowledge measured by a situational judgment test. *Journal of Applied Psychology, 95,* 321–333.

Motowidlo, S.J., Crook, A.E., Kell, H.J., & Naemi, B. (2009). Measuring procedural knowledge more simply with a single-response situational judgment test. *Journal of Business and Psychology, 24,* 281–288.

Motowidlo, S.J., Dunnette, M.D., & Carter, G.W. (1990). An alternative selection procedure: The low-fidelity simulation. *Journal of Applied Psychology, 75,* 640–647.

Motowidlo, S.J., Hanson, M.A., & Crafts, J.L. (1997). Low-fidelity simulations. In D.L. Whetzel & G.R. Wheaton (Eds.), *Applied measurement methods in industrial psychology* (pp. 241–260). Palo Alto, CA: Davies-Black Publishing.

Motowidlo, S.J., Hooper, A.C., & Jackson, H.L. (2006). Implicit policies about relations between personality traits and behavioral effectiveness in situational judgment items. *Journal of Applied Psychology, 91,* 749–761.

Mumford, M.D., & Owens, W.A. (1987). Methodology review: Principles, procedures, and findings in the application of background data measures. *Applied Psychological Measurement, 11,* 1–31.

Mumford, T.V., Van Iddekinge, C.H., Morgeson, F.P., & Campion, M.A. (2008). The Team Role Test: Development and validation of a team role knowledge situational judgment test. *Journal of Applied Psychology, 93,* 250–267.

Nguyen, N.T., Biderman, M.D., & McDaniel, M.A. (2005). Effects of response instructions on faking a situational judgment test. *International Journal of Selection and Assessment, 13*, 250–260.

Nguyen, N.T., & McDaniel, M.A. (2003). Response instructions and racial differences in a situational judgment test. *Applied HRM Research, 8*, 33–44.

Olson-Buchanan, J.B., Drasgow, F., Moberg, P.J., Mead, A.D., Keenan, P.A., & Donovan, M.A. (1998). Interactive video assessment of conflict resolution skills. *Personnel Psychology, 51*, 1–24.

Ones, D.S., & Viswesvaran, C. (1998). The effects of social desirability and faking on personality and integrity assessment for personnel selection. *Human Performance, 11*, 245–269.

Oostrom, J.K., Born, M. Ph., Serlie, A.W., & Van der Molen, H.T. (2010). Webcam testing: Validation of an innovative open-ended multimedia test. *European Journal of Work and Organizational Psychology, 19*, 532–550.

Oostrom, J.K., Born, M. Ph., Serlie, A.W., & Van der Molen, H.T. (2011). A multimedia situational test with a constructed-response format: Its relationship with personality, cognitive ability, job experience, and academic performance. *Journal of Personnel Psychology, 10*, 78–88.

Oostrom, J.K., Born, M. Ph., Serlie, A.W., & Van der Molen, H.T. (2012). Implicit trait policies in multimedia situational judgment tests for leadership skills: Can they predict leadership behavior? *Human Performance, 25*, 335–353.

Paivio, A. (1986). *Mental representation: A dual coding approach*. Oxford, UK: University Press.

Paunonen, S.V., Rothstein, M.G., & Jackson, D.N. (1999). Narrow reasoning about the use of broad personality measures for personnel selection. *Journal of Organizational Behavior, 20*, 389–405.

Peeters, H., & Lievens, F. (2005). Situational judgment tests and their predictiveness of college students' success: The influence of faking. *Educational and Psychological Measurement, 65*, 70–89.

Pereira, G.M., & Schmidt, H.V. (1999, April). *Situational judgment tests: Do they measure ability, personality, or both?* Paper presented at the 14th annual conference of the Society for Industrial and Organizational Psychology, Atlanta, GA.

Ployhart, R.E., Campion, M.C., & MacKenzie, W.I. (2012, April). *Reliability and situational judgment tests: A review of the literature*. Paper presented at the 27th annual conference of the Society for Industrial and Organizational Psychology, San Diego, CA.

Ployhart, R.E., & Ehrhart, M.G. (2003). Be careful what you ask for: Effects of response instructions on the construct validity and reliability of situational judgment tests. *International Journal of Selection and Assessment, 11*, 1–16.

Ployhart, R.E., Porr, W.B., & Ryan, A.M. (2004). *A construct-oriented approach for developing situational judgment tests in a service context*. Unpublished manuscript.

Pulakos, E.D., & Schmitt, N. (1996). An evaluation of two strategies for reducing adverse impact and their effects on criterion-related validity. *Human Performance, 9*, 241–258.

Richman-Hirsch, W.L., Olson-Buchanan, J.B., & Drasgow, F. (2000). Examining the impact of administration medium on examinee perceptions and attitudes. *Journal of Applied Psychology, 85*, 880–887.

Roth, P.L., Bobko, P., & Buster, M. (2013). Situational judgment tests: The influence and importance of applicant status and targeted constructs on estimates of Black–White subgroup differences. *Journal of Occupational and Organizational Psychology, 86*, 394–409.

Ryan, A.M., & Ployhart, R.E. (2000). Applicants' perceptions of selection procedures and decisions: A critical review and agenda for the future. *Journal of Management, 26*, 565–606.

Schmitt, N., & Chan, D. (Eds.) (1998). *Personnel selection: A theoretical approach*. Thousand Oaks, CA: Sage.

Schmitt, N., & Chan, D. (2006). Situational judgment tests: Method or construct. In J.A. Weekley & R.E. Ployhart (Eds.), *Situational judgment tests: Theory, measurement, and application* (pp. 135–155). Mahwah, NJ: Lawrence Erlbaum.

Schoenfeldt, L.F., & Mendoza, J.L. (1994). Developing and using factorially derived biographical scales. In G.S. Stokes, M.D. Mumford, & W.A. Owens (Eds.), *Biodata handbook: Theory, research, and use of biographical information in selection and performance prediction* (pp. 147–169). Palo Alto, CA: CPP Books.

Stemler, S.E., & Sternberg, R.J. (2006). Using situational judgment tests to measure practical intelligence. In J.A. Weekley & R.E. Ployhart (Eds.), *Situational judgment tests: Theory, measurement, and application* (pp. 107–131). Mahwah, NJ: Lawrence Erlbaum.

Vroom, V.H., & Jago, A.G. (1978). On the validity of the Vroom-Yetton model. *Journal of Applied Psychology, 63,* 151–162.

Weekley, J.A., & Jones, C. (1997). Video-based situational testing. *Personnel Psychology, 50,* 25–49.

Weekley, J.A., & Jones, C. (1999). Further studies of situational tests. *Personnel Psychology, 52,* 679–700.

Weekley, J.A., Ployhart, R.E., & Holtz, B.C. (2006). On the development of situational judgment tests: Issues in item development, scaling, and scoring. In J.A. Weekley & R.E. Ployhart (Eds.), *Situational judgment tests: Theory, measurement, and application* (pp. 157–182). Mahwah, NJ: Lawrence Erlbaum.

Whetzel, D.L., & McDaniel, M.A. (2009). Situational judgment tests: An overview of current research. *Human Resource Management Review, 19,* 188–202.

Whetzel, D.L., McDaniel, M.A., & Nguyen, N.T. (2008). Subgroup differences in situational judgment test performance: A meta-analysis. *Human Performance, 21,* 291–309.

11

ASSESSMENT CENTRES

The latest developments on construct validity

Deon Meiring
UNIVERSITY OF PRETORIA, SOUTH AFRICA

Jurgen Becker
UNIVERSITY OF JOHANNESBURG, SOUTH AFRICA

Suzanne Gericke
UNIVERSITY OF PRETORIA, SOUTH AFRICA, AND EOH HUMAN CAPITAL SOLUTIONS, PRETORIA, SOUTH AFRICA

Nadia Louw
STELLENBOSCH UNIVERSITY, SOUTH AFRICA

Assessment Centres (ACs) have a long, rich, and successful history in the domain of personnel selection (Povah & Thornton, 2011). Over the past 60 years, ACs have been used extensively for the selection and development of high-potential employees in diverse organisational settings. There is also an impressive body of research literature concerning ACs that includes scores of book chapters, numerous research articles, regular conference proceedings, and countless doctoral dissertations and master's theses (Howard, 1997; Thornton & Rupp, 2012).

This popularity is mainly attributable to the method's numerous strengths, which include strong correlations with successful job performance (e.g., training success, promotion in rank, managerial performance, extra-role behaviours, salary levels, attendance, and retention) (Arthur, Day, McNelly, & Edens, 2003; Gaugler, Rosenthal, Thornton, & Bentson, 1987; Hermelin, Lievens, & Robertson, 2007; Meriac, Hoffman, Woehr, & Fleisher, 2008; Rupp, Thornton & Gibbons, 2008; Thornton & Gibbons, 2009), high content validity (Dilchert, & Ones, 2009; Gaugler et al., 1987; Iles, 1992), and explaining incremental validity over supervisory ratings, personality tests, biodata, and cognitive ability (Dayan, Kasten, & Fox, 2002; Melchers & Annen, 2010). AC scores are also perceived to be fair by candidates due to the method's high fidelity (Lievens & Schollaert, 2011; Schollaert & Lievens, 2012; Thornton &

Rupp, 2006). ACs also appear to have less adverse impact than standardized psychometric measures (Bernardin, Konopaske, &, Hagan 2012; Bobko, Roth, & Buster, 2005; Dean, Roth, & Bobko, 2008).

Due to the relatively high costs associated with the method as well as the high-stake personnel decisions that are routinely made based on AC ratings, considerable research has been conducted on the utility and validity of the approach (Povah & Povah, 2012). The construct validity debate is a fundamental concern for AC theory and practice, since establishing how well ACs are able to gauge the individual differences they purport to measure and the validity of the inferences that are drawn from these measures speaks directly to the design intention of the approach. Construct-related validity in the context of ACs has been a topic of considerable interest, since the greatest body of research findings, historically at least, suggest that dimension-based AC ratings are dominated by exercise ratings (Bowler & Woehr, 2006; Chan, 1996; Fleenor, 1996; Lance, Lambert, Gewin, Lievens, & Conway, 2004; Schneider & Schmitt, 1992). Lance (2008b) labeled the construct validity controversy the "Achilles heel" of the approach, although other authors have maintained that sufficient evidence exists to support ACs' claims of construct validity (Arthur, Woehr, & Maldegen, 2000; Hoffman, 2012; Kuncel & Sackett, 2013; Thornton, 2013a, 2013b; Thornton & Gibbons, 2009). Although recent research findings seem to provide support for the construct validity of ACs, a great deal of controversy continues to exist concerning the internal structure of ACs.

Against this backdrop, the primary focus of this chapter is to review the historical debate surrounding the construct-related validity of ACs. In order to do justice to the voluminous body of research surrounding the construct-related validity of ACs, the coverage in this chapter is restricted to four main areas. First, the chapter begins with a short description of ACs. Thereafter, the construct validity debate and prevalent methodologies used to assess the internal structure of ACs are discussed. Then the contemporary mixed-method perspective of AC design and interpretation is presented along with some emerging methodologies. The chapter concludes by highlighting a number of existing controversies, emergent questions, and general directions for future research.

The nature of assessment centres

The guidelines and ethical considerations for AC operations (International Task Force on Assessment Centre Guidelines, 2009, p. 244–245) define an AC as follows:

> [An AC] consists of a standardized evaluation of behavior based on multiple inputs. Several trained observers and techniques are used. Judgments about behavior are made, in major part, from specifically developed assessment simulations. These judgments are pooled in a meeting among the assessors or by a statistical integration process. In an integration discussion, comprehensive accounts of behavior – and often ratings of it – are pooled. The discussion results in evaluation of the assessees' performance on the dimensions or other

variables that the AC is designed to measure. Statistical combination methods should be validated in accordance with professionally accepted standards.

In AC theory the behavioural sphere is classified in terms of psychological constructs (Hoffman & Meade, 2012; Lievens & Christiansen, 2012). This means that dimensions are interpreted as constructs that presumably underlie job performance, and these dimensions are operationalized through behaviour/performance on AC exercises (Arthur, Day, & Woehr, 2008). AC dimensions therefore manifest as a group of observable behaviours that are specific and verifiable. Subsequently, these are classified together in a logical and reliable way.

Candidates' performance on AC exercises is assessed based on a predetermined group of dimensions by multiple, trained assessors (Thornton & Gibbons, 2009). Typically, dimension ratings are combined at the conclusion of each exercise, commonly referred to as post-exercise dimension ratings (PEDRs). These PEDRs are subsequently combined, either mechanically or judgmentally, into overall dimension ratings (Guenole, Chernyshenko, Stark, Cockerill, & Drasgow, 2013; Hoffman, Melchers, Blair, Kleinmann, & Ladd, 2011; Kuncel & Sackett, 2013; Lance, 2008b). Alternatively, AC evaluations are postponed until all exercises are completed, at which time the assessors combine dimension-relevant observations across exercises (also referred to as a "wash-up" session) and then arrive at overall dimension ratings (ODRs). The aggregated outcome of this process is referred to as final dimension ratings or post consensus dimension ratings (PCDRs) (Hoffman & Woehr, 2009). Both PCDRs and PEDRs can be further aggregated to arrive at overall assessment ratings (OAR) (Kuncel & Sackett, 2013). Typically the OAR is used to inform selection decisions while PEDRs or PCDRs are used to provide developmental feedback (Guenole et al., 2013).

The construct validity debate in assessment centres

In the context of ACs, the International Task Force on Assessment Centre Guidelines (2009) described validity as the extent to which an AC yields valuable and useful results. Whilst ACs have demonstrated impressive content- and criterion-related validity, the approach has been criticized for not being able to prove that it actually measures the set of predetermined dimensions that it claims to measure (i.e., construct-related validity). Most construct validity studies have tended to focus on the internal structure of ACs and have almost exclusively utilized PEDRs as the unit of analysis (Greyling, Visser & Fourie, 2003; Lance, 2008b, Lievens, 2009). The evidence for construct validity when utilizing PEDRs as the unit of analysis is equivocal at best, since AC ratings generally do not reflect the dimensions they were intended to measure but rather reflect large portions of variance attributed to the simulation format (also known as the exercise effect) (Arthur et al., 2000; Bowler & Woehr, 2006; Lievens, & Conway, 2001). This consistent trend in the literature poses a formidable threat for decision-making based on PEDRs, since it implies that behaviour is cross-situationally specific rather than cross-situationally consistent.

The apparent lack of construct validity has several important implications both for the theory and practice of ACs. It is therefore essential to know whether PEDRs should be conceptualized as exercises or dimensions.

Dimensions versus exercises

Despite decades of discussion as well as numerous influential publications on the construct-related validity of ACs, no single publication has been the source of as much enlightenment and controversy as the seminal article by Sackett and Dreher (1982). On the one hand, the article has been praised for prompting a more probing examination of the construct-related validity of ACs, yet on the other hand, it has been criticized for leading the AC field astray in search of a remedy for a nonexistent problem (Sackett, 2012). In the Sackett and Dreher (1982, p. 406) study, the "within-exercise ratings correlated more highly than the across-exercise ratings of specific dimensions, resulting in a factor pattern in which the factors clearly represent exercises rather than dimensions". In other words, candidates tend to perform more consistently across different dimensions within exercises than across the same dimensions across exercises. The findings reported by Sackett and Dreher (1982) were particularly troublesome at the time of publication, as AC theorists argued that dimensions were related to stable individual differences (trait-like) whereas exercises were merely alternative platforms for dimensions to be measured (Gibbons & Rupp, 2009; Howard, 2008). The lack of cross-exercise dimension consistency was regarded as corroborating evidence against the trait-based foundation of ACs. In response to these troubling findings, numerous researchers undertook to investigate the internal structure of ACs using correlational and factor analytic approaches. These researchers all concluded that observed behaviours are exercise and not dimension specific (Lance, 2008b; Thornton & Rupp, 2012).

More recently, at least four meta-analytic studies have investigated the construct-related validity of AC ratings. Lievens and Conway (2001) reanalyzed 34 multitrait-multimethod (MTMM) matrices of AC ratings and found that exercises and dimensions explain approximately the same amount of variance (34%). However, Lance et al. (2004) argued that the proportions of exercise and dimension variance found in the study by Lievens and Conway may be the result of a statistical artifact. Lievens and Conway utilized a correlated uniqueness factor analytic model, which may have inflated the systemic variance attributable to dimensions. In Lance et al.'s analysis, exercise variance accounted for the majority (52%) of variance in AC ratings. Bowler and Woehr (2006) reanalyzed 35 MTMM matrices containing AC ratings and reported that dimension factors accounted for less variance than did exercises. Bowler and Woehr (2006, p. 1120), however, highlight "that dimensions generally account for more variance (22% vs. 17%) and that exercises generally account for less variance (34% vs. 49%)". Thus, both dimensions and exercises contribute substantially to AC ratings. More recently, Cahoon, Bowler, and Bowler (2012) used a hybrid Monte Carlo resampling approach and subjected AC ratings to generalizability theory analysis. They reported overall, the person, dimension, and person by dimension sources of variance accounted for a combined 34.06% of variance in AC ratings using PEDRs. The largest single effect was found for the person by exercise interaction (21.83%).

The consistent pattern of exercise effect dominance over dimension variance prompted Lance (2008b, p. 84) to contend that "assessment centres do not work the way they are supposed to." Lance and likeminded associates therefore recommended a movement away from dimensions-based interpretations of AC ratings. In addition, Lance (2008a) argued that design fixes (e.g., stronger definition of dimensions, limiting the number of dimensions observed and recorded, rigourous assessor training, as well as the type of evaluation approach) do not provide the expected meaningful improvements in construct validity findings, thus casting further doubt over the cross-situational and temporal stability of dimensions-based interpretations of AC ratings. Finally, Lance (2008a) stated that recurring non-negligible exercise effects represent cross-situational specificity in candidate performance and not method bias, as suggested by previous studies, which made use of MTMM and confirmatory factor analysis (CFA) methodologies.

These findings led Lance (2008b) and others (e.g., Jackson, Stillman, & Atkins, 2005; Joyce, Thayer, & Pond, 1994; Thoreson & Thoreson, 2012) to abandon dimension-based ACs in favour of Task-Based Assessment Centres (TBACs). The TBAC approach to ACs does not seek to relate observed behaviour to stable dimensions, but instead regards AC behaviour as a mixture of knowledge, skills, abilities, and traits unique to each situation. Thus, the exercises themselves are regarded as the conceptual building blocks of the TBAC (Jackson, 2012). Many scholars and practitioners (particularly proponents of dimension-based ACs) have denounced the TBAC approach to AC design for being somewhat myopic and atheoretical (Connelly, Ones, Ramesh, & Goff, 2008; Howard, 2008; Lievens, 2008; Melchers & König, 2008; Rupp et al., 2008; Thornton & Gibbons, 2009). Opponents of the TBAC school of thought argued that the predominant reliance on covariance matrix approaches to analyze AC ratings may be responsible for the lack of construct-related validity of PEDRs.

Howard (2008) as well as Thornton and Rupp (2006) questioned the appropriateness of using the MTMM methodology to investigate AC ratings, since exercises are not designed to be parallel measures of dimensions. Hoffman (2012) argued that MTMM models may not be appropriate for investigating the internal structure of ACs since these models are particularly prone to non-convergence when: (a) each latent dimension only contains a small number of indicators; (b) the sample size is small; and (c) the ratio of indicators to factors is low. He further argued that although research on personality and work attitudes has been dogged by the same CFA-based MTMM problems, it would be absurd to dismiss the existence of these constructs based on non-convergent analytical approaches.

The exercise versus dimension debate with regards to AC ratings bears some resemblance to the person-situation debate in personality research (Mischel, 1973; Mischel & Shoda, 1995). Although there are still personality researchers who vehemently argue in favour of the separation hypothesis, generally consensus exists that the interaction between the person and situation is the most accurate and consistent determinant of human behaviour. Recently, AC research seems to have taken a page from the broader personality literature by assuming that behaviour is a function of both the person and the environment (Anderson, Lievens, van Dam, & Born, 2006; Haaland & Christiansen, 2002; Melchers, Wirz, & Kleinmann, 2012).

Interactionist perspectives on assessment centre design

Evidence presented in the previous section suggests that the three main components of ACs (dimensions, exercises, and assessors) are responsible for most of the variance in AC ratings. Of the three sources, exercise variance seems to be dominant in terms of explaining variance in assessee behaviour. That is not to say that the other components are unimportant (Lievens, Tett, & Schleicher, 2009). On the contrary, more research is needed to elucidate the nature and determinants of exercise and assessor variance. Key to the current discussion is the attempt to establish whether exercise variance represents extraneous error variance or true cross-situational variability in assessee AC performance (Hoffman, 2012; Melchers et al., 2012).

Until recently, exercise variance has been equated to method effects (i.e., measurement error). Method effects are usually seen as undesirable because measurement error impairs the measurement of dimensions (Lance, Dawson, Birklebach, & Hoffman, 2010). However, recent research has focused on discovering the theoretical meaning of the "ubiquitous exercise effect" (Hoffman, 2012, p. 293). Evidence from field and laboratory settings supports the explanation that candidates are likely to behave inconsistently across different exercises (Lance, 2008b, Lievens, 2008). However, inconsistency of behaviour across situations is not endemic only to AC research. Mischel (1973, 1977) has presented numerous examples of behavioural inconsistency of personality and attitude-related behaviour across situations. Thus, research suggests that the situation, or exercise in the case of ACs, moderates the trait-relevant expressions (Haaland & Christiansen, 2002). This view is consistent with the core tenets of interactionist theories such as trait activation theory (TAT) (Tett & Guterman, 2000) and cognitive-affective personality systems (CAPS) theory (Mischel & Shoda, 1995). According to these theories, behavioural consistency across different situations can only be expected if the respondent interprets different situations similarly, so that similar trait-relevant behavioural scripts are activated (Jansen, Lievens, & Kleinman, 2011). Accordingly, exercises are considered to be behaviour-triggering situational indicators and dimensions are seen as conditional dispositions. This implies that stable assessee performances on AC dimensions can only be realistically expected when the situations (exercises) bring forth similar trait-relevant situational triggers (Lievens & Christiansen, 2012). From this perspective AC exercises are no longer considered to be parallel measures but, rather, cues of trait-relevant behaviours (Lievens & Christiansen, 2012).

According to CAPS theory, a distinction is drawn between nominal situations and psychological situations. Nominal situations refer to situations that are perceived in the same manner by different individuals, whereas psychological situations refer to situations as they are perceived and interpreted by a particular individual (Reis, 2008). This distinction is important in the AC context because behavioural consistency across different exercises can only be expected if all candidates perceive the two situations as nominally equivalent. It is then reasonable to assume that behavioural consistency across AC exercises can be promoted by ensuring that trait activation potentials are similar across exercises. Theoretically such interventions should promote the convergent validity of AC ratings across exercises. However, Howard (2008) argued that although this may solve the discriminant validity problem with regards to AC ratings, the final result may be less desirable and may significantly truncate the utility of ACs. According to Howard, AC exercises are not designed to be parallel measures of dimensions. Rather, exercises are intended to assess specific job-related competencies by placing different psychological demands on assessees. For instance, an assessee would be expected to behave differently, even inconsistently, in a one-on-one role play when compared to a group discussion, although the same trait-related behavioural responses are activated. From this perspective, forcing the same dimensions to load on a latent dimension across exercises ignores the fact that different exercises capture unique aspects of dimensions. This scenario poses a potentially irreconcilable problem for those who want to take steps to improve the construct-related validity of ACs, at least in the traditional convergent-discriminant validity perspective, and also want to include a set of relatively different exercises in order to ensure diverse dimension-related behaviour.

Alternatively, different traits can be activated across exercises, with varying degrees of intensity. This would allow candidates to show different kinds of behaviour across dissimilar situations. This approach seems preferable since research supports cross-situational specificity in AC performance (Lance, 2008b; Lievens, Dilchert, & Ones, 2009). In other words, since exercise variance is not regarded as a source of bias but as a valid source of cross-exercise variance, dimensions are viewed as distinguishable within exercises but not necessarily consistent across exercises (Hoffman, 2012). Methodologically speaking, AC performance on dimensions is nested within exercises. This conceptualization of AC dimensions differs sharply from the way in which past models have examined dimensions (Hoffman et al., 2011). This nested conceptualization of dimensions within exercises differs from existing research, which examines the internal structure of ACs in two important ways: (a) exercises are presumed to be unidimensional; and (b) the same dimension assessed in different exercises should correlate strongly. Given the convincing evidence that has been presented recently, it seems likely that Hoffman's viewpoint that exercises are indeed multidimensional, similar to performance, is correct (Borman & Brush, 1993; Campbell, 1992; Hoffman, Blair, Meriac, & Woehr, 2007). Furthermore, cross-situational congruence of dimension ratings, especially when dimensions of conceptually broad traits are activated across different exercises, should not be expected. Clearly, these viewpoints present a radical departure from conventional AC thinking. As such, new methodologies are needed to empirically test these revamped assumptions in AC theory. Although the interactionist approach to ACs is still in its infancy, several promising models have been conceptualized to test the mixed-model perspective.

The subsequent section discusses some of the most prevalent methods available to investigating the internal structure of ACs. Although the focus of the section is on models that operationalize the mixed-model perspective, the coverage also includes some of the more traditional methodologies that may not be relevant to the mixed-model approach. Many of the mixed models are nested variants of the traditional MTMM matrix, and it was therefore considered appropriate to begin the discussion by focusing on the basic MTMM CFA variants and then work towards the latest mixed-model designs.

Construct-related methodology

The multitrait-multimethod (MTMM) framework has been one of the most widely used methods to investigate the internal structure of AC ratings. Campbell and Fiske (1959) proposed an inter-correlation matrix in which dimensions serve as traits and exercises as the methods. According to the theory, MTMM results should demonstrate high convergent validity of dimensions across exercises and high discriminant validity between different dimensions within single exercises. Thus when strong correlations are found between two exercises measuring the same dimension, convergent validity is demonstrated. Discriminant validity is established when weak correlations exist between two different dimensions measured by the same exercise (Campbell & Fiske, 1959; Thornton, 1992).

Despite the frequent reliance on MTMM matrices, the theoretical and analytical appropriateness of these models has been questioned (Hoffman, 2012). From a theoretical perspective, the inability of the approach to recognize and gauge multiple sources of variance constituting AC ratings (e.g., the assessee, the assessor, dimensions, exercises, and the interactions between them) presents an oversimplified view of AC performance (Bowler & Woehr, 2006). From an analytic perspective, problems related to model convergence, admissibility, and replication of known model parameters have prompted researchers to consider simpler nested variants of the MTMM model. Lance, Woehr, and Meade (2007), for instance, experimented with various hybrid models (e.g., CDCE, 1DCE, and UDCE + g)[1] of the traditional MTMM model to investigate AC matrices. From their analysis, Lance et al., (2010) concluded that "true" models may not always appear as the best-fitting models, whereas "false" models sometimes appear to offer better fit than the true models. These findings raised concerns regarding the continued exclusive reliance on CFA-based MTMM approaches for evaluating the internal construct validity of AC PEDRs. Bowler and Woehr (2006) have identified variance partitioning approaches (e.g., generalizability theory) as a viable alternative approach to investigate sources of variance (e.g., rater, dimension, exercise) and the interaction between them (e.g., person by exercise, person by rater by exercise).

Despite the conceptual strength of variance partitioning methodologies in examining the internal structure of ACs (see Woehr, Meriac & Bowler, 2012), many scholars have reverted to latent modelling methodologies (e.g., item response theory and CFA) due to the measurement rigour and flexibility associated with these approaches. In an effort to operationalize and empirically evaluate the

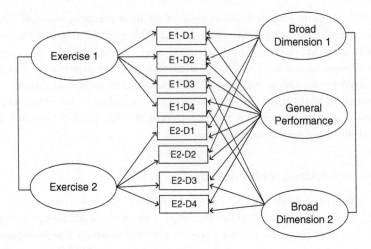

FIGURE 11.1 MTMM-based mixed-model structure

Source: based on Hoffman, Melchers, Blair, Kleinmann, & Ladd (2011)

construct-related validity of AC ratings using a mixed-model approach, Hoffman et al. (2011) conceptualized an alternative MTMM model (see Figure 11.1). The model incorporates broad dimension factors, specific exercise components, and a general performance dimension.

This model remedies some of the problems associated with the traditional MTMM approach by specifying broad dimensions composed of narrow manifest dimensions. By collapsing narrow dimensions into broader dimensions, the number of indicators reflecting each broad dimension is increased whilst the correlations amongst dimensions are reduced. The result is that the potential to arrive at an admissible solution is enhanced. Hoffman et al. (2011) tested the model in four independent samples using a number of broad dimensions and found that the alternative MTMM model provided closer approximations of AC ratings than the traditional MTMM approach. However, the broad dimensions accounted for a relatively small portion of the total variance (15%) and the majority of the variance was still attributed to the general performance dimension (10%) and exercise factors (50%).

With an eye on elucidating the nature and sources of variance endemic to exercise factors, Hoffman and Meade (2012) tested broad dimensions within exercises with a CFA approach. The dimensions within exercises mixed model proposes that (a) convergence of dimension ratings across exercises is not an expected or sufficient criterion for construct-related variance; and (b) exercise performance is multifaceted (Hoffman & Meade, 2012). As can be inferred from Figure 11.1 above, broad dimensions were assessed in each of the two exercises. Factor analytic results found support for the two dimensions measured across exercises. More importantly, equivalence analysis supported the notion that the dimensions were measured on the same psychological rating scales across exercises.

Finally, Kuncel and Sackett (2013) used the theory of composites (Gheselli, Campbell, & Zedeck, 1981) to investigate the proportion of exercise and dimension variance in dimension ratings. Kuncel and Sackett, in agreement with Howard (2008) as well as Thornton and Rupp (2012), argued that PEDRs should not be used as the unit of analysis when investigating the internal structure of ACs because they are not parallel indicators of dimensions in respective exercises. Instead, they argued for the use of final dimension ratings. Based on the theory of composites, Kuncel and Sackett demonstrated that when PEDRs are aggregated into final dimension ratings, dimension variance overtakes exercise variance as the dominant source of variance in AC dimension ratings. The methodology used in this study is based on the well-known psychometric fact that when scores are aggregated, correlated variance accumulates exponentially compared to uncorrelated sources of variance. Kuncel and Sackett identified five sources of variance: two for exercises (exercise general and specific); two for dimensions (dimension general and specific); and one related to error. Drawing on Bowler and Woehr's (2006) meta-analytical results, values were derived for each of the five sources of variance. Applying the estimates derived from the Bowler and Woehr study, Kuncel and Sackett demonstrated that sources of shared variance (i.e., dimension general and specific) increase when final dimension ratings are aggregated across exercises, while sources of unshared variance decrease. The pattern of results reported in the study suggests that dimension general variance is likely to overtake exercise general variance as the dominant source of variance when ratings from multiple exercises are combined. However, ratings from at least five exercises need to be aggregated before dimension specific variance overtakes exercise specific variance. Practically, this may be "a stretch too far" for most practitioners due to the inflated time and financial costs associated with administrating a large number of simulations.

ACs reincarnated: controversies, emergent questions, and future directions

> "When someone seeks," said Siddhartha, "then it easily happens that his eyes see only the thing that he seeks, and he is able to find nothing, to take in nothing because he always thinks only about the thing he is seeking, because he has one goal, because he is obsessed with his goal. Seeking means: having a goal. But finding means: being free, being open, having no goal."
> — Hermann Hesse, Siddhartha

The evolution of the construct validity debate resembles the main character Siddhartha in the classic novel of the same name in many ways. Similar to Siddhartha's tedious and self-depriving search for enlightenment, the AC field has been searching for the missing link in the construct validity paradox. To a large extent, much of the research stimulus directed at the construct-related validity of ACs can be attributed to the seminal work by Sackett and Dreher (1982). Ironically, more than 30 years after presenting their "troubling empirical findings", Kuncel and Sackett

(2013, p. 7) rebutted the original findings by proclaiming: "Our findings indicate that the construct validity issue with assessment centres is generally not an issue." It seems befitting that Sackett, one of the original authors of the seminal article, would lead the field to enlightenment after seemingly leading it astray.

Literature presented in this chapter clearly demonstrates that a paradigm shift has occurred in thinking about ACs over the years. Perhaps the single biggest breakthrough in thinking about AC ratings can be linked to the reconciliation between the "personism" and "situationism" schools of thought. At its height this divide drove a deep and pervasive cleft in AC research and practice. It is now generally recognized that person–situation interactions shape behaviour in ACs (Hoffman & Meade, 2012; Lance, 2008b; Lievens *et al.*, 2009) and that this allows for behavioural inconsistency across different situations. In hindsight, it seems somewhat preposterous that it took the field 30 years to arrive at this conclusion, especially since researchers such as Murray (1938), Lewin (1946), Mischel (1973, 1977), and Allport (1951) previously demonstrated that integrationist principles in work settings clarify how individual traits are translated into work-related behaviour. From the interactionist perspective, consistency would be possible only under relatively rare conditions and the assumption of consistency would be an unreasonable expectation given that exercises are designed to present unique and diverse demands, which call for diverse reactions. However, until recently this is exactly the construct-related criteria against which AC ratings have been judged.

We have argued throughout this chapter against the separation hypotheses in AC thinking. Our approach is based on the assumption that exercises and dimensions are key components of ACs (Hoffman, 2012; Lievens, De Koster, & Schollaert, 2008). Although much research has been dedicated to understanding the psychological processes underlying dimensions, little is known about the important situational characteristics on which AC exercises vary. Regardless of whether inferences from AC performance to actual job performance are based on exercises or dimensions, the heart of such inferences lies in the nature of the exercises. In this regard we agree with Lievens *et al.* (2009), who suggested that research that examines the exercise-dimension link is long overdue. Uncovering the elements of the "ubiquitous exercise effect" seems to be an important next step for AC research (Hoffman, 2012, p. 293). One way of doing this would be to build multiple stimuli into exercises and investigate dimension-relevant responses (Brannick, 2008; Lievens *et al.*, 2009). By implication, key tasks and demands of the job should not be the only focus in designing exercises. Instead, exercises should also target relevant categories of behaviour.

Building on the basic premises of TAT, Brannick (2008, p. 132) argued that researchers and practitioners should "deliberately introduce multiple dimension-relevant items or problems within the exercise to score such items and problems". This approach seems to present a fruitful framework for building trait-activating cues into AC exercises. Based on a domain sampling perspective, Nunnally (1978) warned of the treachery of selecting, or designing, items that may not be representative of the construct domain. Applied to the context of ACs, we argue that TAT could be used as a framework to guide the process of domain sampling in ACs. Thus by manipulating the trait-relevance and strength of simulations in exercises, measurement points akin to items can be designed to triangulate the centroid of a construct in a multidimensional space (Little, Lindenberger, & Nesselroade, 1999). Stated differently, since the exact position of constructs is unknown, the nature and strength of relationships between multiple indicators are used to make inferences about the relative location of constructs in a multivariate space. This multivariate approach to measurement seems to have relevance in the operationalization and measurement of AC ratings. This leads to questions regarding whether trait-relevance and situation strength can be manipulated within exercises to conceptualize manifest variables triangulating the content domain of traits. Clearly this kind of thinking presumes that observed behaviour is linked to underlying trait(s). However, multiple traits may potentially be activated in a given exercise. This could lead to a situation where unidimensional items would be very difficult or even impossible to construct within exercises. As a consequence we would expect within-exercise ratings of these dimensions to be strongly correlated. A potential solution could be to group conceptually related narrow dimensions together to form broader dimensions. If this is done, the sampling domain will clearly be broader, which will have implications for the strength and relevance of dimension-relevant items. The foregoing discussion section highlights the need for further research in order to investigate how TAT processes vary for different types of dimensions embedded in different types of simulations. Although we agree with Howard's (2008) assertion that exercises are not designed to be parallel measures of the same dimensions, we also think that it is important to examine the relationship between manifested behaviours and underlying traits. From a construct validity perspective, this may present one of the most important agendas for AC research, since it could potentially generate a theory of AC performance.

Conclusion

The arguments and debates presented in this chapter point to the multidimensional interpretation of AC performance. Several interesting and exciting theories and models have been presented recently in order to assist scholars in making sense of the complex dynamism between exercises and dimensions in AC performance. We have touched on several important conceptual and methodological developments in AC theory and practice that are likely to continue informing and shaping applied research. We expect the multifaceted interpretation of AC performance to stimulate considerable research interest, since adherence to a single approach is counterproductive and has stifled advances in AC literature for decades. In closing, the following sentence from *Siddhartha* fittingly sums up the current status of AC research:

> We are not going in circles, we are going upwards. The path is a spiral; we have already climbed many steps.
>
> — Hermann Hesse, *Siddhartha*

Note

1. CDCE is a correlated dimensions and correlated exercises model, 1DCE is a single dimension, correlated exercises model, and UDCE + g is an uncorrelated dimensions, correlated exercises, plus g model.

References

Allport, G.W. (1951). *Personality: A psychological interpretation*. London: Constable.

Anderson, N., Lievens, F., van Dam, K., & Born, M. (2006). A construct driven investigation of gender differences in a leadership-role assessment center. *Journal of Applied Psychology, 91*, 555–566.

Arthur, W.A., Day, E.A., McNelly, T.L., & Edens, P.S. (2003). A meta-analysis of the criterion-related validity of assessment center dimensions. *Personnel Psychology, 56*, 125–154.

Arthur, W. A., Day, E.A., & Woehr, D.J. (2008). Mend it, don't end it: An alternate view of assessment centre construct-related validity evidence. *Industrial and Organizational Psychology, 1*, 105–111.

Arthur, W.A., Woehr, D.J., & Maldegen, R. (2000). Convergent and discriminant validity of assessment center dimensions: A conceptual and empirical re-examination of the assessment center construct-related validity paradox. *Journal of Management, 26*, 813–835.

Bernardin, H.J., Konopaske, R., & Hagan, C.M. (2012). A comparison of adverse impact levels based on top-down, multisource, and assessment center data: Promoting diversity and reducing legal challenges. *Human Resource Management, 51*, 313–341.

Bobko, P., Roth, P.L., & Buster, M.A. (2005). Working sample selection test and expected reduction in adverse impact: A cautionary note. *International Journal of Selection and Assessment, 13*, 1–9.

Borman, W.C., & Brush, D.H. (1993). More progress towards a taxonomy of managerial performance requirement. *Human Performance, 6*, 1–21.

Bowler, M.C., & Woehr, D.J. (2006). A meta-analytic evaluation of the impact of dimensions and exercise factors on assessment center ratings. *Journal of Applied Psychology, 91*, 1114–1124.

Brannick, M.T. (2008). Back to basics of test construction and scoring. *Industrial and Organizational Psychology, 1*, 131–133.

Cahoon, M.V., Bowler, M.C., & Bowler, J.L. (2012). A re-evaluation of assessment center construct-related validity. *International Journal of Business and Management, 7*, 3–19.

Campbell, D.T., & Fiske, D.W. (1959). Convergent and discriminant validation by the multitrait-multimethod matrix. *Psychological Bulletin, 56*, 81–105.

Campbell, J.P. (1992). Modeling the performance prediction problem in industrial and organizational psychology. In M.D. Dunnette & L.M. Hough (Eds.), *Handbook of Industrial and Organizational Psychology* (pp. 687–732). Palo Alto, CA: Consulting Psychology Press.

Chan, D. (1996). Criterion and construct validation of an assessment centre. *Journal of Occupational and Organisational Psychology, 69*, 167–181.

Connelly, B.S., Ones, D.S., Ramesh, A., & Goff, M. (2008). A pragmatic view of assessment center exercises and dimensions. *Industrial and Organizational Psychology: Perspectives on Science and Practice, 1*, 121–124.

Dayan, K., Kasten, R., & Fox, S. (2002). Entry-level police candidates assessment center: An efficient tool or a hammer to kill a fly? *Personnel Psychology, 55*, 827–849.

Dean, M.A., Roth, P.L., & Bobko, P. (2008). Ethnic and gender subgroup differences in assessment center ratings: A meta-analysis. *Journal of Applied Psychology, 93*, 685–691.

Dilchert, S., & Ones, D.S. (2009). Assessment centre dimensions: Individual differences correlates and meta-analytic incremental validity. *International Journal of Selection and Assessment, 17*, 254–270.

Fleenor, J.W. (1996). Constructs and developmental assessment centers: Further troubling empirical findings. *Journal of Business and Psychology, 10*, 319–333.

Gaugler, B.B., Rosenthal, D.B., Thornton, G.C., & Bentson, C. (1987). Meta-analysis of assessment center validity. *Journal of Applied Psychology Monograph, 72*, 493–511.

Gheselli, E., Campbell, J.P., & Zedeck, S. (1981). *Measurement theory for the behavioral sciences.* San Francisco: Freeman.

Gibbons, A.M., & Rupp. D.E. (2009). Dimension consistency as an individual difference: A new (old) perspective on the assessment centre construct validity debate. *Journal of Management, 35*, 1154–1181.

Greyling, L., Visser, D., & Fourie, L. (2003). Construct validity of competency dimensions in a team leader assessment centre. *South African Journal of Industrial Psychology, 29*, 10–19.

Guenole, N., Chernyshenko, O.S., Stark, S., Cockerill, T., & Drasgow, F. (2013). More than a mirage: A large-scale assessment centre with more dimension variance than exercise variance. *Journal of Occupational and Organizational Psychology, 86*, 5–21.

Haaland, S., & Christiansen, N.D. (2002). Implications of trait-activation theory for evaluating the construct validity of assessment center ratings. *Personnel Psychology, 55*, 137–163.

Hermelin, E., Lievens, F., & Robertson, I.T. (2007). The validity of assessment centres for the prediction of supervisory performance ratings: A meta-analysis. *International Journal of Selection and Assessment, 15*, 401–411.

Hoffman, B.J. (2012). Exercises, dimensions, and the Battle of Lilliput: Evidence for a mixed-model interpretation of AC performance. In D.J.R. Jackson, C.E. Lance, & B.J. Hoffman (Eds.), *The psychology of assessment centers* (pp. 281–306). New York: Routledge.

Hoffman, B.J., Blair, C., Meriac, J., & Woehr, D.J. (2007). Expanding the criterion domain? A meta-analysis of the OCB literature. *Journal of Applied Psychology, 92*, 555–566.

Hoffman, B.J., & Meade, A. (2012). Alternate approaches to understanding the psychometric properties of assessment centres: An analysis of the structure and equivalence of exercise ratings. *International Journal of Selection and Assessment, 20*, 82–97.

Hoffman, B.J., Melchers, K.G., Blair, C.A., Kleinmann, M., & Ladd, R.T. (2011). Exercises and dimensions are the currency of assessment centres. *Personnel Psychology, 64*, 351–395.

Hoffman, B.J., & Woehr, D.J. (2009). Disentangling the meaning of multisource feedback: An examination of the nomological network surrounding source and dimension factors. *Personnel Psychology, 62*, 735–765.

Howard, A. (1997). A reassessment of assessment centers: Challenges for the 21st century. *Journal of Social Behavior and Personality, 12*, 13–52.

Howard, A. (2008). Making assessment centres work the way they are supposed to. *Industrial and Organizational Psychology, 1*, 98–104.

Iles, P. (1992). Centres of excellence? Assessment and development centres, managerial competencies and human resource strategies. *British Journal of Management, 3*, 79–90.

International Task Force on Assessment Centre Guidelines. (2009). Guidelines and ethical considerations for assessment centre operations. *International Journal of Selection and Assessment, 17*, 243–253.

Jackson, D.J.R. (2012). Task-based assessment centers: Theoretical perspectives. In D. J. R. Jackson, C.E. Lance, & B.J. Hoffman (Eds.), *The psychology of assessment centers* (pp. 173–219). New York: Routledge.

Jackson, D.J.R., Stillman, J.A., & Atkins, S.G. (2005). Rating task versus dimensions in assessment centers: A psychometric comparison. *Human Performance, 18*, 213–241.

Jansen, A., Lievens, F., & Kleinmann, M. (2011). Do individual differences in perceiving situational demands moderate the relationship between personality and assessment centre dimension ratings? *Human Performance, 24*, 231–250.

Joyce. L.W., Thayer, P.W., & Pond, S.B. (1994). Managerial functions: An alternative to traditional assessment center dimensions? *Personnel Psychology, 47*, 109–121.

Kuncel, N.R., & Sackett, P.R. (2013). Resolving the assessment center construct validity problem (as we know it). *Journal of Applied Psychology.* Advance online publication.

Lance, C.E. (2008a). Where have we been, how did we get there, and where shall we go? *Industrial and Organizational Psychology, 1*, 140–146.

Lance, C.E. (2008b). Why assessment centres do not work the way they are supposed to. *Industrial and Organizational Psychology, 1*, 84–97.

Lance, C.E., Dawson, B., Birklebach, D., & Hoffman, B. (2010). Method effects, measurement error, and substantive conclusions. *Organizational Research Methods, 13*, 435–455.

Lance, C.E., Lambert, T.A., Gewin, A.G., Lievens, F., & Conway, J.M. (2004). Revised estimates of dimension and exercise variance components in assessment center postexercise dimension ratings. *Journal of Applied Psychology, 89*, 377–385.

Lance, C.E., Woehr, D.J., & Meade, A.W. (2007). Case study: A Monte Carlo investigation of assessment center exercise factors represent cross-situational specificity, not method bias. *Human Performance, 13*, 323–353.

Lewin, K. (1946). Behavior and development as a function of the total situation. In L. Carmichael (Ed.), *Manual of child psychology* (pp. 791–844). New York: Wiley.

Lievens, F. (2008). What does exercise-based assessment really mean? *Industrial and Organizational Psychology, 1*, 112–115.

Lievens, F. (2009). Assessment centres: A tale about dimensions, exercises, and dancing bears. *European Journal of Work and Organizational Psychology, 18*, 102–121.

Lievens, F., & Christiansen, C. (2012). Core debates in assessment center research: Dimensions 'versus' tasks. In D.J.R. Jackson, C.E. Lance, & B.J. Hoffman (Eds.), *The psychology of assessment centers* (pp. 68–91). New York: Routledge.

Lievens, F., & Conway, J.M. (2001). Dimensions and exercise variance in assessment center scores: A large-scale evaluation of multitrait-multimethod studies. *Journal of Applied Psychology, 86*, 1202–1222.

Lievens, F., De Koster, L., & Schollaert, E. (2008). Current theory and practice of assessment centers. In S. Cartwright & C. Cooper (Eds.), *Oxford handbook of personnel psychology* (pp. 215–233). Oxford: University Press.

Lievens, F., Dilchert, S., & Ones, D.S. (2009). The importance of exercise and dimension factors in assessment centers: Simultaneous examinations of construct-related and criterion-related validity. *Human Performance, 22*, 375–390.

Lievens, F., & Schollaert, E. (2011). Adjusting exercise design in assessment centers: Theory, practice and research. In N. Povah & G.C. Thornton (Eds.), *Assessment centres and global talent management* (pp. 47–60). Surrey: Gower Publishing Limited.

Lievens, F., Tett, R.P., & Schleicher, D.J. (2009). Assessment centers at the crossroads: Toward a reconceptualization of assessment center exercises. In J.J. Martocchio & H. Liao (Eds.), *Research in personnel and human resources management* (pp. 99–152). Bingley, UK: JAI Press.

Little, T.D., Lindenberger, U., & Nesselroade, J.R. (1999). On selecting indicators for multivariate measurement and modeling with latent variables: When "good" indicators are bad and "bad" indicators are good. *Psychological Methods, 4*, 192–211.

Melchers K.G., & Annen, H. (2010). Officer selection for the Swiss armed forces: An evaluation of validity and fairness issues. *Swiss Journal of Psychology, 69*, 105–115.

Melchers, K.G., & König, C.J. (2008). It is not yet time to dismiss dimensions in assessment centers. *Industrial and Organizational Psychology, 1*, 125–127.

Melchers, K.G., Wirz, A., & Kleinmann, M. (2012). Dimensions and exercises: Theoretical background of mixed-model assessment centers. In D.J.R. Jackson, C.E. Lance, & B.J. Hoffman (Eds.), *The psychology of assessment centers* (pp. 237–254). New York: Routledge.

Meriac, J.P., Hoffman, B.J., Woehr, D.J., & Fleisher, M. (2008). Future evidence of validity of assessment center dimensions: A meta-analysis of internal and external correlates. *Journal of Applied Psychology, 93*, 1042–1052.

Mischel, W. (1973). Toward a cognitive social learning reconceptualization of personality. *Psychological Review, 80*, 252–283.

Mischel, W. (1977). The interaction of person and situation. In D. Magnussen & N. Endler (Eds.), *Personality at the cross-roads: Current issues in interaction psychology* (pp. 333–352). Hillsdale, NJ: Erlbaum.

Mischel, W., & Shoda, Y. (1995). A cognitive-affective system theory of personality: Reconceptualising situations, dispositions, dynamics, and invariance in personality structure. *Psychological Review, 102*, 246–268.

Murray, H. (1938). *Explorations in personality*. New York: Oxford University Press.

Nunnally, J.C. (1978). *Psychometric theory*. New York: McGraw-Hill.

Povah, N., & Povah, L. (2012). What are assessment centers and how can they enhance organizations? In D.J.R. Jackson, C.E. Lance, & B.J. Hoffman (Eds.), *The psychology of assessment centers* (pp. 3–24). New York: Routledge.

Povah, N., & Thornton, G.C. (Eds.). (2011). *Assessment centres and global talent management*. Surrey, UK: Gower Publishing Limited.

Reis, H.T. (2008). Reinvigorating the concept of situation social psychology. *Personality and Social Psychology Review, 12*, 311–329.

Rupp, D.E., Thornton, G.C., & Gibbons, A.M. (2008). The construct validity of the assessment center method and usefulness of dimensions as constructs. *Industrial and Organizational Psychology, 1*, 116–120.

Sackett, P.R. (2012). Foreword. In D.J.R. Jackson, C.E. Lance, & B.J. Hoffman (Eds.), *The psychology of assessment centers* (pp. ix). New York: Routledge.

Sackett, P.R., & Dreher, G.F. (1982). Constructs and assessment center dimensions: Some troubling findings. *Journal of Applied Psychology, 67*, 401–410.

Schneider, J.R., & Schmitt, N. (1992). An exercise design approach to understanding assessment center dimension and exercise constructs. *Journal of Applied Psychology, 77*, 32–41.

Schollaert, E., & Lievens, F. (2012). Building situational stimuli in assessment center exercises: Do specific exercise instructions and role-player prompts increase the observability of behavior? *Human Performance, 25*, 255–271.

Tett, R.P., & Guterman, H.A. (2000). Situation trait relevance, trait expression, and cross-situational consistency: Testing a principle of trait activation. *Journal of Research in Personality, 34*, 397–423.

Thoresen, C.J., & Thoresen, J.D. (2012). How to design and implement a task-based assessment center. In D.J.R. Jackson, C.E. Lance, & B.J. Hoffman (Eds.), *The psychology of assessment centers* (pp. 190–217). New York: Routledge.

Thornton, G.C., III. (1992). *Assessment centers in human resource management*. Reading, MA: Addison-Wesley.

Thornton, G.C., III. (2013a, March). *Talent management and alternative centre models: Construct validity evidence for different assessment centres for different purposes*. Paper presented at the 37th International Congress on Assessment Centre Methods and 33rd Annual Assessment Center Study Group Conference, Stellenbosch, South Africa.

Thornton, G.C., III. (2013b, November). *The assessment centre, construct validity debate: Implications for assessment centre design*. Paper presented at the UK Assessment Center Conference: Leading edge science and practice, London, UK.

Thornton, G.C., III, & Gibbons, A.M. (2009). Validity of assessment centers for personnel selection. *Human Resource Management Review, 19,* 169–187.

Thornton, G.C., III, & Rupp, D.R. (2006). *Assessment centers in human resource management: Strategies for prediction, diagnosis, and development.* Mahwah, NJ: Lawrence Erlbaum.

Thornton, G.C., III, & Rupp, D.R. (2012). Research into dimension-based assessment centers. In D.J.R. Jackson, C.E. Lance, & B.J. Hoffman (Eds.), *The psychology of assessment centers* (pp. 141–167). New York: Routledge.

Woehr, D.J., Meriac, J.P., & Bowler, M.C. (2012). Methods and data analysis for assessment centers. In D.J.R. Jackson, C.E. Lance, & B.J. Hoffman (Eds.), *The psychology of assessment centers* (pp. 45–67). New York: Routledge.

PART D
The criterion domain

12

SELECTING FOR INNOVATION

Methods of assessment and the criterion problem

Kristina Potočnik
UNIVERSITY OF EDINBURGH, EDINBURGH, UK

Neil Anderson
BRUNEL UNIVERSITY, LONDON, UK

Felisa Latorre
ITAM, MÉXICO CITY, MÉXICO

Researchers and practitioners alike have acknowledged innovation as an essential ingredient for organizational effectiveness and long-term survival, and as such, innovation in the workplace has been studied extensively over the past decades (see Anderson, Potočnik, & Zhou, 2014; Anderson, De Dreu, & Nijstadt, 2004; West, 2002 for recent reviews). Importantly, in order for the organizations to innovate, they have to employ individuals who are more likely to come up with innovative ideas and implement them to improve their jobs and overall organizational effectiveness (Anderson et al., 2014; Potočnik & Anderson, 2012). Organizations are faced with a number of challenges in their attempt to identify innovative job applicants in the selection process.

First, it is very difficult to predict the criterion that is innovative performance in a valid and reliable way, given that innovation is something novel and unpredictable by its very definition. Second, when screening the candidates for innovation potential, it is important to understand which personality characteristics and abilities are conducive into innovation – however, given that it is difficult to operationalize the

---

Acknowledgments

The writing of this chapter was supported by British Academy grant number SG110409 awarded to the first author, and by Leverhulme Trust grant number IN-2012-095 awarded to the second author. The participation of the third author was supported by Asociación Mexicana de Cultura, A.C.

criterion, it is equally difficult to identify its predictors. In addition, it has widely been acknowledged that individuals' attempts to introduce innovations in their workplaces to a large extent depend on organizational culture and institutional support for innovation (Anderson et al., 2004). Therefore, even though we could select the applicants with higher innovation potential based on robust evidence, their potential might not become realized once employed. Third, the evidence regarding the criterion-related validities of different selection methods when selecting for innovation potential is almost nonexistent. Finally, given that practically all jobs, in addition to engaging in innovative behaviors, also require the fulfillment of routine tasks, it is important to identify the balanced applicant profile and simultaneously select for both overall job performance and innovative performance.

This chapter addresses these issues and challenges by reviewing the assessment of innovative performance and individual-level innovation literature to provide implications for both valid and reliable assessment of innovation on the one hand and selecting for innovation potential on the other. We also analyze the suitability of commonly used selection methods for selecting for innovation potential. In so doing, we attempt to build a link and synergies between innovation and selection literatures – two historically disparate and separate fields. Our chapter concludes with implications for future research and practice.

Assessment of innovative job performance (IJP): the criterion problem

Individual-level innovative job performance (IJP) comprises the generation of novel and useful ideas in the first stage (also called creativity) and their implementation in the second stage (Hülsheger, Anderson, & Salgado, 2009). Compared to overall job performance (OJP), which refers to fulfillment of assigned duties and tasks, IJP implies something novel, unexpected, or unknown beforehand that can occur anytime and therefore it is extremely hard to predict (Potočnik & Anderson, 2013). The first challenge for practitioners concerned with selecting innovative employees hence refers to the reliable and valid assessment of the criterion, that is, individual IJP. To clarify, one recently proposed definition of creativity and innovation gives an unambiguous indication of the criterion-space of IJP:

> Creativity and innovation at work are the process, outcomes, and products of attempts to develop new and improved ways of doing things. The creativity stage of this process refers to idea generation, and innovation to the subsequent stage of implementing ideas toward better procedures, practices, or products. Creativity and innovation can occur at the level of the individual, work team, organization, or at more than one of these levels combined, but will invariably result in identifiable benefits at one or more of these levels-of-analysis.
>
> (Anderson et al., 2014)

TABLE 12.1 Instruments and rating sources used in IJP assessment

Instruments used		N	%
	Zhou & George (2001)	18	25
	Tierney et al. (1999)	11	15.2
	Janssen (2001)	5	7
	Subramaniam & Youndt (2005)	2	3
	Oldham & Cummings (1996)	6	8
	Scott & Bruce (1994)	3	4
	Baer & Oldham (2006)	1	1.4
	Carmeli & Schaubroeck (2007)	1	1.4
	Axtell et al. (2000)	3	4
	Own measure[1]	22	31
Rating sources			
	Self-reports	17	23.6
	Supervisors	35	48.6
	Peer ratings	7	9.72
	Behavior count/expert ratings	1	1.39
	Archival data	3	4.17
	Qualitative analysis	2	2.78
	Mixed[2]	7	9.72

Note: The sample for this summary table consisted of 72 papers on individual innovation and creativity published in top-tier journals in the 2002–2010 periods.
[1] Own measures based either on: (1) entirely own constructed items; (2) adoption of items from different scales; or (3) archival data and behavioral observations.
[2] Peers and expert coders, peers and self-reports, customers and supervisors, self-reports and experts, and self-reports, supervisors, and archival data.

Previous research has applied many different measures to operationalize IJP (Anderson et al., 2014; Potočnik & Anderson, 2012). In Table 12.1 we present the most frequently used instruments. Most research has relied on some sort of self-generated measure to assess innovation, either by combining the items from different scales or by designing entirely new ones. Regarding the specific questionnaires used, past research has mostly relied on the instruments developed by Zhou and George (2001), Oldham and Cummings (1996), Tierney, Farmer, and Graen (1999), Janssen (2001), and Scott and Bruce (1994) to assess employee creativity and IJP. These measures have shown acceptable validity and reliability and could well be used to assess the IJP for selection, assessment, or developmental purposes. Most commonly these instruments were either completed by the employees themselves (e.g., Axtell et al., 2000; Clegg, Unsworth, Epitropaki, & Parker, 2002), their supervisors (e.g., Oldham & Cummings, 1996; Yuan & Woodman, 2010), peers (e.g., Amabile et al., 2002), or experts (e.g., Shalley & Perry-Smith, 2001).

Although self-reports are frequently used in organizational assessment, we have to note that this kind of measure is prone to a wide array of biases that might seriously distort the true scores or ratings (Podsakoff, MacKenzie, Lee, & Podsakoff, 2003).

This is especially important if the assessed phenomenon is valued by the organizations and individuals scoring high on the measure are shown in a more favourable fashion. Because we assume innovation is valued by most if not all organizations, employees might inflate their own ratings of IJP. The lack of validity of self-ratings of innovation was shown in recent research that involved multiple observations of innovation competency within the 360-degree framework (Potočnik & Anderson, 2012). Specifically, the results of this study showed that self-ratings of IJP did not correlate with the ratings of observers (whereas the observers' ratings did exhibit significant correlations). The theory of true score (Becker & Miller, 2002; Borman, 1977) suggests that we can establish the accuracy of self-ratings by comparing them against the average of independent expert ratings (i.e., the true score). Therefore, based on this theory, one obvious conclusion from this study is that self-reports, that is, self-assessment during selection, should be avoided in the assessment of IJP. We suggest IJP be assessed by the independent observers who work closely with the assessed employee. However, employees may not always voice their ideas to others or attempt to implement them in the presence of others, meaning that some innovation-related behaviors are not always visible and the observers might not record and assess them correctly. Therefore, we also suggest the observers should combine their ratings with some sort of objective indicator whenever possible. In fact, previous research has used different indicators to operationalize individual innovation more objectively, such as the number of suggestions submitted or the number of filed patents (e.g., Latham & Braun, 2009). Taking into consideration that only a handful of occupations require employees to submit patents or engage in some sort of radical innovation, we could propose implementing a formal suggestion system to monitor the number of innovative ideas made by each employee could be one way to assess IJP.

It is also clear from our review of these criterion issues that selecting for IJP is quite different to selecting for OJP – that is, innovative job behaviors are distinct from, and likely to be only a subset of, behaviors that relate to OJP. However, given the increasing importance of innovation in organizations, it is becoming vital for firms to be capable of selecting specifically for IJP, in addition to OJP we would argue. In the next section, we review individual innovation research to identify what personality characteristics and abilities were found to predict IJP. Although this research has not been conducted in the context of employee selection, it can provide some valuable insights into individual correlates of innovative behaviors in general and it could be used as a starting point in designing appropriate methods for selecting for innovation potential (Potočnik & Anderson, 2013).

Selecting for innovative job potential

Organizations concerned with hiring innovative talent should address a variety of personality characteristics and abilities in designing their selection and recruitment practices. For instance, the individual-level innovation literature to date has consistently shown that employees who score high on openness and core self-evaluations (CSEs) are more likely to engage in innovative behaviors (e.g., Hammond, Neff,

Farr, Schwall, & Zhao, 2011). Likewise, specific thinking styles and abilities have been linked to higher IJP (e.g., Anderson, Hülsheger & Salgado, 2010). In this section we integrate these findings to provide a clearer picture of what individual characteristics are implicated in individual innovation. We categorize research relating to two such sets of characteristics:

- Personality characteristics
- Abilities and other personal factors

Personality characteristics

Scholars interested in innovation at the individual level have explored the role of different personality characteristics in IJP, including Big Five personality traits, creative and proactive personality, and self-appraisals, such as self-efficacy, creative role identity, and core self-evaluations (CSEs). Recently, primary studies exploring these relationships have also been meta-analyzed (Anderson, Hülsheger, & Salgado, 2010; Hammond et al., 2011). In Table 12.2 we summarize meta-analytical correlations between these personality attributes and IJP. We also included meta-analytical results considering OJP in order to compare the effect sizes considering both types of performance.

The Five-Factor Model of personality or "Big Five" has been one of the most frequently studied personality frameworks in organizational psychology due to its predictive power of diverse outcomes, including performance (Barrick & Mount, 1991), and therefore widely used in employee selection and recruitment. Table 12.2 shows that openness to experience exhibits the strongest correlation with IJP

TABLE 12.2 Meta-analytic results for personality correlates of IJP and OJP

Personality correlates	IJP	OJP
Openness to experience	0.25[1], 0.24[2]	0.07[3]
Conscientiousness	0.00[1]	0.31[3]
Extraversion	0.13[1]	0.13[3]
Agreeableness	−0.06[1]	0.13[3]
Neuroticism	−0.12[1]	−0.13[3]
Creative personality	0.25[2]	/
Proactive personality	0.39[1]	0.38[4]
Core self-evaluations (CSEs)	0.33[1]	0.19[5]
Job self-efficacy	0.26[2]	0.23[6]
Creative self-efficacy	0.33[2]	/

Note: These results were found in [1] Anderson, Hülsheger, & Salgado (2010), [2] Hammond et al. (2011), [3] Barrick et al. (2001), [4] Fuller and Marler (2009), [5] Chang et al. (2012), and [6] Judge and Bono (2001). No meta-analytic evidence was found for the correlations between creative personality and creative self-efficacy and OJP, respectively.

among the Big Five traits, a finding consistently shown in previous research (e.g., Baer & Oldham, 2006; George & Zhou, 2001; Sung & Choi, 2009). Individuals who are characterized with high openness are more imaginative, curious, and flexible and are actively looking for new experience (Barrick & Mount, 1991), and therefore are more likely to engage in innovative behaviors. Openness, however, does not seem to be a significant predictor of OJP. Similarly, different patterns of relationships for each type of performance can be observed for conscientiousness. Whereas this trait is the strongest predictor of OJP (Barrick, Mount, & Judge, 2001), its correlation with IJP is zero (see Table 12.2). In fact, past research has reported mixed results regarding the effect of conscientiousness on IJP (e.g., Furnham & Nederstrom, 2010; Raja & Johns, 2010; Sung & Choi, 2009). These findings overall suggest that conscientiousness is of limited importance for enhancing IJP, although some have argued that self-disciplined, persistent, and hard-working individuals are necessary for the implementation of novel ideas (Wang, Begley, Hui, & Lee, 2012). Apart from conscientiousness, agreeableness also does not seem to be a relevant predictor of IJP (e.g., Anderson, Hülsheger, & Salgado, 2010).

The meta-analytical correlations of extraversion and neuroticism with IJP, respectively, are weak and of the same or similar size as those with OJP (see Table 12.2). Whereas the existing evidence regarding the role of neuroticism in IJP is rather inconclusive, with most of the studies reporting non-significant effects (e.g., Sung & Choi, 2009), the majority of past research observed a positive relationship between extraversion and IJP. This finding could suggest that sociable, assertive, energetic, and talkative employees are more proactive in trying out new ideas, which could improve their IJP (Raja & Johns, 2010; Sung & Choi, 2009).

Other personality attributes that have been linked to IJP are creative and proactive personality and different self-appraisals, such as CSEs and self-efficacy. Table 12.2 shows these characteristics have stronger effects on IJP compared to the Big Five characteristics. Whereas creative personality has been defined in terms of attributes that are common to exceptionally creative people, such as inventive, original, confident, and unconventional, among others, and that differentiate creative from less creative individuals (Gough, 1979), proactive personality refers to the individual tendency to initiate change (Parker, Williams, & Turner, 2006). Past research has consistently confirmed positive effects of both types of personality on IJP (Gong, Cheung, Wang, & Huang, 2012; Oldham & Cummings, 1996; Shalley, Zhou, & Oldham, 2004).

Self-appraisals, such as CSEs, self-efficacy, and creative self-efficacy, comprise another group of personality characteristics that have been related to IJP. These attributes exhibit moderately strong correlations with individual innovation (see Table 12.2). A theory of individual creative action (Ford, 1996) has suggested self-efficacy as a key motivational aspect that impacts the employee ability to engage in creative and innovative behaviors. Past research has provided strong support for this suggestion, showing positive effects of self-efficacy and creative self-efficacy, defined in terms of individual belief of being able to produce novel and useful ideas (Tierney & Farmer, 2002), on IJP (Axtell et al., 2000; Carmeli & Schaubroeck, 2007; Clegg et al., 2002; Tierney & Farmer, 2002, 2011). CSEs, operationalized as a higher order trait comprising concepts such as self-esteem, generalized self-efficacy, locus of control and neuroticism (Judge, Locke, & Durham, 1997) have also been positively linked to IJP (Anderson, Hülsheger, & Salgado, 2010). Based on the theory of core self-evaluation (Judge et al., 1997), these findings could suggest that individuals who feel more confident in their abilities to perform well, who value themselves, and who perceive themselves to be accountable for their actions are more likely to challenge the established procedures and suggest and implement novel ideas to improve them.

Overall, our analysis shows that some personality characteristics, such as creative and proactive personality and CSEs, are important correlates of IJP. Therefore, although rarely assessed in the context of employee selection, these attributes do appear to be promising in identifying applicants with higher innovation potential. In contrast, some attributes, such as conscientiousness, which was found to be the strongest predictor of OJP, do not seem to be that relevant for IJP.

Abilities and other personal factors

Previous research has also examined the role of different abilities, thinking styles, and other personal attributes, such as job knowledge and experience, in IJP. The effects of some of these correlates have already been meta-analyzed (see Table 12.3).

Perhaps the most striking results can be observed for general mental ability (GMA). Whereas this is one of the strongest predictors of OJP (Schmidt & Hunter, 1998; Schmidt, Shaffer, & Oh, 2008), Anderson, Hülsheger, & Salgado (2010) in their meta-analysis observed a non-significant correlation between GMA and IJP (see Table 12.3). These findings support the arguments that intelligence is a necessary but not sufficient element for creativity and innovation and that there might be other, more specific abilities and skills that are predictive of IJP (Potočnik & Anderson, 2013). Creativity scholars, for instance, have explored the effects of creative ability, operationalized in terms of creativity and innovation-relevant skills such as intuitive thinking and use of imagination (Choi, 2004b), on IJP. They provided strong support for positive effects of creative ability on a range of IJP indicators (Choi, 2004a; Choi, Anderson, & Veillette, 2009).

TABLE 12.3 Meta-analytic results for abilities and other personal factors of IJP and OJP

Abilities and other correlates	IJP	OJP
General mental ability (GMA)	0.05[1]	0.51[2]
Job knowledge	0.40[1]	0.48[3]
Job experience	0.01[1], 0.05[4]	0.18[3]
Education	0.15[5]	0.06–0.24[4]

Note: These results were found in [1] Anderson, Hülsheger, & Salgado (2010), [2] Schmidt and Hunter (1998), [3] Hunter and Hunter (1984), [4] Ng and Feldman (2009), and [5] Hammond et al. (2011).

Following the componential theory of creativity (Amabile, 1997), which has suggested creative thinking skill as an important individual ingredient of creativity and IJP, past research has also addressed the role of different thinking styles in IJP, mostly applying the Kirton Adaption-Innovation Inventory, which differentiates between adaptive and innovative cognitive styles, respectively (Kirton, 1976). Individuals with adaptive style are more likely to stick to established procedures and ways of doing work, while those characterized with innovative style are more likely to take risks and develop new ways of fulfilling their tasks (Shalley et al., 2004). The existing evidence has largely confirmed the positive relationship between innovative cognitive style and IJP (Tierney et al., 1999). Recently, some scholars have suggested a positive role of need for cognition defined as "individual dispositional tendency to engage in and enjoy in thinking" (Cacioppo & Petty, 1982 cited in Wu, Parker, & De Jong, 2014, p. 511) in innovative behaviors. Research so far has supported this assumption, arguing that individuals with high need for cognition put more effort in cognitive elaboration and are more confident at voicing their ideas and therefore exhibit higher IJP (Wu et al., 2014).

Although the effects of creative ability, thinking styles, and need for cognition on IJP have not been meta-analyzed yet, these findings seem promising in screening out the applicants with higher/lower innovation potential. Therefore, we would like to suggest that apart from cognitive tests that assess the GMA and are necessary in employee recruitment and selection (Schmidt et al., 2008; Schmidt & Hunter, 1998), selection methods could also cover more innovation-specific ability questionnaires when companies are interested in selecting for innovation potential.

Other individual attributes that have been explored in relation to IJP are job knowledge and job experience (Anderson, Hülsheger, & Salgado, 2010; Hammond et al., 2011). According to the componential theory of creativity (Amabile, 1997), these attributes can be considered as indicators of expertise, which is another key individual factor in enhancing employee creativity and innovation. Although job experience does not seem to be relevant for IJP, job knowledge has a moderately strong effect on IJP, similarly as on OJP (see Table 12.3). Past research in general has provided strong support for the relationships between different aspects of job-relevant knowledge and IJP (Choi, 2004a; Krause, 2004). The level of education an employee has attained can also be considered as one of the indicators of job-related knowledge. Past research has reported a positive but rather weak effect of level of education on IJP (Hammond et al., 2011; Tierney & Farmer, 2011). These findings overall support the componential theory of creativity (Amabile, 1997), suggesting expertise as an important component of IJP. Expertise includes diverse elements such as factual knowledge, technical proficiency and skills, and we could argue that employees should possess a good knowledge base regarding their tasks in order to suggest and implement novel ways of doing their work (Wang et al., 2012). Therefore, job or domain-relevant knowledge and expertise should be considered in selecting for innovation potential. Importantly, one should not simply rely on applicant educational background as presented in curriculum vitae or bio data but rather assess job knowledge more directly.

To conclude, past research provides an unambiguously clear picture of the personal characteristics most strongly associated with IJP. These include openness to experience, CSEs, job knowledge, and creativity and innovation-specific abilities. Empirical evidence also robustly suggests that conscientiousness, agreeableness, and GMA are not correlated with IJP. Our impression is that the research in this area is thus quite well established and provides reasonably clear indicators for selection practices as far as selecting for IJP is concerned. Next, we discuss different selection methods that can be used to select for these established factors and generally for selecting for innovation potential.

Suitability of selection methods in selecting for innovation potential

So far we have analyzed what individual attributes are predictive of IJP in the workplace. In this section we are going to discuss to what extent different selection methods are suitable when selecting for innovation potential. As already noted before, there is virtually no research into criterion-related validity of different selection methods when IJP is studied as the main criterion. We discuss the potential value of different methods based on how individual predictors of IJP have been assessed in selection for OJP. It is important to note the potentially strong influence of job context on future IJP, meaning that what it takes to be innovative in one context might substantially differ from another context (Potočnik & Anderson, 2013). We argue here that the reviewed methods are likely to add value to the selection practices when seeking to identify the innovation potential of job applicants.

There is a range of selection methods that can be used in the assessment of innovation potential (see Table 12.4 for six methods that have been widely used in selecting for OJP and their potential suitability in selecting for IJP). The evidence of criterion-related validity of these methods when used for OJP ranges from moderate (e.g., personality measures) to high (e.g., cognitive ability tests). Also, applicant reactions to these methods vary from most favourable (e.g., interviews) to moderately favourable (e.g., personality inventories). Here, we would like to address each method with respect to how each could be adapted for effective use in selecting for innovation – we consider seven distinct methods overall:

- Application forms, CVs, and bio data
- Cognitive ability tests (or tests of GMA)
- Personality inventories
- Semi-structured interviews
- SJTs and work samples
- Assessment centers
- Innovation potential instruments

Application forms, CVs, and bio data

These methods can be very useful in selecting for innovation potential, allowing the evaluation of applicants' expertise and experience, motivation for applying for a

TABLE 12.4 A review of selection methods and their suitability in selecting for innovation potential

Selection methods	Criterion-related validity – OJP	Applicant reactions to the selection method	Possible suitability for selecting for innovation	Adjustments when selecting for innovation
Application forms, CV, bio data	Moderate	Favourable[1]	Moderate (but only specific elements)	Evaluating candidates' past achievements, experience, and to some extent job knowledge.
Cognitive ability tests	High	Favourable[1]	High	Including tests/measures of creativity and innovation-specific abilities and skills (e.g., creative ability).
Personality inventories	Moderate	Favourable[1]	High	Including measures of CSEs and creative and proactive personality.
Semi-structured interviews	High	Most favourable[1]	Moderate	Asking about applicants' past innovation achievements and their own perception of how creative they consider themselves to be.
Situational judgment tests/work samples	High	Moderate – positive[2]	Moderate	Designing items related to specific job-related situations that will require applicants to engage in innovative behaviors.
Assessment centers	High	Positive[2]	High	Designing different exercises, such as written analyses exercises, mock presentations, or simulation/role-play exercises in which applicants should come up with novel ideas to solve problems.

Note: [1] Anderson, Salgado, & Hülsheger (2010); [2] Arnold et al. (2010).

given post, and to some extent also job-relevant knowledge (Anderson et al., 2008; McEntire & Greene-Shortridge, 2011). As mentioned before, these were found to be significant correlates of IJP (Hammond et al., 2011; Wang et al., 2012). The application form could also include a section in which applicants should list their creativity or innovation-related achievements. Alternatively, applicants could be specifically asked to reflect on their past innovation and creativity successes in their CVs or covering letters.

Cognitive ability tests

Given that cognitive ability tests or tests of general mental ability (GMA) are one of the most consistent and strongest predictors of job performance (Anderson et al., 2008; Schmidt & Hunter, 1998), this method is most likely going to be used and should be used in any selection context. However, when selecting for innovation potential in particular, the assessment of creativity and innovation-related abilities should be added to the battery of cognitive ability tests. These could include divergent thinking tests (e.g., Torrance test of creative thinking) or even short measures of creative ability (Choi, 2004b) that could provide some guidelines regarding how creative job applicants are.

Personality inventories

Most frequently, recruiters assess applicants on the Five-Factor Model (FFM) or Big Five model of personality, measuring conscientiousness, extraversion, agreeableness, neuroticism, and openness to experience with moderate criterion-related validity when it comes to OJP (Anderson et al., 2008; Barrick & Mount, 1991; Barrick et al., 2001). Given that past research on individual innovation has consistently reported significant effects of openness to experience on employee innovation and creativity, FFM measures could be useful for selecting for innovation potential. We would suggest adding creative and proactive personality and CSE measures to the personality assessment battery in this selection context, given that these specific traits have consistently been supported as significant predictors of IJP. For instance, the Adjective Check List (Gough, 1979), the Proactive Personality Scale (Bateman & Crant, 1993), and the Core Self-Evaluations Scale (Judge, Erez, Bono,& Thoresen, 2003), as reliable and valid instruments of these constructs, can be used to this end.

Semi-structured interviews

This method is used in almost any selection context because the questions can be adjusted to fit the post-specific competencies. We would suggest that when selecting for innovation potential, the interviewers should ask the applicants about their past innovation efforts and successes and about their own perception of how creative they consider themselves to be (McEntire & Greene-Shortridge, 2011).

Situational judgment tests (SJTs) and work samples

We would suggest that SJTs and work samples could effectively be used in selecting for innovation potential by designing a set of job-related situations or scenarios with a problem or dilemma requiring the application of creativity and innovation-related KSAOs such as innovative thinking styles, creative ability, and so forth. (McEntire & Greene-Shortridge, 2011).

Assessment centers

Assessment centers (ACs) typically represent a combination of different selection methods; most frequently work samples, ability tests, personality measures, and interviews (Anderson et al., 2008). When practitioners are selecting for innovation potential, they could develop specific exercises for their ACs that would require the application of novel ideas or creative thinking skills (McEntire & Greene-Shortridge, 2011). For instance, a written analysis exercise and mock presentations can be used for assessing applicant creativity. Similarly, simulation or role-play exercises can be designed in which applicants should come up with novel ideas to solve existing problems (Melancon & Williams, 2006).

Innovation potential instruments

Practitioners can also use instruments that have been specifically designed to assess innovation potential. Here we draw attention to two such instruments. The first one is called the "Innovation Potential Indicator" (IPI; Patterson, 2000) and focuses on behaviors that are relevant to the production of novel and useful ideas and their implementation in the organizations. The measure assesses four underlying factors of innovation potential: *consistency of work styles* (the extent to which an individual prefers a strict, methodical, and consistent approach to his or her work), *challenging behavior* (the extent to which an individual actively engages and challenges others' points of view to solve problems at work), *adaptation* (the extent to which an individual strives to improve the status quo and proven work methods), and *motivation to change* (the extent to which an individual is motivated to facilitate and/or adopt change). A range of validation studies with supervisory ratings of innovation performance competency, individuals' propensity for role innovation, and innovative performance as criteria have provided enough support to conclude that the IPI is a reliable and valid measure of innovation potential (Patterson, 2000).

The second instrument developed to capture innovation potential is the "Team Selection Inventory" (TSI; Anderson & Burch, 2003). This tool assesses the individual's preferred team-working climate for innovation and hence it is useful in addressing a person-team fit when team innovation is an important criterion (Burch, Pavelis, & Port, 2008). Developed from the Team Climate Inventory (TCI; Anderson & West, 1999), this tool assesses the same four dimensions of climate as the TCI but in terms of individual team climate preference: *participative safety* (the extent to which an individual prefers working in a team characterized by a climate of psychological safety), *support for innovation* (the extent to which an individual prefers working in a team characterized by climate of support for innovative ideas), *vision* (the extent to which an individual prefers working in a team that has clearly defined objectives), and *task orientation* (the extent to which an individual prefers working in a team that is success driven). Higher scores on these dimensions would imply individual preferences for working in teams that are characterized by climates facilitative of innovation (Burch et al., 2008). This instrument has also been found to be a reliable measure with good construct validity assessing individual preference to work in teams with climates conducive of innovation (Anderson & Burch, 2003; Burch & Anderson, 2004).

Summary

We have analyzed the suitability of a range of commonly used selection methods for selecting for innovation potential. Clearly, some can be more easily adapted to assess innovation-relevant KSAOs (e.g., personality measures, cognitive tests), whereas others might require a much more careful and time-consuming design and sampling of innovation-relevant tasks and exercises (e.g., SJTs, ACs). Importantly, there is no research to date into criterion-related validities of these commonly used methods for predicting IJP. Next, we address these important issues, suggesting various implications for future research and practice.

Implications for future research

Our review of the individual-level innovation and the analysis of suitability of different selection methods for selecting for innovation provides a number of implications for future research. We list three key topics along with their specific research questions in Table 12.5.

First, future research should provide more conclusive evidence regarding the role of some individual predictors of IJP such as job knowledge, extraversion, emotional stability, and cognitive abilities. For instance, there is virtually no research examining the role of personality traits and cognitive abilities in IJP simultaneously to establish the relative importance of each type of individual predictor in IJP. Also, given the strikingly opposing findings regarding the effects of Big Five personality traits on IJP compared to OJP, future research could explore the role of these traits in IJP at the more fine-grained facet level. Such narrower analysis of personality might be especially fruitful in the case of conscientiousness, which apparently does not relate to IJP at all. Another issue that calls for future research is establishing the predictive power of creative and proactive personalities and self-appraisals, respectively, on IJP over and above the effects of Big Five traits. Apart from a few exceptions (e.g., Gong et al., 2012), most of the studies that explored the effects of these variables on IJP have not accounted for the effects of these most commonly used traits in employee selection. Unless these variables show incremental validity beyond that of the Big Five traits, it is pointless to include them as part of the personality assessment for selection purposes.

Second, more research is needed to uncover the interaction effects between individual characteristics and contextual factors to establish the boundary conditions under which employees can excel in innovative behaviors the most. Research to date has explored the interaction effects between different Big Five traits and some contextual variables such as close monitoring and feedback valence (George & Zhou, 2001), job scope (Raja & Johns, 2010), or time pressure (Baer & Oldham, 2006) in predicting IJP. Although their findings are promising, much more research is needed to identify which situational or contextual variables might enhance the

TABLE 12.5 Implications for future research: key topics and specific research questions

Key topic	Research questions
Predictive power of different individual characteristics	1. What are the effect sizes of the relationships between personality traits and cognitive abilities, respectively, and IJP? 2. What is the predictive power of facet-level Big Five characteristics on IJP? 3. How do personality traits interact with cognitive abilities to predict IJP? 4. What is the predictive power of creative and proactive personality on IJP over and above Big Five personality traits? 5. What is the predictive power of CSEs and self-efficacy on IJP over and above personality traits?
Interaction effects between individual characteristics and contextual factors	1. How do personality traits interact with job characteristics (e.g., autonomy, feedback) in predicting IJP? 2. How do personality traits interact with organizational contexts (e.g., culture, climate) in predicting IJP? 3. What are the boundary conditions under which employees with different personality profiles may maximize both their IJP and OJP?
Construct-validity of different selection methods with IJP as a criterion	1. What are the predictive and concurrent validities of traditional selection methods with IJP as criterion? 2. In what way should traditional selection methods be adjusted in order to select for both OJP and IJP simultaneously?

relationships between different personality variables and IJP. Here we suggest future research should look at job characteristics (e.g., autonomy) and wider organizational context (e.g., support for innovation) to predict in what contexts different personality profiles would fit the best in terms of maximizing both their IJP and OJP.

Finally, we would like to highlight the need for more research in "real-life" recruitment and selection settings in order to examine criterion-related validities of different selection methods with IJP as a criterion. In this chapter we have discussed potential suitability of different selection methods and how they can be adjusted when selecting specifically for IJP. However, empirical evidence is needed to attest to both concurrent and predictive validities of these different methods with IJP as a criterion. To this end, future research should employ robust longitudinal designs and, importantly, assess IJP (the criterion) by independent observers using valid and reliable measures (for instance, those presented in Table 12.1).

Implications for practice

Our review also suggests a number of practical implications. First, our analysis suggests there are a number of relevant predictor methods, each of which may well have a role in predicting for the KSAOs we identified as being individual-level characteristics of higher innovation potential in the workplace. We would like to suggest the SJTs and ACs to be particularly relevant tools practitioners may use to screen the candidates for high/low innovation potential. Our view is that whilst organizations may wish to select for IJP more heavily, selection practitioners should not overlook the importance of assessing for OJP or lose sight of the importance of other facets of job performance (contextual performance, helping behaviors in the workplace, etc.). Therefore, the challenge here is how to design a valid and reliable set of selection methods to evaluate IJP that can be run practically alongside a selection procedure that is attempting to predict wider aspects of OJP. For instance, practitioners could add more creativity-specific abilities and personality traits to their already existing batteries of cognitive ability tests and personality inventories. In so doing, selecting for IJP could occur within the borders and overarching framework of selecting for OJP as the primary goal of any selection procedure.

Second, we would like to highlight the importance of following up and monitoring the extent to which employees, once hired, actually engage in innovative and creative behaviors in their workplaces. To this end, we would like to suggest the use of 360-degree feedback systems rather than pure self-reports of IJP to minimize biased ratings. Creating suggestion systems that can be used to submit ideas could also be an option to assess IJP more objectively.

Finally, we would like to highlight the need for wider organizational support for fostering employee IJP. Organizations should enhance innovative climate and performance cultures to support employee innovative efforts. This could be achieved by enhancing diversity in teams and equality in decision-making about new processes, fostering psychological safety and flexibility, providing good communication

TABLE 12.6 Implications for practice

Key areas	Implications for practice
Recruitment and selection	1. Adding proactive and creative personality and CSE measures to personality assessment batteries 2. Adding creative ability measures to cognitive assessment batteries 3. Assessment of innovation-specific KSAOs by means of ACs and SJTs
Assessment of IJP	1. Use of 360-degree feedback 2. Suggestion systems for employees to submit their ideas
Enhancing innovative culture	1. Ensuring diversity in teams 2. Fostering brainstorming 3. Empowering innovative employees 4. Enhancing psychological safety climate 5. Implementing rewards for innovation

systems and open space for employees to meet and brainstorm their ideas, and empowering innovative employees to apply their novel ideas in their workplaces.

Having noted these points, it is certainly the case that organizations are placing greater emphasis upon, and are attempting to select for, IJP over recent years. Therefore, it is beholden upon selection researchers to be able to put forward evidence-based recommendations and suggestions for the design of this element of any selection procedure. In the present chapter, we have endeavored to do precisely that. In drawing synergies between the innovation research findings on the one hand and the selection literature on the other, this chapter provides at least some points of departure and general recommendations for the design of appropriate selection procedures where the assessment of IJP is a declared objective.

References

Amabile, T.M. (1997). Motivating creativity in organizations: On doing what you love and loving what you do. *California Management Review, 40*, 39–58.

Amabile, T.M., Mueller, J.S., Simpson, W.B., Hadley, C.N., Kramer, S.J., & Fleming, L. (2002). *Time pressure and creativity in organizations: A longitudinal field study.* (HBS Working Paper 02-073). Cambridge, MA: Harvard University, Harvard Business School.

Anderson, N., & Burch, G.S.J. (2003). *The Team Selection Inventory.* Windsor, UK: ASE/NFER-Nelson.

Anderson, N., De Dreu, C.K.W., & Nijstad, B.A. (2004). The routinization of innovation research: A constructively critical review of the state-of-the-science. *Journal of Organizational Behavior, 25*, 147–173.

Anderson, N., Hülsheger, U., & Salgado, J. (2010). *Selecting for innovation.* Unpublished manuscript.

Anderson, N., Potočnik, K., & Zhou, J. (2014). Innovation and creativity in organizations: A state-of-the-science review and prospective commentary. *Journal of Management, 40*, 1297–1333.

Anderson, N., Salgado, J.F., & Hülsheger, U.R. (2010). Applicant reactions in selection: Comprehensive meta-analysis into reaction generalization versus situational specificity. *International Journal of Selection and Assessment, 18*, 291–304.

Anderson, N., Salgado, J., Schinkel, S., & Cunningham-Snell, N. (2008). Staffing the organization: An introduction to personnel selection and assessment. In N. Chmiel (Ed.), *An introduction to work and organizational psychology: A European perspective* (pp. 257–280). Oxford: Blackwell.

Anderson, N., & West, M. (1999). *The Team Climate Inventory* (2nd ed.). Windsor, UK: ASE/NFER-Nelson.

Arnold, J., Randall, R., Patterson, F., Silvester, J., Robertson, I., Cooper, C., & Den Hartog, D. (2010). *Work psychology: Understanding human behaviour in the workplace.* Harlow, UK: Pearson.

Axtell, C.M., Holman, D.J., Unsworth, K.L., Wall, T.D., Waterson, P.E., & Harrington, E. (2000). Shop floor innovation: Facilitating the suggestion and implementation of ideas. *Journal of Occupational and Organizational Psychology, 73*, 265–285.

Baer, M., & Oldham, G.R. (2006). The curvilinear relation between experienced creative time pressure and creativity: Moderating effects of openness to experience and support for creativity. *Journal of Applied Psychology, 91*, 963–970.

Barrick, M.R., & Mount, M.K. 1991. The Big Five personality dimensions and job performance: A meta-analysis. *Personnel Psychology, 44*, 1–26.

Barrick, M.R., Mount, M.K., & Judge, T.A. (2001). Personality and performance at the beginning of the new millennium: What do we know and where do we go next? *International Journal of Selection and Assessment, 9*, 9–30.

Bateman, T.S., & Crant, J.M. (1993). The proactive component of organizational behavior: A measure and correlates. *Journal of Organizational Behavior, 14*, 103–118.

Becker, G.A., & Miller, C.E. (2002). Examining contrast effects in performance appraisals: Using appropriate controls and assessing accuracy. *Journal of Psychology, 136*, 667–683.

Borman, W.C. (1977). Consistency of rating accuracy and rating errors in the judgment of human performance. *Organizational Behavior and Human Performance, 20*, 238–252.

Burch, G.S.J., & Anderson, N. (2004). Measuring person-team fit: Development and validation of the team selection inventory. *Journal of Managerial Psychology, 97*, 177–190.

Burch, G.S.J., Pavelis, C., & Port, R.L. (2008). Selecting for creativity and innovation: The relationship between the innovation potential indicator and the team selection inventory. *International Journal of Selection and Assessment, 16*, 177–181.

Cacioppo, J.T., & Petty, R.E. (1982). The need for cognition. *Journal of Personality and Social Psychology, 42*(1), 116.

Carmeli, A., & Schaubroeck, J. (2007). The influence of leaders' and other referents' normative expectations on individual involvement in creative work. *The Leadership Quarterly, 18*, 35–48.

Chang, C.H., Ferris, D.L., Johnson, R.E., Rosen, C.C., & Tan, J.A. (2012). Core self-evaluations: A review and evaluation of the literature. *Journal of Management, 38*, 81–128.

Choi, J.N. (2004a). Individual and contextual dynamics of innovation-use behavior in organizations. *Human Performance, 17*, 397–414.

Choi, J.N. (2004b). Individual and contextual predictors of creative performance: The mediating role of psychological processes. *Creativity Research Journal, 16*, 187–199.

Choi, J.N., Anderson, T.A., & Veillette, A. (2009). Contextual inhibitors of employee creativity in organizations: The insulating role of creative ability. *Group & Organization Management, 34*, 330–357.

Clegg, C., Unsworth, K., Epitropaki, O., & Parker, G. (2002). Implicating trust in the innovation process. *Journal of Occupational & Organizational Psychology, 75*, 409–422.

Ford, C.M. (1996). A theory of individual creative action in multiple social domains. *Academy of Management Review, 21*, 1112–1142.

Fuller, J.B., & Marler, L.E. (2009). Change driven by nature: A meta-analytic review of the proactive personality literature. *Journal of Vocational Behavior, 75*, 329–345.

Furnham, A., & Nederstrom, M. (2010). Ability, demographic and personality predictors of creativity. *Personality and Individual Differences, 48*, 957–961.

George, J.M., & Zhou, J. (2001). When openness to experience and conscientiousness are related to creative behavior: An interactional approach. *Journal of Applied Psychology, 86*, 513–524.

Gong, Y., Cheung, S., Wang, M., & Huang, J. (2012). Unfolding the proactive process for creativity: Integration of the employee proactivity, information exchange, and psychological safety perspectives. *Journal of Management, 38*, 1611–1633.

Gough, H.G. (1979). A creative personality scale for the Adjective Check List. *Journal of Personality and Social Psychology, 37*, 1398–1405.

Hammond, M.M., Neff, N.L., Farr, J.L., Schwall, A.R., & Zhao, X. (2011). Predictors of individual-level innovation at work: A meta-analysis. *Psychology of Aesthetics, Creativity, and the Arts, 5*, 90–105.

Hülsheger, U.R., Anderson, N., & Salgado, J.F. (2009). Team-level predictors of innovation at work: A comprehensive meta-analysis spanning three decades of research. *Journal of Applied Psychology, 94*, 1128–1145.

Hunter, J.E., & Hunter, R.F. (1984). Validity and utility of alternative predictors of job performance. *Psychological Bulletin, 96,* 72–98.

Janssen, O. (2001). Fairness perceptions as a moderator in the curvilinear relationships between job demands, and job performance and job satisfaction. *Academy of Management Journal, 44,* 1039–1050.

Judge, T.A., & Bono, J.E. (2001). Relationship of core self-evaluations traits – self-esteem, generalized self-efficacy, locus of control, and emotional stability – with job satisfaction and job performance: A meta-analysis. *Journal of Applied Psychology, 86,* 80–92.

Judge, T.A., Erez, A., Bono, J.E., & Thoresen, C.J. (2003). The core self-evaluations scale: Development of a measure. *Personnel Psychology, 56,* 303–331.

Judge T.A., Locke, A.E., & Durham, C.C. (1997). The dispositional causes of job satisfaction: A core evaluations approach. *Research in Organizational Behavior, 19,* 151–188.

Kirton, M. (1976). Adaptors and innovators: A description and measure. *Journal of Applied Psychology, 61,* 622–629.

Krause, D.E. (2004). Influence-based leadership as a determinant of the inclination to innovate and of innovation-related behaviors: An empirical investigation. *The Leadership Quarterly, 15,* 79–102.

Latham, S.F., & Braun, M. (2009). Managerial risk, innovation, and organizational decline. *Journal of Management, 35,* 258–281.

McEntire, L.E., & Greene-Shortridge, T.M. (2011). Recruiting and selecting leaders for innovation: How to find the right leader. *Advances in Developing Human Resources, 13,* 266–278.

Melancon, S.C., & Williams, M.S. (2006). Competency-based assessment center design: A case study. *Advances in Developing Human Resources, 8,* 283–314.

Ng, T.W.H., & Feldman, D.C. (2009). How broadly does education contribute to job performance? *Personnel Psychology, 62,* 89–134.

Oldham, G.R., & Cummings, A. (1996). Employee creativity: Personal and contextual factors at work. *Academy of Management Journal, 39,* 607–634.

Parker, S.K., Williams, H.M., & Turner, N. (2006). Modeling the antecedents of proactive behavior at work. *Journal of Applied Psychology, 91,* 636–652.

Patterson, F. (2000). *The Innovation Potential Indicator: Test manual and user's guide.* Oxford: Oxford Psychologists Press.

Podsakoff, P.M., MacKenzie, S.B., Lee, J.Y., & Podsakoff, N.P. (2003). Common method biases in behavioral research: A critical review of the literature and recommended remedies. *Journal of Applied Psychology, 88,* 879–903.

Potočnik, K., & Anderson, N. (2012). Assessing innovation: A 360-degree appraisal study. *International Journal of Selection and Assessment, 20,* 497–509.

Potočnik, K., & Anderson, N. (2013). Innovationsorientierte personalauswahl [Selecting for innovation]. In D. Krause (Ed.), *Kreativität, Innovation, und Entrepreneurship [Creativity, innovation, and entrepreneurship]* (pp. 155–173). Berlin: Springer-Verlag.

Raja, U., & Johns, G. (2010). The joint effects of personality and job scope on in-role performance, citizenship behaviors and creativity. *Human Relations, 63,* 981–1005.

Schmidt, F.L., & Hunter, J.E. (1998). The validity and utility of selection methods in personnel psychology: Practical and theoretical implications of 85 years of research finding. *Psychological Bulletin, 124,* 262–274.

Schmidt, F.L., Shaffer, J.A., & Oh, I. (2008). Increased accuracy for range restriction corrections: Implications for the role of personality and general mental ability in job and training performance. *Personnel Psychology, 61,* 827–868.

Scott, S.G., & Bruce, R.A. (1994). Determinants of innovative behavior: A path model of individual innovation in the workplace. *Academy of Management Journal, 37,* 580–607.

Shalley, C.E., & Perry-Smith, J.E. (2001). Effects of social–psychological factors on creative performance: The role of informational and controlling expected evaluation and modeling experience. *Organizational Behavior and Human Decision Processes, 84*, 1–22.

Shalley, C.E., Zhou, J., & Oldham, G.R. (2004). The effects of personal and contextual characteristics on creativity: Where should we go from here? *Journal of Management, 30*, 933–958.

Subramaniam, M., & Youndt, M.A. (2005). The influence of intellectual capital on the types of innovative capabilities. *Academy of Management Journal, 48*, 450–463.

Sung, S.Y., & Choi, J.N. (2009). Do Big Five personality factors affect individual creativity? The moderating role of extrinsic motivation. *Social Behavior and Personality, 37*, 941–956.

Tierney, P., & Farmer, S.M. (2002). Creative self-efficacy: Its potential antecedents and relationship to creative performance. *Academy of Management Journal, 45*, 1137–1148.

Tierney, P., & Farmer, S.M. (2011). Creative self-efficacy development and creative performance over time. *Journal of Applied Psychology, 96*, 277–293.

Tierney, P., Farmer, S.M., & Graen, G.B. (1999). An examination of leadership and employee creativity: The relevance of traits and relationships. *Personnel Psychology, 52*, 591–620.

Wang, H., Begley, T., Hui, C., & Lee, C. (2012). Are the effects of conscientiousness on contextual and innovative performance context specific? Organizational culture as a moderator. *International Journal of Human Resource Management, 23*, 174–189.

West, M.A. (2002). Sparkling fountains or stagnant ponds: An integrative model of creativity and innovation implementation in work groups. *Applied Psychology: An International Review, 51*, 355–387.

Wu, C., Parker, S.K., & De Jong, J.P.J. (2014). Need for cognition as an antecedent of individual innovation behavior. *Journal of Management, 40*, 511–534.

Yuan, F., & Woodman, R.W. (2010). Innovative behavior in the workplace: The role of performance and image outcome expectations. *Academy of Management Journal, 53*, 323–342.

Zhou, J., & George, J.M. (2001). When job dissatisfaction leads to creativity: Encouraging the expression of voice. *Academy of Management Journal, 44*, 682–696.

13

TYPICAL AND MAXIMUM PERFORMANCE

Ute-Christine Klehe

JUSTUS LIEBIG UNIVERSITÄT GIESSEN, GERMANY

Jessica Grazi

JUSTUS LIEBIG UNIVERSITÄT GIESSEN, GERMANY

Tusharika Mukherjee

JUSTUS LIEBIG UNIVERSITÄT GIESSEN, GERMANY

Job performance – employee behaviors relevant to the goals of the organization (Campbell, 1990; McCloy, Campbell, & Cudeck, 1994) – is a core criterion in human resource decisions. Yet, no one comprehensive model of job performance covers all the multidimensionality and complexity inherent in this criterion (Borman, 1991; Campbell, 1990). This makes job performance a difficult variable to grasp and measure (Austin & Villanova, 1992). Most performance models operationalize performance as a stable or static phenomenon, interpreting deviations from mean performance as a lack of extrinsic and intrinsic reliability (Thorndike, 1949) and thus as task-irrelevant error or noise. These models ignore the temporal multidimensionality and variable nature of individual job performance (Barnes & Morgeson, 2007). Yet, performers not only show idiosyncratic profiles of personal strengths and weaknesses, but performance changes over time as well (Cascio & Aguinis, 2011). Further, there is substantial and meaningful variability of individual performance within the same general time frame of a performer's career and on the exact same task: Stewart and Nandkeolyar (2006) observed the weekly performance of 167 salespeople and found that 73% of the variance in weekly sales was within-person. Fisher and Noble (2004) asked 121 employees to report their task performance five times per day for two weeks and found that 77% of the variance in self-ratings of performance was within-person. Obviously, individuals do not perform at exactly the same level at all times.

Address for correspondence: Ute-Christine Klehe, Work and Organizational Psychology, Justus-Liebig-University Giessen, Otto Behaghel Strasse 10F, 35394 Giessen, Germany

Two main approaches incorporate intra-individual performance variation into performance measurement models. The systems approach tries to identify and combine sources of performance variability inherent to the system (i.e., the organizational context) and the person (Deadrick & Gardner, 2000; Murphy & Cleveland, 1995). Performance variability is therefore explained by changing job requirements, performance expectations, and resources, which in turn change performers' motivation and/or ability (Cascio & Aguinis, 2011). The second approach is the distinction between typical and maximum performance (Sackett, Zedeck, & Fogli, 1988), focusing on variations of motivation on performance on exactly the same tasks. Typical performance is the level of performance achieved over a longer time period ("will do"), while maximum performance refers to the level of performance when highly motivated ("can do").

Typical versus maximum performance

In his 2007 commentary for the *Human Performance* special issue on typical versus maximum performance, Sackett recounts how a chance situation and a surprising finding led to the distinction between typical and maximum performance. Working on an applied validation study for the selection of supermarket cashiers, Sackett and colleagues (1988) had to deal with two versions of their criterion measure, that is, the speed and accuracy with which supermarket cashiers processed items. While some supermarkets at that time were already equipped with electronic monitoring devices that allowed an automatic and unobtrusive assessment of cashier performance, other supermarkets relied on supervisors measuring employee performance via predetermined shopping carts and stopwatches. Unfortunately, these two measures of the supposedly same construct failed to converge, and after ruling out several methodological reasons, Sackett et al. (1988) realized that they were dealing with conceptually distinct dimensions of performance. While the one dimension addressed performance under nonevaluative day-to-day conditions, then labelled *typical* performance, the other dimension rather reflected performance under short but obviously evaluative situations, labelled *maximum* performance. "Thus, the typical versus maximum performance distinction emerged from applied work: We did not dream up the theory and then go test it" (Sackett, 2007, p. 180).

In order to put meaningful labels to their observation, Sackett et al. (1988) borrowed from the personnel selection literature. Cronbach (1960) had used the distinction between typical and maximum performance to differentiate between measures of personality and measures of ability, a distinction that is still used today (Dennis, Sternberg, & Beatty, 2000). Sackett et al. (1988) adapted this to describe variations in actual job performance, thus extending it to the criterion domain on the basis of the following argument:

Job performance is a dynamic function of ability and motivation (Locke, Mento, & Katcher, 1978). The term 'ability' comprises performers' declarative knowledge, procedural knowledge, and procedural skills (Campbell, 1990). Motivation is defined by three choices (Campbell, 1990): (a) to expend effort (direction), (b) which level of effort to expend (level), and (c) whether to persist in the expenditure of that level of effort (persistence). The basic idea underlying Sackett et al.'s (1988) distinction (see also DuBois, Sackett, Zedeck, & Fogli, 1993, and Sackett, 2007) is that performers can differ, depending on the situation, on the direction, level, and persistence of effort they expend on the task at hand. Once motivation is high, goes the argument, performance rises and one can be sure to assess a person's maximum performance, or, as Sackett (2007, p. 182) noted, "Maximum performance is performance when all attentional and motivational resources are dedicated to task performance." He conceptualized maximum performance as "the level of performance in a given domain that one can produce on demand for a short period if one chooses to exert maximum effort" (Sackett, 2007, p. 183). However, in situations in which one cannot be sure that motivation is high (it well may be, but we just can't know), one is more likely to assess a person's typical level of performance. The question then is how one can tell whether someone is currently highly motivated and thus leaning towards maximum performance, or whether that person is currently showing their typical level of direction, effort, and persistence.

Approaches to studying typical versus maximum performance

Performance situations

Sackett et al. (1988) tried to explain such variations in performance motivation via variations in performance situations. More precisely, Sackett et al. (1988; DuBois et al., 1993) argued that during typical performance situations, the day-to-day performance on the job, performers are usually (a) relatively unaware that their performance may be observed or even evaluated, are usually (b) not consciously trying to continually perform their 'absolute best', and are (c) working on their task over an extended period of time.

For many jobs, typical performance represents the broadest part of daily activities. In situations of maximum performance, however, these situational conditions change. Now, performers are (a) very well aware of being evaluated, are (b) aware and accept implicit or explicit instructions to maximize their effort, and are (c) observed for a short enough time period to keep their attention focused on the task.

These situational characteristics in turn will influence the role of motivation and ability. During typical performance situations, the motivational choices of direction, level, and persistence of effort lie with performers: since their performance is not being evaluated, performers can choose to focus on the task or can choose to do something else instead. Since performers have not received or accepted instruction to do their very best, they can choose to invest their full level of effort or just any proportion of it. Finally, as they may tire during the course of the task, performers can choose to persist in that level of effort or can reduce their efforts over time.

However, each of these choices will diminish when a typical performance situation turns into a maximum one. Here, motivation is arguably constrained to be high (DuBois et al., 1993; Sackett et al., 1988): the choice to perform is high due to the performers' knowledge of being monitored and "unless one is inviting disciplinary action, one has little choice but to expend effort on the task in question" (DuBois et al., 1993, p. 206). The level of effort is high, as performers are aware of and accept the instruction to expend effort. Persistence, finally, is neither demanded nor measured in maximum performance situations, as performance is only observed for a period brief enough for performers to stay focused on the task.

Obviously, these three situational conditions are not the only avenue for fostering maximum performance. After all, people may be motivated also for other reasons than external situational constraints, and "the absence of one of more [of these three situational conditions] does not preclude maximum performance" (Sackett, 2007, p. 183). For example, performers may decide to invest their maximum effort out of their free will, for example, when task, personal fitness, working conditions, and other contextual variables support them to do so (e.g., Ryan & Deci, 2000). In this regard, Sackett (2007, p. 182) noted that "In retrospect, I believed we erred in calling the conditions necessary: The better statement is that the three terms are sufficient." Whenever these conditions are present, one can usually assume people will show their maximum performance (though see also Klehe, Anderson, & Hoefnagels, 2007), yet in the absence of the three conditions, it becomes more difficult to judge whether people are already investing their maximum effort or whether they could possibly show higher motivation and thus, likely, higher performance.

Performance distributions

An alternative approach to addressing typical versus maximum performance has been to study performance distributions by comparing performers' average performance under any given circumstance to their highest performance score recorded (e.g., Barnes & Morgeson, 2007; Borman, 1991; Deadrick & Gardner, 2008). The merits of this approach lie in its (a) intuitive logic, (b) conceptual link to earlier research on performance variability, and (c) data-accessibility (something that has proven to be more difficult with Sackett et al.'s [1988] approach; see below). A disadvantage, however, is that one is studying a mere outcome measure without really knowing how this outcome may have come about. This is particularly an issue with the data-points chosen as indicators of 'maximum' or rather 'peak' performance. These can be identified only *post hoc* after the observation of the complete data set, and they may be due to luck and/or to external circumstances just as much as to high motivation.

No studies to date directly compared traditional measures of maximum performance with instances of peak performance, even though these two may well covary. At the same time, even though these terms are regularly used interchangeably in common parlance, both measures differ not only conceptually, but also in terms of research focus. Where traditional approaches to typical versus maximum performance find more resonance in laboratory research and in research using administrative or other regular work tasks, research on peak performance is particularly dominant in the sports domain (e.g., Barnes & Morgeson, 2007).

Relatedly, both lines of research show distinct patterns of covariates and consequences. The relationship between 'traditional' measures of typical versus maximum performance is usually meaningful but modest (ρ = .42; Beus & Whitman,

2012; combining physical, psychosocial, and administrative tasks, assessed by soft as well as hard criterion measures, in both laboratory and field settings across North America, East Asia, and Europe), whereas average and peak performance can correlate considerably higher with one another (e.g., $\rho = .90$; Barnes & Morgeson, 2007). As a consequence, Barnes and Morgeson (2007) found peak performance to be unrelated to the performance evaluations (measured via compensation) as soon as the researchers controlled for performers' average performance. In contrast, Sackett et al. (1988) found that supervisory evaluations of performance correlated more highly with supermarket cashiers' maximum performance than with their typical performance on the job. They explained this originally unexpected finding with supervisors usually being more likely to be around cashiers during periods of high customer demand when all hands were needed at the cash registers and that "their primary concern regarding cashiers is whether the cashier can 'turn it on' during peak periods" (p. 486). Up to now, we still lack a replication of this finding, however, to ensure that this finding was truly due to the importance of high performance under maximum rather than under typical performance conditions, and not necessarily a feature of supervisory performance evaluations in general.

The relevance of typical versus maximum performance

Researchers soon became aware of the major conceptual and empirical consequences that the distinction between typical and maximum performance would bear for different areas of industrial, work, and organizational psychology in general (e.g., Ackerman & Humphreys, 1990; Arvey, & Murphy, 1998; Borman, 1991; Herriot & Anderson, 1997; Viswesvaran, Sinangil, Ones, & Anderson, 2001). Through the distinction from typical performance and the constrained role of motivation during maximum performance, Sackett et al. (1988) argued that the balance between ability and motivation in predicting performance would change. During typical performance ('what people will do', Sackett et al., 1988), both motivation and ability should be relevant predictors of performance. As maximum performance situations constrain motivation to be high, however, maximum performance should be limited primarily by performers' ability ('what people can do', Sackett et al., 1988). Janz (1989, p. 164) argued, "Maximum performance focuses on competencies, whereas typical performance focuses on choices." Guion (1991) proposed that the low correlation between measures of typical and maximum performance may explain the low criterion-related validity of numerous predictors of job performance, and Campbell (1990) argued that basing selection decisions on predictors of maximum performance could be one cause for the weak relationship often found between results of personnel selection procedures and typical performance on the job. Such mismatch could also become quite expensive, as results from utility analyses regarding a selection procedure's prediction of typical job performance are likely biased if the financial value of performance is estimated based on maximum performance criteria, and vice versa (Boudreau, 1991). Consequently, both researchers and practitioners needed to know which of the two aspects of performance they aim to predict, not only in validation studies, but across research situations (Guion, 1991, 1998). Similarly, Sackett and Larson (1990) discussed threats to the generalizability of research findings, including the importance of not generalizing empirical findings derived from typical performance situations to maximum performance situations and vice versa. Chernyshenko, Stark, Chan, Drasgow, and Williams (2001) even applied the distinction to item response theory (IRT) and argued that traditional IRT models may represent well the constrained responding to maximum performance situations, but not the complexity of responding to typical performance situations. Overall, the distinction between typical and maximum performance emerges regularly in the discussion section of empirical manuscripts to outline likely causes for unexpected findings or to suggest boundary conditions to the findings reported.

Findings on typical versus maximum performance

A test of the basic assumptions

At the same time, the empirical basis for the typical versus maximum performance distinction has failed to keep pace with these proposed implications. Even the basic tenets of this literature, namely that the distinction between performance in typical and maximum performance situations lies in the role of motivation (Sackett et al., 1988), wasn't tested until about two decades later. In that study, Klehe and Anderson (2007a) asked 138 psychology students to find hardware prices on the Internet and to enter them into a computer program. While participants worked on this task for close to two hours, they were not obviously observed or evaluated during most of that time (typical performance). The computer unobtrusively recorded all of the participants' actions. Only for a five-minute interval in the midst of the experiment did the experimenter enter the room and look over the participants' shoulders (maximum performance condition). While the experimenter had been instructed to remain as silent and to invite as little interaction as possible, the observatory nature of this intrusion was quite obvious. As expected, results indeed showed that participants did not work significantly smarter, but that they worked harder during the short maximum performance period. They focused more on the task, measured in time working on the task. Their level of effort was higher, measured in task-related clicks per minute, and persistence appears to have been less of an issue during maximum performance, as indicated by the development of level over time. Consequently, their performance during the maximum performance period surpassed their performance during the rest of the experiment. Given such change in direction, level, and persistence of effort, Sackett et al. (1988) had also proposed the relationship of both motivation and ability to change under typical versus maximum performance conditions. And, indeed, given the constrained nature of motivation during the maximum performance period, both proximal (direction, level, persistence of effort) and more distal indicators of motivation (task valence and self-efficacy) correlated significantly higher with performance during the typical performance period than during the short evaluative period in the presence of the experimenter, even though this effect was not as strong as Sackett et al. (1988) might have originally hoped for. The opposite effect was found for a multiple-choice measure of computer-related knowledge and for participants' procedural skills (the degree to which people used smart strategies to solve the task): while these were not the only determinants of performance under maximum performance conditions, they still gained greatly in relevance compared to the typical performance period. Thus, results did not fully support the original assumption that maximum performance would only be accounted for by declarative knowledge and procedural skills. Yet, compared with the assessments of typical performance, the role of ability did indeed increase, whereas the role of motivation decreased, in accounting for performance under the short maximum performance condition.

Motivation and ability predicting typical and maximum performance

Beside this in-depth examination of the distinction's basic assumptions, the differential validities of measures of motivation and ability for typical and maximum performance are the primary interest of subsequent empirical studies on typical versus maximum performance. Different studies indeed found stronger links between measures of ability and indicators of maximum than of typical performance and the reverse for measures of motivation (e.g., DuBois et al., 1993; Klehe & Anderson, 2007a; Marcus, Goffin, Johnston, & Rothstein, 2007; McCloy et al., 1994). The meta-analysis by Beus and Whitman (2012), however, supported this assertion only partially: Although ability, mostly assessed via general mental ability, was a stronger predictor of maximum ($\rho = .32$) than of typical performance ($\rho = .19$), findings on motivation were less conclusive. Here, results did point in the proposed direction (with a validity of $\rho = .40$ for predicting typical and of $\rho = .30$ for predicting maximum performance) but failed to reach statistical significance, possibly because of the few studies available and the relatively high percentage of variance accounted for by sampling error.

Reversing the above argument, Klehe and Latham (2006) used the distinction between typical and maximum performance to address the constructs being assessed in another type of personnel selection procedure, namely structured interviews, which had been argued to assess future intentions (Latham, 1989) or choices made in the past (Janz, 1989), respectively, by their original authors – and which had been argued to measure some form of verbal and inductive reasoning skills or job knowledge by others (e.g., Janz, 1989; Taylor & Small, 2002). Including both typical and maximum performance into a predictive validation study, Klehe and Latham (2006) found that both future- and past-oriented interviews predicted typical performance significantly better than maximum performance, suggesting that both interview formats primarily assessed motivational constructs, such as intentions or choices. Obviously, these motivational variables may still be informed and influenced by interviewees' practical intelligence and job knowledge (Klehe & Latham, 2008).

While future research in this line is clearly needed, this study shows the possibility of using typical versus maximum performance for establishing the construct- and criterion-related validity of specific selection procedures.

The predictive power of personality

On a surface level, linking the distinction between typical versus maximum performance to its original counterpart in the personnel selection domain (Cronbach, 1960; Dennis et al., 2000), one might argue for a close link between maximum performance predictors (i.e., ability) and maximum performance as a criterion and between typical performance predictors (i.e., personality) and typical performance as a criterion. After all, ability is proposed to address *can do* aspects of performance, while personality is proposed to address *will do* aspects of performance. Yet, a closer examination of different personality dimensions suggests that such a direct link is too simplistic. Not even conscientiousness, conceptually closely linked to the motivation to perform well, emerges consistently as a significantly better predictor of typical than of maximum performance (Beus & Whitman, 2012). Nor did any such results occur for extraversion, agreeableness, or emotional stability. Yet, openness to experience, sometimes also labelled 'intellect' and related to general mental ability (Judge, Higgins, Thoresen, & Barrick, 1999), emerged as a stronger predictor of maximum relative to typical performance. When interpreting these findings, however, one needs to be aware that results rely on only three to five studies each, with one of them (Ployhart, Lim, & Chan, 2001) dominating the overall sample size with 71% to 87%. As this study in particular, however, is rather atypical of the typical versus maximum performance literature, comparing vastly different performance situations with one another (see below), results will be difficult to generalize in the absence of further studies.

Moderators to the correlation between measures of typical and maximum performance

Another relevant area addresses the relationship between measures of typical and maximum performance and the conditions under which their overlap will be more or less pronounced. While research on this is still in its infancy, some factors have already gained meta-analytic attention, namely the complexity of the task, the objective versus subjective nature of the performance rating, and the study's setting.

Sackett et al. (1988) argued that more complex tasks usually require a greater level of ability also for typical performance – with the result that typical and maximum performance should thus share a stronger relationship. Thus, the distinction between typical and maximum performance may be less vital in a dynamic setting requiring continuous learning and mutual adaptation than in a relatively static job. Relatedly, Sternberg (1999) conceptualized ability as developing expertise, arguing that the main constraint in achieving this expertise is not some fixed capacity, but deliberate practice. Thus, an individual's ability to perform a complex task may depend on that person's prior motivation to learn how to perform this task effectively. Thus, high typical performance may even become a prerequisite for high maximum performance for complex tasks, and the distinction between the two may become less clear. In line with such thoughts, Beus and Whitman (2012) found that the average relationship between measures of typical versus maximum performance ($\rho = .42$) is usually stronger for more complex ($\rho = .46$) than for simple tasks ($\rho = .36$).

Further moderators studied to date are primarily methodological in nature. First, Beus and Whitman (2012) argued that the criterion deficiencies and poor reliability of objective performance criteria might attenuate the relationships found between objective measures of typical and maximum performance. Results indeed suggest smaller relationships between objective indicators of typical and maximum performance ($\rho = .37$) than between subjective indicators ($\rho = .45$). Second, they addressed the distinction between field and military settings on the one hand and laboratory or classroom settings on the other hand. The former are more in line with Sackett et al.'s (1988) own approach and Sackett and Larson's (1990) concern that laboratory studies in general are often assessments of maximum rather than of typical performance. Yet, laboratory settings often allow for cleaner experiments free of external noise or alternative possible explanations but the manipulation involved. In either case, results indeed revealed stronger links between assessments of typical versus maximum performance in laboratory ($\rho = .59$) than in field or military settings ($\rho = .35$).

Beus and Whitman (2012) also proposed other moderators, such as length of assessment under both typical and maximum performance conditions or the time lag between those two assessments. Yet, the database currently available is still too small to render meaningful results, leaving the authors with nothing but nonsignificant tendencies.

Methodological issues in studying typical versus maximum performance

Overall, the empirical basis for the study of typical versus maximum performance is thus still rather modest and it certainly falls short of the numerous implications proposed. Considering this relatively scarce research base, Sackett (2007, p. 181) acknowledged "that Sackett et al. contributed to the relatively slow rate of work on this issue by presenting an imposing set of conditions for an appropriate comparison of typical and maximum performance measures." More specifically, Sackett et al. (1988) argued that in order to present a non-confounded comparison of any measure of typical versus maximum performance, these measures should be comparable in: (a) the modality of measurement (using the same measurement source and standard), (b) the level of specificity (e.g., speed of performance in both instances, rather than relying on speed of performance in one instance and a global measure of performance in another), (c) the time of assessment in an individual's job tenure, and (d) they should both be reliable.

The goal of these conditions is to ensure that results obtained are truly a function of participants' knowledge of being evaluated, their acceptance of instruction to invest effort, and the time duration (Sackett et al., 1988). While these demands sound logical and straightforward, Sackett (2007, p. 181) himself acknowledged that "studies in field settings generally do not meet these conditions". One of the reasons may be that a clear comparison between performance under typical versus maximum performance conditions implies that the task that is being performed is fully comparable as well – a requirement that may not even be feasible in many occupations. For example, when comparing the typical performance of pilots with their performance in a maximum-performance flight simulator (Smith-Jentsch, Jentsch, Payne, & Salas, 1996), one must also consider that flight simulations oftentimes do not mirror pilots' average flight but rather particularly challenging/dangerous crisis situations. Similar cases could be made about many other occupations (doctors, firefighters, soldiers, etc.). Here, the dominant distinction may be far less between instances of typical and maximum performance than between performance during typical versus crisis situations. Even parts of Sackett et al.'s (1988) own results could be a function not of typical versus maximum performance per se, but of varying job demands during typical performance situations. During a typical performance period, which oftentimes also includes slow periods, speed of processing items might be less indicative of good cashier performance than, for example, establishing friendly interpersonal relationships with customers.

Some studies on typical versus maximum performance make explicit usage of different task requirements under typical versus maximum performance conditions. Building on the finding that agreeableness, openness, and extraversion correlate with transformational leadership (Judge & Bono, 2000), Ployhart et al. (2001) argued that transformational leadership would be more relevant during maximum performance conditions than under typical performance conditions – resulting in higher criterion-related validities of these personality dimensions for transformational leadership under maximum performance conditions. For testing their assumptions, they subsequently compared military recruits' transformational leadership during a two-day assessment center developed primarily to assess leadership skills (maximum performance situation) with their performance during their basic military training, which in turn had been primarily developed to train recruits' physical fitness (typical performance situation). Thus, the assessments of typical and maximum performance posed explicitly different task demands to performers and thus differed in more aspects than the three motivational conditions differentiating typical and maximum performance situations.

As a consequence of the difficulties in establishing clean comparisons between typical versus maximum performance in field settings, and thus in ensuring the internal validity of any comparison made, other researchers turn to laboratory settings (Klehe & Anderson, 2007a; Klehe et al., 2007). They ask research participants to perform exactly the same task under differing conditions (e.g., monitored vs. unmonitored, timed vs. untimed) and thus ensure the establishment of truly parallel situations of typical and maximum performance under an otherwise relatively controlled research setting. Laboratory findings (Klehe & Anderson, 2007a) supporting

Sackett et al.'s (1988) assumptions suggest the viability of such an approach. Yet, Sackett (2007, p. 181) correctly notes that "although the effects of varying these conditions can be examined, the 'performance over the long term' aspect of typical performance is not amendable to study in short-duration lab studies". In other words: Laboratory studies may fall short in terms of external validity to the organizational context.

In the end, typical versus maximum performance situations represent a continuum (Sackett et al., 1988), and any comparison between the two is relative. Potentially more troublesome, however, is that only a few field (Klehe & Latham, 2006) or laboratory (Klehe et al., 2007) studies on typical versus maximum performance include even a basic manipulation check, empirically testing whether the 'more typical' and the 'more maximum' performance situations truly differ in their perceived evaluation, instruction, and duration.

To facilitate future research in this regard, Klehe and Anderson (2005) developed the typical-maximum-performance-scale (TMPS), a scale to distinguish the degree to which a situation is perceived as rather typical or maximum on six distinct dimensions: the three situational criteria of (a) knowledge of evaluation, (b) receiving and acceptance of instructions to maximize effort, and (c) perceived duration, and the three motivational consequences of (d) direction, (e) level, and (f) persistence of effort. Generally, subscales show decent internal consistencies and have successfully distinguished between situations of clearly typical and clearly maximum performance, while being unaffected by gender, age, cognitive ability, and most facets of personality.

At the same time, a mere manipulation check using the TMPS does not preclude the existence of alternative possible explanations that may easily account for the effects found. A more comprehensive manipulation check would not only include the proposed differences between typical versus maximum performance instances but would also ensure their comparability in regard to the performance objectives and specificities, as well as the measurements' modality and reliability. To our knowledge, only Klehe and Latham (2006) went through the effort to not only argue but actually test whether the criterion used in that study (peer evaluations of team playing performance) were comparably important and observable under both the typical and the maximum performance conditions studied.

Conceptual links to other motivational theories and their consequences for the study of typical versus maximum performance

Given that the empirical literature on typical versus maximum performance is still small compared to the hopes and promises raised (Sackett, 2007), our final objective of the current chapter is to point at some directions of potential promise. Actually, we may already know quite a bit more about this literature than we possibly think we know as soon as we study typical versus maximum performance not only from its own perspective, but also from those of other – and frequently quite fundamental – psychological theories. In the following, we will introduce three such theoretical approaches, namely VIE theory, social loafing and facilitation, and self-determination theory.

VIE theory

In terms of classic motivational theories, the distinction between typical and maximum performance is likely best explained via Vroom's (1964) valence-instrumentality-expectancy theory (VIE), which posits that people will be more motivated to enact a certain behavior (e.g., to work hard) the more they believe that their effort will result in effective performance (expectancy) and that such performance will be rewarded (instrumentality), and the more they value those rewards (valence). Following DuBois et al.'s (1993) arguments, the variable most influenced through a change from a typical to a maximum performance situation is likely instrumentality, the belief that high performance will be rewarded or, alternatively, that low performance will be punished. During typical performance situations, instrumentality is likely relatively weak and will depend on performers' ability to set goals and rewards contingent on the achievement of those goals (that is, to create the missing instrumentality themselves). During situations of maximum performance, however, when performers are encouraged to invest their full effort and are evaluated on the basis of their performance, the link between performance and extrinsic rewards becomes highly apparent, leading performers to be highly motivated.

Social loafing, facilitation, and inhibition

VIE theory has already served to explain effects in the conceptually related literature on social loafing, that is, the tendency for individuals to expend less effort when working collectively than when working alone (Karau & Williams, 1993). Like typical and maximum performance, social loafing depends on the evaluation potential existent in the situation. Latané, Williams, and Harkins (1979) proposed that people only loaf when they think that their performance is not identifiable and thus believe that "they can receive neither precise credit nor appropriate blame for their performance" (p. 830). Indeed, Karau and Williams (1993) meta-analytically confirmed that people engage in social loafing if they feel unaccountable for the outcome, but not if they feel that they can be evaluated for their results. DuBois et al.'s (1993) argument that "unless one is inviting disciplinary action [under maximum performance conditions], one has little choice but to expend effort on the task in question" (p. 206) follows the exact same train of thought, suggesting that social loafing will only happen under typical but not under maximum performance conditions.

Karau and Williams (1993) further integrated the literature on social loafing via VIE theory, showing that loafing usually occurs in the absence of an evaluation, but particularly under certain conditions (e.g., on tasks of low valence or with work groups of low valence). Taking these findings into account, Klehe and Anderson

(2007b) created a series of scenario cases and asked participants to respond to them under either typical or under maximum performance conditions, largely replicating findings from the social loafing literature also for the case of typical versus maximum performance conditions.

Yet research on social loafing also suggests that evaluative conditions do not always enhance motivation and subsequent performance. More specifically, social loafing, social facilitation, and social inhibition share the same underlying processes (Sanna, 1992), with the primary distinction defining the performance result of a highly evaluative situation being performers' task-related self-efficacy. Given high self-efficacy, expectation of evaluation usually improves or has no effect on performance. Yet evaluation expectation inhibits performance among performers with low self-efficacy (Bond, 1982; Sanna, 1992; Sanna & Shotland, 1990). Klehe et al. (2007) found comparable effects for typical versus maximum performance. After a manipulation of their self-efficacy through feedback on a multiple-choice test, 93 first-year psychology students explained three topics from one of their lectures to a confederate (typical performance condition) and three related topics to the experimenter in the presence of a camera and a microphone (maximum performance condition). Performance was assessed in the form of the content and the communicative quality of the explanation. In line with above research on social loafing and inhibition, but contradicting Sackett et al. (1988), the performance of low self-efficacy participants in the maximum performance condition fell significantly short of their performance in the typical performance condition.

Conceptually, this implies two things: First, via the conceptual links to the literature on VIE theory and on social loafing, facilitation, and inhibition, we apparently know more about typical versus maximum performance than the literature focusing explicitly on this distinction would suggest. Second, the link between situational conditions and resulting performance isn't quite as linear and straightforward as originally proposed. The literature on self-determination theory could provide another interesting link.

Self-determination theory

Sackett et al. (1988) and DuBois et al. (1993) argued that the typical versus maximum nature of a given situation influences performers' level of motivation, that is, the choice of direction, level, and persistence of effort (Campbell, 1990). However, looking at the performance distinction from the perspective of self-determination theory (SDT; Deci & Ryan, 1985; Ryan & Deci, 2000), typical versus maximum performance situations might not only alter performers' level, but also type (intrinsic versus extrinsic) of motivation (Deci et al., 2001; Ryan & Deci, 2000). SDT proposes (besides the possibility of amotivation, i.e., nonexistent motivation) a continuum ranging from an externally regulated motivation (people doing things because they have to; the control lies fully external to themselves) via different degrees of internalization (e.g., people doing things because they would have guilty conscience if they didn't, or doing them because they see them as valuable and important) to a fully autonomous and possibly even intrinsic motivation. During typical performance situations, employees are relatively autonomous in their choices of direction, level, and persistence of effort, while maximum performance situations force the three motivational factors to be high (Sackett et al., 1988; DuBois et al., 1993) and the usual manners presented for achieving this (evaluation, instruction, short duration) are rather extrinsic in nature. This idea is also represented by DuBois et al.'s (1993, p. 206) notion that "unless one is inviting disciplinary action [in maximum performance situations], one has little choice but to expend effort". As we know from SDT that situational factors like surveillance (Lepper & Greene, 1975; Plant & Ryan, 1985) and evaluation (Ryan, 1982) diminish feelings of autonomy and foster externally regulated, that is, externally controlled forms of motivation, maximum performance situations likely raise performers' situational extrinsic motivation, likely at the detriment of their situational amotivation but possibly also at the detriment of their situational intrinsic motivation (Deci et al., 2001; Ryan & Deci, 2000). Therefore, the link found between changes from a typical to a maximum performance situation and performers' enhanced direction and level of effort (Klehe & Anderson, 2007a) might be mediated by an increase in externally regulated motivation.

Suggestions for future research and conclusions

The above conceptual links are important for two core reasons: for one, they point at the great potential that the distinction between typical and maximum performance has on informing different areas of our literature, and for the other, the empirical study of typical versus maximum performance itself may thus gain further inspiration from these related literatures. Thus, these literatures offer multiple suggestions for mechanisms (e.g., from SDT and VIE theory) and moderators (e.g., from social loafing) to the study of typical versus maximum performance. Such inspiration also appears needed, given the dearth of research on typical versus maximum performance, and where research has been done, of replication. Thus, we hardly know about the links between maximum and peak performance and the reasons for the diverging findings between these two literatures. Similarly, we also still lack conclusive insights into some basic predictors of typical versus maximum performance, be it on the basis of the broad personality dimensions discussed above or of more specific performance-related predictors such as goal orientations, perfectionism, or fear of failure (see also Klehe & Anderson, 2005). Given the relevance of the distinction for diverse areas of work and organizational psychology, from personnel selection (Boudreau, 1991; Guion, 1991, 1998) to performance appraisal (Campbell, 1990) to research methods (Chernyshenko et al., 2001; Sackett & Larson, 1990), such research is direly needed.

References

Ackerman, P.L., & Humphreys, L.G. (1990). Individual differences theory in industrial and organizational psychology. In M.D. Dunnette & L.M. Hough (Eds.), *Handbook of industrial and organizational psychology, Vol. 1* (2nd ed., pp. 223–282). Palo Alto, CA: Consulting Psychologists Press.

Arvey, R.D., & Murphy, K.R. (1998). Performance evaluation in work settings. *Annual Review of Psychology, 49*, 141–168.
Austin, J.T., & Villanova, P. (1992). The criterion problem: 1917–1992. *Journal of Applied Psychology, 77*, 836–874.
Barnes, C.M., & Morgeson, F.P. (2007). Typical performance, maximal performance, and performance variability: Expanding our understanding of how organizations value performance. *Human Performance, 20*, 259–274.
Beus, J.M., & Whitman, D.S. (2012). The relationship between typical and maximum performance: A meta-analytic examination. *Human Performance, 25*, 355–376.
Bond, C.F. (1982). Social facilitation: A self-presentational view. *Journal of Personality and Social Psychology, 42*, 1042–1050.
Borman, W.C. (1991). Job behavior, performance, and effectiveness. In M.D. Dunnette & L.M. Hough (Eds.), *Handbook of industrial and organizational psychology, Vol. 2* (2nd ed., pp. 271–326). Palo Alto, CA: Consulting Psychologists Press.
Boudreau, J.W. (1991). Utility analysis for decisions in human resource management. In M.D. Dunnette & L.M. Hough (Eds.), *Handbook of industrial and organizational psychology, Vol. 2* (2nd ed., pp. 621–745). Palo Alto, CA: Consulting Psychologists Press.
Campbell, J.P. (1990). Modeling the performance prediction problem in industrial and organizational psychology. In M.D. Dunnette & L.M. Hough (Eds.), *Handbook of industrial and organizational psychology, Vol. 1* (2nd ed., pp. 687–732). Palo Alto, CA: Consulting Psychologists Press.
Cascio, W., & Aguinis, H. (2011). *Applied psychology in human resource management* (7th ed.). Upper Saddle River, NJ: Pearson Prentice Hall.
Chernyshenko, O.S., Stark, S., Chan, K.Y., Drasgow, F., & Williams, B. (2001). Fitting item response theory models to two personality inventories: Issues and insights. *Multivariate Behavioral Research, 36*, 523–562.
Cronbach, L.J. (1960). *Essentials of psychological testing* (2nd ed.). New York: Harper & Row.
Deadrick, D.L., & Gardner, D.G. (2000). Performance distributions: Measuring employee performance using total quality management principles. *Journal of Quality Management, 4*, 225–241.
Deadrick, D.L., & Gardner, D.G. (2008). Maximal and typical measures of job performance: An analysis of performance variability over time. *Human Resource Management Review, 18*, 133–145.
Deci, E.L., & Ryan, R.M. (1985). *Intrinsic motivation and self-determination in human behavior.* New York: Plenum.
Deci, E.L., Ryan, R.M., Gagne, M., Leone, D.R., Usunov, J., & Kornazheva, B.P. (2001). Need satisfaction, motivation, and well-being in the work organizations of a former eastern bloc country: A cross-cultural study of self-determination. *Personality and Social Psychology Bulletin, 27*, 930–942.
Dennis, M.J., Sternberg, R.J., & Beatty, P. (2000). The construction of "user-friendly" tests of cognitive functioning: A synthesis of maximal- and typical-performance measurement philosophies. *Intelligence, 28*, 193–211.
DuBois, C.L., Sackett, P.R., Zedeck, S., & Fogli, L. (1993). Further exploration of typical and maximum performance criteria: Definitional issues, prediction, and White-Black differences. *Journal of Applied Psychology, 78*, 205–211.
Fisher, C.D., & Noble, C.S. (2004). A within-person examination of correlates of performance and emotions while working. *Human Performance, 17*, 145–168.
Guion, R.M. (1991). Personnel assessment, selection, and placement. In M.D. Dunnette & L.M. Hough (Eds.), *Handbook of industrial and organizational psychology, Vol. 2* (2nd ed., pp. 327–397). Palo Alto, CA: Consulting Psychologists Press.
Guion, R.M. (1998). *Assessment, measurement, and prediction of personnel decisions.* Mahwah, NJ: Lawrence Erlbaum.

Herriot, P., & Anderson, N. (1997). Selecting for change: How will personnel and selection psychology survive? In N. Anderson & P. Herriot (Eds.), *International handbook of selection and assessment* (pp. 1–38). Chichester, UK: Wiley.

Janz, J.T. (1989). The patterned behaviour description interview: The best prophet of the future is the past. In R.W. Eder & G.R. Ferris (Eds.), *The employment interview: Theory, research, and practice* (pp. 158–168). Newbury Park, CA: Sage.

Judge, T.A., & Bono, J.E. (2000). Five factor model of personality and transformational leadership. *Journal of Applied Psychology, 85,* 751–765.

Judge, T.A., Higgins, C., Thoresen, C.J., & Barrick, M.R. (1999). The Big Five personality traits, general mental ability, and career success across the life span. *Personnel Psychology, 52,* 621–652.

Karau, S.J., & Williams, K.D. (1993). Social loafing: A meta-analytic review and theoretical integration. *Journal of Personality and Social Psychology, 65,* 681–706.

Klehe, U.-C., & Anderson, N. (2005). The prediction of typical and maximum performance. In A. Evers, N. Anderson, & O. Smit-Voskuijl (Eds.), *Handbook of personnel selection* (pp. 331–353). Oxford, UK: Blackwell.

Klehe, U.-C., & Anderson, N. (2007a). Working hard and working smart: Motivation and ability during typical and maximum performance. *Journal of Applied Psychology, 92,* 978–992.

Klehe, U.-C., & Anderson, N. (2007b). The moderating influence of personality and culture on social loafing in typical versus maximum performance situations. *International Journal of Selection and Assessment, 15,* 250–262.

Klehe, U.-C., Anderson, N., & Hoefnagels, E.A. (2007). Social facilitation and inhibition during maximum versus typical performance situations. *Human Performance, 20,* 223–239.

Klehe, U.-C., & Latham, G. (2006). What would you do – really or ideally? Constructs underlying the behavior description interview and the situational interview in predicting typical versus maximum performance. *Human Performance, 19,* 357–382.

Klehe, U.-C., & Latham, G. (2008). Predicting typical and maximum performance with measures of motivation and abilities. *Psychologica Belgica, 48,* 67–91.

Latané, B., Williams, K., & Harkins, S. (1979). Many hands make light the work: The causes and consequences of social loafing. *Journal of Personality and Social Psychology, 37,* 822–832.

Latham, G.P. (1989). The reliability, validity, and practicality of the situational interview. In G. Ferris & R. Eder (Eds.), *The employment interview: Theory, research and practice* (pp. 169–182). Newbury Park, CA: Sage.

Lepper, M.R., & Greene, D. (1975). Turning play into work: Effects of adult surveillance and extrinsic rewards on children's intrinsic motivation. *Journal of Personality and Social Psychology, 31,* 479–486.

Locke, E.A., Mento, A.J., & Katcher, B.L. (1978). The interaction of ability and motivation in performance: An exploration of the meaning of moderators. *Personnel Psychology, 31,* 269–280.

Marcus, B., Goffin, R.D., Johnston, N.G., & Rothstein, M.G. (2007). Personality and cognitive ability as predictors of typical and maximum managerial performance. *Human Performance, 20,* 275–285.

McCloy, R.A., Campbell, J.P., & Cudeck, R. (1994). A confirmatory test of a model of performance determinants. *Journal of Applied Psychology, 79,* 493–505.

Murphy, K.R., & Cleveland, J.N. (1995). *Understanding performance appraisal: Social, organizational, and goal-based perspectives.* Thousand Oaks, CA: Sage

Plant, R.W., & Ryan, R.M. (1985). Intrinsic motivation and the effects of self-consciousness, self-awareness, and ego-involvement: An investigation of internally controlling styles. *Journal of Personality, 53,* 435–449.

Ployhart, R.E., Lim, B.C., & Chan, K.Y. (2001). Exploring relations between typical and maximum performance ratings and the five factor model of personality. *Personnel Psychology, 54*, 809–843.

Ryan, R.M. (1982). Control and information in the intrapersonal sphere: An extension of cognitive evaluation theory. *Journal of Personality and Social Psychology, 43*, 450–461.

Ryan, R.M., & Deci, E.L. (2000). Self-determination theory and the facilitation of intrinsic motivation, social development, and well-being. *American Psychologist, 55*, 68–78.

Sackett, P.R. (2007). Revisiting the origins of the typical-maximum performance distinction. *Human Performance, 20*, 179–185.

Sackett, P.R., & Larson, J.R. (1990). Research strategies and tactics in industrial and organizational psychology. In M.D. Dunnette & L.M. Hough (Eds.), *Handbook of industrial and organizational psychology, Vol. 1* (2nd ed., pp. 419–490). Palo Alto, CA: Consulting Psychologists Press.

Sackett, P.R., Zedeck, S., & Fogli, L. (1988). Relations between measures of typical and maximum job performance. *Journal of Applied Psychology, 73*, 482–486.

Sanna, L. (1992). Self-efficacy theory: Implications for social facilitation and social loafing. *Journal of Personality and Social Psychology, 62*, 774–786.

Sanna, L., & Shotland, R.L. (1990). Valence of anticipated evaluation and social facilitation. *Journal of Experimental Social Psychology, 26*, 82–92.

Smith-Jentsch, K.A., Jentsch, F.G., Payne, S.C., & Salas, E. (1996). Can pretraining experiences explain individual differences in learning? *Journal of Applied Psychology, 81*, 110–116.

Sternberg, R.J. (1999). Intelligence as developing expertise. *Contemporary Educational Psychology, 24*, 359–375.

Stewart, G.L., & Nandkeolyar, A.K. (2006). Adaptation and intraindividual variation in sales outcomes: Exploring the interactive effects of personality and environmental opportunity. *Personnel Psychology, 59*, 307–332.

Taylor, P.J., & Small, B. (2002). Asking applicants what they would do versus what they did do: A meta-analytic comparison of situational and past behaviour employment interview questions. *Journal of Occupational and Organizational Psychology, 75*, 277–294.

Thorndike, R.L. (1949). *Personnel selection: Test and measurement techniques*. New York: Wiley.

Viswesvaran, C., Sinangil, H.K., Ones, D.S., & Anderson, N. (2001). Where we have been, where we are, (and where we could be). In N. Anderson, D.S. Ones, H.K. Sinangil, & C. Viswesvaran (Eds.), *Handbook of industrial, work and organizational psychology, Vol. 1*, (pp. 1–9). London: Sage.

Vroom, V.H. (1964). *Work and motivation*. Oxford, UK: Wiley.

INDEX

Page numbers in *italic* indicate tables and figures.

ability to identify the criteria (ATIC) 158
Academy of Management (AoM) 2
Ackerman, P. L. 103
Actor-Network Theory (ANT) 75
Adjective Check List 219
adverse impact 63, 72–3, 91, 191
Ajzen, I. 51
Allen, D. 106
Allport, G.W. 200
Anderson, N. 84–5, 215, 233, 238, 239–40
Annual Review of Psychology 1, 87
antecedent-behavior-consequence (A-B-C) method 173
applicant attraction *see* recruitment processes
applicant reactions to selection methods 80–93; effects of 85–7; future research 87–92; literature review 80–1, *81*; methodological advances 91–2; practical implications 92–3; predictors of 84–5; role of Internet 87–91; theoretical perspectives 81–7
Armed Services Vocational Aptitude Battery 103
Arthur, W. 46, 145, 146, 147
Arvey, R.D. 82
Assessment Centres (ACs) 190–202; construct-related methodology 197–201; construct validity debate 192–3; dimensions vs. exercises 193–5; future research 199–201; guidelines for 191–2; interactionist perspectives on design 195–7; selecting for innovation *218*, 220, 223
attraction *see* recruitment processes

Back, M.D. 71
Bangerter, A. 156
Barnes, C.M. 232
Barnum effect 125
Baron, H. 136–7
Barrick, M.R. 117–18, 160
Bauer, T.N. 82, 83, 85, 86
Beier, M.E. 183
Berchtold, M. 54
Bergman, M.E. 175
Bertolino, M. 85
Beus, J.M. 234, 236
Biddle, D.A. 21
Biderman, M.D. 179
Big Five Personality Inventory (NEO) 119, 120–1, 124, 125, 129, 221 *see also* Five-Factor Model (FFM) of personality
Black, S. L. 73, 90
Bledow, R. 182
Bliese, P. 103
Bobko, P. 88–9
Bochum Inventory for profession-related personality description (BIP) 120, *121*
Bodner, T.E. 85
Bohnert, D. 71
Born, M. 182, 183
Borodenko, N. 28
Bosco, F. 106

Boudreau, J.W. 150
Bowler, J. L. 193–4
Bowler, M.C. 193–4, 197
Braddy, P.W. 31–2
Bradley, J.C. 172
branding 34
Brannick, M.T. 11, 18, 200
Briggs, K. 125
Bruce, R.A. 211
Buckley, M.R. 84
Buyse, T. 177

Cable, D.M. 166
Cahoon, M.V. 193–4
California Psychological Inventory (CPI) 119
Campbell, J.P. 197, 232
Campion, M.A. 19, 28, 85, 162, 173, 175
Carroll, J. 101
Carroll, S.A. 29
Cattell, R. 101
Cattell–Horn–Carroll (CHC) model of intelligence 101–2
Caughron, J.J. 15
Chamorro-Premuzic, T. 103
Chan, D. 176, 178, 180
Chan, K.Y. 233
Chapman, D.S. 28, 29, 32, 33–4, 36–8
Chen, B. 74
Chernyshenko, O.S. 233
Chow, S. 36–7
Christian, M.S. 172, 177
Christopher, J. 73
Classmates.com 63
Clayton, A.C. 74
Cober, R.T. 22
cognitive-affective personality systems (CAPS) theory 195–6
Cognitive Assessment System (CAS) 107
Competence Modelling (CM) 11–12
componential theory of creativity 216
confirmatory factor analysis (CFA) methodology 194, 197
content validity (Wernimont) 20
Conway, J.M. 193
core self-evaluation (CSE) theory 212–15, 217, *218*, 219
Core Self-Evaluations Scale 219
Critical Incident Technique 11
Cromheecke, S. 33
Cronbach, L. J. 229
Crook, A.E. 183
cross-battery assessment approach (XBA) 101–3

culture, defined 31
Cummings, A. 211

Dalessio, A.T. 174
da Motta Veiga, S.P. 84
Daniel, T. 36
Davison, H.K. 70
Day, D.V. 82
De Meijer, L.A.L. 182
deontic outrage 83, 88
Derous, E. 51–3, 54, 56
Dictionary of Occupational Titles (DOT) 18
digital divide 56
Di Milia, L. 120
DISC (Dominance, Influence, Steadiness, and Conscientiousness) 120, *121*, 125
Downes, P.E. 73
Drasgow, F. 144, 145, 180, 233
Drauden, G. 82
Dreher, G.F. 193, 199
DuBois, C. L. 239, 240–1

Edwards, J.C. 172
Ehrhart, M.G. 175–6
Elaboration Likelihood Model (ELM) 34, 38
employee recruitment, selection, and assessment 1–6
employee testimonials *see* online recruiting
Equal Employment Opportunity Commission (EEOC): Uniform Guidelines on Employee Selection Procedures 68
equal opportunity, and work analysis 21–2
ethnic score differences *see* situational judgment tests (SJTs)
European Association of Work and Organizational Psychology (EAWOP) 2
European Network of Selection Researchers (ENESER) 2
European Union (EU): Council Directive 75/117/EC (equal pay) 21; Council Directive 76/207/EEC (equal treatment in employment and training) 21–2; Council Directive 2002/73/EC (legislative objective of equality) 21–2; Council Directive 2006/54/EC (discrimination) 22; Privacy Directive (1998) 147

Facebook 37, 93; SNW screening 62, 63–5, 68–70, 72, 73, 74, 75, 89, 91
face validity perceptions, and video résumés 52

Fagan, J. 109–10
faking behavior: in interviews 162–3, 168; and personality testing 118, 119, 140; and situational judgment tests (SJTs) 178–9, *181*; and social networking websites (SNWs) 71–2
Farmer, S.M. 211
FastPitch 62
Feldt, T. 85
Fifteen Factor Questionnaire 120
Fink, L. 80
Fischer, A.H. 31
Fisher, C.D. 228
Fiske, D.W. 197
Five-Factor Model (FFM) of personality 16, 65, 67, 68, 74, 85, 117–18, 177, 213–14, 219 *see also* Big Five Personality Inventory (NEO)
Flanagan, D. 101
Fleishman, E.A. 15
Fleishman Job Analysis Survey (F-JAS) 15
Ford, J.K. 11–12
Freedle, R. 109
Freeman, M. 73–4
Frese, M. 182
Friendster 62
Furnham, A. 103

Gael, S. 11, 14
gamification of recruiting *see* recruitment processes
Gavin, M.B. 84
General Aptitude Test Battery (GATB) 17
general mental ability (GMA) *see* innovation, selecting for
George, J.M. 211
GEVA Personality test *121*
Gilbreth, F. 10
Gilbreth, L. 10
Gilliland, S.W. 80, 81, 82–3, 86, 87
Gissel, A.L. 50, 51
Glassdoor.com 88
Glaze, R.M. 146, 147
Goldstein, I.L. 11–12
Google+ 63
Graen, G.B. 211
Grewe, K. 173
group-values motive 83
Guder, J.E. 12
Guion, R.M. 232
Gustafson, D.A. 73

Hackman, J.R. 28
Hadouch, M. 173

Haefner, R. 70
Hamilton, L. 50
Harkins, S. 239
Harold, C.M. 28
Harris, M. 80
Hausknecht, J.P. 82, 87, 92
headhunting 34–5, 38
Helms-Lorenz, M. 109
Herriot, Peter 83
Herrmann, Ned 125
Herrmann Brain Dominance Instrument (HBDI) 120, 125
Hesse, Hermann 199, 201
Hiemstra, A.M.F. 51–2
Higgins, D. 104–6
Hoffman, B.J. 194, 196, 198
Hogan, J. 15–16
Hogan Personality Inventory (HPI) 16, 120, *121*
Holland, C. 109–10
Hollenberg, S. 173
Honkaniemi, L. 85
Hooper, A.C. 183–4
Horn, J. 101
Howard, A. 194, 196, 199, 201
Huffcutt, A.I. 157, 159, 161, 166
Hülsheger, U.R. 84–5, 215
Human Performance 229
Humphrey, S.E. 28
Hunter, D.R. 173
Hurtz, G.M. 22–3
Hymes, R. 51

image theory 34
I-Meet 62
implicit trait policy (ITP) theory (Motowidlo, Hooper, and Jackson) 183–4
impression management (IM), defined 156 *see also* social situation in interviews
individual-level innovative job performance (IJP) assessment *see* innovation, selecting for
innovation, selecting for 209–24; abilities and personal factors 215–17, *215*; and applications/CVs/bio data 217–18, *218*; and Assessment Centres (ACs) *218*, 220, 223; and cognitive ability tests *218*, 219; future research 221–2, *222*; individual-level innovative job performance (IJP) assessment 210–12, *211*; innovation potential instruments 220–1; innovative job potential 212–17, *213*, *215*; personality characteristics

248 Index

213–15, *213*; and personality inventories 218, 219; practice implications 223–4, *223*; and semi-structured interviews *218*, 219; and situational judgment tests (SJTs) and work samples *218*, 219, 223
Innovation Potential Indicator (IPI) 220
Insights Discovery 120, 125
intelligence quotient (IQ) 65
intelligence theory and assessment 99–111; cognitive approaches 104–7; neuropsychological approaches 104–6; non-domain-relevant and cultural content in tests 109–10; and personnel selection 100; Planning, Attention-Arousal, Simultaneous and Successive (PASS) theory 104, 107; psychometric approaches 100–4; theory-driven cognitive ability tests 108–9; use of novel or non-entrenched tasks 110–11
International Congress of Applied Psychology (ICAP) 2
International Journal of Selection and Assessment 87
International Labour Organization (ILO) 19
International Task Force on Assessment Centre Guidelines 191–2
interviews: comparison to video résumés 46–50, *49*; faking behavior in 162–3, 168; selecting for innovation *218*, 219; in work analysis 14 *see also* social situation in interviews
invasion of privacy model (Bauer) 83
ISCO-08 (International Standard Classification of Occupations) 19
item response theory (IRT) 233

Jackson, H. L. 183–4
Janssen, O. 211
Janz, J.T. 232
Jeanneret, P.R. 17
job analysis *see* work analysis (WA)
Job Analysis Manual 17
job boards 91
Job Characteristics Model (JCM) 28
job descriptions 22–3
job design 28
job fit *see* person-organization (P-O) fit
job interviews *see* interviews
job-task inventories 14–15
Johnson, A.F. 73
Johnson, E.C. 20
Jones, D.A. 29

Journal of Management 61
Judge, T.A. 85
Junco, E. 69, 91
Jung, C.G. 125

Kanning, U.P. 173, 180
Karau, S.J. 239
Kelly, J. 50
Kirton Adaption-Innovation Inventory 216
Klehe, U.-C. 54, 139, 233, 234, 238, 239–40
Kleinmann, M. 54
Klotz, A.C. 84
Kluemper, D.H. 65, 66, 68–9, 74, 88–9, 90
knowledge, skills, abilities, and other characteristics (KSAOs) 10; Competence Modelling (CM) 11–12; Equal Employment Opportunities (EEO) and 21–2; Fleishman Job Analysis Survey (F-JAS) 15; innovation-related 219; SNW screening for 66, 68, 69–70
König, C.J. 54, 128, 140–1, 159
Kraichy, D. 33–4
Kristof-Brown, A. L. 20
Kroustalis, C.M. 31–2
Kuncel, N.R. 199–200
Kuthy, J.E. 21

Lance, C.E. 191, 193–4, 197
Lang, J. 103
Lanivich, S.E. 69, 91
Larson, J.R. 233, 236
Latané, B. 239
Latham, G. 234, 238
Legree, P.J. 177
Levashina, J. 160, 161, 162
Levine, E. L. 9, 11, 12, 18
Lewin, K. 200
Lievens, F. 33, 36, 161, 172, 175, 176, 177, 179, 193, 200
Light, L. 50
LinkedIn 37; SNW screening 62, 63–5, 69–70, 74; testing trends survey respondents 137
London Symphony Orchestra 47

Machiavellianism 161
MacKenzie, W. I. 175
MacLean, P.D. 125
Malda, M. 109
Marcus, J. 74
Marr, J.C. 166
Marston, William 125
Martin, C, 82
Martinko, M.J. 14

Master Person Analysis (MPA) 120
maximal performance tests *see* situational judgment tests (SJTs)
maximum performance *see* typical and maximum performance
McAuslan, P. 51
McCarthy, J.M. 86
McCormick, E.J. 17
McDaniel, M.A. 159, 172, 176–9
McFarland, L. 136–7
McGrew, K. 101
McPhail, S.M. 14
Meade, A.W. 31–2, 73, 89, 127, 197, 198
Mecham, R.C. 17
mergers and acquisitions 35–6
Metcalf, G. 36
Metsapelto, R. L. 85
Minnesota Multiphasic Personality Inventory (MMPI) 119
Mischel, W. 195, 200
Mitchell, T.R. 165
Mobley, W.H. 35
model of psychometric *g* (Spearman) 101
Monahan, C.J. 21
Morgeson, F.P. 18, 19, 28, 173, 232
Motowidlo, S.J. 183–4
Mount, M.K. 117–18
Muchinsky, P.M. 21
multitrait-multimethod (MTMM) framework 193, 194, 197–8, *198*
Mumford, M.D. 15
Mumford, T.V. 173
Murray, H. 200
Myers, Isabel Briggs 125
Myers-Briggs Type Indicator (MBTI) 119, 120–1, 124, 125
MySpace 62

Naglieri, J. 104, 107
Nahrgang, J.D. 28
Nandkeolyar, A.K. 228
nested-factor models of intelligence 103
Nguyen, N.T. 177–8, 179
Nikolaou, I. 85
Ning 62
Noble, C.S. 228
Nolan, K.P. 28
nominal situations, defined 195–6
non-entrenchment *see* intelligence theory and assessment
Nunnally, J.C. 200–1

O*NET OnLine 18
O*NET Questionnaires 18–19

O'Brien, E. 50
observation, in work analysis 13–14
Occupational Information Network (O*NET) 11, 18–19
Occupational Personality Profile (OPP) 120
Occupational Personality Questionnaire (OPQ) 119, 120, *121*
Oldham, G.R. 28, 211
Olson-Buchanan, J.B. 180
online recruiting 36
Oostsrom, J.K. 51, 52, 159, 183
openness to experience *see* innovation, selecting for
open systems theory 32
O'Reilly, C. 31
organizational citizenship behaviors (OCBs) 90
organizational image, defined 29–30
organizational justice framework (Gilliland) 81, 82, 83, 89
outsourcing 149
overall dimension ratings (ODRs) *see* Assessment Centres (ACs)
overall job performance (OJP) *see* innovation, selecting for

Page, R. 136–7
Paronto, M.E. 85
Pearlman, K. 13
Peeters, H. 161, 172, 179
Performance Improvement Characteristics Job Analysis (PIC) 15–16, *16*
performance measures *see* typical and maximum performance
Personal Characteristics Inventory (PCI) 120
personality-based job analysis 15–17
Personality-Related Position Requirements Form (PPRF) 16, *17*
personality testing 117–30; comparison of questionnaires 122–9, *123*; and faking behavior 118, 119, 140; future research 129–30; model of delivery 126–7; practice of 119–22, *121–2*; presentation of results 123–6; quality criteria 127–8; selection criteria 128–9 *see also individual test instruments*
Personal Profile Analysis 125
person-organization (P-O) fit: defined 31; SNW screening for 67–8; in work analysis (WA) 20–1
Piasentin, K.A. 29
Pike, J.C. 71
planned behavior theory (Ajzen) 51

Planning, Attention-Arousal, Simultaneous and Successive (PASS) theory 104, 107
Plaxo 62
Ployhart, R.E. 1, 87, 149, 175–6, 182, 184
Porr, W.B. 182
Position Analysis Questionnaire (PAQ) 17
post consensus dimension ratings (PCDRs) *see* Assessment Centres (ACs)
post-exercise dimension ratings (PEDRs) *see* Assessment Centres (ACs)
Predictive Index (PI) 120, *121*
privacy issues 37, 57, 73, 83
Proactive Personality Scale 219
proctoring practices *see* testing trends survey
Project A 103
Psotka, J. 177

Queensland Tourist Board 51

Raymark, P.H. 16, 162
reaction generalizability hypothesis 84–5
Realistic Accuracy Model (RAM) 74–5
recruiter effects *see* recruitment processes
recruitment processes 27–39; attractive job characteristics 27–9; company location 32; culture and attraction 31–2; for employed candidates 34–5; future research 38; gamification of recruiting 36–7; job design for 28; mergers and acquisitions 35–6; methodological issues 37–8; online recruiting 31–2, 36; organizational characteristics 29–32; pay levels and attraction 29; persuasion and message attributes 33–4; recruiter effects 32–3; social media 37
Reeve, C. 103
ResearchGate 62
résumés *see* video résumés
retake policies *see* testing trends survey
Richman-Hirsch, W. L. 180
Roberts, K. 73–4
Rosen, P. 65, 66
Ross, W.H. 71
Roth, P. L. 69, 88–9, 91, 159, 162
Roulin, N. 91, 160, 163
Rupp, D.E. 194, 199
Ryan, A.M. 1, 87, 136–7, 149, 182
Rybicki, S. 15–16

Sabet, J. 106
Sackett, P.R. 176, 177, 193, 199–200, 229–31, 232, 233–4, 235–8, 240
Salgado, J.F. 84–5, 215

Sánchez, J. I. 9, 12, 13
Sanchez, R.J. 73–4, 90–1
Schein, E. 31
Schinkel, S. 86, 87
Schlenker, B.R. 156
Schmitt, N. 176, 178, 180
Schneider, W.J. 101
Schollaert, E. 172
Schuler, H. 81–2
Scott, S.G. 211
selection research, overview 1–2
self-determination theory (SDT) 240–1
self-serving bias mechanism 82–3, 86
Serlie, A.W. 183
Siebert, S. 73
signaling theory 30, 156–7
situational judgment tests (SJTs) 172–85; alternative response formats 182–3; construct-based approach 180, 182; construct-related validity 176, *181*; criterion-related validity 176–7, *181*; ethnic score differences 177–8, *181*, 182–3; fakability 178–9, *181*; future research 184; implicit trait policies 183–4; item stem development 173; reliability 175–6, *181*; response instructions 173–4, 178; scoring methods 174–5; selecting for innovation 218, 219, 223; test taker perceptions 179–80, *181*; video-based 173, 177, 178, 180, *181*, 182
16 Personality Factor Questionnaire (16PF) 119, 120, *121*
Snow, R.E. 103
social identity theory 30
social loafing *see* typical and maximum performance
social media 37, 54 *see also specific sites*
social networking websites (SNWs) 61–76; applicant reactions to selection methods 87–93; construct validity 67–8; content validity 68; criterion-related validity 68–9; fairness issues in screening 72–4; future research 69, 72; generalizability 69–70; internal consistency reliability 66; interrater reliability 64–5; measurement error 66; online identity/impression management 70–2; screening 62–3; standardization 63–4; test-retest reliability 65–6; theoretical perspectives 74–5; utility 70; validity of screening 66–9
social psychological theories 83
social situation in interviews 154–68; effects of interviewee IM 160; effects of

interviewer behavior 163–6; face-to-face vs. electronic methods 166–7; faking behavior 162–3; future research 167–8; influences on interviewee IM 161–2; interviewee perceptions of 158–9; models of interviewee performance 157; self-presentation behavior 159–60; signaling processes 155–7
social validity concept (Schuler) 81–2
Society for Industrial and Organizational Psychology 50
Society for Industrial and Organizational Psychology (SIOP) 2
Spearman, C. 100, 101
Steiner, D.D. 80, 82–3, 86, 87
Stemler, S.E. 176
Sternberg, R.J. 110–11, 176, 235–6
Stevens, C.K. 165
Stewart, G. L. 228
Stone, D. L. 73
Stoughton, J.W. 73, 89–90
Strickland, W. 82
subject matter experts (SMEs) *see* situational judgment tests (SJTs)

Takach, S.E. 73
Task-Based Assessment Centres (TBACs) 194
Task Inventory/ Comprehensive Occupational Data Program (TI/CODAP) 11
Taylor, F.W. 10
Team Climate Inventory (TCI) 220
Team Selection Inventory (TSI) 220–1
technology: applicant reactions to selection methods 87–92; personality testing 126–7; recruitment processes 36–7; testing trends survey 142–9; video résumés 45–58
technology acceptance model (TAM) 75
Test Attitude Scale 82
testing *see* intelligence theory and assessment; personality testing; situational judgment tests (SJTs); *individual test instruments*
testing trends survey 136–51; overview 138; assessment content 142; data protection and security *145–7*; limitations 150; proctoring practices 143–4; rationale for using/not using tests 139–41, *139–40*; research implications 150; respondents 137–8; summary recommendations 150–1; test policies and practices 148–9, *149*; test program descriptions

141–2, *141*; use of technology 142–9, *142–7, 149*
test-taking motivation model (Arvey, Strickland, Drauden, and Martin) 82, 83
Thatcher, J.B. 88–9
Thomas, S.C. 82
Thomas Assessment/Personal Profile Analysis (PPA) 119, 120, *121*
Thompson, L. F. 73, 89
Thornton, C.G., III 194, 199
Tierney, P. 211
Time and Motions Study, Functional Job Analysis 11
Tippins, N.T. 143
Tolvanen, A. 85
trait activation theory (TAT) 195, 200–1
Tripp, T.M. 165
triune brain theory (MacLean) 125
true score theory 212
trust and trustworthiness 84
Truxillo, D.M. 85, 86
turnover model (Mobley) 35
Twitter 37, 62, 63–5, 70, 93
typical and maximum performance 228–41; comparison of 229–30; correlation between measures of 235–6; findings on basic assumptions 233–4; future research 241; methodological issues 236–8; motivation and ability predictors 234–5; performance distributions 231–2; performance situations 230–1; predictive power of personality 235; relevance of distinction between 232–3; self-determination theory 240–1; social loafing 239–40; VIE theory 239, 240
typical-maximum-performance-scale (TMPS) 238
typical performance tests *see* situational judgment tests (SJTs)

Uggerslev, K. L. 29, 32
unfolding model of turnover (Lee and Mitchell) 35
Uniform Guidelines on Employee Selection Procedures (EEOC) 68
U.S. Office of Personnel Management 14
U.S. Safe Harbor Provisions (2000) 147
utility, defined 70

valence-instrumentality expectancy theory (VIE) 239, 240
Van der Molen, H.T. 182, 183
Van Dierendonck, D. 86
Van Hoye, G. 33, 36, 93

Index

Van Iddekinge, C.H. 69, 88–9, 91, 161, 162, 173
Van Vianen, A.E. 31, 86
Van Zielst, J. 182
video résumés 45–58; administration medium of 47–8, *49*; comparison to job interviews 46–50, *49*; comparison to paper résumés 53, 55, 57; cost-effectiveness of 55–6; ease of use 56; format of 47, *49*; future research 53–7; goal and content of 47, *49*; interactivity of 47–8, *49*; research findings 50–3; standardization 47; standardized procedures for *49*; structure of 47, *49*
Villado, A.J. 46
Vroom, V. H. 175, 239

Walker, H.J. 84–5
Warshawski, E. 50
Waung, M. 51, 52, 53, 56
Web of Science 50–2, *81*
Webster, J. 32
Weekley, J.A. 177, 179
Wernimont, P.F. 12, 20
Weschler, D. 100–1
Whetzel, D. L. 172, 177–8

Whitman, D.S. 234, 236
Wikipedia 62
Wilhelmy, A. 164
Williams, B. 233
Williams, K.D. 239
Woehr, D.J. 193, 197
Wonderlic Personnel Test 102, 106
work analysis (WA) 9–23; databases 18–19; defined 10; Equal Employment Opportunity 21–2; job fit 20–1; qualitative methods for 13–14; quantitative methods for 14–17; recruitment 22–3; reliability and validity 19–20; sources of information 12; task-oriented job analysis 11; worker-oriented job analysis 11–12
Work Performance Survey System 11
Wright, C.W. 22–3

Yonce, C.A. 85
Yost, A.P. 177
YouTube 47
Yusko, K. 111

Zhou, J. 211
Zimmerman, R.D. 20